A New History of English Metre

LEGENDA

LEGENDA, founded in 1995 by the European Humanities Research Centre of the University of Oxford, is now a joint imprint of the Modern Humanities Research Association and Maney Publishing. Titles range from medieval texts to contemporary cinema and form a widely comparative view of the modern humanities, including works on Arabic, Catalan, English, French, German, Greek, Italian, Portuguese, Russian, Spanish, and Yiddish literature. An Editorial Board of distinguished academic specialists works in collaboration with leading scholarly bodies such as the Society for French Studies and the British Comparative Literature Association.

MHRA

The Modern Humanities Research Association (MHRA) encourages and promotes advanced study and research in the field of the modern humanities, especially modern European languages and literature, including English, and also cinema. It also aims to break down the barriers between scholars working in different disciplines and to maintain the unity of humanistic scholarship in the face of increasing specialization. The Association fulfils this purpose primarily through the publication of journals, bibliographies, monographs and other aids to research.

MANEY
publishing

Maney Publishing is one of the few remaining independent British academic publishers. Founded in 1900 the company has offices both in the UK, in Leeds and London, and in North America, in Boston. Since 1945 Maney Publishing has worked closely with learned societies, their editors, authors, and members, in publishing academic books and journals to the highest traditional standards of materials and production.

A New History of English Metre

Martin J. Duffell

LEGENDA

Studies in Linguistics 5

Modern Humanities Research Association and Maney Publishing

2008

Published by the
Modern Humanities Research Association and Maney Publishing
1 Carlton House Terrace
London SW1Y 5AF
United Kingdom

LEGENDA is an imprint of the
Modern Humanities Research Association and Maney Publishing

Maney Publishing is the trading name of W. S. Maney & Son Ltd,
whose registered office is at Suite 1C, Joseph's Well, Hanover Walk, Leeds LS3 1AB

ISBN 978-1-905981-91-5

First published 2008

Printed in Great Britain

Cover: 875 Design

Copy-Editor: Polly Fallows

CONTENTS

To Dawn
and my illustrators
Hazel and Jasmine

ACKNOWLEDGEMENTS

I am deeply indebted to Anne Birrell, Thomas Carper, Donka Minkova, Derek Pearsall, Gerald Smith, and Robert Stockwell for the advice that they gave at various stages in the preparation of this book.

M. J. D.

The author would like to thank the publishers and copyright holders for their permission to quote lines from the following poems:

'On this Island', copyright 1937 and renewed in 1965 by W. H. Auden, 'The Quest', copyright © 1976 by Edward Mendelson, William Meredith and Monroe K. Spears, Executors of the Estate of W. H. Auden. 'The Wanderer', copyright © 1934 and renewed 1962 by W. H. Auden, from COLLECTED POEMS by W. H. AUDEN. Reprinted by permission of Faber and Faber Ltd and Random House, Inc.

'take it from me, kiddo' and 'in time's a noble mercy of proportion', reprinted from COMPLETE POEMS 1904-1962 by E. E. CUMMINGS, edited by George J. Firmage, copyright © 1991 by the Trustees for the E. E. Cummings Trust and George J. Firmage. Reprinted by permission of W. W. Norton & Company.

'The Love Song of Alfred J. Prufrock' and 'The Waste Land: The Burial of the Dead', from COLLECTED POEMS 1909-1962 by T. S. ELIOT, copyright © 1963. Reprinted by permission of Faber and Faber Ltd and Harcourt Inc.

'Howl', from COLLECTED POEMS 1947-1980 by ALLEN GINSBERG, copyright © 1955, 1956, and 1996 by Allen Ginsberg. Reprinted by permission of Harper Collins Publishers and Penguin Group (UK).

'Glanmore Sonnets' and 'Sunlight', from NEW SELECTED POEMS 1966-1987 by SEAMUS HEANEY, copyright © 1990. 'Beowulf', from 'BEOWULF': A NEW TRANSLATION by SEAMUS HEANEY, copyright © 1999. Reprinted by permission of Faber and Faber Ltd and Farrar, Straus and Giroux, LLC.

'Ode on an Engraving by Casserius' and 'Letter from the Line', from SELECTED PROSE AND POETRY by A. D. HOPE, edited by D. Brooks, Halstead Classics (Sidney), copyright © 2000. Reprinted by permission of Halstead Press.

'The Jaguar', from NEW SELECTED POEMS 1957-1994 by TED HUGHES, copyright © 1995. 'Fingers' from BIRTHDAY LETTERS by TED HUGHES, copyright © 1998. Reprinted by permission of Faber and Faber Ltd and Farrar, Straus and Giroux, LLC.

'An Arundel Tomb', 'The Trees', This Be the Verse', 'Ambulances', and 'The Whitsun Weddings', from COLLECTED POEMS by PHILIP LARKIN, edited by Anthony Thwaite. Reprinted by permission of Faber and Faber Ltd and Farrar, Straus and Giroux, LLC.

'For Sale', by Robert Lowell, from SELECTED POEMS by ROBERT LOWELL, copyright © 1963. Reprinted by permission of Farrar, Straus and Giroux, LLC.

'Hugh Selwyn Mauberley I, E.P. Ode pour l'élection de son sépulcre' and 'Sestina Altaforte', from PERSONAE by EZRA POUND, copyright © 1926 by Ezra Pound, reprinted by permission of the New Directions Publishing Corp. 'Canto I' and 'Canto XLV' by Ezra Pound from THE CANTOS OF EZRA POUND, copyright © 1934, 1937, 1940, 1948, 1956, 1959, 1962, 1963, 1966, and 1968 by Ezra Pound, reprinted by permission of the New Directions Publishing Corp.

'The Steeple-Jack', copyright © 1951 by Marianne Moore, renewed © 1979 by Lawrence E. Brinn and Louise Crane, Executors for the Estate of Marianne Moore, from THE COMPLETE POEMS OF MARIANNE MOORE by Marianne Moore. Reprinted by permission of Viking Penguin, a division of Penguin Group (USA) Inc., and Faber and Faber Ltd. 'Poetry', from THE POEMS OF MARIANNE MOORE, edited by Grace Schulman, copyright © 2003 by Marianne Craig Moore, Executor of Marianne Moore. Reprinted by permission of Viking Penguin, a division of Penguin Group (USA) Inc., and Faber and Faber Ltd.

'Mirror' and 'Lady Lazarus', from COLLECTED POEMS by SYLVIA PLATH, edited by Ted Hughes, copyright © 1981. Reprinted by permission of Faber and Faber Ltd and HarperCollins Publishers.

'Sonnet', from THE WANT BONE by ROBERT PINSKY, copyright © 1990 by Robert Pinsky, reprinted by permission of Ecco Press, a division of HarperCollins Publishers. 'The Figured Wheel', from THE FIGURED WHEEL: NEW AND COLLECTED POEMS by ROBERT PINSKY, copyright © 1996. Reprinted by permission of Farrar, Straus and Giroux, LLC.

'The Force that through the Green Fuse Drives the Flower' and 'From Love's First Fever to Her Plague' by Dylan Thomas from COLLECTED POEMS 1934-1952 by DYLAN THOMAS. Reprinted by permission of David Higham Associates. 'From Love's First Fever to Her Plague' (excerpt) and the 'The Force That Through the Green Fuse Drives the Flower' (excerpt), copyright © 1939 by New Directions Publishing Corp. Reprinted by permission of New Directions Publishing Corp.

'The Snow Man', 'Sunday Morning', 'Notes Toward a Supreme Fiction', 'The Man with the Blue Guitar', and 'An Ordinary Evening in New Haven' reprinted from THE COLLECTED POEMS OF WALLACE STEVENS by WALLACE STEVENS, copyright © 1954 by Wallace Stevens and renewed 1982 by Holly Stevens. Reprinted by permission of Faber and Faber Ltd and Alfred A. Knopf, a division of Random House, Inc.

'The Crimson Cyclamen' and 'The Widow's Lament in Springtime' by William Carlos Williams from COLLECTED POEMS: 1909-1939, VOLUME I, copyright

ABBREVIATIONS

ABRSM	Associated Board of the Royal Schools of Music
ANTS	Anglo-Norman Texts Society
BHS	*Bulletin of Hispanic Studies* (Liverpool)
BRH	Biblioteca Románica Hispánica
C	consonant
CE	*College English*
CILT	Current Issues in Linguistic Theory
CNRS	Centre National de la Recherche Scientifique
CR	*Chaucer Review*
CSIC	Consejo Superior de Investigaciones Científicas
CT	Colección Támesis
CUP	Cambridge University Press
EETS	Early English Texts Society
ELS	English Language Series
ES	Extra Series
F	feminine (ending)
LIn	*Linguistic Inquiry*
M	masculine (ending)
MAe	*Medium Aevum*
MLA	Modern Language Association of America
MPh	*Modern Philology*
MRTS	Medieval & Renaissance Texts and Studies
NS	New Series
OS	Original Series
OUP	Oxford University Press
P	proparoxytonic
PMHRS	Papers of the Medieval Hispanic Research Seminar
PMLA	*Publications of the Modern Language Association of America*
PUF	Presses Universitaires de France
QMW	Queen Mary and Westfield College
s	strong (element)
σ	standard error
SS	Second Series
SUNY	State University of New York
UP	University Press
V	vowel
[v]	void (position)
w	weak (element)

INTRODUCTION

The story this book tells is not new, but it can only now be told from a modern perspective and for a twenty-first-century audience. Almost a hundred years have passed since George Saintsbury produced his great three-volume *History of English Prosody*, and in that time there have been many changes in the ways that poets versify, and even more in the methods critics use to approach texts. Saintsbury, of necessity, stopped short at the outset of one of the most exciting and innovative periods in the history of versifying in English, yet no modern author would wish simply to add a fourth volume to bring his work up to date. This is, first, because of Saintsbury's method: he cites numerous poems and poets exemplifying the same metrical features, which leads to prolixity and repetition, and he requires frequent summaries, inter-chapters, and appendices in order to develop the narrative and argument. Secondly, a modern sequel could hardly preserve the gross imbalance between the number of opinions Saintsbury expresses and the amount of evidence he presents. Finally, no author today would want to continue in the elitist and chauvinistic tone of Saintsbury's three volumes, typified by the constant use of the terms 'doggerel' and 'foreign' as pejoratives to apply to any line that offends the author's personal taste and any research that conflicts with his own views.[1] This narrowness of outlook reduces Saintsbury's credibility in the eyes of modern readers and is certainly inappropriate to the history of versifying in the period that followed, when the development of free verse ignored national and linguistic boundaries.[2]

The final volume of Saintsbury's work appeared in 1910, which also marked the publication of his *A Historical Manual of English Prosody* and Jakob Schipper's *A History of English Versification* (which had first appeared in German in 1896). Saintsbury's manual, like R. S. Brewer's *Orthometry* (1893), presented a theory of English metre on which there was then a fair measure of agreement among scholars on both sides of the Atlantic (see, for example, Baum 1922), and gave it a historical dimension. (In the present volume I shall refer to that broad consensus as 'traditional English metrics', and modern research into metre has more often confirmed than contradicted its conclusions.) Schipper's history covered the same ground as Saintsbury's, but did so in a much more systematic fashion, particularly in its explanation and illustration of Old and Middle English metre. But both histories appeared in English as Britain was preparing for war, and that probably influenced the subsequent preference shown by English academia for Saintsbury's less rigorous but more chauvinistic work. Nevertheless, the period 1880–1910 may be regarded as a Golden Age of English metrics: T. S. Omond's *English Metrists* lists more than 120 authors who made significant contributions in this period (1921: 312–24); Omond's book, subtitled *A Sketch of English Prosodical Criticism from Elizabethan Times to the Present Day*, has deservedly become a classic.

A number of metrists working in the second half of the twentieth century made important additions to the story that Saintsbury and Schipper told: John Thompson focused on a crucial period in the development of English stress-syllabic verse and identified its most influential pioneers; Seymour Chatman showed the value of non-literary research in the analysis of verse texts; Marina Tarlinskaja introduced sophisticated statistical analysis to the study of English historical metrics; Derek Attridge developed a theory of verse rhythm that could be applied to all types of English poetry; M. L. Gasparov refined the tools for the statistical analysis of metre and set English historical metrics within a broader European context; and a series of American scholars, from Morris Halle to Paul Kiparsky and Kristin Hanson, developed and tested metrical rules to match the latest developments in comparative linguistics. In this period a number of scientific fields provided rich insights in areas where Saintsbury had struggled: cognitive science supplied data on how people count and recognize stress; statistics provided new tools for analysing texts, both in verse and in prose; and linguistics offered new theories of linguistic rhythm and of universal constraints on language output. Linguistics also helped metrists develop new and more precise terms for some metrical features: for example, while Saintsbury used the term 'the line' confusingly to refer to several different things, Roman Jakobson has taught us to distinguish between 'verse design', 'verse instance', and 'delivery instance'. All these developments must be taken into account in a modern history of versifying in English, and they form the subject of the opening chapters of this volume.

More than a thousand years have passed since the composition of the first literary texts in the modern languages of Western Europe, and throughout that period a very high proportion of authors have chosen to follow the tradition of writing in verse.[3] For most of it verse was an all-purpose medium: thus it was employed for extended narratives, textbooks on physics, and manuals of agriculture. But today there is so much information available, and there are so many alternative ways of spending leisure-time, that few writers or readers want to combine the process of data transfer with the pleasure of verse. Modern authors and readers have therefore reserved versifying for a narrow range of genres (e.g. lyric, elegiac, or humorous), and the status of metre has also been undermined by the alleged 'freedom' of much modern verse, which can lead the uninformed to confuse it with chopped-up prose. But there is no risk that metre and rhyme will disappear from our culture, since popular songs have never been able to dispense with them. While written texts have become less important, oral verse still dominates the world of mass entertainment, and young people today, wired to their Walkmen and iPods, are bombarded by metre more than any previous generation. One of the scientific definitions of metre is 'low-grade musical material', which is to say that it has rhythm but only limited melody (the tonal variation of normal speech); other members of the class *low-grade musical material* are percussion and dancing, and it would be difficult to regard as human any culture that lacked any of these.[4] Verse texts are universal because they help satisfy two basic human needs, the first for security and the second for stimulation (*sécurité* and *surprise*, in the terms of Auguste Dorchain 1919: 22–23).[5] They can satisfy these needs better than prose texts because they have an added layer of regularity (metre), which poets may choose to supply or withhold at any given point.

In his presidential address to the Modern Humanities Research Association in the year 2000 the eminent Russianist Gerald Smith concluded that 'to make and study good poetry is the best that human beings can attempt to do with their most valuable and distinctive common attribute, which is language'. A corollary of this is that the craftsmanship that has gone into creating two and a half thousand years of European poetry is a subject highly deserving of detailed study. The technical term for that craftsmanship is *poetics*, and an essential part of it is the mechanics of versifying, or *metrics*. If poetry is worth our study, so is the technology that underpins it: and the importance of metre to poets has been constantly reaffirmed by the meticulous care the greatest have taken in crafting their lines. Although most literary critics have recognized this, they have often disagreed on the nature of that craftsmanship, and few issues generate more heated debate.[6] There are a number of reasons why there is so much room for disagreement; the first is that versifying is mostly intuitive, it is a music played by ear, and metres pass from one poet to another by example not by precept; a second reason is that there is room, within certain linguistic norms, for readers to differ in their performance of the same line; and a third is that very few poets have left directions on their preferred delivery.[7] These factors combine to make the scansion of some lines ambiguous, but this ambiguity can usually be resolved by context. It is nevertheless incumbent upon metrists to check their conclusions constantly against the relevant text (including its variants) and to give due weight to the views of other metrists.

The process whereby a metre passes from one poet to another is a further variable in historical metrics: only a few poets have had the benefit of personal coaching in English verse composition, although many have been formally taught to versify in the dead languages of Greece and Rome. There are some examples of personal and professional contact between poets, such as that between Chaucer and Gower, Sidney and Spenser, Wordsworth and Coleridge, or Pound and Eliot. But all poets have in common the fact that they hear a great deal of verse before they compose any, and they seek to imitate or improve on what they have heard. This is usually how metres are transmitted between generations, and in the chapters that follow I shall often employ an evolutionary metaphor for this process.[8] This metaphor will prove valuable providing we bear in mind the differences between metrical and biological evolution: the mutations of metre are not random, they represent poets' individual choices, and the agents of selection for metres include sociological factors as well as changes in the linguistic environment. Politics, fame, fashion, and faith help determine whether a metrical experiment becomes a canon or a curiosity.

English metre represents a coherent system that has developed steadily over the last thousand years and is still developing; because of this continuity I have presented its history as a running narrative, from the earliest surviving example of versifying in a Germanic language to some of the most complex and subtle modern metrical experiments. Since the progress made in linguistic research in the last hundred years provides much of the justification for a new history of English metre, the first two chapters of this book define the essential features of a metrical system according to that research. In these chapters I shall explain the concepts concerned in both the new terminology and the old, and in the narrative itself I shall employ the new terms where they are more precise, or concise, but retain more traditional ones where they seem appropriate. I shall also pay much more attention to the way that poets versify in other languages than Saintsbury did in his highly nationalistic era. Metrics has become more global in the last hundred years: we can now recognize that English metrics is a subset of European metrics and that the pioneers of English metre were strongly influenced by models in the verse of other languages. Moreover, the search for metric universals has revealed that many of the nuances that English versifiers have tried to introduce are captured more fully and clearly in the metrical traditions of other, sometimes unrelated, languages. Where I use verse texts in other languages to demonstrate either models or parallels for English versification I shall append prose translations and use scansion aids to help the reader appreciate the structure and rhythms of the original.

The narrative chapters in this volume cover periods that vary from roughly a century to several hundred years, because the development of English metre has not proceeded uniformly either in time or in place. The length of the chapters reflects the varying pace of metrical change, and their location is similarly variable: when the locus of metrical innovation moves to Scotland or the New World my narrative follows. Inevitably this focus on change leads to inequality in the attention I pay to individual poets: metrical innovations are examined in greater detail, the refinement of existing technique is described in less, and many highly competent poets who versified in pretty much the same way as their contemporaries receive no mention. I have traced the story of English metre in the work of just over ninety poets because I believe that invoking several hundred more would not change the story materially. The ninety poets chosen provide ample evidence of the endless experiment and refinement, and of the roles of both conservation and revolution in the growth of a complex and varied system. Because most of those poets are still widely read I have included only the briefest biographical note on each, and I would urge readers who wish to know more about them to consult the latest edition of Margaret Drabble's *Oxford Companion to English Literature* for details of recent biographies.

To conclude this introduction I should like to say something of the purpose and the intended audience of the present volume. The book's first aim is to provide teachers and students of English literature with a historical account of how poets have versified in English right up to the present day. Its second aim is to familiarize this literary audience with some of the latest linguistic research into metre and to compare the traditional explanation of how various types of line are crafted with the metrical analyses offered by a number of modern writers. This comparison will have the ancillary benefit of introducing readers who are familiar with one variety of modern linguistic metrics to other varieties, and I know of no other work that has attempted this cross-fertilization. Finally, I hope that my efforts will provide a bridge between literary history and linguistics, because as university departments become larger and more specialized the two disciplines risk drifting apart. Combining the insights obtained from each can only increase the reader's understanding of literary texts and the enjoyment to be derived from them.

Notes to Introduction

1. Thus, for example, he ridicules the analyses of the German scholar Josef Schick and the American Charlton Lewis (although many of their conclusions seem valid to modern metrists), and he dismisses the polished versification of the Scots poet William Dunbar with the curious statement that it was somehow easier for a foreigner to compose good English verse (1906: 1, 300).
2. Unfortunately, including the twentieth century in any history of English metre brings complex copyright problems: today someone, somewhere, owns a poet's words until the seventieth anniversary of his or her death. There are usually two owners, one of the rights for the USA and another of those for the rest of the world, and quoting even a single line requires the permission of both. While most publishers will generously allow an author to quote isolated lines in academic debate, some will demand payment, and a few will ignore the author's requests, presumably because they doubt whether he is able to afford a sufficient sum to satisfy their shareholders. I have tried to minimize the impact of these problems on the final chapter of this book, but the acknowledgement page above gives some idea of their scale.
3. That verse accounts for a high proportion of surviving medieval texts is particularly true of English: while only 40 per cent of the works named in a medieval history of Spain (Deyermond 1971) are in verse, the corresponding figure for English is over 70 per cent (Bennett 1986).
4. I borrow the term *low-grade musical material* and the comparison with percussion from Donald Justice (1979: 269); Pietro Beltrami notes that the comparison of metre with dancing goes back to Plato (1991: 17). Perhaps metrics would become a popular discipline if renamed 'word-dancing'.
5. This observation is an improvement on the three human needs noted by Baudelaire in his 'Projet de préface' for the *Fleurs du mal*: *monotonie*, *symétrie*, and *surprise*.
6. F. L. Lucas noted the passion that animates the debates between metrists (1927: IV, 250), and Derek Pearsall linked the rancour to the difficulty and importance of their discipline (1991: 41).
7. Among the earliest recordings of poets delivering their own lines are those of Tennyson and Browning. Few readers today would emphasize the rhythms of the poems concerned in the way that the two nineteenth-century poets did.
8. Kristin Hanson and Paul Kiparsky describe metres evolving so as to be a good fit for the language in which they are employed (1996: 294). Steven Pinker has also applied the evolutionary metaphor to language itself (1994: 26–31).

CHAPTER 1

Linguistic Metrics

Linguistics and Metrics

This attempt to recount the history of English metre will be greatly aided by the adoption, at the outset, of agreed terms and definitions which will be employed consistently in the narrative chapters that follow. Some of the terms I shall employ have been in use for centuries while others are the result of modern researchers' attempts to make the discipline of metrics more scientific. Many of them derive from the Ancient Greeks, and consequently have had to be radically adapted to fit English practice. Beginning in the sixteenth century, English writers gradually developed from this Classical base a vocabulary for discussing metre that I shall refer to as the 'traditional', and, since much of it has passed into general use, I shall employ it wherever no more precise term has been introduced. But the twentieth century saw the emergence of the discipline of *linguistics*, the study of the structure of language, or of language as a system, which began with the work of Ferdinand de Saussure (b. 1857, d. 1913), a professor of Sanskrit, who taught in Geneva in the years that Saintsbury was writing his *History of English Prosody*. In the second half of the century linguistics departments were set up in most universities, and linguistics researchers found themselves increasingly involved in the study of the mind itself. This was recognized in the establishment of Chairs in *Cognitive Science* at a number of universities in the 1990s. A twenty-first-century treatise can therefore examine metre within a wider cognitive context, but it has to contend with the fact that linguistic researchers have introduced a vast number of new terms that describe many aspects of metre more precisely.

Varieties of linguistic metrics

Unfortunately, modern linguistic metrists do not share a single set of terms and procedures; in particular there are radical differences between the outputs of two important groups of scholars, one trained in Russia (or on Slav metrics) and the other in the USA. The first group use the term *statistical* to describe their brand of linguistic metrics, and the second style themselves *generative* metrists. It is an unfortunate legacy of the Cold War that many US generative metrists know little of the work of Russian statistical metrists and vice versa. The great achievement of the statistical approach to metre has been to categorize large bodies of verse, and it was first exemplified in a study published in 1910 by the poet Andrei Bely (b. 1880,

d. 1824). Boris Tomashevsky refined his method (see Tomashevsky 1929) and M. L. Gasparov is the leading member of the third generation to employ it. His major contributions to comparative metrics include a single-volume history of European metre (Gasparov 1996) and a technique termed *probability modelling* (Gasparov 1980a, 1980b, & 1987). This technique helps establish the poet's metrical intention by comparing the frequency of any given linguistic feature in his or her verse with its frequency in the language itself.[1] The impressive Russian progress in metric typology and stylistics probably owes something to the size of the published corpus of verse in Russian, which is nowhere near as daunting as its equivalent in English.

In contrast, the prime concerns of generative metrists have been (a) establishing the universals of metre and (b) defining the boundary between metrical and unmetrical utterances. Both projects have met with considerable success, although much of the research has been devoted to the versifying of a few well-known poets, such as Shakespeare, Donne, Milton, and Hopkins. The methodology of generative metrics is to hypothesize a poem's verse design and then test individual lines against the hypothesis.[2] This is the antithesis of the statistical method, where researchers log all the metrical features of a vast number of lines before deriving a hypothesis from their statistics. Critics of generative metrics complain that it has mostly generated impenetrable jargon, but many of the terms it has introduced are both concise and precise, and I shall employ them gratefully in this volume. For a number of English metres, however, the terms employed by traditional or by statistical metrics are simpler and raise fewer difficult questions. I have not hesitated, therefore, to be eclectic in my use of terms, or to employ synonyms for the sake of variety. In this I am not alone: a number of important modern works on European metrics have drawn impartially upon traditional, statistical, and generative concepts, and their analysis has been the richer for it.[3] I shall first employ this eclectic approach to offer answers to some fundamental questions: what is verse? Why and how do poets produce it? Which features of their language can English poets employ in this process?

Verse and Versifying

Verse is a *stylization* of language, which is to say that it is language used in a specific context (Allen 1973: 103–04): the context in which the present volume will study verse is poetry, but verse is also the language of song lyrics, memory aids, greetings card messages, and utterances that accompany bodily movements such as marching. Verse, whether oral or written, differs from other utterances (prose) by being 'numerically regulated' (Lotz 1960: 135), that is, it involves some form of counting. The basic unit of verse, the *line*, extends from the point where the counting begins to the point where it ends (Fabb 2002a: 48–49), and in modern editions of verse texts orthography separates the individual lines. The word *verse* itself is derived from the Latin for a turn of the plough, the moment when it was *reversed* and the ploughman began again. Composing verse predates literacy and is a universal human activity (see Bowra 1963: 14–17), and explanations offered of why humans versify include the biological, practical, and even supernatural. The most credible is that counting provides intellectual stimulation, while the more regular rhythms of the language it produces give sensory satisfaction. Rhythm can be perceived by all the human organs and by the central nervous system itself, and regular motion is a feature of most biological processes; humans also reproduce it in many of their activities, such as dancing, marching, and singing.[4]

Another credible motivation for versifying is that it provides a memory aid for non-literate performers, enabling them to reproduce a text with great verbal precision (see Gaur 1984: 25). This is vital in religious contexts: primitive animists believe that spells and prayers work only if every word is in the correct place and most of the world's principal religions preserve this tradition.[5] There may be a religious element even in secular verse; thus epic poems always open with a prayer or invocation, and many poets have pursued their craft with religious intensity. The poet's (and artist's) desire for transcendence is explained by Justice (1979: 271) as follows:

> One motive for much if not all art [...] is [... that] emotion needs to be fixed, so that [... it] may become as nearly permanent as possible, allowing it to be recalled back again and again at pleasure.

The deepest and most detailed study of the relationship between metre, meaning, and cultural memory has so far appeared only in Russian (Gasparov 1999), but there can be no doubt that one of the greatest achievements of the finest poetry is a fusion of these three.

Structure and Design

The second half of the twentieth century developed a body of theory that used linguistic analysis to identify many different types of structures in literary texts (see Rivkin & Ryan 1998). Many of these structures applied equally to both verse and prose texts, but metre is a layer of structure specific to verse. The study of the language of poetry, or *poetics*, includes in its field all these structures plus a wide range of other features. Some very important books on poetics make little or no mention of metre (for example, Culler 1975 and Birrell 2004), but others do not make this separation (see, for example, Leech 1969 and Preminger et al. 1975). Similarly, most works on metrics pay some attention to structural features of the poem that have little to do with the counting that goes on within lines or with the rhythms that it produces. Such structures may be based upon semantics or imagery, when metrists tend to ignore them, or they may be syntactic, in which case metrists often take a keen interest in how they interact with line structure.

Syntax and metre

The relationship between metrical and syntactic structures in a poem is an important one. Allen argues that the line is a 'metrically normalized sentence' (1973: 113), and the norm in verse is for metrical and syntactic boundaries to coincide at the end of each line (when they are termed *end-stopped*). But in practice syntactic and metrical boundaries don't always coincide: sometimes the sentence overlaps the line and sometimes the line contains material that belongs to two different sentences. It is important to distinguish between the systematic and random subdivision of lines: when all the lines of a poem are divided in the same place (or in one of a fixed number of places) the division can be termed a *caesura*; but when some lines have no such division, or the position of any subdivision is random, it is more correct to refer to the line as containing two *cola*, thus emphasizing the grammatical as distinct from metrical nature of the subdivision. The way that poets have employed caesura and cola play an important part in the history of English metre, and I shall often return to this subject in the course of the chapters that follow.

The severance of a syntactic unit by a line boundary is termed *enjambment*, and may involve a sentence, a clause, a phrase, a syntagm, or even a word (thus in Chapter 10 we shall encounter an example of the word *A-me-ri-ca* occupying four lines). Syntactic units may also be divided between strophes, although such enjambment is much rarer than within strophes. There have been many attempts to define the degrees of enjambment (see, for example, Quilis 1964 and Beltrami 1986) but, as Robert Pinsky notes, 'there are as many different kinds of line ending as there are ways one word can follow another [... because] every line ending slices into the sentence a little differently' (1998: 29–30). Nevertheless, there are significant differences in the frequency of enjambment, at least of some types, between poems, genres, and poetic styles. In the chapters that follow, therefore, I shall adopt a simple definition of enjambment that enables me to demonstrate these differences in comparative tables: 'the severance by a line boundary of a phrase or nuclear clause'.[6]

Enjambment emphasizes the individual words in the enjambed phrase, and is also an important source of variety in long poems (as is the subdivision of lines into cola).[7] Enjambment is of particular significance in free verse, where the division of the text into lines is sometimes the only metrical constant. The frequency of enjambment and the changes in it are often the result of fashion and emulation, but sometimes they are related to linguistic factors. Thus, for example, verse that depends for its rhythm on line-end phrasal stress, like French syllabic verse, favours the end-stopping of lines. Similarly, the heroic couplet favours the end-stopping of even-numbered lines to emphasize its structure, while dramatic blank verse favours enjambment (and thus more closely mimics the language of normal speech). I shall comment on the use of enjambment in many of the texts that I discuss in this volume, and note how often it occurs, in the same way that I measure purely metrical features.

Poem design

The purely metrical structures of a poem are based on the numerical regulation of specific features of its language. Such regulation occurs at various levels: a poem contains a number of lines, those lines may be grouped into *strophes* or *stanzas*, and each line contains a number of smaller linguistic units. Modern metrics describes the regulation at these three levels as *poem design*, *strophe design*, and *verse design*, respectively. Although the number of lines a poem contains is often arbitrary, many poems are in set forms, for which there is a traditional formula, and long poems are usually divided for convenience into sub-units called *books, cantos,* or even *fits.* The earliest long poems had to be divided into such sub-units because they were performed before audiences, and the sub-unit probably represented the maximum practical limit of a single performance. More sophisticated poems sometimes employ symbolism in their poem design; thus, for example, the three books of Dante's *Commedia* (Petrocchi 1975) are subdivided into 100 *cantos,* the three symbolizing the Trinity and 100 in numerology being the perfect number.[8] Although some isolated studies relating numerology to long medieval verse texts were published in the last century, poem design is rarely studied in a systematic way. Set forms, on the other hand, are easily listed, and many popular primers of metre provide such lists (see, for example, Stillman 1966: 41–79 and Fry 2005: 191–274). Most of the set forms originated in ancient Greece or Rome, or in medieval France or Italy, but some modern poets have employed them, or devised new variations upon them. I shall do no more than note these set forms as they occur in my narrative, because modern metrical research has found very little new to say about them. Thus the section on set forms in Fry 2005 could have been a written a century ago. A great deal of modern research, however, has been devoted to the systematic study of strophe design.

Strophe design

Ancient Greek metrists divided verse into two classes: *stichic,* in which there are no intermediate metrical structures between the poem and the line, and *strophic,* in which there are. Strophe design and the device of rhyme, which has characterized it for almost a millennium, are not as important in English as in French, where the poverty of structure within the line has led both poets and critics to focus on that of the larger unit. Thus a number of modern metrists have produced works that catalogue the strophe forms found in substantial bodies of Romance verse (see n3), but I know of no study of this type devoted to English poetry. While such a study would add significantly to our knowledge of versifying in English, lack of space prevents me from attempting to include an inventory, or even a checklist, of strophe forms in the present volume. The aims of this section are therefore to note general principles and to supply some terms and definitions as background to a historical narrative focused on English line structure.

In strophic verse each strophe usually comprises the same number of lines; these may differ in structure, but each must have the same structure as the corresponding line in the poem's other strophes.[9] The linguistic features that have been most frequently employed in strophe design are line length and rhyme. Spenser's *Faerie Queene* (Kirschbaum 1961) is an example of a poem in which both play a part in the strophe structure. Spenser's poem design divides into seven books (the last unfinished), each of twelve cantos, which vary in length around fifty strophes; his strophe design consists of nine lines, the first eight of which have ten syllables, while the final one has twelve; the rhyme scheme is ababcdcdd.[10] This form subsequently became known as the Spenserian stanza and is a fairly complex structure, but strophes can be much simpler, and even pairs of lines meet the definition. The couplet of Chaucer's *Canterbury Tales* is a minimum strophe based on rhyme, and the Latin elegiac couplet that Chaucer's friend Gower employed in his *Vox clamantis* is a minimum strophe based on line length: it combines a line of six durational feet with one of five. Both types of couplet are repeating structures intermediate between poem and line.

Features other than line length and rhyme may be used to group lines into strophes, including the following devices: (1) the use of *refrains* (a line, or lines, may be repeated at regular intervals, thus creating a series of similar units); (2) the use of verbal repetition (the same word(s) may be used to close a series of lines occurring at regular intervals), and (3) the opening letters of either lines or strophes may be used to spell a word. An example of a refrain is Shakespeare's song 'It Was a Lover and his Lass' from *As You Like It*, v. 3 (Hughes 1971: 47), which has a three-line refrain. The tour de force of final-word repetition is an Occitan form called the *sestina*, where six words rotated in a fixed order end all the lines and divide the poem into strophes; Pound's 'Altaforte' (Eliot 1959: 53–55) is a modern English example. Acrostic poems have been composed throughout recorded history: the initial letters of the strophes in Psalm 119 represent the Hebrew alphabet and those of Chaucer's *ABC* (Benson 1988: 637–40) the Roman. The initial letters of lines, as well as of strophes, have been used in this way; the Latin playwright Plautus often used the initial letters of a prologue's lines to spell out the name of his play, as in the *Miles gloriosus* (Tyrrell 1881: xlvii), and Ben Jonson is among the English playwrights who have imitated this (Preminger et al. 1975: 4). Many acrostic poems contain a name in the initial letters of their lines; for example, the poems by Edgar Allan Poe that spell out the first two names of his beloved (Wilbur 1959: 115–16). But structural devices such as refrains, the repetition of final words, and acrostics should probably be regarded not as metrical features (because they could equally well be used in prose sentences), but as compositional choices of an author who happens to be writing verse.

Strophic structure based on line length and quantitative patterns reached its zenith in the Ancient Greek ode (Levi 1985: 114–32), and that based on line length and rhyme was at its most impressive in medieval Occitan poetry (Ricketts 2001). The earliest surviving strophes in French and Spanish are *laisses*, which consist of a varying number of lines of the same structure linked by the same assonance. In the eleventh century, however, Occitan poets, or troubadours, began to invent highly complex strophe forms based on rhyme, and their Northern contemporaries were quick to follow; Billy 1989 appropriately uses the metaphor of *architecture* to describe these elegant constructions of the Occitan troubadours, who took great care not to use the same strophe structures as their rivals. But most later European poets preferred to cultivate 'fixed forms', many of which are international. French poetry offered English poets models for strophe design of almost every conceivable length (listed in Mazaleyrat & Molinié 1989): for example, a seven-line design that has proved enduringly popular in English is *rhyme royal* (rhymed ababbcc). The Italians also bequeathed English poets a number of strophe designs, including *terza rima* (rhymed aba bcb etc.) and the eight-line *ottava rima* (abababcc). The most popular import from Italy, however, has been a poem design, the fourteen-line *sonnet*, which divides 8 + 6 and has a variety of rhyme schemes.

Syllable structure

A linguistic feature that poets may regulate numerically in their poetry is the quality of the sounds in certain parts of the line, usually at its close. The technical term for such regulation is *phoneme repetition*, but the general public often term it loosely, and inaccurately, 'rhyme'. Measurement with modern instruments shows that human speech more closely resembles a continuous chain than a series of separate sounds, and the minimum segments of that chain used to distinguish meaning (for example, the initial sounds in *cat* and *mat*) are termed *phonemes* (see Crystal 1985: 228–29). Speakers of all languages, however, intuitively sense that phonemes are grouped in *syllables*, and metrists find the concept of the syllable invaluable in their analysis. There is, of course, a relationship between syllables and phonemes in the speech chain (see Crystal 1985: 297–98 and Hogg & McCully 1987: 35–41), and we can see what it is if we represent syllable structure by a tree diagram:

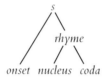

Each of the terminal nodes in this diagram corresponds to a phoneme or phonemes, a consonant, or consonants, in the case of onset and coda, a vowel or diphthong in the case of the nucleus. Of these sub-units of syllable structure only the nucleus is mandatory: although many syllables have all three elements (notation CVC), a syllable may lack an onset (making its notation VC), a coda (notation CV), or both (notation V). The four possibilities can be exemplified by the words *mat*, *at*, *ma*, and *a*, respectively. Note that syllables may be divided into two classes according to whether they have branching rhymes (CVC or CV if the V of the latter represents a long vowel or diphthong). Syllables with non-branching rhymes are termed *short* in traditional and *light* in linguistic metrics, and their duration is described as being of one *mora*. Syllables with branching rhymes are similarly termed *long* or *heavy*, and are held to occupy two moras. I shall return to the concept of syllable weight later in this chapter.

Phoneme repetition

Poets can link any number of syllables in a passage of verse by filling the same element of syllable structure with the same phoneme. Because there are three possible places (onset, nucleus, and coda) and two possible situations (repetition or non-repetition), phoneme repetition may take eight (2^3) forms, for each of which there is a technical term.[11] Although some of these have passed into common parlance, others have not, and so I shall list them here using binary numbers to demonstrate their complementary nature. If a similarity at any point between two syllables is indicated by the binary digit *1* and a difference by *0*, the eight possibilities can be presented as a simple paradigm (with repeated phonemes underlined):

(1) *000* = zero repetition [cat/dog]   (2) *001* = consonance [dog/pig]
(3) *010* = assonance [b<u>a</u>t/m<u>a</u>n]   (4) *011* = rhyme [c<u>at</u>/m<u>at</u>]
(5) *100* = alliteration [<u>c</u>at/<u>c</u>up]   (6) *101* = pararhyme [<u>b</u>at/<u>b</u>it]
(7) *110* = reverse rhyme [<u>ma</u>n/<u>ma</u>t]   (8) *111* = full repetition [<u>man</u>/un<u>man</u>]

There are a number of conventions associated with rhyme that vary from language to language: for example, to English ears full repetition (8) is scarcely rhyme at all (it is sometimes termed *echo rhyme*), but French poets regard it as the most perfect and term it *rime riche* (see Leech 1969: 92 and Grammont 1937: 354). The lack of an onset or coda creates a sort of zero phoneme, which is also subject to repetition: thus the monosyllables *go* and *no* have no codas yet clearly rhyme. Similarly, zero onsets are sometimes held to alliterate in English, as in the second line of Henry King's 'Sic Vita' (Gardner 1972: 251): 'Or as the flights of eagles are'. It should also be noted that any of these types of repetition may or may not be systematic: it may be a compositional feature in one poetic tradition, but a metrical feature in another.[12]

In the Romance and Germanic languages rhyme usually involves stress and may affect up to three syllables; it is therefore traditionally classed as being of three types: *masculine* (M), *feminine* (F), and *proparoxytonic* (P). Masculine rhymes involve phoneme repetition (*011*) in a final stressed syllable; feminine rhymes involve a penultimate stressed syllable, which must be followed by full repetition (*011* + *111*); proparoxytonic rhymes involve a stressed antepenultimate syllable, which must be followed by two full repetitions (*011* + *111* + *111*). Assonance (*010*) may similarly be M, F, or P. The first Western poets to employ rhyme in this way (and the first metrists to analyse it) did so in Arabic, using the terms *qāfiya* for 011 and *radīf* for 111.[13]

Verse design

Most modern works on metrics have replaced the traditional word *line* by a series of less ambiguous terms first proposed by Roman Jakobson (1960: 364–65). A *verse design* is the abstract theoretical scheme also known as metre, a *verse instance* is an actual line, and a *delivery instance* is a particular performance of it; a verse instance is thus 'the common-denominator of all meaningful delivery instances' (Chatman 1965: 96).[14] I shall use the word *line* primarily to describe a specific verse instance (which will be numbered in my examples), and where there is any risk of ambiguity I shall use the longer and more precise terms. A *verse design* is made up of an abstract pattern in the poet's head (the *template*) and any rules or constraints (s)he observes in realizing this pattern in verse instances (*correspondence rules*). Although modern poets' delivery of their own lines can be valuable evidence, we usually have to infer a verse design from the instances based upon it. A template comprises a series of *positions*, each corresponding to a different piece of linguistic material in the verse instance, and longer templates may contain a mandatory word boundary, a constraint preventing adjacent positions containing syllables from the same word (termed a *caesura* by traditional metrics). The correspondence rules govern the quantity and quality of linguistic material that may fill each position in verse instances; for example, the rules may state that a given position must be filled by a single syllable, or by a stressed syllable. Since the templates and correspondence rules of counting metres are usually less complex than those of patterning metres, I shall begin my examination of verse design with the former.

Counting Metres

Poets versify by counting, and the line begins where the counting begins, and ends where it ends; in modern works this is usually signalled by the orthography, but I shall note a few exceptions in the course of this volume. Poets count linguistic units, and one of the strengths of statistical linguistic metrics is that it leads researchers to check just what is being counted in any given verse text. Since much of the controversy and confusion in modern metrics results from differing assumptions, I shall begin by examining the limited number of options that the poet has. These limits are imposed by language itself and may be listed in what linguisticians term the *prosodic hierarchy*.

The prosodic hierarchy

Poets can count only the units that language provides, and those units may be listed in descending order, as in the following table derived from Getty 2002: 7:

Phonological utterance
|
Intonational phrase
|
Phonological phrase
|
Word
|
Foot
|
Syllable
|
Mora

We can thus redefine a verse text as a series of utterances that are numerically regulated at one or more of these levels: a verse design's rules may stipulate the number of phrases, words, feet, syllables, or moras in a line.[15] Some verse is regulated at more than one level, and its lines may contain a regular number of both phrases and words, or phrases and syllables, or of feet and moras. I shall discuss each of these types of verse briefly and then focus my analysis on the units that most (but by no means all) English poets have counted.

Phrasal metres

One of the most widespread forms of numerical regulation found in verse is at phrase level: poets may regulate the number of intonational phrases in the line and, within them, the number of phonological phrases, as in (1) to (3) below. The major sub-units of the line so created are usually known as *cola* (sing.: *colon*); their most common number by far is two, when they are termed *hemistichs* and the boundary between them the *caesura*. The eighteenth and nineteenth centuries saw isolated attempts to introduce phrasal metres into English and phrasal metres were employed frequently in the twentieth as one of the categories of free verse. But they have an extremely long history: phrase-level regulation is first found in verse texts of the third millennium BC; it is the most important and invariable structural principle of Sumerian, Egyptian, Babylonian, and early Semitic verse, and also of the earliest surviving verse text in an Indo-European language.[16] The large body of poetry contained in the Hebrew miscellany that we call the Bible is regulated in this way, and such a metre translates very readily into other languages, as the following examples show:[17]

(1) They part my garments among them,
       and cast lots upon my vesture.   (Psalm 22. 18)

(2) The conies are but a feeble folk,
       yet make they their houses in the rocks.   (Proverbs 30. 26)

(3) Stay me with flagons,
       comfort me with apples:
          for I am sick of love.   (Song of Solomon 2. 5)

Note that instance (3) is an example of the less common, three-part structure. The technical term for this type of metre is *parallelismus membrorum*, and the parallel units comprising the line are of three types (Preminger et al. 1975: 337): instance (1) is an example of *sameness*, (2) of *contrast*, and (3) of *complementary* parallelism.

Phrase-level regulation can be found in the verse of most languages, if only because poets sometimes want to employ lines longer than the typical phrase in their language. Thus French metrists have always held that lines of more than eight syllables must contain a caesura dividing them into at least two cola (Cornulier 1995: 47). The lines of Old English epic metre are clear examples of a two-part structure, or phrase-level regulation but, like most two-part lines in most languages, their linguistic material is also numerically regulated in other ways. Phrase-level regulation is usually reinforced at lower levels because, on its own, it cannot satisfy the human appetite for ever more elaborate structures. Cola are quite large units of linguistic material and, while audiences readily identify multiples of two or three of them, they would find lines containing six cola (and no other regulation) amorphous and confusing.

Word-based metres

English poets have shown little interest in counting the number of words in the line, probably because it is difficult to distinguish individual lines composed in this way from accentual verse (the number of lexical words in any line is the same as the number of primary stresses). It is, nevertheless, worth looking briefly at verbal metres, because they may be the precursors of the earliest English metres; verbal metres certainly have a long enough history. Phrase-level regulation in verse tends to be reinforced at lower levels, and the poetry of the Old Testament is no exception: in the original Hebrew it is reinforced often, but not invariably, by word-level regulation. In the English of the AV the translator replaces this with accentual regulation; following an old English tradition, he gives each colon two stresses (my bold typeface):

> (4)   A **time** to **weep**,
>   and a **time** to **laugh**.   (Ecclesiastes 3. 4)

But the Hebrew original regulated the number of words in each colon (my emphasis by word separation):

> (5)   Et li-Bekot || we-'Et li-Sehok

This line comprises two cola, each of two words, but three- or four-word cola may equally well be balanced in this way. Preminger et al. note the perfect symmetry of such lines and say that the Hebrew poet's aim was 'symmetric perfection in form and content' (1975: 337c2).

Word-level numerical regulation is undoubtedly one of the oldest and most basic modes of versifying; thus, for example, Bowra 1963: 32 gives an example of a chant in the native Australian Aranda language that is regulated at this level (my emphasis by word separation):

> (6)   ngkinjaba iturala albutjika
>   [turn home in the afternoon when the sun is bright and hot]

Word-level regulation is employed in some of the oldest texts in Western Europe: the earliest surviving Celtic verse has lines comprising hemistichs of three words (Pighi 1970: 18), and the verse design of the oldest Italic verse may also be based on the number of words. The few fragments of what is termed *numerus italicus* reveal no quantitative pattern, but show some regularity in the number of words and accents (Gildersleeve & Lodge 1953: 462). As I shall show in Chapter 2, Latin poets seem to have counted words in two different periods, and poets in a number of cultures have changed quite rapidly from counting one linguistic unit to counting another.

Syllabic and moraic metres

The smallest linguistic units that poets may count are *moras*, the units that describe the duration of the shortest syllables. Attempts to compose Classical quantitative verse in English are the only clear examples of moraic metres in the language, but at the end of the nineteenth century and beginning of the twentieth some English poets made a determined effort to introduce a metrics in which syllable weight played a part as well as stress. A simple, but perfect, example of moraic verse can be found in Japanese metrics, although it is usually described as syllabic (see, for example, Henderson 1958, Bownas 1964, and Preminger et al. 1975: 423–31). Brower (1972: 38), Fabb (1997: 58), and Getty (2002: 10), however, point out correctly that Japanese verse is based on the numerical regulation of moras.[18] The only heavy syllables in Japanese are those with long vowels, which are regarded as double syllables (see Dunn & Yanada 1958: 3), and a seven-syllable line has only six syllables if one of them is heavy, and only five if it contains two heavy syllables. All Japanese lines contain either five or seven moras and the two most popular verse forms combine the two lengths: the 17-mora *haiku* has lines of 5, 7, and 5, and the 31-mora *tanka* has lines of 5, 7, 5, 7, and 7.[19]

In Indo-European verse the counting of moras has always been combined with that of syllables, and I shall postpone discussion of syllabic metres to the next chapter, because syllable counting is a major element in the versification of those languages that have most influenced English metrics.

Patterning Metres

Modern cognitive science has demonstrated that humans instantly recognize (for which the technical term is subitize) not only single units, but also duples and triples, pairs and groups of three (Hurford 1987: 93–97; see also Fabb 2002a: 51). This is reflected in language by the existence of duals and plurals as well as singulars; and it seems to be mirrored in other species, because nesting birds can distinguish between two eggs and three, but not between three and four. Numbers beyond three even humans need to learn to count. Poets of many cultures have learned to count the number of contrasts in their lines, contrasts between a linguistic unit and its (one or two) neighbours. Modern linguistic metrics has borrowed the term feet from Classical metrics to describe contrasts, duples, and triples, and Nigel Fabb describes metres that count these more complex entities as patterning metres (1997: 59–60).

The inventory of feet

Roman Jakobson once argued that all verse is based on binary contrasts, because even in syllabic metres the nuclei of syllables were contrasted with their boundaries (1960: 359–60), but it is difficult to demonstrate that poets and audiences are aware of such nuclei and boundaries. What is undeniable is that poets employ the contrast between two different types of syllable when composing patterning metres.

One such contrast is between heavy and light syllables, and the verse so produced is usually termed *quantitative*. The poets of many ancient languages composed quantitative verse, including Sanskrit (see Mukherji 1976), Ancient Greek (see West 1982), Classical Latin (see Raven 1965), and Arabic (see Arberry 1965). Quantitative verse has also been composed in English, in imitation of Classical models, but not entirely successfully.

Modern linguistic metrics has borrowed the Greek term *feet* to describe the contrasts used in patterning metres, but recognizes that properties other than syllable weight may be patterned in describing the contrasted elements as strong (s) and weak (w). Modern writers also employ the Greek terms for the five types of foot that can constitute a duple or a triple: the *iamb* [w s], *trochee* [s w], *anapaest* [w w s], *amphibrach* [w s w], and *dactyl* [s w w]. Ancient Greek metrists also coined terms for non-contrastive feet, such as the *pyrrhic* (two short syllables), and for contrastive combinations of four or more syllables, such as the *choriamb* (a trochee followed by an iamb), and some popular works on modern English metre still refer to these (for example, Fry 2005). Most linguistic metrists, however, follow the insights of cognitive science and restrict feet to duples and triples (see Fabb & Halle 2005). I shall often find it convenient in this volume to describe combinations of two or three contrastive syllables as feet and give them their Greek names.

Verse and rhythm

Justice describes verse as 'low-grade musical material' (1979: 269), which is to say that it has rhythm, like music, but only very limited tonic variation, like percussion or dancing.[20] Chatman offers an analysis of the nature of rhythm and of the types of rhythm found in English verse (1965: 19–26), Gross compares metre with music (1972: passim), and Attridge discusses the use of musical analogies in the analysis of verse and notes their limitations (1982: 20–27). Rhythm is produced when a series of events occurs at what is perceived by the human ear as regular intervals.[21] A *simple primary rhythm* is produced when a single event is repeated at regular intervals, for example, the ticking of a clock, and the language produced by counting metres has this type of rhythm: its lines contain an undifferentiated series of events, which may be phrases, words, syllables, or moras. In contrast, the language of patterning metres has a *complex secondary rhythm*: its lines contain two different types of event in a regular sequence (Chatman 1965: 29). There are traditional metrical terms for the rhythms produced by different types of feet: *duple time* is used to describe the rhythm produced by a series of binary and *triple time* that produced by a series of ternary feet. Similarly the rhythm produced by a series of *left-strong* feet (trochees or dactyls) is described as a *falling* and that produced by a series of *right-strong* feet (iambs or anapaests) as a *rising rhythm*.

Accent and rhythm

The feet and the rhythms of Ancient Greek verse were quantitative, based upon the distinction between long and short syllables. That language also had another type of contrast available: the contrast between *accented* and *unaccented* syllables. Accent is a property that distinguishes some syllables from others, and it has acoustic correlates that vary from language to language. Phonologists tend to simplify this situation by dividing languages into those with *melodic* and those with *dynamic* accent. In languages with melodic accent accented syllables are delivered with a change in pitch, which may rise, fall, or rise and fall again. In languages with dynamic accent (more commonly termed *stress*) accented syllables exhibit a combination of pitch change with greater volume and duration (see Fry 1958 and Quilis 1971). Ancient Greek had a melodic accent that its poets did not employ to pattern their versification, but we know that they could have done so because the poets of ancient China did.[22] Moreover, Chinese poets sometimes used melodic accent to create a larger pattern by giving adjacent lines contrasting rhythms (for example, a trochaic line may follow an iambic). Lines used in this way produce a similar effect to the phrases in phrasal metres: one line balances another; this can be termed *linear verse*. In modern times *linear free verse* has been composed in many languages, and in English the linear contrasts often involve line length as well as rhythm, a short line being juxtaposed to a series of long ones, or vice versa.[23] In English, changes in pitch are used for other purposes than to produce contrasts between syllables (see Bolinger 1958), and the rhythms and feet of English verse are based upon one of the language's more obvious features, stress.

Stress and metre

The acoustic correlates of stress (pitch, volume, and duration) are not zero–sum properties, and many metrists have been uneasy with the concept of only two types of syllable, stressed and unstressed. The traditional terminology recognizes three levels of stress (primary, secondary, and non-stress), but Trager & Smith (1951) argued that English contains four, and their hypothesis soon found many adherents. They also had doubters, among whom Seymour Chatman pointed out that he could identify eight levels in the word *anti-disestablishmentarianism*, the only candidate in English for a one-word decasyllable (1965: 13). More recent research has concluded that stress is a continuum, and that the number of levels of stress identifiable in utterances varies. Metrists consequently abandoned the four-level theory in favour of the relative stress principle: the hypothesis that the aspect of stress most relevant to verse is whether a syllable has more stress than its neighbours.[24] This property of having greater stress than neighbouring syllables is called *prominence* and is of great importance to versifying in English, because some poets have counted and others have patterned the prominent syllables in their verse.

Stress is assigned to the most important syllable in every phrase, when it is termed *phrasal stress*, and to at least one syllable of lexical words (nouns, verbs, adjectives, adverbs, and some pronouns), when it is termed *lexical stress*. In polysyllabic words one syllable always has more stress than the other(s), and this is used to distinguish meaning, as in the English words *insight* [s w] and *incite* [w s]. As noted, the term *strength* is used to describe the property of having greater stress than neighbouring syllables in the same word. Thus, for example, both syllables of the word *reptile* usually receive some stress in delivery, but only the first syllable is strong. In some longer words there is more than one strong syllable; thus, for example, in *confidential* the third syllable is strongest and is said to have *primary stress*, but the first syllable also has more stress than its neighbour, and is said to have *secondary stress*. In modern English this usually falls two places from primary stress, but in some words (for example, *fortification*) the interval between the stresses is three syllables. If primary stress is indicated by 'S' and secondary by 's', the stress profile of *confidential* can be represented as [s w S w] and that of *fortification* as [s w w S w]. Note that, in English, trisyllabic words may have one strong syllable, like *insightful* [w s w], two, like *commandant* [S w s], or be ambiguous, like *misery*, which may be pronounced either [s w w] or [S w s].

Lexical monosyllables also usually receive stress, but there is no fixed strong/ weak relationship between them and their neighbours; thus, for example, in *John thought* the relative stress depends on context and the monosyllable that receives it may be regarded as having *phrasal stress*. Some English metres prescribe the position of the strong syllables of polysyllabic words more strictly than that of other stresses, because the relative prominence of such syllables is fixed by the lexicon. Some combinations of monosyllables also have a predictable stress relationship in normal speech: for example, *on fire* and *the house* are usually [w s], and *ask for* and *play with* [s w]. Poets who regulate strength more strictly than stress in their metre, therefore, will rarely violate the normal [w s] prominence relationship of *incite*, be more relaxed about that of *on fire*, but place *John thought* wherever it fits most conveniently into the line.[25]

Approaches to English Metre

Many of the difficulties the general reader finds in metrics are the result of differing terminology: metrists often have several different terms for the same feature and sometimes employ a term inconsistently. There is also intense rivalry between modern metrists and there have been few attempts to reconcile their differences. But the variety of directions from which linguistic metrists approach their subject can be seen as an advantage, since one approach may offer the clearest account of one type of English verse, and a second approach the most convincing explanation of another. In the present volume I shall be unashamedly eclectic because I believe that we can learn more by paying heed to many teachers. The number of concepts and terms I shall employ is, of course, increased by this eclecticism, and in order to introduce them I shall devote this section to comparing four different descriptions of the English long-line canon. The first description is traditional, the second rhythmic, the third generative, and the fourth statistical. I shall illustrate each approach by analysing four lines (11–14) from the epigram (no. 14) 'To William Camden' (Donaldson 1975: 13) by Ben Jonson (b. 1572, d. 1637).[26]

(7)   Pardon free truth, and let thy modesty,
(8)   Which conquers all, be once overcome by thee.
(9)   Many of thine this better could than I;
(10)   But for their powers accept my piety.

The traditional approach

Traditional metrics classifies the metre of Jonson's poem as *stress-syllabic*, implying that its design regulates both stresses and syllables, in contrast to *accentual* metres, where the poet counts only stresses, and *syllabic* metres, where the poet counts only syllables. This particular metre is traditionally termed an *iambic pentameter* because the ideal line comprises five unstressed syllables, each followed by a stressed syllable, as in line 4 of the same poem:

(11)   The <u>great</u> re-**nown** and <u>name</u> where-**with** she <u>goes</u>

In (11) I have placed strong syllables in bold typeface and underlined stressed monosyllables to emphasize the iambic (w s) alternation. But none of the other lines quoted is made up of five iambs in this way. Traditional metrists account for this discrepancy by the concept of tension, permitted variance from the metrical pattern (see Allen 1973: 110–13). The appeal of tension to poets and audiences probably results from the human mind's quest for variety as well as regularity: as Auguste Dorchain noted, people seem to crave *surprise* as well as *sécurité* (1919: 22–23). In modern cognitive theory the concept of *ostension* from pragmatics has been used to explain tension: Nigel Fabb argues that poets use it communicate the message 'this is my metre' (2001: 786). According to this hypothesis, tension stimulates the mind by presenting it with two things that are the same but different (the invariant design and the deviant instance).

Two of Jonson's lines, (7) and (9), open with a trochee (S w), '**Par**-don' and '**Ma**-ny'; this feature, termed *inversion* by traditional metrics, is quite common at line openings (*initial inversion*), but elsewhere is rare except after a major mid-line syntactic boundary (when it could be regarded as *initial inversion* applied to the second hemistich). The iambic regularity of the other two lines, (8) and (10), is threatened by an extra syllable if the words are pronounced 'o-ver-**come**' and '**po**-wers'. But the first may also be pronounced 'o'er-**come**' and the second '<u>powers</u>'; English poets make considerable use of the ambivalence of words like these with flimsy boundaries between syllables (note that 'au-tho-ri-ty in' counts as four syllables in line 9 of the same poem). Instance (8), however, is held by traditional metrists to be metrical even if 'overcome' is trisyllabic, because it would be allowed by another type of tension, *resolution* or *substitution*, which allows two (usually light) syllables to replace a single unstressed syllable in exceptional cases.

There are two other types of tension that are rather less obvious, but which occur in Jonson's four lines. The third syllable of (7) is not unstressed, but a stressed monosyllable ('free'), and traditional metrics explains this as *incursion*, arguing that its stress is neutralized by that of an adjacent word ('truth'). In iambic metres such incursive stresses are always monosyllables and they are by no means uncommon: many metrists have noted the multiple example in *Paradise Lost* (II. 621; Leonard 1998) by John Milton (b. 1608, d. 1674), where the lexical monosyllables 'rocks', 'lakes', and 'bogs' are all incursive:[27]

> (12)   Rocks, <u>caves</u>, lakes, <u>fens</u>, bogs, <u>dens</u>, and <u>shades</u> of <u>death</u>

Another form of tension occurs in instance (10), where the second syllable is not stressed (the grammatical monosyllable 'for'), and the term I prefer for this type of tension is *erosion*, a geological metaphor that captures the dynamic contour of the line involved.[28] Grammatical monosyllables and secondary stresses often serve instead of stresses in the iambic pentameter, even the line-final stress (as in (10), where the secondary stress of '**pi**-e-<u>ty</u>' serves this purpose).

Traditional metrics can thus explain almost all instances of the iambic pentameter by a metrically ideal line plus the various types of tension. Even if this explanation does not apply as satisfactorily to other types of English verse, I shall find the terms stress-syllabic, accentual, syllabic, tension, inversion, resolution, incursion, and erosion extremely useful in pointing out the features of verse instances in the chapters that follow.

A rhythmic approach

In 1982 Derek Attridge proposed an alternative approach to English metre, based on rhythmic principles, which assumes that the poet counts neither feet nor syllables, but *beats*, a musical term sometimes applied to the prominent syllables in a passage of verse. Intuitively this seems very plausible, because feet are abstractions (see Wimsatt & Beardsley 1959) and English lines often have ten syllables, a number beyond the range that humans can learn to count rapidly (see Miller 1956). Attridge argues that the English line is a series of rhythmic contrasts between *beats* and *offbeats*, and he uses his own notation to describe these constituents. Each beat is provided by a single syllable, which may be a primary stressed syllable (denoted by 'B') or an atonic monosyllable or secondary stress that is 'promoted' to a beat (denoted by 'b'). Offbeats are provided by the linguistic material between beats, which varies in its number of syllables: one syllable provides a *single* offbeat (denoted by 'o'), two a *double* offbeat (denoted by 'ŏ'), zero syllables an *implied* offbeat (denoted by 'ô'), and three a *triple* offbeat (denoted by '~o~'). An Attridgean scansion of my instances from Jonson's poem is thus:

(7)a   Pardon free truth, and let thy modesty,
       B   ŏ   B   o   B   o   B   o   b

(8)a   Which conquers all, be once overcome by thee.
       o   B   o   B   o   B   ŏ   B   o   B

(9)a   Many of thine this better could than I;
       B   ŏ   B   o   B   o   B   o   B

(10)a But for their powers accept my piety.
       o   b   o   B   ŏ   B   o   B   o   b

Note that '<u>powers</u>' may be delivered as a monosyllable, making the third offbeat of (10)a single not double. Attridge's theory describes this difference as varying the size of the offbeat in performance, and thus dispenses with the concept of resolution.

The other forms of tension are also covered by this theory: incursion, as found in 'free' in (7)a, is the *ictus demotion* of a stressed syllable so that it forms an offbeat; erosion is the *ictus promotion* of an unstressed syllable to form a beat; and inversion is simply a question of balancing consecutive offbeats, following a zero by a double. Initial inversion, as in (7)a and (9)a, is not marked in this scansion by a 'ŏ' because this theory dispenses with feet and does not see the line as a series of iambic contrasts. In Attridgean theory iambic and trochaic pentameters are merely syllabically regular variants of *five-beat verse*. This hypothesis is ingenious in that it explains all types of English metre in the same terms, but it ignores history: by the sixteenth century English poets believed that they were counting syllables, and that by alternating stressed syllables to form feet they had devised an ingenious method of doing so rapidly, instinctively, and more or less accurately. It also ignores the insight of modern linguistics that languages themselves may be foot-based (see Hogg & McCully 1987 and Hayes 1995).

In this volume I shall often find it useful to employ Attridge's concept of English verse rhythm, and the terms beat and offbeat, particularly when I come to analyse those English metres in which the lines do not have a regular number of syllables. I shall also note Attridge's explanation of some lines where the scansion according to other approaches is problematic.

A generative approach

The earliest published example of generative metrical analysis is Halle & Keyser 1966 and the most recent exposition that of Fabb & Halle 2005. The simplest and most concise generative account of metre, however, is that of Hanson & Kiparsky 1996 and this is the theory I shall use to illustrate the difference between generative and other analyses. Hanson & Kiparsky term theirs a *parametric theory* of metre because it argues that just five variables (*parameters*) can be used to define all metres:

(1) *position number* (the number of positions in the template); (2) *orientation* (whether the template is left- or right-strong); (3) *position size* (the maximum quantity of linguistic material that may occur in each type of position); (4) *prominence site* (whether s, w, or both positions are constrained from containing a given quality of linguistic material); (5) *prominence type* (the specific quality of material that is constrained from appearing in relevant positions). Hanson & Kiparsky argue that the quantity of linguistic material specified in the position-size parameter may be a syllable, a foot (a pair contrasting elements), or a word. The qualities of material that may be constrained by the prominence-type parameter include heavy, stressed, and strong syllables.

Hanson & Kiparsky use the English iambic pentameter to exemplify parametric theory, and they argue that its template has ten right-strong positions and that the maximum size of each may be either one syllable (syllable-based metres) or one *phonological foot* (foot-based), at the poet's discretion. Foot-based metres allow a series of unstressed light syllables to occupy a single position. Hanson & Kiparsky also argue that the prominence site of the iambic pentameter is weak positions, and its prominence type is syllable strength: weak positions are subject to a constraint against the strong syllables of polysyllabic words. This analysis explains resolution by making the metre foot-based, incursion by making strength the prominence type (thus allowing stressed monosyllables to appear anywhere), and erosion by leaving strong positions unconstrained. This leaves only one type of tension, inversion, which parametric theory explains as *permissible mismatches* between the template and a particular instance: a trochee in the instance may correspond to an iamb in the template under specific conditions.

I shall illustrate the generative approach by scanning the four instances by Jonson that I have quoted above. I place a (w s) template below each line, mark mismatches by underlining in the template, and indicate a position size greater than a single syllable by enclosing the symbol in hyphens:

> (7)b Pardon free truth, and let thy modesty,
> <u>W S</u>   W   S   W   S   W   S W   S
>
> (8)b Which conquers all, be once overcome by thee.
> W   S   W   S   W   S   –w– S   W   S
>
> (9)b Many of thine this better could than I;
> <u>w s</u> W   S   W   S W   S   W   S
>
> (10)b But for their powers accept my piety.
> W   S   W   S   –w– S   W   S W   S

Instances (7)b and (9)b each contain a mismatch and (8)b and (10)b each contain a weak position greater in size than one syllable. The mismatches here are both line-initial, which Hanson & Kiparsky explains in terms of the *closure principle* (Smith 1968), whereby linguistic rules are stricter at the end of units and laxer at their beginning. This principle may also be invoked to explain mid-line mismatches that follow a major syntactic boundary, which are obviously colon-initial. Other mismatches are rare and they must be of words that correspond exactly with foot boundaries; Hanson & Kiparsky term this last rule the *bracketing condition* (1996: 333).

Parametric theory is both concise and rigorous, but since its introduction weaknesses have inevitably been identified. Even its authors acknowledged that it made no attempt to account for *ternary*, or *triple-time*, verse, in which three syllables normally occupy two positions (Hanson & Kiparsky 1996: 300n21). But parametric theory also left important questions unexplored with regard to the iambic pentameter itself, because it *underdetermines* the properties of the line: it makes no attempt to predict some of the important and statistically verifiable features of metrical lines. First, as Nigel Fabb points out, it says nothing of the distribution of weak syllables in the line, although this is far from random (2001: 780), and secondly it ignores the position of mid-line word boundaries, which are also not random (see Duffell 2002b: 305). Finally, parametric theory ignores such important questions as whether parameters interact (for example, does the setting of position size affect the prominence type and site), or whether constraints are sometimes cumulative (applying to consecutive positions), or interlinear (applying not to individual lines but to a series). Despite these shortcomings, parametric theory offers valuable new insights into the way that poets versify in this and some other metres; I shall find it useful when explaining the essential features of many English metres in this volume, because the concepts and terms orientation, position size, foot-based, prominence site, prominence type, and closure principle are both concise and convenient.[29]

A statistical approach

Tarlinskaja 1976, arguably the most important work on English historical metrics since Saintsbury and Schipper two-thirds of a century earlier, is an eminent example of linguistic metrics employing statistical methods in the Russian manner. Tarlin-skaja shows that counting syllables evolved gradually in English verse, and that this produced a continuum of metres from the accentual to the stress-syllabic. The only criticism that can be directed at her book is that it offers different levels of detail with respect to different periods, and excludes modern free verse from its analysis. Although her work won great respect, its influence on generative metrics has been negligible, partly because it employs a four-level theory of stress that fell from fashion within a year of her book's publication (see Liberman & Prince 1977).

Russian metrists are much more willing to retain the traditional terms for the features they observe — they are more concerned with measuring them than re-labelling them. The Greek names for feet are examples of a more general conservatism in modern metrics, but in most Russian works the older term is nearly always preferred: thus Attridge's beats and generative theory's strong positions become *ictuses*, while offbeats and weak positions become *inter-ictic intervals*. Incursion becomes *non-ictic stress*, erosion *ictic non-stress*, while inversion (in the English sense) is not a feature of Russian verse at all. To illustrate the Russian approach I scan below the four lines by Jonson quoted above, marking ictuses by acute accents, intervals greater than one syllable by a circumflex, and stresses by bold typeface (if they are provided by strong syllables) or underlining (if they are monosyllabic or secondary).

(7)c   **Pardón** free <u>trúth</u>, and <u>lét</u> thy **módestý**,

(8)c   Which **cón**quers <u>áll</u>, be <u>ónce</u> o ^ ver**cóme** by <u>thée</u>.

(9)c   **Maný** of <u>thíne</u> this **bétter** <u>coúld</u> than <u>Í</u>;

(10)c   But <u>fór</u> their **pówers** ^ ac**cépt** my **píetý**.

Instances (7)c and (9)c open with a non-ictic stress followed by an ictic non-stress, something that does not occur in Russian iambic pentameters. Russian metrists explain this difference between the versification of the two languages by stating that only *non-initial* stressed syllables are constrained from appearing in weak positions in English iambic verse. This accounts at one stroke for both incursion and the closure principle.

A statistical analysis of Jonson's (14-line) poem quoted above shows that 21 per cent of its lines have initial stress and 7 per cent of the intervals between ictuses are disyllabic, making it a very iambic pentameter indeed. This clear statement is exactly what is required about many of the controversial examples of English metre that I shall encounter in the course of my narrative. All the statements made in the traditional, rhythmic, and generative analyses I have outlined would be much more meaningful if they were quantified so as to demonstrate whether the frequency with which the observed phenomena occur changed with time, or varied by poet or poem. I shall therefore borrow two techniques from Russian statistical metrics: the precise measurement of the frequency with which metrical features occur and the comparison of verse samples with prose, termed *probability modelling*, which helps separate specifically metrical from purely linguistic features. In this volume I shall also use the terms ictus, ictic, and (inter-ictic) interval whenever I believe it appropriate to employ or compare the Russian statistical approach.[30]

Samples and tables

The corpus of published English poetry is much vaster than that of Russian, and this has discouraged English metrists from mass measurement and broad comparison between poems, poets, and periods. Yet Tarlinskaja 1976 & 1993 demonstrate how much valuable information can be obtained in this way, and how much clearer the statements made about English metre can be as a result. I shall tackle the problem of corpus size partly, as Tarlinskaja did, by selecting individual well-known poems, but mainly by employing samples of lines from longer poems. I shall seek a minimum of three hundred lines for these because experience has shown me that samples of this size provide *statistically significant* differences (see Duffell 1991: 302–28 & 2002b: 305). When statisticians draw conclusions from samples they calculate *standard errors* (σ) on the numbers involved; they can then quantify the chance that any differences within the figures could be the result of sampling error (selecting one particular sample rather than another). A difference equal to 2σ has only a one-in-twenty chance, and a difference of 3σ only a one-in-hundred chance of being the result of sampling error. A difference of 2σ is termed *significant* and a difference of 3σ highly significant, while a difference of 4σ or greater is very highly significant and is almost certainly not the result of choosing one sample rather than another (see any primer of statistics; for example, Clarke & Cooke 1983: 40–52). In the chapters that follow I shall note and comment on the statistical significance of the differences I observe between samples of verse instances.

I shall deal with the quantity of information my calculations produce by following Russian practice and presenting many of my conclusions in the form of tables at the end of this volume. The metrical features I shall measure include ictus number, interval size, inversion, resolution, caesura, enjambment, and non-ictic stress and ictic non-stress. This last feature I shall express not as Russian metrists do, by *stressing tables*, but by giving percentage figures for erosion, that is, the proportion of ictuses that fall on unstressed syllables. This will have two advantages: the erosion figure will be directly comparable with that for the other types of tension, inversion and resolution, and the figure will be much smaller, and therefore easier for the reader to register and assess. For example, ictic non-stress figures of 90 and 95 per cent do not seem too dissimilar, but erosion figures of 5 and 10 per cent represent a doubling that may be statistically significant. I shall also append to my tables a note of the poems, lines, and editions concerned so as to help readers check my figures for themselves.

Conclusions

The survey of linguistic metrics in this chapter shows that it is now possible for researchers to provide more rigorous and scientific information on how English poets have versified than they could a century ago, and to describe their findings in a more precise and consistent fashion. But English metres are many and various and the way that poets have versified has frequently been modified by both linguistic change and literary fashion. A number of different linguistic approaches to the analysis of metre have been developed in the last forty years, and some offer a simpler and clearer explanation of some metres, others of others. For that reason I shall be eclectic in my choice of analytical tools in the narrative chapters of the present volume, but wherever possible I shall quantify my conclusions and test them statistically. Before I commence that narrative, however, I must deal with one of the chief sources of change and innovation in English versifying. The metrical system that I have described in this chapter, using four different approaches, differs dramatically from that of the earliest English verse: this is almost entirely the result of foreign influence, the fact that many of the most innovative versifiers in English versified first in Latin or French, while a few went to Italy, seeking a metrics that would be more congenial to English than either found in those two languages. Before examining the earliest English verse, therefore, I shall discuss briefly some modes of versifying employed on the European mainland that antedate our native metrics, and which have repeatedly influenced the way that English poets versify. This will involve a short excursion into the discipline known as comparative historical metrics.

Notes to Chapter 1

1. Examples of the statistical method applied to Russian verse can be found in English in Bailey 1968, 1973a, & 1973b, and in Smith 1983, 1985, 2000b, & 2002; it has also been applied to verse in other languages, including English (see Tarlinskaja 1976 & 1993, Bailey 1987, and Gasparov 1987 & 1996). Russia has also produced a number of eminent metrists whose research makes little use of the linguistic-statistical method, and some of their work has appeared in English (see Zhirmunsky 1925 and Jakobson 1952 & 1960).

2. Studies that employ the methodology of generative metrics include Halle & Keyser 1966 & 1971, Kiparsky 1975, 1977, & 1989, Liberman & Prince 1977, Nespor & Vogel 1986, Hanson 1995b, 1996, & 2001, Hanson & Kiparsky 1996, Fabb 2002a, and Fabb & Halle 2005.

3. Tarlinskaja 1976 is the prime example of the statistical method applied to English verse, while Attridge 1982 takes careful account of the generative method before offering his own rhythmic analysis of English metre. Generative theory has been applied to the metrics of the Romance languages by Roubaud 1971, Piera 1980, and Oliva 1980; and statistical methods have been used for the same purpose by Macrí 1979, Beltrami 1986, Billy 1999, 2000a, & 2000b, Dominicy 2003, Domínguez Caparrós 2002, and Duffell 1991 & 2000b. A statistical approach is also the basis of the inventories of strophe designs and rhyme schemes produced by Frank 1953–57, Tavani 1967, Chambers 1985, Billy 1989, and Gómez-Bravo 1998. Works that employ an eclectic approach to European metres include Beltrami 1991, Dominicy 1992, Menichetti 1993, Cornulier 1995, and Domínguez Caparrós 2000 & 2001.

4. For a discussion of the biological aspects of rhythm see Chatman 1965: 23n15 & 24. One of the oldest surviving Indo-European texts, the *Rig Veda*, proclaims that all metres were created at the same moment as the universe itself (x. 90. 9; Zaehner 1966: 9); this is true insofar as rhythms are mathematical possibilities that have always been available for expression by human limbs or speech. Even the most primitive cultures that have not developed song employ chants and prayers that are delivered rhythmically (Bowra 1963: 14–17).

5. See Bowra 1963: 39 and Gaur 1984: 93 & 32. Other writers who have discussed the religious influence on the development of verse include Elwert (1965: 17), Deloffre (1973: 58), and Beltrami (1981: 13).

6. Thus my definition includes severances like 'the | reason', 'good | reason', 'God | knows', 'God knows | the reason', but not ones like 'man knows in his heart | that god is in his heaven', or 'the force that through the green fuse drives the flower | drives my green age'. My choice of a working definition for enjambment has necessarily been arbitrary, but I have made every effort to apply it consistently, and I have found that in many cases it produces differences between poems and poets that meet the standard tests of statistical significance.

7. French metrists, who coined the terms *césure* and *enjambement*, also have terms to describe the sub-units of the dissected phrase: the material consigned to the second line is termed the *rejet*, making that left hanging at the end of the first the *contre-rejet*. Both sub-units attract the reader's special attention.

8. In the Middle Ages numerology (like astrology) was one of the best-developed sciences, and an even more remarkable example of numerology applied to poem design can be found in the great national epic of fifteenth-century Spain, Juan de Mena's *Laberinto de Fortuna* (Kerkhof 1995). Its 297 strophes and 2376 lines are at first sight very odd numbers, but the digital sum of both is the magic number nine, the square of the Trinity (see Clarke 1973: 79–84).

9. Many set forms are introduced or closed by an abbreviated strophe that bears some structural resemblance to the full strophes.

10. Identical lower-case letters denote lines linked by phoneme repetition and identical upper-case letters those ending in the same word.

11. Leech 1965: 89 notes only six of these possibilities and Preminger & Brogan 1993: 1054 seven, but all the variants in my octal matrix play an important part in versifying in English: zero repetition is one of the devices that poets can use to make their lines sound more like normal speech. *Blank verse*, which is systematic zero repetition, has therefore often been employed in drama.

12. Thus, for example, alliteration is compositional in Classical Latin (see Jackson Knight 1944: 249–52), but systematic in Old English verse, where two to three alliterating syllables per line are stipulated by the verse design (see Wrenn & Bolton 1988: 55).

13. Arabic rhymed quantitative verse of the highest technical complexity was composed at least as early as the sixth century AD (see Gibb 1963: 13 and Arberry 1965: 13–14). It is tempting to speculate that the Arabs may have borrowed rhyme, like mathematics, from India, where rhyme had been a compositional feature of Vedic verse and was widely employed in Prakrit verse by the second century AD (see Preminger et al. 1975: 385 & 394). But pre-Islamic Arabic verse rhymed perfectly long before the earliest Muslim invasions of India, making an Indian origin unlikely.

14. Jakobson also coined the term *delivery design* (1960: 366) for the poet's intended performance, but I have found this concept much less useful. Although some modern poets have left (phono-)graphic evidence of their verse design in the form of a 'scanning' delivery of their own lines, the performance itself is no more a feature of that design than the prosaic delivery of Edmund Kean (b. ?1787, d. 1833) was a feature of Shakespeare's. A poet's personal preference for a 'sing-song' delivery is rather like Mozart's rating of the violin above the flute: one is as irrelevant to the theory of metre as the other is to the theory of music.

15. It may be argued that the phoneme represents a prosodic level below the mora, and that some verse numerically regulates specific phonemes in the line, either those in certain syllable onsets (alliteration), or those in certain nuclei and codas (internal or *Leonine* rhyme; see Preminger et al. 1975: 446). Phoneme-level regulation, however, is usually ancillary (it is a feature of verse designs that also regulate material at other linguistic levels), and is peripheral to the themes of the present volume.

16. The phrasal metre of the Hittite *Song of Ullikummi* (second millennium BC) is discussed in Chapter 3. The only Hebrew poem in which a syllabic pattern has so far been identified is Psalm 137, the architecture of which is linked to the Temple of Jerusalem by Halle 1997a.

17. The text I have used is that of the King James Bible, or 'Authorised Version' (Smith et al. 1611), which contains some of the greatest and most influential poetry in the English language. While later translations of the Old Testament are sometimes more faithful to the meaning of the original Hebrew, none captures the resonance of the AV's magnificent versification.

18. Accent, of any type, is of little significance in Japanese (Dunn & Yanada 1958: 5), and Japanese metre imitates the language in this respect (Brower 1972: 39). The earliest (pre-literate) Japanese verse was rather less regular than the metres described here (Bownas 1964: xlvi; Preminger et al. 1975: 423).

19. The length of Japanese lines seems to confirm the limits on human perception discovered by modern cognitive science, which concludes that we are able learn to recognize quickly and easily numbers of events up to a maximum of only about eight (Miller 1956; see also Duffell 1999b: 156). Whether poets use phrases, words, syllables, feet, or moras to regulate their verse, eight appears to be the maximum number of units in an undivided line.

20. Dance is, perhaps, an even better analogy for metre than percussion, because *rhythm* is a term derived from the Greek word for *balanced movement*. The earliest comparison between dance and verse rhythm was made by Plato (Beltrami 1991: 17n5) and Greek metrics borrowed its most basic terms, *podes*, *arsis*, and *thesis*, from dancing.

21. Chatman notes that the human ear perceives intervals as equal providing there is no more than 14 per cent variation in their objective length (1965: 30–40).

22. The oldest surviving Chinese verse is purely syllabic and the most common line length is four syllables (see Kennedy 1980); in later ('Old Style') verse this became five and seven, and tone began to play a role. There are four tones in the traditional Chinese phonology: (1) level (upper and lower), *ping*; (2) rising, *shang* (3) departing, *qu*; and (4) entering, *tu*. (These transliterations are in *pinyin*.) Later Chinese verse regulated some positions in the line with regard to the tone they should contain (see Frankel 1972). In some periods Chinese syllables with level tone may have been perceived as heavier than those with deflected tones, thus making some Chinese verse quantitative (see Fabb 1997: 77).

23. Pitch-change has not been exploited in the versification of any European language as it has in Chinese, but some writers have argued that it plays a role in French (Pensom 2000), or in Spanish and Italian verse (Piera 2001). It is perhaps significant that the intonational patterns found in French by Pensom, like those of Chinese, offer variety, not regularity.

24. The *relative stress principle*, that the stress contrasts between adjacent syllables are the only ones relevant to metre, was first argued by Otto Jespersen in a paper published in 1900 (Preminger & Brogan 1993: 1019–20). It is supported by a considerable weight of modern metrical research; see Halle & Keyser 1966, Tavani 1974: 135–36, Liberman & Prince 1977: passim, and Kiparsky 1977: 194.

25. In practice, syntagms like *a note* almost always occur as [w s] contrasts in iambic verse. An article most often occupies an s position at the beginning of the line, or when a qualifier is involved, as in the phrase *on a sweet note* [w s w s]; see Fabb 2001: 780–82.

26. In each description I employ the terminology of its proponents because there are subtle differences in meaning between their terms; for example, an *offbeat* differs from a *weak position* by not forming a *foot* with the material either to its left or to its right.

27. In this example, and throughout this volume, I have underlined the monosyllables in those positions in the line where a prominent syllable is expected (strong or ictic positions). Whether 'caves' is made more prominent than 'rocks' in this line, however, will vary from delivery to delivery.

28. Some examples of erosion could be described as the inversion of two monosyllables, but many cannot. Confusing erosion with inversion leads Pinsky to state that both are more common at the beginning of lines (1998: 30–32); the statistics given later in this volume show that this statement is not true of erosion.

29. In the course of this volume I shall also have occasion to use another term employed by the earliest generative analyses, a *stress maximum*, a syllable with greater stress than both the syllables that surround it. Halle & Keyser 1966 used this concept to explain initial inversion, arguing that a stressed first syllable does not break their correspondence rules for the iambic pentameter: it is not a stress maximum because it does not have other syllables on both sides.

30. Note that dividing the line into ictuses and intervals avoids the problem faced by generative metrics of deciding how to allocate three syllables between two positions.

CHAPTER 2

Comparative Metrics

Language and Metre

As noted, metre is a stylization of language employed in specific contexts, the most important of which is poetry. Hanson & Kiparsky argue that there is a 'principle of fit', which ensures that metres evolve in such a way as to accommodate most of the lexicon and reflect the major phonological features of the language concerned (1996: 294 & 325). Although this principle confirms the insights of earlier scholars (in particular, Thompson 1961 and Jakobson 1973), there are notable exceptions to it. For example, the adoption of the Greek quantitative dactylic hexameter denied Roman poets access to a large portion of their lexicon (Raven 1965: 11), and the cultivation of syllabic metres in Spanish and Russian in various periods has involved ignoring those languages' strong word stress within the line (Duffell 2000c: 114–16 and Gasparov 1996: 227–35). Nevertheless, most metrical systems are based on the salient phonological features of the language concerned (Hanson 2001: 41); metres also adapt rapidly to linguistic change: thus, for example, the loss of vowel-length distinctions in Late Latin undoubtedly led to the decline of quantitative versifying (see Lote 1939: 229–36).

Phonology

An obvious corollary of the principle of fit is that poets can employ only the phonological features of the language in which they are versifying and, when poets attempt to adapt a metre from another language into their own, only the shared features will survive the adaptation. From the time of the Norman Conquest French poetry and versifying have had a great influence on English, and before studying that interaction it will prove instructive to examine some of the principal differences between the phonologies of the two languages. Next to French, Latin has been most influential: most of the pioneers of the English metrical system were taught to versify in Latin and then had to learn how do so in English by trial and error. The third language that has proved influential is Italian, because at vital stages in the development of English metre the most famous poems in Europe were Italian and a few fortunate Englishmen visited Italy and learned to appreciate its rhythms. I shall come to Latin and Italian in due course, but the three major phonological differences between French and English that affect how poets versify are timing, orientation, and stress strength.

Delivery

Modern linguistics identifies two opposing tendencies in speech delivery: *syllable-timing* and *stress-timing*. In the first the speaker allots what audiences perceive as equal time to all syllables, while in the second the intervals between stressed syllables are made perceptibly equal by varying the time allotted to unstressed ones, termed *accentual isochrony* (see Giegerich 1980 & 1985, Roach 1982, and Toledo 1988). Syllable-timing predominates in most Romance languages and stress-timing in most Germanic ones, and the interaction after the Norman Conquest between left-strong, stress-timed English and right-strong, syllable-timed French will be examined in Chapter 4.[1] The rhythm of French poetry depends upon syllable-timing, which enables poets to create a simple primary rhythm with phrasal stress. Since the lines and hemistichs of French poems are isosyllabic and each must close in a stressed syllable, these final stresses arrive at regular intervals (see Cornulier 1995: 111–13). Since word stress was probably always weaker in French than in other European languages, and in modern French it has disappeared altogether, phrasal stresses have greater impact in both speech and verse. The lines of French verse also rhyme (or assonate), which emphasizes the line-final phrasal stresses and the regularity with which they occur.

Most French verse is isosyllabic and rhythmic in this way, but English poets struggled for centuries to compose lines of exactly eight syllables, whether in English or in French, as I shall show in Chapter 4. The biggest problems that English poets faced in this enterprise were the presence of much stronger word stress and the absence of syllable-timing. They also inherited a situation in which their audiences were used to counting word stresses, not syllables, as I shall show in Chapter 3. English poets solved the problem of producing isosyllabic lines by alternating prominent and non-prominent syllables in their verse, as in Medieval Latin. Not only do English lines contain prominence peaks, but the tendency to stress-timing means that we perceive them as occurring at equal intervals, regardless of whether what lies between them is a single syllable, as in iambic or trochaic verse, or two, as in ternary metres, or even a mixture, as in an important class of English metres examined in Chapter 3.

In Old English verse the varying amount of linguistic material between the metrically relevant stresses can be regarded as an intrinsic part of the interval between events. Certainly the obvious rhythm of Old English verse derives from one pair of strong stresses being balanced by another pair of a different alliterative pattern. Stress-syllabic verse, on the other hand, converts those intervals into events of another type, offbeats. But implicit in Attridge's rhythmic analysis is the idea that English poets and audiences continue to count stress peaks or beats, not feet or syllables, even in the iambic pentameter. As I shall show in the chapters that follow, the native English tendency to count stresses has frequently reasserted itself in the face of an imported fashion for counting syllables.

Orientation

Language sometimes appears to dictate the metrical features that its poets employ; and this seems to be the case with phoneme repetition. Alliteration tends to become systematic in left-strong languages (those with initial stress) as is shown by Old Latin (Raven 1965: 53 and West 1973: 177), Old English (Fussell 1972: 197), and Welsh (Preminger et al. 1975: 109–10). In contrast, right-strong repetition (rhyme) becomes most extensively cultivated in right-strong (oxytonic languages), like French; the origins of the systematic use of rhyme in Latin may also be connected to the habit of artificially stressing the final (inflected) syllable (the pedagogic French accentuation; see Lote 1939 and Marouzeau 1931). Systematic rhyme first appeared in English under the influence of French, as phrasal stress, which had been left-strong in all the Old Germanic languages (see Lehman 1993: 136–37), became right-strong in Middle English. The accentual profile of the majority of Modern English lines is right-strong, like that of Modern English phrases (see Hayes 1995: 368–70), and right-strong repetition clearly emphasizes this. Rhyme is of fundamental importance to versifying in French because it helps provide French verse's only rhythm, that between lines. There is no rhythm (in the sense of a regular occurrence of events) within French lines because of the loss of word stress, which has become no more than a potential for prominence in delivery when the word concerned is phrase-final. And even in Old French word stress was probably weaker than in the other Romance languages (see Ewert 1943: 104–08). Many metrists have argued that this is why French poets have never cultivated *blank verse*, which is devoid of any form of systematic line-end phoneme repetition (see, for example, Dorchain 1919: 101 and Scott 1980: 77). If lines have no discernible stress pattern, blank verse becomes very difficult to distinguish from prose; it is only an accentual structure within lines that makes blank verse viable, as it is in English and those Romance languages with strong word stress.

Phoneme repetition

Preminger et al. gives a brief history of rhyme in Western Europe (1975: 705–10), which dismisses the possibility that our rhyming tradition derives, like so much of European civilization, from the Arabs.[2] Rhyme occurs as a compositional feature in Ancient Greek, where it was known as *homoeoteleuton* or *homoeoptoton*; it also occurs in Classical Latin verse, especially at the caesura and line end of elegiac couplets. Note that single-syllable (M) rhyme in Latin usually involves secondary stressed syllables, since only monosyllables can be oxytonic in that language. Masculine rhyme began to be used systematically in Latin hymns of the second century and was enthusiastically adopted by the monks of Ireland in the seventh.[3] The earliest feminine rhymes in Latin appear only at the end of the eleventh century (Beare 1957: 288). In the eleventh and twelfth centuries a number of secular poets, or troubadours, began using both types of rhyme in Occitan and developed a skill in rhyming that has never been surpassed (see Pound 1961: 52–55).

Meanwhile in other Romance languages many poets continued to employ assonance: rhyme is, of course, only a special case of assonance: some assonating words in a long series usually have the same coda by chance. Until rhyme became systematic it occurred at random among assonances, and it was probably aesthetic selection that led to its systematic use: the repetition of two elements in the syllable provided a more striking and pleasing pattern. Rhyme became the predominant form of systematic phoneme repetition throughout Western Europe in the thirteenth century; systematic alliteration survived in English until the end of the fifteenth century, by which time assonance had fallen from use in French. Assonance has enjoyed periodic revivals in Spanish verse, but later poets who employed it, unlike their medieval predecessors, avoided chance rhymes among the assonances (Gornall 2000: 402–05). In the later chapters of this volume we shall see that in the twentieth century many poets avoided full rhyme, either preferring the other types of repetition listed in Chapter 1 or eschewing repetition altogether.

Metrical Phonology

Although word stress may be weak or non-existent in French, it is an important feature of most other languages and the study of linguistic rhythm has made rapid advances in the last twenty years. The discipline has become known as *metrical phonology* (Hogg & McCully 1987) or *metrical stress theory* (Hayes 1995), and one of its most important findings is that the various levels of stress form a hierarchy. The stress hierarchy within polysyllabic words can be illustrated using a vertical grid where each layer carries the symbol × (Hayes 1995: 29):

```
                      ×
  ×                   ×
  ×         ×         ×
  ×    ×    ×    ×    ×    ×
  1    2    3    4    5    6
  re - con - ci - li - a - tion
```

The operation of phrasal stress in combination with word stress can be seen from the following phrase, which I have adapted from an example given in Hayes 1995: 369:

```
                           ×
              ×            ×
  ×           ×       ×    ×
  ×     ×  ×  ×    ×  ×  ×    ×
  1     2  3  4    5  6  7
  Bel - gian far - mers grow tur - nips
```

These findings make it particularly important for metrists to think of prominence peaks rather than stresses in their deliberations. Note that the discovery that language is metrical has led some metrists to insert the word *poetic* before *metre* in their statements about versification.

Stress hierarchy in verse

The stress hierarchies proposed by metrical phonology can also be applied to lines of English verse (see Hayes 1989). Some generative metrists build their stress hierarchies upwards, as in Hayes 1995 and the diagram above, while others construct a grid beneath the text with parentheses grouping pairs of constituents, or feet (Fabb

2002a and Fabb & Halle 2005). Individual metres in a number of languages have been analysed in this way (see, for example, Piera 1980 and Hanson 1996) and this is undoubtedly appropriate in the analysis of stress-syllabic metres. This can be illustrated by a simple example, an iambic tetrameter that opens a poem (Gill 1984: 295) by William Wordsworth (b. 1770, d. 1850):

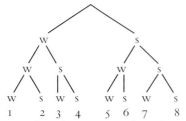

(1)   Strange fits of pas – sion I have known

The hierarchical structure proposed can be justified by both the stress profile of this line and the statistical profile of the poem that contains it. In normal delivery the stress in position 8 is stronger than that in 4, which in turn is stronger than those in 2 and 6. The relative salience of each position thus corresponds to the number of strong nodes at the levels above it. Moreover, a statistical analysis shows that position 8 always contains a strongly stressed syllable, and position 4 does so more often than 2 or 6, while the weakest strong position (2) is most likely to suffer from (initial) inversion.

If, however, we try to apply this structure to a French *octosyllabe*, both these justifications are absent, as can be seen from the following line (2) from *Balade* XXXVII (Champion 1907: 56) by Charles d'Orléans (b. 1394, d. 1465):

proposed structure:		w	s	w	s		w	s	w		s
stress profile:		w	w	s	w		s	w	w		s
		1	2	3	4		5	6	7		8

(2)   Pour sa – voir com – ment se por – toit
[To find out how he was bearing up]

It can be seen that every strong syllable but the last one in this line is in the wrong place according to the hypothesized structure (technically termed a *mismatch*). Generative metrists (for example, Piera 1980 and Hanson 1996) defend the application of this hierarchical model to Romance syllabic metres by explaining that the latter have different correspondence rules, and describe the first seven positions in (2) as unregulated or *unconstrained*. There is, however, another explanation: that metres contain such a stress hierarchy only in languages with word stress. The metres poets employ are thus at least partly determined by the phonological features of the language in which they are versifying.

Linguistic rhythm

In Chapter 1 I noted that syllables are of either one or two moras' duration, and are termed light or heavy. Moras seem to belong in pairs, since no English lexical monosyllable comprises a single mora, and metrical phonologists use the term a *phonological foot* to describe the contrast between a pair of moras, whether they occur in the same (heavy) syllable, or in pairs of consecutive light syllables. In English, phonological feet branch strong–weak and the basic rhythm of the language is said to be one of moraic trochees. Metrical phonology argues that all languages may be divided into two types rhythmically, iambic and trochaic, according to the rules for assigning accent to syllables within them. In iambic languages accented syllables form rhythmic feet with the syllables that precede them, in trochaic ones accented syllables combine rhythmically with the syllables that follow (Hayes 1995: 62–84). Trochaic languages, which are by far the most common, may be subdivided into two types: those based on syllabic and those on moraic trochees. In syllabic-trochaic languages pairs of syllables form a binary strong–weak contrast, in moraic-trochaic languages pairs of moras do.

The list of languages based on moraic trochees includes Germanic languages, such as English and German, Romance languages including Latin itself, Ancient Greek and Sanskrit, and non-Indo-European languages, such as Hebrew and Arabic (Hayes 1995: 125–82). Although English is a trochaic language, most of its sentences and lines of verse are iambic, because it is a trochaic language with pre-position: monosyllables, both unaccented (articles, conjunctions, and prepositions) and accented (adjectives and auxiliaries), normally precede rather than follow the words they qualify. As will emerge in the course of the chapters that follow, these properties are reflected in the versifying of English poets, and the fact that some of them are shared with Latin, French, or Italian aided the imitation and absorption of modes of versifying that were not native in English.

Foreign Influences on English Metre

Medieval English literature was the product of a literate minority, at first clerics and later laypersons, who were more familiar with Latin texts than with English ones (see Curtius 1953: passim and Whinnom 1994: 97–98), and who conducted their public business in French. It would, indeed, be surprising if Latin and/or French versification had not strongly influenced the pioneers of English verse.

Most historical metrists have realized this, and George Saintsbury identified five 'mothers' of English prosody, two of which, Scandinavian and Celtic versification, he noted were of very minor importance (1906: I, 11–12); the others were Anglo-Saxon, Latin, and French metrics, which he discussed in a little more detail (1906: I, 12–23). Saintsbury's hypothesis that English metre was simply a fusion of those parts of these three metrical systems that suited the language (1906: I, 162) is a glib assumption that was stoutly challenged by Fitzroy Pyle (1935: 22). Saintsbury's nationalism (in 1906 the greatest ever conflict of nations was imminent) and his desire to portray English versifiers as the heirs to Roman and Greek ones combined to affect his judgment on the influence of foreigners (for a more balanced, American, view see Lewis 1898). Saintsbury admitted that he neither knew nor cared about the nature of accent, or whether it differed from syllable length (1906: I, 5), but he nevertheless assumed that this feature he did not understand was a single property, and that poets could equally well use it in all languages. This is a mistake that modern linguistics can correct, and in the next sections of this chapter I shall present a more up-to-date and analytical account of Latin and French historical metrics.[4] How the Anglo-Saxons (and other Germanic speakers) versified will be the subject of the next chapter and form the starting point for my historical narrative.

Versifying in Latin

In medieval Western Europe most adults were familiar with hymns in Latin, and a powerful literate minority also knew poems in what was the universal language of instruction, worship, and diplomacy. By the time the earliest surviving English poems were written down Latin verse had a thousand years' history. During that time the Latin language, and the way that its poets versified, changed very considerably. The metres of Old Latin (before 200 BC), Classical Latin (200 BC to AD 300), and Medieval Latin (after AD 300) are therefore of very different types.

Word-based metres

The only surviving Latin verse that may be argued to antedate Greek influence (Raven 1965: 17) is in the Saturnian metre, of which fewer than two hundred lines have survived (Koster 1929). Although both syllabic and accentual verse designs have been proposed for this metre (see, for example, Nougaret 1948: 20 and Gildersleeve & Lodge 1953: 463), there are difficulties and exceptions that undermine both explanations (see Raven 1965: 33–36, West 1973: 175–79, and Preminger & Brogan 1993: 1117). Word-level regulation, however, offers a satisfactory explanation of all the surviving lines in the Saturnian metre: they comprise 3 (± 1) + 2 words (see Nougaret 1948: 23 and Pighi 1970: 24). But the speed and totality with which Greek metres replaced native ones have convinced some modern scholars that the Saturnian metre must also have been based on the number and weight of its syllables, even though it exhibits considerable irregularities in both (see, for example, Koster 1929 and Cole 1969).

Word-based metres, however, were employed in the Latin of a much later period: as Norberg points out, early Medieval Latin versifiers also composed lines in which the number of words, rather than syllables, was regulated (1958: 131–33). The lines of these poems contained 3, 4, 2 + 2, or 3 + 3 words, and they date from a period when instinctive knowledge of vowel length and accent in Classical Latin was restricted to a tiny minority of speakers and writers (Lote 1939: 219–71). These linguistic conditions bear an interesting similarity to those in the period from which the oldest Italic verse dates. Word-based metres are the exception in Latin, and many medieval English poets would have been unaware of them, but other types of Latin verse, quantitative, syllabic, and stress-syllabic, undoubtedly influenced the way that English metre developed, and merit discussion in more detail.

Quantitative metres in Latin

The duration of syllables is either one or two moras depending on whether they have branching rhymes. Ancient Greek poets sensed this difference in length intuitively and employed it in patterning the language of their verse, and ancient Greek theory soon caught up with practice. In the second century BC Rome imported vast areas of Greek culture including its poetry, and Roman poets were converted to versifying in the Greek fashion. Quantitative verse dominated Latin poetry for around five hundred years; by AD 300 immigration had led to great changes in the language of the Roman empire, and one of these, the loss of the phonemic distinction between long and short vowels, proved almost fatal to this system of versifying. Quantitative versifying in Latin thereafter depended upon learning by rote which vowels were long and which short, and so it became the province of the learned and the bored. It also became a pedagogical tool: until the mid-twentieth century many English schoolboys were taught how to compose quantitative verse in Latin and Greek, and this was the only formal training in composition that English poets received. Some poets have attempted to introduce quantitative verse into both modern Romance (see Domínguez Caparrós 2001) and modern Germanic languages (see Hanson 2001) but with limited success: in particular, English poets were hampered by the fact that syllable weight in their language is far less stable than in either of the Classical languages.[5]

Classical quantitative verse is of two types, termed by the Greeks *Ionic* and *Aeolic*. In Ionic verse all lines are of the same total duration but, since some positions may be filled by either one long or two short syllables, they vary in syllable count (Gasparov 1996: 65–87); In Aeolic verse, by contrast, lines have a fixed number of syllables but the length of each syllable is prescribed by the verse design (Raven 1965: 133–50). Gasparov describes Aeolic metres as 'syllabo-metrical' (1996: 49–64); Fabb, on the other hand, classifies both Aeolic and Ionic metres as quantitative, noting only that some metres allow resolution while others do not (1997: 61–64).

Ionic quantitative verse

Ancient Greek metrics, which was derived from music, divided lines of verse into a number of *feet*, or binary contrasts between an *arsis* ('upbeat') and *thesis* ('downbeat' or 'ictus'). But lines of Ionic verse, in addition to a regular number of beats and feet, also contain a regular number of moras; and their verse design regulates not only the number of moras, as in Japanese, but also the position in the line of two-mora syllables. Such patterning becomes viable when two-mora syllables are sufficiently numerous, as they are in Greek, Latin, and English. Greek versifiers, like Japanese, recognized that the duration of their long syllables was approximately double that of short. The Ancient Greeks cultivated a very large number of different metres, but the most famous Ionic metre was that of the traditional epic, the *dactylic hexameter*. I shall summarize its parameters and exemplify it briefly.

The dactylic hexameter's template has twelve positions, constituting six feet; its orientation is left-strong; strong positions must contain a long syllable, weak ones either one long or two short; its prominence-type parameter is thus syllable length. When both strong and weak positions contain a long syllable the foot produced is termed a *spondee*, which is very common in Latin verse because the language is rich in heavy syllables. Spondees are a feature of most dactylic hexameters, but the fifth foot in the line almost invariably contains a dactyl and the sixth a disyllabic foot (a spondee or trochee).[6] The dactylic hexameter line comprises twenty-four moras (or twenty-three, if the last foot is a trochee), and regulating moras can produce extremes of syllable count, as in the following lines (*Aeneid*, VIII. 452 & 596; Hirtzel 1900) by Virgil (P. Virgilius Maro, b. 70, d. 19 BC):[7]

$$- \ -/- \ -/- \ // \ \ - \ / -- \ / \ - \ \ \smallsmile \smallsmile \ / - \ -$$
(3)   Ill[i] in–ter se–se   mul–tā vī brac–chi–a tol–lunt

$$- \ \smallsmile \smallsmile \ / - \ \smallsmile \ \smallsmile \ / - \ \ // \ \smallsmile \ \smallsmile /- \ \ \smallsmile \ \smallsmile /- \ \smallsmile \smallsmile \ / - \ \ -$$
(4)   Quad–ri–pe–dan–te pu–trem   so–ni–tū qua–tit un–gu–la cam–pum

[They raised their arms with great force; | The hoof beats the dust of the plain with a four-footed rhythm]

Instance (3) is an example of a line containing five spondees, while (3) contains five dactyls followed by a spondee; the rhythm of both lines mimics the actions described in them: smiths striking alternate blows on an anvil, and horses in mid-gallop.[8] Virgil's verse design has two other important features: the first is a mandatory word boundary (caesura) after position 5, as in (3) and (4), or after position 7 (when it must be supplemented by another after position 3). The second is that Virgil, like other Latin poets, almost always ensured that in the last two feet ictus coincided with lexical accent, as in these examples (accented 'brácchia tóllunt', 'úngula cámpum').[9]

Aeolic quantitative verse

Lines of Aeolic verse contain a regular number of both quantitative feet and syllables. Surviving fragments of folk verse suggest that it may predate Ionic, although literary texts show that both types of metre were in use as early as the ninth century BC (West 1973: 166).[10] Roman poets did not adopt all of the numerous Greek metres, but nevertheless a great deal of Aeolic verse in various metres can be found in Latin. I shall illustrate this type of verse by the *Phalaecian hendecasyllable*, a metre that was much more popular in Latin than in Greek: thus Catullus (G. Valerius Catullus, b. *c*. 84, d. *c*. 54 BC) employed it in two-thirds of his surviving poems. Its template may be divided into an opening of two syllables, a nucleus of four, and a close of five (a division marked by / in my scansion). The quantity of the first two syllables varies, while that of the remainder is fixed; this can be illustrated by the following three lines (I. 2–4; Mynors 1958):

$$- \ \smallsmile \ /- \ \ \smallsmile \ \ \smallsmile \ // - \ / \ \smallsmile \ \ - \ \ \ \smallsmile \ - \ \ -$$
(5)   a–ri–da mo–do   pu–mi–c[e] ex–po–li–tum

$$- \ \ -/- \ \smallsmile \ \smallsmile \ \ // \ \ - \ / \smallsmile \ \ - \ \ \ - \ \smallsmile \ - \ \ -$$
(6)   Cor–ne–li, ti–bi: nam–que tu so–le–bas

$$\smallsmile \ \ -/- \ \ \smallsmile \ \smallsmile \ \ - \ / \ // \ \ \smallsmile \ \ - - \smallsmile \ \ \ - \ \ -$$
(7)   me–as ess[e] a–li–quid   pu–ta–re nu–gas

[(To whom shall I give my new book) | polished with dry pumice stone? | To you, Cornelius, because you always | thought my trifles worth something]

Note that the caesura in this metre falls after either position 5, as in (5) and (6), or position 6, as in (7). By opening (5) with a trochee, (6) with a spondee, and (7) with an iamb, Catullus reveals that the syllable count of these lines is more important to his metrical intention than the total line length (which varies between seventeen and eighteen moras). The rules of Catullus's metre allow one syllable to be substituted for another (of a different duration), those of Virgil's allow only two moras to replace two moras (except after the final ictus). In Ionic verse the regulation of syllable quantity is paramount and syllable count is immaterial, but in Aeolic the two compete, and in Catullus's line quantity loses the contest.[11] Note that, although lexical accent does not appear to be regulated by this verse design, in the second half-line of the quoted examples the trochaic quantitative pattern is strongly reinforced by an accentual one ('èxpolítum', 'tù solébas', 'putáre núgas'; here grave accents mark secondary stresses).

The Evolution of Stress-Syllabic Metres in Latin

By the fourth century AD, speakers of Latin (many of whom in the West were of Germanic origin) no longer had an instinctive sense of syllable length, and thus the basis on which Classical poets had versified was lost.[12] Some poets persisted with the quantitative system of versifying, but did so very badly, while others, pragmatically, rendered the old metres syllabic by ignoring quantity and preserving only the syllable count of the lines.

Medieval Latin syllabic verse

This new syllabic Latin verse required the prop of rhyme to distinguish it from prose, and poets counted all the syllables in the line (and, indeed, all the written vowels). There was some concern for stress in this process: most poets avoided mixing paroxytonic lines with proparoxytonic, so that the final stress in the line fell regularly when delivered with syllable-timing. But some medieval poets undoubtedly introduced more accentual regularity than this into their verse (see for example, Raby 1934: II, 190–219 and Gasparov 1996: 107). Nevertheless, some modern scholars have argued that accent played little or no part in Medieval Latin verse design (for example, Lote 1939 and Beare 1957), and even Gasparov expresses doubt as to whether the poets concerned actually planned these regularities (1996: 92–96). Norberg is probably correct, however, when he states that, although some Medieval Latin verse designs are syllabic, others are stress-syllabic (1958: 119–31).[13] Even when the metre of a Latin poem seems analogous to a French syllabic metre it tends to have greater regularity of accent. For example, Lote 1939: 273 classifies the *Chant pour la mort du Guillaume le Conquérant* (Du Méril 1843: 294) as a Latin *vers de dix* of 4 + 6 syllables.[14] Its metre can be seen from the following lines (1 & 4):

(8) Fle-te, vi-ri; || lu-ge-te **pro**-ce-<u>res</u>!

(9) rex Gui-llel-mus || bel-lo for-**tis**-si-<u>mus</u>

[Weep, warriors, and mourn, chiefs! | King William, most valiant in war]

Note that the final syllable in each line has only secondary stress and the eighth has primary, so that according to the Romance method of counting these lines have the formula 3F + 8P.[15] The first hemistichs of (8) and (9) are both trochaic, and the hemistichs they are paired with could be regarded as having an iambic rhythm with an initial inversion in (9). The metre of this poem may, indeed, represent one stage in the evolution of syllabic into stress-syllabic metres and, since the nature of Latin accent was vital to that process, I shall digress briefly in order to discuss it.

The nature of Latin accent

As I have noted, Latin accent seems to have been subject to change: while linguisticians generally agree that it was dynamic by the end of the third century AD, they disagree on whether this was the case in Classical Latin (see, for example, Palmer 1954: 211–14, Norberg 1958: 87, Elcock 1975: 51, and Penny 2002: 42). Classical writers described Latin accent as being one of pitch, like that of Greek, but they did so in words that are patently translations of Greek accounts of Greek accent; as a result many modern scholars discount them (see Allen 1973: 151).[16] Their doubts are strongly supported by linguistic evidence: Latin of all periods resembles other languages with dynamic accent by being subject to *syncope*, the loss of medial unstressed syllables.[17] Moreover, all the languages descended from Latin, from East to West, have dynamic accent, and it seems more reasonable to assume that the typology of Latin accent remained constant than that it changed from dynamic (Old Latin) to melodic (the Classical language) and then back again. The evidence from versification also supports the view that Latin had something more than the melodic accent of Greek. When Roman poets adopted Greek metres they introduced correspondence rules unknown in the original language, making metrical ictus and accent coincide in all, or part, of the line (Allen 1973: 166–67). Such a correlation of ictus and accent appeared in Greek verse only when accent had changed from melodic to dynamic (Palmer 1954: 214).[18] On balance, therefore, it is reasonable to conclude that ancient authors were mistaken (as they were about the function of the heart), and that Latin had always had a dynamic accent.[19]

Early Latin stress-syllabic verse

This conclusion leads to another: that the metre of some Latin popular verse that has survived from the Classical period is stress-syllabic. Like their imperial successors from the USA, Roman legionaries chanted as they marched, and historians have preserved a number of such texts, collated by Du Méril (1843: 106–10). The rhythm of these marching songs is preponderantly trochaic, as the most famous of them shows:[20]

> (10)   Ec-ce, **Cae**-sar <u>nunc</u> tri-**um**-phat, || <u>qui</u> su-**be**-git **Gal**-li-<u>as</u>
>
> (11)   <u>Ur</u>-**ba**-<u>ni</u>, ser-**va**-t[e] u-**xo**-res, || **moe**-chum **cal**-v[um] ad-**du**-ci-<u>mus</u>

[Behold, Caesar now triumphs, who conquered the Gauls | Home we bring the bald whoremonger; Romans lock your wives away]

Although these lines contain no quantitative pattern, (10) consists entirely, and (11) predominantly, of accentual trochees (providing secondary stressed syllables and monosyllables may represent beats). A trochaic verse design is thus a reasonable hypothesis, and the iamb that opens (11) is no more than the first-foot inversion (licensed by the closure principle) that is typical of most stress-syllabic metres. Moreover, the word 'Ur-**ba**-ni' was probably wrenched in delivery: soldiers of all eras have marched in duple time because they have two hind-limbs, scanned by drill sergeants as left and right, but serving the rhythm as beat and offbeat.

Whether this accentual patterning is the result of chance can be confirmed by the statistical technique known as probability modelling.[21] This shows that in prose approximately 66 per cent of beats are separated by exactly one syllable; that is, they form accentual trochees. From this we can calculate that the odds against seven consecutive accentual trochees occurring by chance in Latin is 17:1, and that the chance against fourteen is 2557:1. Yet almost all the lines (and pairs of consecutive lines) in these soldiers' chants defy these odds. It seems reasonable to conclude that Romans of the first century BC could use their language's dynamic accent to compose accentual trochaic tetrameters. As the next section will demonstrate, a variant of this metre was still a favourite among Latin speakers more than a thousand years later.

Medieval Latin stress-syllabic metres

Most scholars agree that much of the Latin verse composed in Western Europe after AD 1100 was stress-syllabic, and that its most illustrious practitioner was Walter of Châtillon (b. Lille, 1135). He composed scrupulously correct and exceptionally elegant Latin verse, and was master of two modes of versifying: quantitative (metrical) and stress-syllabic (rhythmical).[22] Raby 1934: II, 196 gives a widely admired and imitated poem that contains both; its 'Goliardic' measure *cum auctoritate* was a series of quatrains comprising three rhythmical lines of 7M + 5F syllables followed by a quantitative dactylic hexameter, all having the same rhyme. The hexameter was quoted from a Classical author, and employing this metre clearly required a great deal of erudition. The poem given by Raby comprises 15 strophes, of which the first opens:

(12)   **Mis**-sus <u>sum</u> in **vi**-ne-<u>am</u> || **cir**-ca **ho**-ram **no**-nam,

(13)   **su**-am **quis**-que **ni**-ti-<u>tur</u> || **ven**-de-<u>re</u> per-**so**-nam;

(14)   **er**-go **qui**-a **cur**-si-<u>tant</u> || **om**-nes <u>ad</u> co-**ro**-nam

[I entered the vineyard at about nine; | everyone strives to promote himself; | therefore because all seek status]

Each of these three lines contains six trochees, divided midway by a secondary stress, producing eighteen consecutive trochees in all. The odds against this accentual configuration occurring in Latin by chance are well over a thousand to one; yet it occurs many times in Goliardic verse.[23] Since all poets using this metre shared this strong preference for trochaic rhythm, it must be regarded as a feature of its verse design.

But many nineteenth- and twentieth-century writers argued that only the hemistich-final stresses (as in French verse) are metrically significant in this metre. Yet, as these examples show, a high proportion of those final stresses are secondary, and it seems unlikely that poets would base their metre upon them while ignoring primary stresses.[24] As with my earlier Latin examples, (10) and (11), the objectors to a stress-syllabic explanation of Goliardic verse point out that the lines are far from perfectly trochaic. Once again, initial inversion and the use of monosyllables or secondary stresses to provide beats, both typical of stress-syllabic verse, can explain the imperfection. Some 18 per cent of the hemistichs of this Latin poem are not perfectly trochaic: this is sometimes the result of an initial inversion, but more often it involves an initial monosyllable; for example, in line 13:

> (15)   cur se-qui ves-ti-gi-a || ve-te-rum re-fu-tem
>
> [Why should I refuse to follow in the footsteps of the ancients?]

If phrasal stress is employed to make 'cur' more prominent than the lexically stressed 'se-', the weak syllable '-qui' then corresponds to the second ictus, and is an unusual inversion, but it interferes minimally with the prevailing trochaic rhythm. This monosyllabic feature occurs in some 12 per cent of hemistichs, compared with only 6 per cent that contain polysyllabic initial inversions like that in the second hemistich of line 46 of the poem:

> (16)   pau-per-ta-tem fu-gi-ens || vi-tam-que mi-sel-lam
>
> [fleeing poverty and a miserable life]

Even here it is possible that twelfth-century readers would have restored the pre-enclitic stressing of the first syllable of 'vi-tam'.

At the very least, Goliardic metre must be seen as transitional between syllabic and stress-syllabic verse; indeed, it is much closer to the latter than to the former. But there is also a case for arguing that it is a trochaic metre with a level of tension that is high, but by no means unusual. As I shall show in Chapter 8, the most famous trochaic poem in English, *The Song of Hiawatha*, contains more tension: 40 per cent of its hemistichs do not open with a strong–weak contrast. And in Chapter 4 I shall demonstrate that one of the earliest English stress-syllabic poems is in a metre that is clearly derived from the Latin Goliardic.

The Evolution of Syllabic Metres in French

The verse of many languages is numerically regulated at the level of the syllable and some writing systems represent one syllable by one sign, thus reinforcing the process visually.[25] Verse based entirely on the number of syllables in the line, however, accounts for only a small minority of texts in most of those languages. In some languages the composition of such verse seems to have followed a period in which syllable count was distinctly less rigorous; for example, in Chinese (see Frankel 1972: 25), Japanese (see Bownas 1964: xlvi), and the Romance languages (see Baehr 1970: 177). In the verse traditions of most languages syllabism came to be compounded or replaced by the regulation of some other suprasegmental feature, such as duration/weight (as in Sanskrit and Ancient Greek), pitch (as in Chinese), or stress (as in Iranian, Greek, Romance, and the Slavonic languages), and some evidence of such regulation is often present in the earliest surviving texts in these languages.[26] It may therefore be argued that counting syllables alone provides too fragile a metrical system to compete with more complex modes of composition, ones that employ features of syllables more obvious to listeners than their number.

Accentual patterns in Old French verse

Since French monks were among those who composed Latin verse that regulated word stress, it is not surprising that some of them attempted to do the same in the vernacular. Of the few such experiments that have survived two are texts dating from the eleventh century, the *Passion of Clermont* and *Vie de Saint Léger* (Henry 1953: 6–13). The following examples are lines 14–17 of the *Vie de St Léger*, and the scansion here assumes a right-strong template of eight positions:

> (17)   Al rei lo **duis**-trent || soi pa-**rent**,
> (18)   Qui donc reg-**ne**-vet || a ciel di,
> (19)   Cio fud Lo-**thiers**, || fils Bal-de-**qui**.
> (20)   Il l'e-na-**mat**, || Deu lo co-**vit**,

> [They took him to his father, | who was king at the time, | Lothiers, son of Baldequin; | he was his enemy, but God protected him.]

This metre differs from later (syllabic) French *octosyllabes* in that the fourth as well as the final syllable in the line invariably has stress. Moreover the only odd-numbered positions in the line that contain stressed syllables are positions 1 and 5, the first in each hemistich, and thus can be interpreted as initial inversion (licensed by the closure principle). This metre is virtually an iambic tetrameter, and should probably be classified as stress-syllabic.

Lewis 1898: 69–70 argues that word stress once played a major role in French versification, and the text of the earliest surviving poem in French supports this. The *Sainte Eulalie* (Aspland 1979: 4–6), which dates from *c.* 882, has a verse design that is even further from modern French practice: its lines have a regular number of stresses (two per hemistich) but not a regular number of syllables (see Duffell 1999a: 100–01). Purczinsky 1965: 271 attributes this peculiarity to the influence of Germanic verse (the manuscript's provenance is Valenciennes, and contains both Latin and German verse). But the two eleventh-century poems from Clermont Ferrand have no such Germanic connections. All three texts point to a time when French word stress was stronger than it is now, and when poets were tempted to employ it in the same way as they employed stress in their Latin verse. But the weakening of French word stress in subsequent centuries favoured a new metrics based on phrasal stress, and the eventual disappearance of word stress ensured that early French experiments in regulating it were not repeated, and were often not even recognized.

Old French metres employing only phrasal stress

Cornulier includes French verse together with pure syllabic metres in his term 'the metrics of undifferentiated syllables' (my translation; 1995: 111). But the syllabic metres of French differ from those of Japanese in that the final position of each French line must contain an accented syllable, and in longer lines the final position of the first hemistich usually does so. The three most common lengths of line in French are the *octosyllabe*, *décasyllabe* (or *vers de dix*), and the *dodécasyllabe* (or *alexandrin*). I shall describe each briefly, since these three metres were very influential at different points in the evolution of English metre.

The poems in *octosyllabes* that post-date the *Passion de Clermont* and the *Vie de Saint Léger* no longer employ word stress: the metre's template has eight positions with no caesura, or mandatory word boundary . Only the final position in the line is constrained: it must contain a stressed syllable and may also contain a post–tonic one, giving the line a syllable formula of 8M/F. The following lines (1659 & 1661) from the *Roman de la Rose* (Woledge 1961: 149) by Guillaume de Lorris (*fl.* 1240) demonstrate the absence of any caesura after position 4 and the random placement of non–final stressed syllables; for examples (21) to (26) only the phrase–final stresses are marked in my scansion:

(21)   Car u–ne co-lor l'en-lu-**mi**ne
(22)   Com Na-tu-re la pot plus **fai**re

[For one colour illuminates it | As much as Nature can make it]

In (21) the mid–line stressed syllables occupy positions 2 and 5, and in (22) they occupy 3 and 6; but the only stress that is mandatory is in position 8. This metre, although it regulates phrasal stress, is termed syllabic in traditional French metrics, and an *octosyllabe* with just such a syllabic verse design remained the most popular short French line in the centuries that followed. As we shall see in Chapter 4, this metre also accounted for a substantial proportion of the French verse composed in England between 1066 and 1363.

French long-line metres

As noted, French lines of more than eight syllables contain a caesura dividing them into at least two cola (Cornulier 1995: 47), and this is the chief difference between the verse designs of French long-line metres and that of the *octosyllabe*. The template of the *vers de dix* is divided into 4 + 6 and that of the *alexandrin* into 6 + 6 positions.[27] Thus the *vers de dix* has a mandatory word boundary that constrains the syllables in positions 4 and 5 from belonging to the same word. The *Vie de St Alexis* (Meunier 1933), dated *c.* 1020, is the earliest surviving French poem in this metre, which is a strongly divided *vers de dix*, as can be shown by lines 20 & 33:

| (23)   Des melz gen-**tils**   ‖ de tu-te la con-**tre**the | 4M + 6F |
| (24)   Puis ad es-**cole**   ‖ li bons pe-dre le <u>mist</u> | 4F + 6M |

[Of the best people in all the land | Then his good father sent him to school]

The syllabic formula of the poem's lines is 4M/F + 6M/F and the two hemistichs are metrically independent. Only the final stress of each is governed by the verse design: other stressed syllables, including the strong syllables of polysyllabic words, may occur in any position in the line. The final stress of either hemistich may be followed by a post-tonic syllable that is not included in the syllable count. When, as in instance (24), the first hemistich has such an uncounted syllable, the line is said to have an *epic caesura*, so termed because this method of accommodating feminine words at the caesura was a feature of widely disseminated epics, or *chansons de geste*.

Epic caesura, however, meant that in setting poems to music two syllables had to be fitted to one note in some lines. This inconsistency seemed to irk poets composing lyrics for singing, since they found alternative ways to accommodate feminine words at the caesura, as exemplified by two lines (34 & 19) from a *chanson* (Woledge 1961: 156–57) by Thibaud IV, Roi de Navarre (b. 1201, d. 1252):

(25)   D'en-tre-**pren**-dre || cho-se des-me-su-**re**e
(26)   La plus tres **bel**[e] || et la mei-lleur aus-**si**

[To attempt a rash thing | The most handsome and also the best]

Instance (25) has what is termed *lyric caesura*, or inversion in positions 3–4; in singing, and also perhaps in recitation, the first hemistich would be wrenched to make its final schwa prominent ('D'en-tre-pren-**dre**'). The other way of accommodating a feminine word mid-line in French verse is to elide its final schwa before an initial vowel after the caesura, as in (26), and this was the only one employed in French verse after 1500. In modern French the deletion of all word-final schwas has rendered feminine words oxytonic in normal speech (*e-atone* has become *e-muet*), but poets and actors have preserved the convention of counting and pronouncing all unelided word-final schwas in verse.

The *alexandrin*'s verse design differs from that of the *vers de dix* in only one parameter, a position number of 6 + 6, which offers greater regularity of phrasal stress than the line of 4 + 6. The *vers de dix* dominated French long-line verse composition in the eleventh and twelfth centuries, but then gave way to the *alexandrin*, which remained in favour until the fourteenth. It was followed by a revived, more unified *vers de dix* that invariably contained ten actual syllables, because it eschewed epic caesura. In the sixteenth century this metre was rejected as the French long-line canon in favour of a new, unified *alexandrin*, which also accommodated feminine words at the caesura only by eliding them before a following vowel (see Kastner 1903: 142–48). The emergence of syllabic verse in the eleventh century suggests that Old French word stress was weaker than phrasal stress even at that early date. But the fact that syllabic verse is such a good fit for the phonology of French caused a variety of problems for poets who sought to imitate these metres in other languages.

Pan-Romance syllabic metres

Poets in many other languages, ranging from Italian and Spanish in the South to Polish and Russian in the North, have imitated French syllabic (or, more accurately, phrasal-stress) versification (see Gasparov 1996: 217–29). In the Romance languages of Western Europe the imitation of French syllabic verse was aided by an important phonological similarity, syllable-timing, and hindered by an important difference, strong word stress. Nevertheless, Occitan poets mastered syllabic metrics early in the eleventh century, and Catalan poets were equally successful when they began to versify in their own language in the fifteenth.[28] But Italian poets had to make many adjustments to the *vers de dix* in the thirteenth before it emerged as the *endecasillabo*. Exported to the Iberian Peninsula in the sixteenth century, this metre evolved into the Spanish *endecasílabo* and Portuguese *decassílabo* and became the long-line canon for the poets of three nations.[29]

In the course of this expansion, poets working in languages with strong word stress met, and brought their own solutions to, several problems. The first was that their language's word stress hindered audience's perceptions of the regularity of phrasal stress in this type of verse.[30] This made it difficult to count syllables by ear, and there is evidence that some of the first poets of the Iberian Peninsula to imitate French syllabic metres were reduced to counting on their fingers or on the page (see Duffell 2007: 37n28). These methods led to what may be termed *anti-rhythmic* counting: the inclusion of line-final post-tonic syllables in the count, thus making 8M = 7F syllables. This equivalence forfeits the regularity of phrasal stress on every eighth syllable in delivery (a key feature of verse in which 8M = 8F), but anti-rhythmic counting became widespread in thirteenth- and fourteenth-century Castilian and Galician-Portuguese verse.[31] Although short-line verse in these languages had overcome these problems by the fifteenth century, long-line verse did not, and poets reverted to traditional accentual metres that fell from favour only when Italian metrics was introduced.[32] Many metrists, however, in both Italy and the Iberian Peninsula, have defined all the metres of these three languages entirely in terms of their syllable count.[33]

A second problem was that presented by lyric caesura: recession, or wrenching, may be tolerable in sung verse, or in languages with weak word stress, but it sounds ugly, clumsy, and unnatural in those where word stress is a major feature. From Italy to Catalonia, poets shunned lyric caesura and cultivated other methods of accommodating feminine words at the caesura. One of these was to abandon a fixed word boundary in their longer lines and rely instead on a limited number of rhythms provided by word stress to give the correct number of syllables in total. This modification led back towards stress–syllabic metres and, as a result, the Italian and Iberian long-line canons became transitional between syllabic and stress–syllabic.[34] This development was of considerable significance in the history of English metre, as I shall show in Chapter 4.

Conclusions

This chapter began by considering a number of linguistic features that are relevant to versifying where English differs from some other languages. It then discussed which other languages have most influenced English metrics, and focused on Latin and French. It showed that the two language's metrical systems had changed considerably over time, Latin towards stress–syllabic verse and French towards syllabic, and that French syllabic metrics was imitated and adapted in the other

Romance languages. From this analysis it is clear that English libraries and, even more importantly, schoolrooms have always offered a variety of foreign metrical models: foot-based verse in Classical Latin, stress-syllabic verse in Medieval Latin, verse based on syllable count in Old French, and rhymed verse in both the medieval languages. New foreign influences have also appeared at various points in time: from verse in a peculiar variety of French between the eleventh and fourteenth centuries, from Italian verse in the fourteenth and sixteenth, from French and American experiments in the nineteenth, and from repeated attempts to reproduce the phrasal rhythms of Hebrew verse. Each of these I shall discuss in the relevant place in my narrative, but the above account of versifying in Latin and French should prove sufficient to explain most of the differences between the English metrical system I described in Chapter 1 and the versification of the earliest poetry in the language. This will be the subject of the next chapter, which offers an account of Old English metre and traces its legacy in the verse of Middle and Modern English.

Notes to Chapter 2

1. I doubt whether the delivery of Old English was as stress-timed as that of modern speech. In Old English verse some consecutive stresses are separated by five syllables while others are back-to-back; delivering such verse with stress-timing would have been rather difficult. Evidence that stress-timing evolved with the phonology of Middle English includes the appearance of hemistichs with a third stress (Andrew & Waldron 1987: 48), and the subsequent development of types of verse with a maximum interval of two syllables (Tarlinskaja 1976 & 1993).

2. Texts containing rhymed verse in both Romance and Arabic have survived in Spain from the eleventh century (see Hitchcock 1977 and Corriente 1997: 270–335), but the earliest surviving texts composed entirely in Spanish or in Portuguese (Michael 1987 and Nunes 1926–28) suggest that assonance preceded rhyme in all the Romance languages, whereas even the earliest Arabic poems have full rhyme in all its manifestations.

3. Preminger et al. note that Irish was the first modern European language where rhyme was employed systematically at the line or hemistich end (1975: 708); it was also used compositionally within hemistichs. Irish rules for rhyme allow the codas of rhyming syllables to contain consonants of the same class, and alliteration remained a feature of Irish verse for many centuries (see Meyer 1909: 5–10). In Welsh poetry an elaborate system (termed *cynghanedd*) of combining alliteration, rhyme, assonance, and pararhyme was developed in the Middle Ages (see Graves 1961: 18 and Abley 2005: 169). Cynghanedd combines both left- and right-strong features, as does the language itself, which experienced accentual change in the Middle Ages and now combines stress on penultimate syllables with a rise of fundamental frequency on final syllables (see Rowland 1876: 10–14).

4. Saintsbury devotes eight pages to Latin (including Greek), less than a page to French and Provençal, and half a page each to Scandinavian and Celtic metrics (1906: 1, 14–24).

5. For example, the word *controversy* has two current pronunciations: one makes the penultimate syllable (-*ver*-) heavy and stresses it, the other makes this syllable light and stresses the preceding syllable.

6. The final syllable in the line (the second in position 12) is optionally long or short: this is an example of *boundary indifference*, which applies to a number of metres that I shall discuss. Boundary indifference allows deviance in the number and quantity of the syllables before the first ictus and after the last. The Classical terms for these syllables are *anacrusic, catalectic,* and *anceps*; more modern terms are *extramusical, extrametrical,* and *optional* (see Duffell 2000a: 238–41).

7. I employ the following visual aids to scansion in the instances that follow: (1) separately counted syllables are separated by a hyphen; (2) word-final vowels that are not included in the syllable

count are in superscript; (3) caesura is marked by extra space. (4) For Latin texts I have also marked long vowels, and placed the conventional scansional symbols above the line: − denotes a long syllable, ⌣ denotes a short one, / denotes a foot boundary, and // denotes a caesura. Word-final vowels may be excluded from the syllable count of a line for a number of reasons. In Classical Latin verse such vowels were subject to elision ('a striking out') before another vowel or diphthong, but in Medieval Latin verse every written vowel was counted as a syllable and its delivery involved hiatus. In French verse elision also became the most frequent treatment of adjacent vowels in adjacent words; in the verse of other Romance languages it is *synaloepha* ('a smearing together') of the two vowels.

8. French metrists term the use of metre to echo and reinforce a passage's meaning *expressivité* (see, for example, Grammont 1937: 39, Wright 1988, and Carper & Attridge 2003). I shall note numerous examples of this phenomenon in English verse in the chapters that follow.

9. Greek poets had not taken this precaution, probably because of differences between the nature of Greek and Latin accent, which I shall discuss later in this chapter.

10. Mukherji refers to Sanskrit verse of the Ionic type as 'moric' and shows that it post-dates that of the Aeolic type (1976: 172–213), but this is less clearly the case in Greek. West, following Meillet, suggests that the Greek dactylic hexameter may have been derived from a metre in an earlier Mediterranean language (1973: 169n10). Since we know of no Mediterranean culture earlier than Greek that employed quantitative verse, this is unsatisfactory: it attempts to explain a mystery by a bigger mystery.

11. The moraic length of the Phalaecian hendecasyllable was subsequently regularized by Horace (Q. Horatius Flaccus, b. 65, d. 8 BC; Garrod 1947), who opened all his lines in this metre with a spondee, thus giving them a fixed total length of eighteen moras, but later poets reverted to Catullus's verse design.

12. For the metrical implications of these linguistic changes see Lote 1939: 219–71; for a traditional account of how Latin became Romance see Elcock 1975: 225–311, and for a more challenging modern hypothesis see Wright 1982, 1994, & 2003.

13. Thus, Gasparov 1996: 104 argues that a ninth-century Latin poem composed in Modena is an example of a syllabic line of twelve syllables, but in no line has the poet placed a stressed syllable in any odd-numbered position other than the first. A careful scansion of this poem demonstrates that stress-syllabic Latin verse dates from well before the twelfth century.

14. This particular poem, composed soon after 1089, cannot be the model for the Romance metre, since it dates from sixty years after the earliest surviving examples in French and Occitan. Burger 1957 derives the *vers de dix* from the Latin iambic trimeter or *senarius*, and Avalle 1963 from the Latin *tropes* that were often inserted into the Mass.

15. French metrists denote line length by an arabic numeral for the number of syllables to the final stress plus M or F to indicate whether the line is oxytonic or paroxytonic; Latin lines, like English ones, can also be proparoxytonic, which I indicate here by P.

16. When Greek accent changed from pitch to stress at the end of the second century AD, contemporary writers continued to describe the stressed syllables as higher (Palmer 1954: 211). Similar confusion about the acoustics of stress persisted in Europe until at least the fifteenth century: thus, for example, Lydgate described stressed/unstressed syllables as 'long/short' (Schirmer 1961: 71).

17. Thus, for example, syncope makes the English word *me-di-cine* disyllabic; in Latin *ae-vi-tas* became *ae-tas* very early (Palmer 1954: 212), but *po-si-ta* became *pos-ta* relatively late (Elcock 1975: 53).

18. Ictus and accent coincide in the last two feet of the Classical dactylic hexameter and throughout the line in dramatic verse. Some Medieval Latin dactylic hexameters, particularly those composed in France, dispensed with this precaution: some lines have a word-final long syllable in position 9 (Taylor et al. 1998: 361–62). This may have been because the poets concerned stressed the final syllable of Latin words, as they did of French (e.g. *rosarúm* and *rosís*). Such an accentuation of Latin (known as the 'French pedagogic') is common in modern French schoolrooms and is defended by Marouzeau 1931. For a history of the pronunciation of Latin in medieval and modern Europe see Kelly 1986 & 1988 and Waquet 2001: 160–71.

19. The Romans based many of their beliefs on Greek texts rather than direct observation: for example, that the heart is the centre of human intelligence and that flies have four legs.

20. In this and all subsequent examples I indicate the strong syllables of polysyllabic words by bold typeface and other types of syllable occupying strong positions by underlining.

21. I have used the technique of probability modelling to compare the accentual disposition in Du Méril's text with that of a sample of Latin prose. For this control I have used Koster's essay on the Saturnian metre (1929), chosen by the random process of looking on my desk and appropriate because of its plain, unpoetic style.

22. Walter's quantitative masterpiece, the *Alexandreis* (Migne 1844), is in dactylic hexameters in which ictus and accent coincide at the line end, as they do in Virgil's and Ovid's.

23. My figures are based on a probability analysis similar to that used by Gasparov 1980a, and my Latin prose control is the text of the introduction to Koster 1929. On average 66 per cent of intervals between stresses in the prose control contained exactly one syllable, so that the chance of eighteen consecutive stresses having this configuration is 1:1667 ($1:1.515^{18}$).

24. Secondary stress in Latin polysyllabic words usually falls two places from primary stress, as in English.

25. For Chinese versifiers a syllable has the advantage of being not only one sign, but also one word. Note that in Chinese the same word (*chü*) is used to describe a sentence and a line; the lines of the earliest surviving Chinese verse in the *Book of Songs* (tenth to seventh centuries BC) are arranged syntactically in couplets with an intricate rhyme scheme, and the majority of lines contain four syllables (Frankel 1972: 23–25).

26. For the growing role of accent in these languages see Pighi 1970: 40–41, West 1973: 164–65 & 169, and Gasparov 1996: 140–41; for evidence of an element of quantitative or accentual regulation in the earliest Greek, Iranian, and Sanskrit verse see Pighi 1970: 6–7, West 1973: 164–66, and Mukherji 1976: 32–43.

27. The ubiquitous 4 + 6 *vers de dix* was not the only type employed by medieval French poets: poems in 6 + 4 and 5 + 5 decasyllables have also survived, of which the earliest examples also ignore any post-tonic syllable at the caesura in their syllable count. French poets did not combine these different types of *vers de dix* in the same poem and they should therefore be regarded as separate metres.

28. Some two and a half thousand Occitan poems composed between the eleventh and the thirteenth centuries have survived in syllabic metres of almost every length (see Ricketts 2001). Both the content and the form of these poems were influential throughout Europe and they demonstrate great skill in syllable count, rhyme, and strophe architecture (see Billy 1989). In the thirteenth and fourteenth centuries Catalan poets also composed in Occitan (see, for example, Cabré 1999) or in an intermediate language (see Duffell 1994: 297). The first poems employing the Catalan language (Bohigas 1952–59) were by Ausias March (b. 1400, d. 1459); the widespread influence and lasting popularity of March's syllabic verse delayed the introduction of Italianate metres into Catalan (see Ramírez 1985: 77–83).

29. Since most Italian words have a post-tonic syllable, Italian metrists describe a line of ten syllables to the final stress as an *endecasillabo*. This term became even more appropriate as Italian poets soon came to avoid lines of 10M (*bruschi*) and 10P syllables (*sdruccioli*) and to use only lines of 10F (*piani*). Note that Spanish metrists follow the Italian convention for counting syllables and naming metres, and that Catalan and Portuguese metrists follow the French.

30. The part played by accent in the versification of the Galician-Portuguese *trovadores* is shown by Parkinson 2006, and a detailed discussion of accent in various types of medieval Castilian verse can be found in Cano 1931 and in Duffell 1999c, 2002a, & 2003. Duffell 1999c argues that the earliest syllabic metre in Castilian (dating from *c.* 1200) is adapted from the French *alexandrin*. A much greater variety of syllabic metres appeared later in the thirteenth century in Galician-Portuguese (see Hanssen 1913 and Clarke 1955).

31. Anti-rhythmic counting is termed 'Mussafia's law' by Hispanic metrists, but calling it a law does not stop its being a mistake, at least as far as creating and recognizing a primary rhythm is concerned; see Duffell 2007: 94 & 99.

32. The development of the Castilian *verso común* into a strictly counted *octosílabo* is described in Clarke 1964: 18–50, and the conversion of the accentual *verso de arte mayor* into a *dodecasílabo* of

5F + 5M/F syllables by one influential fifteenth-century poet is discussed in Duffell 2000c. An accentual metre, the *verso de arte mayor*, displaced the Castilian equivalent of the *alexandrin* soon after 1380 and became stress-syllabic in the hands of some poets (see Duffell 1999b).

33. Dante Alighieri (b. 1255, d. 1321) writes of Italian lines as if their structure were identical with that of French or Occitan ones. He makes no mention of accent in the *De vulgari eloquentiâ* (Howell 1973) and Italian poets soon learned to ignore word stress within short lines. For the modifications required in the *vers de dix* to produce the *endecasillabo* see Beltrami 1986 and Billy 1989.

34. Zhirmunsky (1966: 86) and Gasparov (1987: 330–32) argue that these metres are intermediate between syllabic and stress-syllabic, because almost all their lines have an iambic second hemistich (see also Domínguez Caparrós 2000: 152–55, Carvalho 1965: 32, and Bandeira 1962: 3243). Fabb, on the other hand, categorizes the Italian *endecasillabo* as *accentual*, because of its two mandatory accented syllables in positions 4 and 10, or 6 and 10 (1997: 72–74); Fabb's terminology risks confusion with metres that contain a fixed number of accents per line and much greater variation in the number of intervening syllables.

CHAPTER 3

English Historical Metrics: The Germanic Inheritance

Old Germanic Accentual Verse

English is a Germanic language and is descended from the speech of the tribes who first arrived in the British Isles in the fifth century AD and subsequently settled in England (except for Cornwall). A new wave of Germanic sea raiders from Scandinavia settled in the North and East of England between the eighth and eleventh centuries, which triggered a major migration of the Northumbrian English into Southern Scotland. The two major languages of England between the ninth and eleventh centuries, Old English and Old Norse, were mutually intelligible and had similar literary traditions. The Germanic peoples of Northern Europe had developed a mode of versifying that differed significantly from those discussed in Chapter 2. Among the surviving verse texts composed in this way are the Old German *Ludwigslied* (Braune & Helme 1928), the Old Icelandic Elder (Poetic) Edda (Dronke 1969), and many Old English poems (Hamer 1970).[1] The syllabic irregularity and accentual regularity of such texts can be seen from the following lines (96–99) from the Old English *Battle of Maldon* (Scragg 1991), probably composed fairly soon after 991 when the battle was fought:

(1) **Wo**-don þa **wæl**-wul-fas || for **wæ**-te-re ne **mur**-non
(2) **wi**-cin-ga **we**-rod || <u>west</u> **o**-fer **Pan**-tan
(3) **o**-fer <u>scir</u> **wæ**-ter || **scyl**-das **we**-gon
(4) **lid**-men to **lan**-de || **lin**-de **bæ**-ron

[Wolves of war, unmindful of ocean, | the Viking horde surged west over Pante, | carrying their shields over shining water, | seafarers, bearing to land the linden (my translation)]

These lines contain an irregular number of syllables (between nine and thirteen actual syllables) and their most obvious regularity is in the number of prominent syllables: there are four strong stresses in each line, two in each half-verse. One nineteenth-century writer described this metre as a line in which stressed syllables (2 + 2) are numerically regulated, but unstressed ones are not (Wackernagel 1879). There is, however, much more to this verse design than the number of strong positions and the prominence type, stress. First of all, of the four strongly stressed syllables in the line, the first three are linked and emphasized by alliteration; the final stress, being the weakest in a left-strong line, lacks it. The alliteration in the passage quoted confirms the intuitive analysis that stress, not syllable strength, is the prominence type: the stressed monosyllables 'west' and 'scir' form part of the alliterative pattern, but the strong syllable of the grammatical word 'ofer' does not.

Although most modern analyses of this metre accept that the verse design stipulates four strong stresses, they disagree with the idea that the material between them (the content of weak positions) is unregulated. Many different analyses of Old Germanic verse design (often referred to as *accentual metre*) have been offered, almost all of them based on the same text, *Beowulf* (Wrenn & Bolton 1988).[2] This, the most famous poem in the metre, may have been composed as early as the beginning of the ninth century, but we know it from a single manuscript in a language that seems to date from the end of the tenth (see Wrenn & Bolton 1988: 9–13). Stockwell & Minkova 1997 gives an admirable synopsis of the modern debate on the metre of *Beowulf*, and I have drawn heavily on their work in the sections below. First I shall examine the two most widely held theories of Germanic metre, then I shall discuss two recent linguistic accounts of it, and finally I shall attempt to set the Old Germanic mode of versifying in the context of the modes I have examined in the course of Chapters 1 and 2.

Musical theories

A number of modern scholars have proposed that the numerical regulation in *Beowulf* was that of music (now lost) to which the text was set. Musical rhythm is the product of units (*bars*) each containing material (*notes*) of the same total duration. These equal units are marked by *beats*, which always coincide with the opening note in each bar, and introductory notes before the beat of the first bar are regarded as *anacrusis*, or striking-up notes, and do not contribute to the rhythm (ABRSM 1958: 18). Any verse design can be described in musical terms, even a right-strong one, because the contents of its opening weak position can be labelled anacrusis. But a musical analysis of left-strong Germanic metres has seemed particularly appropriate to many writers; for example, Heusler 1891, Pope 1942 & 1966, and Creed 1966 & 1990. A musical analysis enables metrists to regularize the extreme syllabic irregularity of this metre by inserting rests, where there are too few syllables, and reducing the length of the note allotted to each, where there are too many. The problem with such musical scansion is that we don't know how this verse was delivered, whether it was sung, or chanted, or recited.

Modern experience of oral epic delivery is confined almost entirely to the 'singing of tales' in Serbo-Croat (Lord 1960), and specialists in English verse have mostly been critical of any attempt to extrapolate these findings to the ancient Germanic tradition (see, for example, Campbell 1962). Traditional Serbo-Croat oral verse is quite unlike Old Germanic in one most important respect: the former is syllabically regular (lines have 9F syllables) and thus fits the isochrony of music extremely well. Germanic epic verse, on the other hand, is extremely irregular in syllable count; while it can be sung in the manner of Gregorian chant (that is, not isochronously), this is not the type of musical scansion that has usually been proposed.[3] Stockwell &

Minkova rightly dismiss hypotheses of *Beowulf*'s 'performance' as 'hazardous' (1997: 59). The one element of musical scansion that most metrists find useful, however, is the concept of anacrusis. In many types of verse syllables before the first stress seem to be optional; they are allowed but not demanded by the verse design. Indeed, they may be termed *extramusical* in the same way that syllables after the final stress in the line are termed *extrametrical*, the two categories combining to produce what I have called *boundary indifference* (see Chapter 2, n. 6).[4] On the whole, however, our uncertainties about delivery have made another, non-musical, method of analysis the prevailing orthodoxy of Old English metrics, the *reference theory*.

Reference theory

Sievers 1885 first argued that the verse design of *Beowulf* allows certain configurations of stressed and unstressed syllables, but not others, and he identified five permissible types (subdivided by subsequent writers into six). This hypothesis and its many sub-sequent ramifications are known as *reference theory*. Stockwell & Minkova illustrate the permissible structures by alliterating Modern English phrases and by half-verses of *Beowulf*, using '!' to describe a void position (where my scansion elsewhere uses [V]), as follows (1997: 69):

Type	English phrase	Scansion	'Beowulf' half-line	No.
A	Arnie's army	[s w / s w]	*lāðan līges*	83a
B	in briny baths	[w s / w s]	*nē lēof nē lāð*	511a
C	by cost-cutting	[w s / s w]	*beloren lēofum*	1073a
D_1	dumb dog-catchers	[s ! / s s w]	*flōd fæðmian*	3133a
D_2	dry daisy-chain	[s ! / s w s]	*eall ēðelwyn*	2885a
E	egg-laying hen	[s s w / s !]	*fēasceaftum men*	2285a

All of these basic types have four actual syllables, and some 80 per cent of *Beowulf*'s half-lines conform exactly to one of the six patterns. Most of the remainder can be explained with the aid of the concepts of anacrusis (the presence of one or more striking-up syllables before the first metrically significant stress) and resolution (the equivalence of [s !] and [s w]). There then remain a small number of hypermetrical half-lines, which Sievers argued contain a third foot (1885: section 94), but which are open to other interpretations. Sievers's categorization is by no means perfect or complete, and subsequent writers added a great deal more detail. The most important advances were those of Bliss (1958 & 1962), which subdivided the five Sievers types into 130 sub-types and provided an invaluable index of lines by type, and of Cable 1974 & 1989, which offered the most convincing explanations to date of why the Sievers types were permissible and other configurations not.

Cable pointed out that the pattern [w s w / s w], Type A with single-syllable anacrusis, is one of the most common in Old English, yet the *Beowulf* poet avoided it, probably because it presents five stress contrasts rather than four (1974: 32–44). He also showed that the list of permissible types, like the phonology of the lexicon, excludes stress contours with two consecutive rises in relative stress (1974: 84–93). Cable thus identified important ways in which the rules governing the metre of the poem either differed from or resembled those governing the language itself. The most important developments in the analysis of Old Germanic metrics in the last twenty years have built on this foundation of comparing metrical and linguistic norms. The two new theories I shall discuss here are both derived from generative linguistics: the first is a *syntagmatic* theory, and the second is an application of *optimality theory* to the study of metrics.

The 'word-foot' in Old Germanic verse

Russom 1987 argues that the configurations of stress and syllable in Old English verse are closely related to the word structure of the language, and he coined the term *word-foot* to describe what he believes to be the basic constituent of the line. In Russom's analysis foot and word boundaries always coincide, and he argues that nine configurations of stress and syllable are found in Old English words and are permissible feet in its verse. I give them below, using his notation (S = primary stress, s = secondary stress, x = non-stress) and his word examples (1987: 13).

> x: *ond* ('and')
> S: *gōd* ('good')
> xx: *oþþe* ('or')
> Sx: *dryhten* ('lord')
> Ss: *sǽ-mann* ('sailor')
> Sxx: *bealdode* ('he encouraged')
> Ssx: *sǽ-mannes* ('sailor's')
> Sxs: *middan-geard* ('middle earth')
> Sxxs: *sibbe-ge-driht* ('band of kinsmen')

Some of these word-feet differ from the feet of traditional explanations of the metre: the two types of light foot that correspond to unstressed monosyllables [x] and disyllables [x x], and the tetrasyllabic foot [S x x s]. At the same time some traditional feet are excluded, most importantly the rising foot (iamb) that characterizes Sievers types B and C, but corresponds to no word in the language. Russom shows that all normal half-lines in *Beowulf* comprise two of his word-feet, in any of twenty-five possible combinations (1987: 20–23), and he explains hypermetric lines in terms of 'overlapping feet', the expansion of a foot into a half-line on the model of compounding in the lexicon (1987: 59–63). Like earlier theories, Russom's recognizes anacrusis and allows extrametrical words to appear before either foot in a half-line (1987: 19–20). He notes that the word-feet found most often in verse are the most common structures of words in the lexicon (as we should expect, since he has made feet of words), and he describes less common structures as more complex (1987: 48–49).

Russom 1998 applies the word-foot theory to the four-beat verse of three languages: Old English, Old Norse, and continental West Germanic. He concludes that differences in foot structure in the three verse traditions are linked to differences in the strength of stress (strongest in Old Norse, weakest in continental West Germanic) and offers an account of the evolution of four-beat verse in the three languages that relies heavily on linguistic determinism (1998: 206–15). Russom also uses his cross-linguistic comparison to demonstrate inadequacies in reference theory, in particular Sievers's reliance on numerous ad hoc principles in order to accommodate all the half-lines in his typology (1998: 195–204). Russom's theory is more than an alternative description of Old Germanic metre that uses different sub-units to account for line structure, because it offers a credible explanation of how the poems came to be composed. Reference theory provides a menu explanation of the process of composition: the poet had a number of variants to choose from in constructing the next line (five, according to Sievers, 130 according to Bliss); this seems an unlikely way for poets to work and is contra-indicated by modern experience. In contrast Russom's theory allows the poet to perform a simple repetitive act: to produce lines of four word-equivalents (linked by alliteration), using the inherent knowledge of possible word shapes that is part of his linguistic competence.

Optimality theory: constraints in 'Beowulf'

Getty 2002 analyses the metre of *Beowulf* using optimality theory, which replaces the idea of linguistic *rules* with that of a series of universal *constraints*. These are hierarchical, and the position of any given constraint in the hierarchy (which may change over time) determines its influence on linguistic output.[5]

Getty 2002: 10–15 offers an analysis of *Beowulf*'s template based on parametric theory (Hanson & Kiparsky 1996): *position number*: 8; *orientation*: left-strong; *position size*: one foot (or moraic trochee); *prominence site*: strong positions; *prominence type*: strength (the weak syllables of polysyllabic words are constrained from appearing in strong positions). This verse design can be recognized as the trochaic tetrameter of traditional metrics but, while Getty describes four trochees as the 'optimal' realization of the pattern, he argues that a number of other realizations are licensed by the poet's need to employ all the words in the Old English lexicon (the principle of fit). Thus non-optimal feet and non-optimal half-lines occur; Getty hypothesizes four types of foot, all of them left-strong (since any initial weak syllable is anacrusis), as follows (2002: 12):

a	b	c	d
S	S W	S W W	S W W W

In addition to sub-optimal feet, sub-optimal half-lines, with three feet instead of two, make up 20 per cent of total in the poem (2002: 13).

Getty's theory, which he supports with examples from *Beowulf*, can equally well be illustrated by the passage from *The Battle of Maldon* quoted above.

```
        s     w  w / s   w   w  // (w) s w w w / s w
(1)a  Wo-don þa wæl-wul-fas || for wæ-te-re ne mur-non

        s  w  w / s  w        //  s   w  w / s  w
(2)a  wi-cin-ga we-rod        || west o-fer Pan-tan

        s  w / s / s   w       //  s   w / s  w
(3)a  o-fer scir wæ-ter       || scyl-das we-gon

        s   w  w / s  w        //  s   w / s  w
(4)a  lid-men to lan-de       || lin-de bæ-ron
```

Instance (1)a thus comprises four feet: c, c / anacrusis, d, b; (2)a comprises four feet:

c, b / c, b; (3)a comprises five feet: b, a, b / b, b; and (4)a comprises four feet: c, b / b, b. In this passage 10 of the 17 feet are optimal and 7 of the 8 half-lines have the optimal two feet (the first of (3)a has three).[6]

Having established his parameters Getty moves on to optimality theory and constructs his hierarchy of ranked constraints that will generate lines of the structure and frequency with which they appear in *Beowulf*. He lists forty-three constraints in all (2002: 311–13), and high on that list are (c) half-lines occurring in the same line must be linked by alliteration, (d) the maximum size of a metrical position is that of a phonological foot, and (e) stressed syllables are barred from occupying weak metrical positions.[7] At the top of the list, however, are two that over-ride all others: (a) languages select metres in which their entire vocabularies are usable in the greatest variety of ways, and (b) metrical boundaries should be maximally distinct. The first of these elevates the principle of fit to a constraint: it is contentious in that it can be applied to all verse and licenses all exceptions to other metrical rules, as long as those exceptions constitute words. Nevertheless, Getty's book is a highly significant contribution to the debate on Old English metre, elegantly combining several important innovations in linguistics: parametric theory, the principle of fit, and optimality theory. Most importantly of all, as Getty 2002: 6 points out, this theory frees Old English verse from its isolation: it is not a metrical curiosity, but an early example of the same type of verse we find later in English.

The Rhythmic Typology and Origins of Old Germanic Verse

The foregoing synopsis enables us to place Old Germanic verse in context: to classify it rhythmically within the framework of earlier chapters, to compare it with the other metres found in Western Europe, and to account for its evolution from primitive Indo-European metres.

The rhythm of Old Germanic verse

One interpretation of Old English verse is that it has a simple primary rhythm, a regular series of identical events produced by four (2 + 2) stresses per line: that is, the poet versified by counting stresses and emphasizing them by alliteration. This is the analysis of Wackernagel 1879, which ignored the remaining linguistic material in the line, treating it as an intrinsic part of the interval between the four rhythmic events. Such an analysis can be defended against the claims of reference theory by arguing that the allowable configurations of stress and syllable (whether six or 130) are a source of variety, not of regularity. In contrast, Russom's theory and, even more clearly, Getty's theory imply that a complex secondary rhythm is present (as in modern English stress-syllabic verse), a series of trochees, contrasts between two different types of event, stress and non-stress. What *Beowulf*'s audience made of the metre is an interesting question: they would surely have been aware of the 2 + 2 stresses, and they may have recognized the lack of alliteration on the fourth stress as a line-end marker (see Sapora 1977: 18). It is more doubtful, however, whether they would have registered that 130 combinations of stress and non-stress were employed, while the remainder were excluded. Nevertheless, modern research has demonstrated that the poet was observing more rules than those that produce 2 + 2 stresses: consciously or subconsciously the poet created a trochaic text, one that instinctively echoed the process of word formation in the language.

The evolution of accentual verse

The hypothesis of Meillet 1923 that all Indo-European metres have evolved from syllabic originals has become the orthodoxy of European metrists (see West 1973: 161 and Gasparov 1996: 7–10). The explanation of syllabically irregular verse in this group of languages is attributed to syllable loss (syncope and final-vowel deletion) in the languages concerned, which would have ensured that new pronunciations of old lines would destroy their regularity. The antiquity and wide distribution of such irregular verse, however, should cause us to re-examine this hypothesis.

As I have noted, pre-literate verse antedates literate verse, and the folk poems (proverbs and nursery rhymes) of many European languages are not only syllabically irregular, they also contain accentual patterns (for Romance examples, see Milá y Fontanals 1893, Bayo 1999, and Duffell 2002a). The evidence for Meillet's hypothesis, on the other hand, comes from written texts: the Old Iranian *Avesta*, the Sanskrit *Rig Veda*, and some Greek inscriptions, which are as regular in syllable count as Greek Aeolic metres. Although the oldest Indo-European verse text of all, the Hittite *Song of Ullikummi*, is irregular, it is dismissed as the product of Semitic influence by the supporters of Meillet's hypothesis (see, for example, West 1973: 182). They also discount as a later development the quantity contrasts that characterize the second half of the earliest Sanskrit lines and pervade all Greek ones. But the fact that most of the surviving ancient texts are syllabic proves only that ancient Indo-European peoples used this mode of versifying, not that it was the only mode, nor that all others must be derived from it.

That the texts that have survived are syllabic cannot be dissociated from the method of preservation: the oldest scripts in which the verse is written are open syllabaries, where one syllable equals one sign (Gaur 1984: 14–17).[8] Such scripts make syllabic verse (but no other) perfectly regular to the eye as well as the ear, and would give it a clear evolutionary advantage. Texts already syllabically regular would probably have gained aesthetic preference from the invention of writing, and irregular ones could easily have been regularized (see Duffell 1999c: 166–67 and 2003: 115). The *Avesta* and *Rig Veda*, in particular, were products of a priesthood in possession of a revolutionary new technology, a syllabic script, which may have led to the selection of one of several existing types of metre, or even to the invention of modes of versifying that were previously unknown.

The oldest surviving Germanic line of verse, which dates from *c.* 400 AD, is an inscription on a horn in a language that was probably an early form of Old Norse. It is given in Russom 1998: 1, as follows (except that I have used ř to represent the sound between *z* and *r*, for which Russom uses R):

   (5)   ekhlewagastiř : holtijař : horna : tawido :

        [I Hlewagast, Holt's son, made this horn; Russom's translation]

This inscription, with its four strong stresses and alliterative pattern, is unmistakably in the same metre as *Beowulf*. Hlewagast's metrical intention is not thirteen syllables, but four words, as the colons and the inclusion of the pronoun 'ek' in the first word clearly show.[9] This example of word-based metre, geographically distant from Semitic influence, suggests that at least one ancient Indo-European people employed a mode of versifying other than the syllabic. Since counting by ear up to four is easy, and to thirteen impossible, it seems very likely that, when ancient Indo-European poets wanted lines of this length, they would have based them on word count. The alternative would have been to subdivide all the lines in the same place (for example, into 5: 3: 2: 3 syllables, as in (5)). This alternative, which requires much greater effort, would have been attractive only once writing (in an open syllabary) had given it the advantage of visual regularity.

Old Germanic verse seems to have been based on words from its very beginning (hence the appropriateness of Russom's term, *word-foot*). Moreover, all the languages in which I have instanced accentual metres in this chapter are synthetic and highly inflected ones; for them syncope and schwa-loss lie in the future, and it is difficult to envisage that such lines once had additional syllables, which eroded to make them irregular. Bringing Old Germanic metre back into the mainstream of European historical metrics (Getty 2002: 6) has important repercussions: it brings strong evidence against Meillet's hypothesis that all Indo-European verse was originally syllabic and that other types evolved from it.

Middle English Alliterative Verse

Although only forty-five lines of Old English verse composed after the Norman Conquest have survived, the traditions of alliteration and strong-stress rhythm were preserved in the prose of the period. As Rosamund Allen notes (2002: 251n1), Middle English alliterating verse probably owes more to the homilies of Aelfric (b. *c.* 955, d. *c.* 1020) than to any memory of Old English epic. But, although Aelfric's work (Pope 1967–68) was still being copied in the twelfth century, the Middle English alliterative poems that have survived date from the second half of the fourteenth century, and are in the dialect of the north and west Midlands. Among the most important are the poems of the *Pearl* manuscript (Andrew & Waldron 1987), *The Wars of Alexander* (Duggan & Petre 1989), and *Piers the Plowman* (Skeat 1886) by William Langland (b. ?1330, d. ?1386). By the late fourteenth century, however, a metre based on strong stress and alliteration was no longer as good a fit for the language. English had changed in many ways (Barber 1993: 151–63), some of which were metrically very significant: Middle English contained a steadily increasing number of monosyllables (Strang 1980: 286–87), fewer weak syllables, as a result of syncope and word-final schwa deletion (Minkova 1991), and many right-strong French loan words (Tarlinskaja 1976: 86). Nevertheless, some literate Middle English poets chose to versify in the Old Germanic mode, basing their verse on beats and employing alliteration. The revival of these features was clearly influenced by the fact that the English language was beginning to reassert itself socially in this period; this seems to have outweighed any difficulty in combining them with right-strong phrasal stress and rhyme.

Strophe design

Middle English alliterative, or *strong-stress*, verse also has two metrical features imported from France, strophes and rhyme. Thus in *Sir Gawain and the Green Knight*, the longest of the poems in the *Pearl* manuscript, groups of between twelve and thirty-six alliterating lines are punctuated by a strophe of five shorter, rhyming lines. This rhymed strophe is known as a *bob* and *wheel*: a one-stress line followed by a quatrain of three-stressed lines, rhyming ababa, as can be seen from the following lines (174–78).

(6)   Ser-**tayn**:
(7)   A <u>grene</u> hors <u>gret</u> and <u>þikke</u>,
(8)   A <u>stede</u> ful <u>stif</u> to <u>strayne</u>,
(9)   In **braw**-den **bry**-del <u>quik</u>:
(10) To þe <u>gome</u> he <u>watz</u> ful <u>gayn</u>

[brawden: 'woven'; gome: 'knight'; gayn: 'suited']

The first three lines of this particular wheel contain six syllables as well as three beats, but other wheels in the poem are syllabically less regular; for example, 'iche lede as he loued hymselue' (126) and 'For wonder of his hwe men hade' (147) have at least seven and eight syllables respectively.

Strophe structure varied considerably from poem to poem in this metre: thus *Piers the Plowman* has neither bob nor wheel, but is interspersed with rhyming lines in Latin, and, while the number of long lines between wheels in *Sir Gawain and the Green Knight* varies, other poems have strophes of a fixed length. The most popular lengths were thirteen and fourteen lines (see Kennedy 2000a); an example of the former is discussed in Chapter 5, and an example of the latter is the *Katherine Hymn* (Kennedy 1991), which rhymes abab abab ccb ccb, with the last six lines containing only two stresses. I shall return to the subject of Middle English strophe design in Chapter 4.

Verse design

The verse design of the Middle English metre has received rather less critical attention than the metre of *Beowulf*, but modern scholars have made significant progress in its analysis. The traditional account of the metre can be compared with the findings of two modern pieces of research. The structure of the Middle English alliterative line can be seen from the following extract (lines 85–89) from *Gawain*, which is from the unrhymed part of the strophe:

(11) Bot **Ar**thure wolde not **ete** || til <u>al</u> were **ser**ued
(12) He watz so **joly** of his **joyf**nes, || and **sum**quat **child**gered.
(13) His <u>lif</u> liked hym <u>ly3t</u>; || he louied þe <u>lasse</u>
(14) Auþer to **lon**ge <u>lye</u> || or to **lon**ge **sitte**
(15) So **bi**sied him his <u>3</u>onge <u>blod</u> || and his <u>brayn</u> **wyl**de.

[jofnes: 'youthfulness'; childgered: 'boyish'; ly3t: 'active']

A concise summary of the traditional interpretation of Middle English alliterative verse design appears in Andrew & Waldron 1987: 45–50.[10] The major differences between this and the Old English metre are that (1) the line, rather than the half-line, has become the principal syntactic unit, (2) a high proportion of lines have a fifth prominence peak, and (3) although many lines alliterate on their first three stresses, other alliterative patterns are not uncommon; for example, instance (13) above has five alliterations of 'l'. This traditional analysis suggests that the Middle English alliterative line was less strictly regulated than its antecedent, and modern generative metrists have endeavoured to produce a more elaborate set of rules that could account for all the line variants. More recent research, however, indicates that the alliterative line was regulated in rather different ways, as I shall outline below.

Generative analysis

Keyser 1969 had applied generative theory to Old English metre and in 1977 Robert Sapora extended this to the Middle English alliterative line. Sapora described the latter as a line of four to five stresses, of which a minimum of two and a maximum of five must alliterate (1977: 17–28). He also argued that the Middle English line did not employ a non-alliterating syllable in the last strong position as a line marker because, unlike its Old English antecedent, it contained no caesura and was predominantly end-stopped (1977: 17–18). Using the (ambiguous) symbols S and W for feet containing alliterating and non-alliterating stressed syllables, respectively, Sapora described the line with the Old English pattern SSSW as the least complex form of the Middle English metre. The minority of lines that have other formulae (such as SSSS, SSWW, or SWSW) or a fifth stress (such as WSSSW or SSSSW) thus became metrically more complex rather than irregular, and Sapora listed them in order of complexity (1977: 26–27). He then quantified the frequency with which lines of each type occurred in six of the most important poems in this metre (1977: 47–62). In his 1000-line sample from *Sir Gawain* the simplest realization of the metrical pattern (SSSW) accounted for 61 per cent of lines, five-stress lines accounted for 25.5 per cent, and SSSS lines accounted for 3 per cent. In other poems SSSW lines reached 88 per cent of total, with a corresponding reduction in the proportion of five-stress lines, but SSSS lines did not exceed 4 per cent.

Although Sapora's research brought greater precision to the analysis of this metre, it confirmed rather than modified traditional conclusions. In the following decade, however, linguistic metrics combined with textual criticism to produce important new insights into the structure of Middle English alliterative verse.

Modern hypotheses based on textual criticism

Thomas Cable argued that some alliterative poets had strong preferences for certain rhythms (1988 & 1991), and other scholars have elaborated this. Hoyt Duggan developed the hypothesis that the authors of these poems had restricted the accentual patterns in their second hemistichs, after analysing a number of texts that have survived in two or more witnesses (1986, 1987, & 1988). He found that those second hemistichs that are identical in all extant manuscripts contain only two accentual patterns, while those that have different readings are more varied. This hypothesis was confirmed by a computer analysis of *The Wars of Alexander* (Duggan

& Petre 1989: xxvi–xxiv), which showed that in the common or 'authorial' lines the pattern (w) S w w S (w) accounted for 85 per cent of all second hemistichs, and the pattern w w S S (w) for 14 per cent. Duggan subsequently, and more controversially, extrapolated his conclusion that metrical irregularity is the product of scribal error to other Middle English texts (1996: 232–33). More recently, Ruth Kennedy has shown that the scribal errors concerned produced rhythms that were more, rather than less, regular than the authors' preferences (1999: 134–35). Nevertheless, she points out how easily surviving Middle English verse texts of all types can be regularized, and she hypothesizes that syllabically regular English verse may have appeared much earlier than has been previously thought (1999: 139–44).

I shall return to Kennedy's hypothesis in Chapter 4, but it seems clear that the English four-beat line had evolved considerably by the fourteenth century, and that this new generation of poets found new sources of regularity that either followed imported fashions or were a better fit for their changed language. In addition to introducing rhyme and strophe form, they produced patterns in their language that employed both syllable count and word stress. The primacy of the latter was a legacy from Old Germanic metrics, and traditional modes of versifying did not die out with the Norman Conquest. Moreover, although they have lain dormant for long periods, accentual metres have repeatedly resurfaced under the right cultural conditions, as I shall demonstrate in the chapters that follow.

Early Modern English Verse with Old Germanic Features

The changes in the language that had already begun to make the metre of *Beowulf* a bad fit for Middle English continued into the early modern period. As syncope, schwa-deletion, and the simplification of inflected forms brought stresses closer together, long sequences of unstressed syllables became rare in normal speech. This reduction in the interval between stresses increased the tendency towards stress-timing in English speech. The increasing number of monosyllables of all types also meant that fewer syllables had a lexical stress relationship to their neighbours, and placing phrasal stress at regular intervals became easier. Alliteration also became less conspicuous in lines that might consist of eight or more monosyllables and yielded further ground to rhyme. These changes combined to ensure that native English metres would evolve into forms containing complex secondary rhythms, alternating beats and offbeats; but other Germanic metrical feature persisted, such as anacrusis and the primacy of the four-beat line. This combination is evident in *tumbling verse* and *ballad metre*, which survived into the early modern period and beyond.

Tumbling verse

In the course of the fifteenth and sixteenth centuries the alliterative metre gradually merged with a style of folk composition called tumbling verse (Andrew & Waldron 1987: 46). We have noted that one of the preferred structures in the second hemistich of fourteenth-century alliterative poems was [(w) S w w S (w)]; later poets extended this triple-time rhythm to the whole line, and to long passages of lines.

This combined with a less systematic use of alliteration and a strong preference for rhyme to make the metre indistinguishable from *tumbling verse*. This predominantly triple-time metre was used in folk and popular poems, many of which were not committed to writing, and I shall illustrate it with some lines by Thomas Tusser (b. ?1528, d. 1580); although they were composed in the middle of the sixteenth century, their content is traditional wisdom and their mode of versifying probably seemed antiquated even to Tusser's contemporaries. The following lines are from Chapters 10 (81–82) and 13 (1–2) of the 1580 edition of Tusser's *Five Hundred Points of Good Husbandrie* (Payne & Heritage 1878), the shorter first edition of which had been published in 1557.

> (16)   Good **hus**-band he **trud**-geth, || to <u>bring</u> in the <u>gaines</u>
> (17)   good **hus**-wife she **drud**-geth, || re-**fu**-sing no <u>paines</u>
> (18)   [V] <u>North</u> winds send <u>haile</u> [V], || [V] <u>South</u> winds bring <u>raine</u>
> (19)   East <u>winds</u> we be-**wail** [V], || West <u>winds</u> blow a-**maine**

Many of Tusser's lines contain multiple alliterations, as in (19), and many have internal rhyme; all have a preponderantly triple-time rhythm, although (18) and (19) indicate that the initial and final weak syllables in each hemistich are optional. As Ker 1898 first pointed out, the line structure of tumbling verse is very similar to that of the *verso de arte mayor*, the most popular long line in Castilian and Portuguese between 1380 and 1550 (see Chapter 2, n32). The parameters of Tusser's metre are not entirely clear: the verse design has a template of eight positions, but its orientation may be left-strong with anacrusis, or right-strong allowing void initial weak positions. There are similar doubts on position size: by far the most common interval between prominence peaks is two syllables, and this means that either weak or strong positions, but not both, can contain two syllables. Tusser's prominence parameters are equally unclear: since beats, or ictuses, are never represented by atonic monosyllables, strong positions seem to demand stress; but, since disyllabic words (and thus their strong syllables) do not appear between ictuses, weak positions seem to be constrained with regard to strength. It was doubtless ambiguities such as these that deterred Hanson & Kiparsky from applying their parametric theory to ternary metres when it first appeared (1996: 300). I shall attempt to resolve them by a detailed analysis of the structure of ternary metres in Chapter 8.

The strong triple-time rhythm that runs through the quoted lines gives them a sing-song effect in stress-timed English; in syllable-timed Spanish such a rhythm appears 'sonorous but not melodious' (Lázaro Carreter 1972: 377). This metre doubtless reminded its English readers of proverbs and traditional sayings, and was therefore admirably suited to Tusser's content, helping endow it with rustic charm. The distinctive rhythm of tumbling verse survived in English nursery rhymes (for example, in the odd-numbered lines of 'Little Miss Muffet') and humorous verse (for example, the third line of the limerick). After Tusser, however, poets employed this rhythm in serious verse only for special effects; thus Spenser used tumbling verse for the speech of rustics in *The Shepheardes Calender* (see Chapter 6) and Browning used the same rhythm to imitate the galloping of horses in 'How They Brought the Good News from Ghent to Aix' (which I shall discuss in Chapter 8).

Ballad metre

The word *ballad*, as Graves 1957: vii points out, derives from a metaphor: it means a 'dance' or, if we weaken the metaphor, a 'word-dance', and in modern popular culture it has come to mean a sentimental song. The Old French term *balade* refers to a poem design in which the last line of each strophe is the same and which closes with a condensed strophe, or *envoi*.[11] The term widened to cover a poem with narrative or dramatic content, usually of uncertain authorship, that was performed (sung or recited) before a popular, and not necessarily literate, audience. The largest extant corpus of ballads in Western Europe is in Spanish (*romances*; see Wright 1987 and Chicote 2002), but a large number of ballads have been composed in England and Scotland, and many of them have survived (for a selection edited with modern spelling see Graves 1957). Although a systematic attempt to record such ballads was made only in the eighteenth century, they were in circulation in the sixteenth, and their form and content indicate that they originated far earlier.

English and Scottish ballads have systematic rhyme in the French fashion, and alliteration only as a compositional feature. The most common strophe form is the quatrain and the most common rhyme scheme is the same as that of its Spanish equivalent, the *romance*: xaxa, xbxb. Scottish and English ballads are in metres that are clearly derived from the Old Germanic tradition, and they resemble Old Icelandic verse in that their lines do not always contain four beats.[12] Ballad metre in which all the lines contain four beats is termed *long measure*, and that in which four- and three-beat lines are alternated is termed *common measure*. More than half of the thirty-eight ballads included in Graves's selection are in common measure, and almost a quarter are in long measure: 'Sir Patrick Spens' (1957: 17–21) is an example of common measure (4/3) and 'King John and the Abbot' (1957: 64–68) an example of long measure (4/4). Most of the remaining ballads contain other mixtures of three- and four-beat lines, or have three beats in odd-numbered lines and either two or three beats in the even-numbered ones. 'Loving Mad Tom' (1957: 71–74) is an example of the former and 'The Cherry Tree Carol' (1957: 25–28) an example of the latter.

Some ballads have a predominantly triple-time rhythm; for example, 'Lord Rendal' (1957: 5–7), which contains the following lines (1, 4, 17, & 33):

> (20) 'O <u>where</u> have you <u>been</u>, Lord **Ren**-dal my <u>son</u>,
> (21) 'For I'm **wea**-ried with **hun**-ting and <u>fain</u> would lie <u>down</u>.'
> (22) [V] '<u>Who</u> got the **lea**-vings, Lord **Ren**-dal my <u>son</u>,'
> (23) 'What will you <u>leave</u> to your **fa**-ther, my **jo**-lly young <u>man</u>?'

All the strophes in this ballad have the same four words (*son, man, soon, down*) at line end, the Welsh device of cynghanedd (Chapter 2, n3), rather than full rhyme. Each line of the poem has four beats (strong positions), which must fall on stressed syllables. The inter-ictic intervals (non-initial weak positions) may contain one syllable, as in the second interval of (20), two syllables, as in all the intervals of (21), or three, as in the anacrusis (initial weak position) of (23). In total 89 per cent of the poem's inter-ictic intervals contain two syllables, giving the poem a predominantly triple-time rhythm. In contrast, only 32 per cent of the poem's anacruses are disyllabic, as in (21); in other lines the first beat is preceded by one syllable, as in (20), zero syllables, as in (22), or three, as in (23). Seven of the poem's inter-ictic intervals (5 per cent) also contain three syllables, but it contains no example of a zero interval. This poem's metre is accentual, but the poet avoids clashing stresses; in other respects it resembles tumbling verse.

The lines of most ballads, however, contain a mixture of rhythms, like normal speech, and this natural, informal quality is one of the characteristic features of the genre. In that mixture, duple-time rhythms (created by inter-ictic intervals of a single syllable) usually outnumber triple-time (created by an interval of two), again as in normal speech or prose. The rhythm of 'Sir Patrick Spens' (Graves 1957: 17) is the converse of that of 'Lord Rendal': 88 per cent of its inter-ictic intervals are of one syllable, giving it a predominantly duple-time rhythm. It tells of a disaster of 1290 and is likely to have been composed while that event was still fresh in Scottish memories; it is in common measure, four beats alternating with three, as the opening lines show:

> (24)   The <u>King</u> [V] <u>sits</u> in Dun-**ferm**-line <u>town</u>
> (25)   [V] **Drin**-king the **blood**-red <u>wine</u>: [V] [V]
> (26)   'O, <u>where</u> will I <u>get</u> a **ski**-lly **ski**pper
> (27)   'To <u>sail</u> this good <u>ship</u> of <u>mine</u>?' [V] [V]

In my scansion I have marked a double void ([V] [V]) at the end of each of the three-beat lines in order to show what Attridge terms an 'unrealised beat'. He describes this rhythmic phenomenon in detail, and notes that we perceive all English lines with an odd number of stresses as having such a missing beat, thus confirming the essentially binary nature of linguistic rhythm (1982: 84–102).

Another major difference between this poem's metre and that of 'Lord Rendal' is that an atonic grammatical monosyllable may represent a beat, for example the preposition 'in' in (24). This makes the metre's prominence type strength rather than stress in terms of parametric theory: the weak syllables of polysyllabic words are constrained from appearing in strong positions, not those lacking lexical stress. There are two other features of 'Sir Patrick Spens' that can help us classify its metre: the first is the absence of inter-ictic intervals of three syllables; the second is the rarity of void positions: only three lines have no syllable in anacrusis and four have a zero interval between beats; the latter include:

> (28)   [V] <u>loth</u>, [V] <u>loth</u>, were our **Sco**-ttish <u>lords</u>   (65)
> (29)   O <u>lang</u>, [V] <u>lang</u>, may the **la**-dies <u>sit</u>   (69)

An unnatural delivery of these lines would make 'were' and 'may' ictic, and there are a number of disyllables in the poem that seem to require stressing in a way that is no longer permissible; for example sai-**lor** (line 7) and mas-**ter** (line 9). But the delivery with beats on adjacent syllables, as shown by my scansion, is much more likely and in no way interferes with perception of the four-beat pattern. Most ballads, however, have no lines with beats on adjacent syllables like (28) and (29); their intervals are of either one or two syllables, and either rhythm may predominate, Thus, for example, in 'King John and the Abbot', 61 per cent of intervals contain two syllables, giving the poem a mixed rhythm that favours triple time, but in 'Johny of Cockley's Well' (Graves 1957: 43–47) and 'Johny Faa, the Lord of Little Egypt' (1957: 60–64) 75 per cent of intervals contain just one syllable, making these poems predominantly duple-time.

Ictic verse and the dolnik

The foregoing analysis shows that it in some types of English verse *atonic* (unstressed) monosyllables may represent beats, the strong elements in the lines' strong–weak contrasts (a relatively rare feature in Old English epic metre). As noted in Chapter 1, I shall employ the term *erosion* for this lack of stress on ictic syllables, and I shall use the term *ictic* to describe metres that count the number of beats, rather than of stresses or syllables, in the line. In English, as in Russian, the most common type of ictic metre restricts the size of the intervals between beats to a maximum of two syllables, and Russian metrics terms such a metre a *dol'nik*. Modern metrists have used a wide variety of different terms to describe analogous metres in English: for example, according to Attridge (1982) they are simply metres with no compensation between the size of adjacent offbeats; other writers call such metres 'iambic-anapaestic' (Hanson 1991), 'strict stress-meter' (Tarlinskaja 1993, following Bailey 1976), 'sprung verse' (Hobsbaum 1996), or 'loose iambic metres' (Fabb 2002a). In this book I shall employ the simpler, disyllabic Russian term, and Anglicize it by dropping the apostrophe and giving it a normal English plural, *dolniks*.[13] As Tarlinskaja notes (1976: 13), the English *dolnik* differs from its Russian equivalent by allowing an occasional *zero interval* between beats (thus just over 2 per cent of the intervals in 'Sir Patrick Spens' are void).

Tarlinskaja 1976 classifies dolnik lines in two ways: (a) by the number of beats (from 'three-ictic' to 'six-ictic'), and (b) by whether the line comes from a poem where all the lines have the same number of beats (*homogeneous dolniks*), or from a poem where some have a different number (*heterogeneous dolniks*). Dolniks are metres intermediate between accentual and stress-syllabic, and their existence shows that these two types of verse form a continuum rather than constituting watertight categories (Tarlinskaja 1993: 11–12).[14] Tarlinskaja argues that in the English dolnik one syllable is the normal position size, just as it is in iambic verse, but that the two types of metre differ in their proportion of disyllabic inter-ictic intervals (1993: 19): she defines the 'canonical iamb' as having up to 3 per cent disyllabic intervals, the 'transitional iamb' as having 3–12 per cent, and the dolnik as having above 20 per cent (1976: 128).[15] She also argues that the higher the proportion of disyllabic intervals in the two types of metre, the higher the proportion of beats that are realized by a stressed syllable. The poems she includes in her own analysis vary in their proportion of disyllabic intervals from 1 to 83 per cent (1993: 212–13). The higher figures in her tables indicate poems that are almost entirely in triple time, showing that the categories duple-time and triple-time verse also disguise a continuum. If we accept Tarlinskaja's criteria for definition, the metres of 'King John and the Abbot', 'Johny of Cockley's Well', and 'Johny Faa, the Lord of Little Egypt' are dolniks, while those of 'Sir Patrick Spens' and 'Lord Rendal' are transitionally iambic and anapaestic, respectively.

Tarlinskaja's work demonstrates the continuity not only of metric typology, but also of English historical metrics. All the types of verse that have been composed in the language are related and have developed over a long period of time; and, when a new species of versification has evolved, it has not necessarily displaced earlier ones. Survival has depended upon fitness for the new linguistic environment and appeal to the latest poetic fashion. Ictic metres have survived because they are a good fit for the English language, where the strength of stress and stress-timing make it easier to count beats than syllables. Indeed it can be argued that English poets and audiences perceive all lines of verse as a series of beats: thus Attridge 1982 describes English stress-syllabic lines as if they were a variety of ictic verse in which every disyllabic weak position must be balanced by a void so as to produce the regular number of syllables.[16]

The Survival of Old Germanic Features in English Verse

Although a number of important features of foreign metrics have been successfully introduced into English poetry, Old Germanic modes of versifying have continued to be influential on the practice of English poets. Perhaps even more importantly, the English language has retained many of the features that make such an accentual metrics viable: strong word stress, many left-strong polysyllables, and a host of tonic monosyllables. The vestiges of its old accentual metrics can be found in many places in modern English: in nursery rhymes, proverbs, liturgical texts, deliberately archaic poems, parodies, and modern translations of ancient works.

Nursery rhymes and proverbs

The alliterative revival of the late fourteenth century is evidence that Old Germanic modes of versifying survived in widely known oral texts, which would have enabled poets to employ such metres and audiences to recognize them. Those oral texts almost certainly included nursery rhymes and proverbs, and many English texts of this type, based on beats and offbeats, have survived to the present day. The survival of ictic metres in English has been greatly aided by the fact that they provide almost all children with a pre-school education in metrics. This education may be relegated to the unconscious when they learn another system of versifying (stress-syllabic) later, but it remains available. As a result, when poets find canonical metres restricting, they can revert to features of the verse imprinted in their childhood.

The English language contains a very large number of nursery rhymes, as any dictionary of them shows (Opie & Opie 1967 is an extensive modern collection). Although some nursery rhymes are very ancient indeed, others refer to personages or events of more recent centuries, but even the latter were probably constructed on rhythmic models of earlier rhymes. English nursery rhymes have ictic metres like those of English traditional ballads: they regulate the number of beats, or prominence peaks, not syllables, and three-beat and four-beat lines are the most common lengths. The metres of many nursery rhymes qualify as dolniks, because fewer than 5 per cent of their inter-ictic intervals are void, and some lines, as in ballads, happen to be syllabically regular, which also gives them a regular rhythm (most often iambic or trochaic, or a combination of both). The most common line lengths, and the use of contrasting rhythms, can be seen in the following lines from 'Jack and Jill':

(30)	[V] <u>Jack</u> and <u>Jill</u> went <u>up</u> the <u>hill</u>	(1)
(31)	To <u>fetch</u> a <u>pail</u> of **wat**er	(2)
(32)	With **vi**-ne-gar <u>and</u> brown <u>pa</u>-per	(12)

Instance (30), which opens with the first beat, is trochaic in rhythm; (31) has one syllable in anacrusis and is iambic; (32), the last line in the poem, contains a disyllabic interval and a mixed rhythm. The metre of this particular nursery rhyme is clearly a dolnik, because all its inter-ictic intervals contain either one or two syllables. Some nursery rhymes, however, contain zero inter-ictic intervals, for example, 'Sing a Song of Sixpence':

(33)	[V] <u>Four</u>-and-**twen**-ty **black**birds	(3)
(34)	[V] <u>Baked</u> [V] <u>in</u> a <u>pie</u>	(4)
(35)	O <u>was</u>-n't <u>that</u> a **dain**-ty <u>dish</u>	(7)
(36)	And <u>pecked</u> [V] <u>off</u> her <u>nose</u>	(16)

Instance (33) has a zero anacrusis, giving it a falling (trochaic) rhythm, while (35) has one syllable before its first beat, giving it a rising (iambic) rhythm. Instances (34) and (36) have a zero interval, or void position, between their first and second beats, and their second beat is provided by an atonic monosyllable ('in' or 'off'). In total just over 9 per cent of inter-ictic intervals in this nursery rhyme contain zero syllables, so it does not meet the strict definition of a dolnik that I have proposed. Its metre is accentual and it must be classified as ictic, not strong-stress, because atonic monosyllables represent beats.

   Like that of 'Jack and Jill', the strophe design of 'Sing a Song of Sixpence' mixes three-beat with four-beat lines, the staples of common measure. A design that combines lines of 3–3–4–3 beats is known as *poulter's measure*, and both nursery rhymes, such as 'The Grand Old Duke of York', and ballads, such as 'Loving Mad Tom', have survived in that metre. A smaller number of nursery rhymes employ long measure (four-beat lines throughout); for example, 'The Old Woman in a Shoe'. Many nursery rhymes, however, comprise lines shorter than three beats; thus 'Solomon Grundy' has two-beat lines and 'Old Mother Hubbard' and 'Little Miss Muffet' have a combination of two- and three-beat lines (2–2–3–2–2–3). An example of a nursery rhyme that is trochaic throughout is 'Goosey, Goosey Gander'.

   Another type of traditional English text is metrically very similar to nursery rhymes: proverbs, which have also survived in large numbers; these are not always recognized as verse, however, because many do not rhyme. Their antiquity is evidenced by the obsolete language in which they are couched and their predilection for alliteration (for example, 'Many a mickle makes a muckle'). Such proverbs are also in ictic metres, and the four-beat line is by far the most common; some version of the following is likely to have been in circulation since the prevailing English wind first became south-westerly:

(37)   [V] <u>Red</u> sky at <u>night</u>, [V] **shep**-herd's de-**light**;
(38)   Red <u>sky</u> in the **mor**-ning, **shep**-herd's **war**ning

In these lines the monosyllables 'red' and 'sky' are ambivalent: they can represent either a beat or offbeat. Very few English speakers can have been entirely ignorant of nursery rhymes and proverbs, and most thus had an ability to compose and recognize ictic verse that they developed at an early age.

Psalms and sermons

For well over a millennium, most English speakers pursued a path that led inexorably from cradle to pew to grave. They were forced to learn prayers and listen to sermons, both composed in a language that was as much a stylization as is literary verse. As noted above, the alliterative revival of the fourteenth century probably owes more to prose sermons than to any memory of OE epic (or even to Welsh poetry, which shared some of the OE features). Medieval preachers regularized their language's natural rhythms to make their sermons more memorable and pleasurable. At least one preacher went as far as composing sermons in verse and inventing a new accentual metre for them, as I shall show in the next chapter. From the fifteenth century onwards translators of the Bible dignified their language by employing stress patterns that reminded readers of the Latin liturgy, as can be seen from innumerable passages in the Authorised Version (Smith et al. 1611). Many lines subdivide into three-beat phrases, like the following, which has 3 + 3 beats:

(39)   [V] <u>Man</u> that is <u>born</u> of <u>wo</u>man
         is of <u>few</u> days, and <u>full</u> of **trou**ble.   (Job 14. 1)

Many others combine four- and three-beat phrases, like common measure; for example, the following lines:

(40)   [V] <u>One</u> ge-ne-**ra**-tion **pas**-seth a-**way**,
         and a-**no**-ther ge-ne-**ra**-tion **co**-meth
            but the <u>earth</u> a-**bi**-deth for **ever**.   (Ecclesiastes 1. 4)

(41)   [V] <u>When</u> I was <u>child</u>, I <u>spake</u> as a <u>child</u>,
         I un-der-**stood** as a <u>child</u>, I <u>thought</u> as a <u>child</u>:
            But <u>when</u> I be-**came** a <u>man</u>,
               I <u>put</u> a-way **chil**-dish <u>things</u>.   (II Corinthians 13. 11)

Instance (40) subdivides 4 + 4 + 3 (or 4 + 3 + 3 if the first syllable of 'generation' in its second phrase does not become a peak in delivery), while (41) subdivides 4 + 4 + 3 + 3. It is clear from these examples that ictic and phrasal rhythms can be used to stylize a text so as to give it religious significance, and the preachers of sermons soon exploited this potential. Thus in late medieval and early modern times English speakers were constantly exposed to language with much older rhythms, even as their poets sought to develop new metrical systems that produced syllabic regularity.

Psychological beats and double audition

Nursery rhymes, prayers, biblical quotes, and sermons all teach English speakers to appreciate accentual regularity. This conditioning combines with linguistic factors, strong word stress, and a tendency towards stress-timing to ensure that English speakers perceive lines of verse as a series of beats (or, as generative metrists would say, *feet*) before they recognize them as containing a given number of syllables. As we shall see in the next chapter, when English poets began to compose lines that were more regular in syllable count around AD 1200, they (and their audiences) perceived those lines as four beats rather than eight syllables. Even today we call an iambic line of ten syllables a pentameter, indicating that its essence is five beats, yet most iambic pentameters do not contain five stresses (because some beats are realized by unstressed monosyllables). Audiences can hear five beats in what is actually a three-, four-, or six-stress line because metre exists not in acoustic events, or in written signs, but in the hearer's or reader's head: it is a psychological phenomenon. This process, whereby the English reader hears, but does not hear, five beats in an iambic pentameter line, has been termed double audition (see Lewis 1938: 30–32 and Duffell 2000c: 14–15); it seems quite unnatural to anyone whose language lacks word stress, and indeed to anyone who has failed to acquire the habit of registering beats subconsciously. Many of the misunderstandings between English and French metrists emanate from this source.

The literary dolnik

In the latter part of the eighteenth century some English poets began to employ traditional ballad metres in literary verse and, although some of their ballads were in syllabically regular versions of old three- and four-beat lines, others were in ictic metres, mostly dolniks. I shall examine the revival of the dolnik and its subsequent use for longer poems and different genres in more detail in Chapter 8. Tarlinskaja's most recent analysis of the English dolnik gives statistics for 157 poems (13,160 lines) by fourteen different poets (1993); the earliest of these poets was born in 1770 and the latest died almost two hundred years later. Poets have used, and continue to use, this type of metre in order to create special effects (antiquity or rusticity), or from the desire to make their verse resemble ordinary speech with its varying inter-ictic intervals. In Chapters 9 and 10 of this volume I shall examine contemporary ictic verse and its relationship with the free verse of various languages. The dolnik is also a cross-linguistic phenomenon, as Tarlinskaja 1993 demonstrates: it came into Russian from German. In these languages, as in English, the dolnik has long made the transition from a folk to a literary metre, and more recently it has become a feature of French metrics with the advent of free verse (see Chapter 9).

Archaism and imitation

Conscious metrical archaism is something rather different from the influence that Germanic modes of versifying have exerted on imported metres. A number of poets working in modern English have employed archaic versification skilfully and effectively, and none more so than Rudyard Kipling (b. 1865, d. 1936). His 'Harp Song of the Dane Women' (1990: 431) is in ictic metre, and this is wholly appropriate to the content of the poem: its opening lines immediately transport the reader to a former era in North–West Europe:

(42) [V] <u>What</u> is a **wo**-man || that <u>you</u> for-**sake** her,
(43) And the <u>hearth</u> [V] –<u>fire</u> || and the <u>home</u> [V] –acre,
(44) To <u>go</u> with the <u>old</u> || grey **Wi**-dow-**ma**ker?

Here the compounding of words, the clashing of stress, and the historically correct use of alliteration combine to produce rhythms that are typical of an earlier stage of the English language; these lines are admirably suited to evoke a heroic age of suffering and endeavour.

Somewhat less appropriate, but almost as skilful, is the versification of a poem by W. H. Auden (b. 1907, d. 1973), where the archaic features were probably suggested by the title rather than the subject matter. Although 'The Wanderer' (Auden 1966: 51) contains some lines that are not strikingly archaic, the following lines (1 & 16) employ three of the staples of Old Germanic metre: four beats, irregular line length, and alliteration (the latter with a non-traditional pattern):

(45) <u>Doom</u> is <u>dark</u> || and **dee**-per than **a**-ny sea-**din**gle
(46) **Wa**-ving from **win**-dow, || <u>spread</u> of **wel**come

Auden's choice of diction in the first line is as archaic as his metre, and throughout the poem he finds ancient echoes for his mood of the moment.

The lines that I have quoted from Kipling and Auden show that versifying in the Old Germanic mode remains a resource available to modern English poets, one that will remain as long as the language retains its combination of strong word stress and an abundance of left-strong words and accented monosyllables.

Parody and translation

What is perhaps the most mannered and curious modern use of the features that characterize Old Germanic verse can be found in the prose of James Joyce (b. 1882, d. 1941). In the 'Oxen of the Sun' section of *Ulysses* Joyce describes a birthing in language that demonstrates the development of English style: he opens with a Latinate invocation to a fertility god and introduces a Dublin maternity hospital in the style of a Roman historian, before imitating a chronological series of English prose styles. The first of these is that of the Anglo-Saxon sermons of Aelfric (see Johnson 1993: 367); Joyce begins the passage with ten words (from 'Before' to 'wor-ship') that are a parody of Old English epic metre, and they can be read as two four-beat lines, each of which has four alliterations instead of three. The excessive and non-traditional alliteration signal that we are dealing with parody rather than poetry, but there can be no doubt that the whole section is strongly influenced by Joyce's study of the original texts and of Saintsbury's commentary on them (see Johnson 1993: 907).

Joyce shows that the legacy of Old Germanic metre can embellish modern prose as well as verse; but there is one field in which it is pre-eminently appropriate to employ the features of ancient metre: the translation of old Germanic texts. The twentieth century saw a number of modern English translations of Old and Middle English poems, including *Beowulf* (Raffel 1963 and Heaney 1999), and *Pearl* and *Sir Gawain* (Tolkien 1975). These translations were in what may be taken as free verse; Heaney, like Tolkien, but unlike Raffel, incorporated such features of the original as four beats and alliteration. It is interesting to compare his translation with the original; for example, line 3139 (Wrenn & Bolton 1988: 211 and Heaney 1999: 98):

(47)a **helm**[um] be-**hen**-ges || **hil**-de borden
(47)b <u>hung</u> with <u>hel</u>-mets || <u>hea</u>-vy <u>war</u>-shields

In this line the translator has captured the poet's music as well as his meaning. It shows how after a millennium the Old Germanic mode of versifying can still work aesthetically. It also shows that the ancient metre has more in common with modern versifying practice than the highly elaborate systems developed between 1200 and 1900: both the ancient and modern metres exploit the rhythmic riches of their lexicon in a more direct way than the modes of versifying that intervened.

Conclusions

This chapter has examined the accentual metrics of the oldest surviving English poems and discussed the role of accent in medieval epic, ballad, nursery rhyme, proverb, and holy writ, and in modern parody and translation. As the chapters that follow will show, accentual verse has not only endured into modern times, it has exerted a strong influence on poets who have sought to naturalize the imported metres that largely superseded it. This chapter has shown that in Middle English accentual verse evolved from strong-stress metre into ictic metre, and that the latter contained a complex secondary rhythm, in which the material lying between two beats became less an interval than an alternative event, an offbeat. Linguistic change helped this evolution: syncope, inflexion loss, and schwa deletion all reduced the average syllabic interval between stresses. But fashion and aesthetic effect also play a role in the historical development of metres, and from 1066 the language of fashion in England was French. I shall now, therefore, turn to the attempts made by the poets of England after that date to import continental modes of versifying and the compromise between the metrics of the two languages that resulted.

Notes to Chapter 3

1. A few very early Romance texts contain verse constructed on similar principles: the Latin *Poema de Almería* (Martínez 1975), the Old French *Sainte Eulalie* (Aspland 1979: 4–6), and the Old Spanish *Poema de Mio Cid* (Michael 1987). Duffell 2002a debates whether this similarity is the result of Germanic influence or convergent development.
2. The relatively minor differences in verse design between *Beowulf* and *The Battle of Maldon* are discussed by Russom 1998: 157.
3. Luecke 1978 proposes such a setting, which results in something far from isochrony. Cable 1974: 94–110 also discusses musical performance without regard to isochrony.
4. Navarro 1974 confirms this concept in his analysis of Spanish verse, where he includes only the syllables from one stress to the next in the *período rítmico* ('rhythmic unit').

5. Hammond 1997 provides a concise introduction to the application of optimality theory in the area of prosody. Among his examples of constraints on English prosody is the following account of syncope (the loss of unstressed syllables, as when 'chocolate' become 'choc'late' in normal speech): constraint 1 = FAITH (σs) (pronounce stressed vowels), 2 = *FOOTLESS (no unfooted syllables), and 3 = FAITH (σw) (pronounce unstressed vowels). Syncope occurs because the second of these constraints ranks more highly than the third (1997: 48–49).

6. Getty argues that line-initial grammatical words like 'ofer' form (trochaic) metrical feet of their own (2002: 13); for a discussion of the metrical status of words of this type see Duffell 1999b: 27–29. Note that this left-strong interpretation of a sequence of syllables without lexical accent is supported by the 'core' theory of Indo-European accentuation: words not otherwise accented attract initial stress (Halle 1997b: 276). The loss of (melodic) accent (on one of the last three syllables) in lexical words probably explains the initial stress that is a feature of a number of ancient and modern Indo-European languages.

7. Here I assume that the word 'unstressed' (Getty 2002: 311) is a typographical error.

8. This contrasts with Egyptian hieroglyphs and Chinese ideograms, where one sign generally equals one word, and alphabets of the Semitic type, where one sign equals one consonant.

9. The division into four units is that of the original inscription; the colons printed here were lines of four points on the horn itself.

10. There has been much recent debate on whether Middle English texts should be divided into verse and prose at all. They all employ alliteration in a profuse but unsystematic fashion, and they all show considerable regularity in the number of stresses (combined with irregularity in the number of unstressed syllables that separate them). For a discussion of the ill-defined boundary between verse and artistic prose in this period see Allen 2002: 251n1.

11. Many English ballads also have a refrain, often nonsensical, repeated at the end of each strophe to suggest musical accompaniment; for example, 'King John and the Abbot' (quoted below) has the refrain 'Derry down, down hey, derry down'.

12. Old Icelandic *chant metre* has a 4/3 beat structure like common measure (Salus & Taylor 1973: 18); Preminger et al. note the occurrence of three-beat lines in Old Norse *ljóðaháttr* verse (1975: 459–60); for a thirteenth-century Icelandic exposition of Old Germanic poetics see Faulkes 1995: 165–220.

13. I have chosen the term *dolnik* by a process of elimination. Hobsbaum's term (1996: 53–70) risks confusion, because *sprung rhythm* is the usual term for a much more complex metre (see Chapter 9 below); Bailey's term carries the same risk, because *strong-stress metre* is the more precise term for Old and Middle English alliterative metres (see, for example, Kennedy 2000a); Hanson's term would waste a great deal of space in the chapters that follow; Fabb's term is inappropriate for metres in which as many as 75 per cent of intervals may be disyllabic; Attridge's terms for these metres, 'five-beat verse', 'four-beat verse', etc., fail to distinguish them from other metres: the iambic pentameter also has five beats and the trochaic tetrameter and Old English line also have four.

14. There are other types of intermediate metre besides the dolnik: for example, the Russian *taktovik* in which weak positions are limited to three syllables (Tarlinskaja 1993: 13), and Romance metres in which stress is regulated only in the latter part of the line.

15. Poems with between 12 and 20 per cent disyllabic intervals fall through the gap in this categorization; they doubtless represent a less advanced stage of the transition from dolnik to stress-syllabic, and I shall include them in the transitional or intermediate category in the chapters that follow.

16. Note that one type of generative metrics does the opposite to Attridge and describes the dolnik in terms of stress-syllabic metres: according to parametric theory, the five-ictic dolnik is an iambic pentameter in which the position-size parameter is set at one prosodic foot (Hanson & Kiparsky 1996: 290).

CHAPTER 4

Versifying in Bilingual England

Politics and Language in England AD 1066–1455

Two invaders, both of Scandinavian origin, seized the throne of England in the eleventh century. The Danish king Cnut, who ruled from 1017 to 1035, was the greatest of all England's kings: he won all his battles, ruled wisely and well, and reconciled the English and Danish elements in the population. He was elected to the throne by the English nobility and preserved an English court and English institutions, the most important of which was the English language. Under Cnut England was richer and safer than it had been for centuries, but both his sons died young and in 1042 the throne reverted to Edward, the son of Cnut's English predecessor. Edward had been raised by his mother's family in Normandy, and when he died childless one of his cousins mounted a successful invasion to claim the English throne. William of Normandy, who reigned from 1066 to 1087, was the worst of England's kings: he also won all his battles, but he killed a quarter of his subjects and enslaved most of the rest. William built a great chain of castles and used military force to subdue his people, laying waste whole counties when they rose against him. His only positive achievements were an inventory of his spoils, *The Domesday Book*, and numerous stone churches where his subjects could pray for his bloodstained soul.

   The Normans were Vikings who had rapidly adopted French customs and the French language, both of which William brought to England. He divided the land between his followers and, in order to administer their new kingdom, he and his successors imported almost a quarter of a million French to replace the half-million Anglo-Danes he had killed.[1] William's French successors ruled England for more than four hundred years, throughout which there was almost continuous civil war, as kings fought their closest kin and were challenged by their barons, who steadily restricted royal power. The arrival of the Black Death in the 1340s wiped out a large proportion of the population but revived the fortunes of the Anglo-Danish underclass. Able serfs and tradesmen who had learned French filled the many gaps in the social hierarchy left by the pestilence. In 1337, however, the king of England had inherited the crown of France and his rejection by the French nobility led to more than a hundred years of warfare between the two countries. The French kings of England finally lost that war in the 1450s, and the last of them died in battle in 1485 fighting against a Welshman whose French troops helped win him the English crown.

Bilingual England

The English language was one of the first victims of the Anglo-Danish defeat in 1066: very few texts in Old English have survived from after that date. When English reappears a century later it is a new language, which we term Middle English, and half its lexicon is clearly of French origin. But, although some Parisians may regard modern English as a variety of French spoken by people who cannot pronounce it, English grammar and phonology have remained stubbornly Germanic. Although the Norman conquerors made French the official language of England, English remained the mother tongue of the vast majority of the king's subjects, and there were advantages for both rulers and ruled in learning the other's language. As a result, by 1200 most people in England were to some extent bilingual (Vising 1923: 12–18 and Legge 1963: 4n2). The variety of French they spoke, however, had developed somewhat from the dialect of Normandy; I shall refer to it as 'Insular French', but it is also sometimes called 'Anglo-Norman' or 'the French of England'. We can only reconstruct the phonology of Insular French, since it ceased to be spoken in the late fifteenth century, but it is reasonable to assume that the differences in phonology between Insular French and Francien (the Parisian variety) were at least as great as those in accidence and syntax (Vising 1923: 27–33). Centuries of daily contact with oral English undoubtedly caused Insular French to diverge considerably from the language of the mainland, so much so that Vising describes what happened to French in England as 'la ruine générale qui fondit sur la langue' (1884: 57). The phonological features of Insular French could hardly escape this ruin, including some that are vital to versifying, such as the strength of word stress, the syllabification of final schwa, and any tendencies to syllable- or stress-timing (see Duffell 2005: 122).

The distinctive features of Insular French (listed by Vising 1923: 27–33) were something of which many of its speakers were aware; thus in the 1160s a nun from Barking states 'un faus franceis sai d'Angleterre' (Legge 1963: 63). This awareness may have been increased by the arrival of a different variety of French in 1154, when Henry II, his Queen, and their courtiers spoke varieties of French that were very different from that spoken by their English nobles.[2] Thereafter snobbery, combined with the influx of speakers from the mainland, ensured that the Plantagenet court spoke Francien, just like its Valois rival. The difference between the two varieties was commented upon by Chaucer, who says of his Prioress: 'Frenssh she spak ful faire and fetisly | after the scole of Stratford atte Bowe; | the Frenssh of Parys was to hire unknowe' (*Canterbury Tales: General Prologue* (*CT: GP*), 124–26; in Benson 1988: 56). Since he was a royal lackey who spoke the French of Paris and his Plantagenet masters, Chaucer doubtless regarded Insular French as an inferior variety, and Gower and Lydgate both felt it necessary to excuse their 'rude' French on the grounds that that they had been born in England (see Pyle 1935: 35–36). Nevertheless, Gower employed the Insular variety (albeit laced with mainland forms acquired from his reading) for major poems long before he risked writing in the upstart language English, and Legge argues that Gower's was the finest French poetry of his time (1963: 71).

French was challenged in the fourteenth century and supplanted in the fifteenth by a new English rich in words borrowed from the French lexicon (see Barber 1993:

145–50). The emancipation of the English language was gradual: in 1363 it became possible for defendants to plead 'not' in English before being found 'guilty' in French, and a few years later Chaucer was able to risk composing poetry in English, trusting that posterity would be able to read it. In 1399 a new king addressed parliament in English (its first royal public endorsement since the final 'ouch' of the last English king a third of a millennium earlier), and in 1417 his son penned the first royal letter in the language.[3] This change signalled the final unification of the French and Anglo-Danish elements of the population and transformed military rivalry between two dynasties into war between nations. The new patriotism naturally led to a decline of French in England, and the final English defeat of the Hundred Years War in 1453 sounded the death knell of the Insular variety. But the English language remains as its enduring monument.

Versifying in Insular French

French was the official language of England for the same length of time that Britain has existed, and French kings ruled England for almost twice as long as the USA has elected presidents. It is therefore not surprising that the culture and language of England was transformed almost beyond recognition by the Norman and Angevin experience. Although poets at the royal court composed Francien verse using the same forms, strophes, and verse designs as their mainland contemporaries, most English poets versified in Insular French. Only a minority attempted to compose in the new hybrid that was Middle English, but by the thirteenth century their numbers were increasing and two versions of some poems were composed, one in each language. The Insular French verse texts that have survived may be divided into two groups, and their metrics differed significantly.

Counting syllables in Insular French

Some of the poets who composed in Insular French counted syllables, and Vising divided the published verse texts into two groups, one of which follows the rules of French metrics (1884: 71–78). It would, however, have been surprising if the continuous import of literate French-speakers from the mainland had allowed the rules of versifying to be forgotten. Thus Pyle quotes a number of Insular French and English texts in which the poet acknowledges not counting syllables, and in some cases even names it as a fault (1935: 35–38). One place where people seem to have known the rules was the royal abbey at Barking.[4] The nun quoted above as being aware as early as the 1160s that the French she spoke was different from mainland varieties may have been the Clemence who appended her name to a poem (Vising no. 11) composed a decade later, the *Life of St Catherine* (MacBain 1964). This poem is in the metre that was the clear favourite of Insular French, the *octosyllabe*, and MacBain's text is, for the most part, syllabically regular, although he hesitates to emend all the lines with the wrong number of syllables in the manuscript (1964: xxiv). An unusual feature of Clemence's verse is the equivalence of 8M and 8F syllables, suggesting that she counted by ear, when most of her contemporaries in England did not (see Vising 1923: 23 and Legge 1963: 12).[5] But the regularity of her lines is exceptional, and, although many other poets paid lip service to the idea that the mainland practice was a virtue, few bothered to cultivate it.

Vising also lists the surviving Insular French poems that are syllabically irregular (1884: 78–87), and in many scarcely half the lines have the correct number of syllables. Vising 1884: 28 notes that manuscripts copied on the mainland often contain both syllabically regular poems (composed on the mainland) and irregular ones (composed in England).[6] After detailed discussion of the problem, he concludes that only a minority of irregular lines are likely to be the result of scribal errors (1884: 24–50). It is also surely more than fortuitous that English poetry composed at this time was equally irregular in syllable count, and only emendation on the same massive scale can regularize both. Under these circumstances, it seems reasonable to accept the authenticity of syllabically irregular lines in both languages, providing they are semantically and grammatically satisfactory. Fitzroy Pyle first pointed out the significance of this similarity: since the earliest Insular French poems predate any in Middle English, the way of versifying that we think of as typically English was first developed in French (1935). This accounts for many of the features of medieval English verse that have puzzled and vexed some modern English metrists: for example, the differences between fifteenth-century Scottish and English versification, the reluctance of medieval English poets to count syllables, and their preference for lines with four rather than five prominent syllables.

Syllabic irregularity

Syllabic regularity in bilingual England also varied with time: Vising analysed all the Insular French poems published at his time of writing, and concluded that 58 per cent of those dating from the twelfth century were metrically correct, but only 7 per cent of those from the thirteenth (1884: 56 & 68–91). Later Insular French verse texts are thus considerably more likely to be irregular than earlier ones, but Vising does not draw the obvious conclusion that the norms of versifying changed over time and may be linked with the proportion of people who were bilingual in this period. The anonymous poem 'Thomas Turberville' (Vising no. 301, in Aspin 1953: 51–53), which was probably composed between 1295 and 1297, exemplifies the irregularity of most thirteenth- and fourteenth-century Insular French verse, as the following lines show:

(1)	[V] <u>e</u> ju-**ré** par <u>Seint</u> De-**nys**	(6)
(2)	<u>Teu</u> ga-ri-**son** ad pur <u>son</u> la-**bour**	(62)
(3)	O-re sunt <u>tuz</u>, jeo **quid**^e neëz	(79)
(4)	Ly <u>Ducs</u> Lo-**wys**, [V] <u>ton</u> pa-**rent**	(93)

[And I swear by St Denis | Your garrison has for its effort | Now are all, I reckon, born | The Duke Louis, your father]

All of these lines are unacceptable according to French metrics: (1) and (4) contain seven syllables, and (2) contains nine; (3) may also contain nine, but can be regularized by deleting one (but not both) of its word-final schwas, as shown here. All four lines, however, scan perfectly as four-beat ictic verse: they may be terrible *octosyllabes*, but they are excellent dolniks.[7] The poets concerned may have been composing in French, but they seem to have been counting beats.

By my calculation, only 56 per cent of lines in Aspin 1953 have 8M/F syllables, while 100 per cent contain four beats.[8] When these lines are analysed as four-beat verse, 91 per cent of beats correspond to stressed syllables, of which 9 per cent are secondary stresses, and the remaining 9 per cent are represented by atonic monosyllables. This proportion of primary stresses is more than sufficient to give the verse a pulse recognizable to any audience that speaks a language with strong word stress. Analysis on this basis also shows that 79 per cent of non-initial weak positions contain a single syllable, giving all three poems a predominantly iambic rhythm. These results are remarkably similar to those found by Tarlinskaja in seven Middle English poems (1976: 256–58). The figures for the Insular French sample also show that void positions occurred mostly in position 1 or 5, just as in Middle English, where metrists use the terms *headless* and *broken-backed* to describe lines with such colon-initial voids.

Vising dismissed the view of many scholars that Anglo-Norman poets copied certain features of the English metrical system'(1923: 81), and he preferred the explanation that these poets were attempting *octosyllabes*, but were 'ignorant', or 'careless', or both (1884: 53).[9] But there is at least one Insular French text where syllabic irregularity cannot be attributed to either carelessness or ignorance: 'Against the King's Taxes' (Vising no. 286, in Aspin 1953: 108–11). This macaronic poem is composed in lines in which a hemistich of Insular French is followed by a second in Latin, and its metre is a development of the medieval Latin Goliardic metre that employs anacrusis. This metre can be compared with Orm's, which I discuss below, but the Insular French poet clearly has a livelier mind and is a better versifier. Over all, the evidence of my analysis weighs heavily against Vising's conclusion. The hypothesis that medieval English poets versified in the same manner in two different languages becomes even stronger if we examine what happened after 1366.

Middle English Short-Line Verse 1200–1400

The mode of versifying employed by Middle English poets thus seems to have been developed first in French, but many of these poets, and in particular those in holy orders, were also aware of Latin metrics. Moreover, those whose mother tongue was English must have known nursery rhymes and proverbs in which the rhythm depended upon word stress and was emphasized by alliteration. This contrasted with the French practice of counting syllables and emphasizing the regular phrasal stresses with rhyme. It is tempting to try to classify the individual poems that have survived according to which of these two different traditions most influenced their versification, but to label them examples of either 'alliterative verse' or 'rhymed verse' is simplistic. Some Middle English poems employ both rhyme (which English versifiers knew long before the Conquest from Latin hymns) and alliteration, and many lines of rhymed verse contain four word stresses. Moreover, by the fourteenth century at least one poet had mastered both modes of versifying, since the alliterative *Sir Gawain* and the preponderantly octosyllabic poem *Pearl* are almost certainly the work of the same author (see Andrew & Waldron 1987: 15–16).

It is easy to see why an octosyllabic metre should be the first to develop under French influence: it represents a combination of two traditional parameters, French position size (one syllable), and Germanic position number (eight). Thus the earliest surviving stress–syllabic poem in a Germanic language, the medieval Dutch *Life of Saint Lutgart*, is octosyllabic: its lines are iambic tetrameters (see Zonneveld 2000). But the English 'octosyllabic' poems are syllabically much less regular than this, and many of their lines have seven syllables, not eight, and a trochaic rather than an iambic rhythm.[10] Mainland French poets would have regarded these trochaic variants as *heptasyllabes*, and would not have randomly permutated them with *octosyllabes*; but these lines share both their rhythm and syllable count with first hemistichs of the Latin Goliardic metre (see p. 41 above). One of the earliest Middle English poems clearly derives its metre from the Latin one.

The Goliardic metre of 'Ormulum'

Ormulum (Holt 1878), the work of a monk of Scandinavian origin (Orm or Ormin), probably dates from the end of the twelfth century, and it consists of a series of sermons in verse. Elements of Orm's system of English spelling (doubled consonants indicating short preceding vowels) have survived better than his fame as a poet. The poem is repetitive and monotonous but, as Bennett 1986: 33 notes, its sermons are written for different days of the year and congregations would have had to digest only one at a time. The Preface opens with the following lines (given here with my scansion):

(5) Þiss <u>boc</u> iss **nemm**-nedd **Orr**-mu-<u>lum</u>
(6) Forr-þi þatt <u>Orrm</u> itt **wrohh**te

[This book is entitled Ormulum | Because Orm wrote it]

Orm's metre is stress-syllabic, that of Latin Goliardic verse with an extra syllable in anacrusis in both hemistichs [w s w s w s w s — w s w s w s w]. The English poem, unlike its Latin models, is usually laid out as a series of couplets, and lacks any systematic use of rhyme or alliteration. The poem alternates four- and three-beat lines in which beats are sometimes realized by atonic monosyllables; in terms of parametric theory, *Ormulum*'s prominence type is strength: only the weak syllables of polysyllabic words are constrained from appearing strong positions.[11]

Ormulum is preserved in a single, very ugly manuscript in which almost one in four of its lines is defective. Holt's edition marks the defective lines, most of which (19 per cent of total) have the same fault: a missing initial syllable. They thus resemble the metre of their Latin model even more closely than the full lines, and it may have been Orm's metrical intention to make his added anacrusic syllable optional in the traditional English way. The poem's full lines are strictly iambic: the odd-numbered lines are tetrameters and the even-numbered trimeters. Although a Latin model could offer the two lengths in combination, other early Old English poems containing iambic tetrameters may have been influenced by French *octosyllabes*, some of which have their accented syllables in even-numbered positions (as did almost all the lines of the earliest surviving poems in this metre).

Thirteenth-century ictic verse: 'The Owl and the Nightingale'

Like Orm, the author of the Dutch *Life of Saint Lutgart* solved the problem of counting syllables in a Germanic language by alternating stress and non-stress in the Goliardic manner. Most Middle English poets, however, seem to have struggled with linguistic factors, such as syncope, schwa-loss, and a tendency towards stress-timing. How these problems affected both rhythm and syllable count can be seen from the following lines from the anonymous *Owl and the Nightingale* (Stanley 1972). This poem, which was composed around 1200, is considered by Bennett to be the first poetic masterpiece of Middle English (1986: 1).[12]

(7) þat **fu**-leþ his [V] **o**-wne nest	(100)
(8) he cuþ wel **who**-nen^e he is i-**cume**,	(138)
(9) he is wis an war of **wor**de,	(192)
(10) & 3et Al-ured **seid**^e an **o**-þer side	(299)

Instance (7) has seven syllables to the final stress only if the final schwa of 'owne' is syllabified; instance (8) can be counted as eight only if 'whonene' is pronounced as if it were the simple 'whan'; (9) definitely contains only seven syllables; and (10) is octosyllabic only if 'oþer' is reduced by syncope to a monosyllable. My attempt to scan these lines with four beats is rather more successful, providing the void marked in (7) is allowed. Tarlinskaja's tables show that 95.5 per cent of lines in *The Owl and the Nightingale* have four ictuses, while only 70 per cent have eight syllables (1976: 256–57). The latter figure is, nevertheless, much higher than the average (55 per cent) for the six Middle English rhymed poems that Tarlinskaja analyses. Many of the beats in *The Owl and the Nightingale*'s lines are realized by atonic monosyllables, as in *Ormulum*, showing that its prominence type is strength, and 83 per cent of inter-ictic intervals contain just one syllable, making the metre Tarlinskaja's 'transitional iamb'.

The fourteenth-century dolnik: 'Pearl'

Pearl, which Kennedy calls 'the sacred jewel in the crown of Middle English literature' (1999: 143), was composed almost two centuries after *The Owl and the Nightingale*. In some respects the versification of the later poem seems more developed: thus, *Pearl*'s strophe is longer and more complex, comprising twelve lines (in French, a *douzain*) rhymed abab abab bcbc. But, as it stands in the unique witness, only 55 per cent of *Pearl*'s lines have eight syllables (although 100 per cent have four ictuses, as shown by Tarlinskaja 1976: 257). Kennedy argues that the poet's metrical intention was an iambic tetrameter, and attributes the many irregularities to inaccurate copying (1999: 143). But to make all *Pearl*'s lines syllabically and accentually regular would be greater libertinism than any that can be proved against the witness's scribe. It would also produce stylistic and grammatical problems, as the following lines show:

(11) [V] Perl^e ple-**saunt**^e, to **pryn**-ces paye	(1)
(12) Of þat **pre**-cios perl^e wy-**thou**-ten spot	(36)

To make (11) octosyllabic we must either add an initial 'O' (as in line 10 of the poem), or syllabify one final schwa (either of 'plesaunte' or of 'perle'). But the vocative is used without 'O' elsewhere in the poem (for example, in line 189), and most of its lines are octosyllables only if their mid-line final schwas are deleted. It might be argued, however, that schwa loss occurred unevenly in Middle English and that the poet's treatment of final schwas might have been as inconsistent as the spelling of the manuscript. But in (12) regularizing syllable count is far less defensible: the preceding line clearly requires the preposition 'of', and the pronoun 'þat' is a grammatical necessity. Moreover, the poet closes the first five strophes with subtle variations of instance (12); the care that he takes to make each slightly different suggests that variation is one of his aesthetic aims. Since three of these variant lines have an extra syllable, it is reasonable to conclude that syllabic variation was equally part of his intention.

When taken together, the best explanation of these two lines is that the poet's verse design accepts the anacrusic principle: the first position may contain two syllables or a void, as in my scansion here. On this assumption 79 per cent of lines have one syllable in anacrusis, 11 per cent have two syllables, and 10 per cent have zero. But, even as an example of a tetrameter that allows *headless* lines, *Pearl* falls far short of regularity: only 68 per cent of lines contain the required seven or eight syllables. This is because there are also many lines in the manuscript text where weak positions other than the first contain two syllables, as in the following lines:

> (13)   <u>Oft</u>^e haf I **way**-ted, **wy**-schand^e þat <u>wele</u>   (13)
> (14)   O <u>moul</u>, þou **mar**-rez a **my**-ry ju-**ele**   (23)

Shedding a syllable in either of these two lines is as difficult as in (12), and 14 per cent of inter-ictic intervals in the poem are similarly disyllabic. Only 2 per cent of intervals, on the other hand, contain zero syllables, which is within the limits I have proposed for the English dolnik in Chapter 3. These percentages combine to place the poem's rhythm in Tarlinskaja's category 'transitionally iambic'.

Since atonic monosyllables sometimes represent beats in *Pearl*, the metre's prominence type is strength: as in *Ormulum* and *The Owl and the Nightingale*, only the weak syllables of polysyllabic words are constrained from appearing in strong positions. The parameters that differentiate the Middle English short line from the long are thus prominence type and position size; the long line requires stress in strong positions, and its weak positions are not limited to two syllables. The parameter shared by both types of line is position number, eight, and an overwhelming proportion of lines in both metres contain four beats. From this point the fates of the Middle English long and short lines diverged. The long evolved into triple-time (tumbling) verse, and was eventually superseded by a new long line with five beats; the short line retained its four beats and developed into duple-time (iambic and trochaic) metres; but as late as the fourteenth century the two metres had more in common than is generally acknowledged.

The principle of fit in Middle English

My analysis of *The Owl and the Nightingale* and *Pearl* confirms Owen's observation that all Middle English short-line verse seems to be based on four beats rather than eight syllables (1994: 412n5). Kennedy's opposing argument requires a puzzling combination of carelessness and fastidiousness on the part of the scribe: he needed to change the syllable count or rhythm, or both, of 45 per cent of his original's lines, while preserving the number of beats in 100 per cent. It is therefore far more likely that the poems concerned were never perfectly regular, and that the poet, like the scribe, was counting beats, not syllables. The phonological features of Middle English that are most relevant to versifying make ictic verse a much better fit for the language than any stress-syllabic metre: ictic verse is indifferent to the loss of word-final schwa and of weak syllables in syncope; it allows either accentuation of French loan words; it allows any monosyllable to represent a beat, making versifying easier in an increasingly monosyllabic language.

Some of the advantages of ictic verse lessened with time: final-schwa loss became complete, syncope became standard, the tendency to stress-timing became stronger, the old French accentuation of loan words died out, and new poly-syllabic words were imported from Latin, Romance, and Greek. Ictic verse was thus chronologically transitional, as well as typologically intermediate between accentual and stress-syllabic verse in English. The process can be described by the evolutionary metaphor: accentual verse became ictic when poets employed atonic monosyllables to represent beats and limited inter-ictic intervals to a maximum of two syllables; ictic metres then became various lengths of dolnik when poets avoided zero intervals, and iambic or trochaic metres when they further restricted intervals to one syllable.

Gower and Chaucer

The last third of the fourteenth century witnessed striking new developments in both Insular French and Middle English versification. Two men were responsible for the experiments that radically changed the history of English metrics: Geoffrey Chaucer (b. ?1340, d. 1400) and John Gower (b. ?1330, d. 1408). Each poet produced both a new octosyllabic line and a new decasyllabic one, and their innovations, after many vicissitudes, became the canonical short and long lines of English verse. Gower was born into a family of very prosperous landowners and as a young man bought, sold, and managed his estates in various parts of the country. In middle age he moved into the Priory of St Mary Overeys in Southwark, probably having paid for its rebuilding, and devoted the remainder of his life to writing. His verse found a growing audience, as he turned from Latin and French to English in the late 1380s and courted the favour of the Lancastrian party, which eventually seized the throne in 1399. Gower married in 1398, possibly because he needed a carer to help him cope with his encroaching blindness, and he died ten years later.

Chaucer was the son of a London wine merchant, a trade that brought many Italians to London and introduced young Geoffrey to their language. He was enrolled at an early age into a noble household, where he served as page and courtier. The contacts he gained opened the way to a coveted career in the civil service of his day, first in the Diplomatic Corps, and then in Customs and Excise. He composed poetry between arduous bouts of foreign travel, or after busy days at the office, until his retirement from the Civil Service in 1386, when he moved to Kent, became an MP, and began to write *The Canterbury Tales*. This vast work, his crowning enterprise, was still unfinished when he died in 1400. The two men were undoubtedly close friends for some time. Gower was one of two confidants to whom Chaucer entrusted his property when he made his second trip to Italy in 1378. He also dedicated the literary fruit of that trip, *Troilus and Criseyde*, to Gower in 1386, a compliment that was returned in Gower's *Confessio Amantis* of 1390. Gower changed this dedication in a subsequent recension (1393), and some writers have speculated that there was a rift between the two men (see Pearsall 1992: 132–33). The reason for the change, however, is more likely to have been political: Gower had dedicated the first version of the poem to Chaucer and to King Richard II; he dedicated the later one to the man who would eventually murder Richard and usurp his throne as Henry IV. On balance, therefore, it is highly unlikely that the two poets' metrical experiments were conducted independently (see Duffell & Billy 2004 and Billy & Duffell 2005).

Gower divided his early poetic output between two languages, Latin and French, and he took the risk of composing in English only after Chaucer had achieved success and fame with *Troilus and Criseyde*. The French in which Gower composed his poetry was not the Francien of the royal court, but the Insular variety, interspersed with many neologisms and words usually found only in mainland dialects (see Merrilees 2003). But his morphology and syntax were typically Insular and, like the structure of his lines, is evidence that he spoke French with the strong stress and stress-timing of Insular speakers (Duffell 2005: 122). As a courtier, Chaucer must have become fluent in French, and he was clearly familiar with the work of his most famous French contemporaries, some of whom visited the English court. Although the only French poems that may have been composed by Chaucer are of uncertain attribution, he certainly translated at least part of the *Roman de la Rose* into English (Sutherland 1968). His knowledge of Latin is something we can infer from his use of terms and tags, and from the large number of Latin works on which he drew for his material. His knowledge of Italian, which was unusual in fourteenth-century England, is attested by three pieces of evidence: he retained Italian friends from his youth, he spent some months in Italy, and he translated long passages of the *Filostrato* almost word for word in his *Troilus and Criseyde* (see the parallel texts in Windeatt 1984).

Chaucer's Metrics

Chaucer's earliest works are in his short-line metre: his section of *The Romaunt of the Rose* and *The Book of the Duchess* (*BD*) date from 1368–69; but *The House of Fame* (*HF*), completed in 1378, was his last major short-line work.[13] The period 1378–81 saw his first experiments with a new long-line metre: they included *Anelida and Arcite* (*AA*), *The Parliament of Fowles* (*PF*), and the short poems 'An ABC' (*ABC*) and 'Complaint unto Pity' (*CP*). Three major works in the new metre followed: he worked on *Troilus and Criseyde* (*TC*) between 1381 and 1386, *The Legend of Good Women* in 1387–97, revising its prologue in 1394–95, and *The Canterbury Tales* (*CT*) between 1387 and 1400.

Contemporary Francien norms

References, borrowings, and translations make it clear that Chaucer and Gower admired the work of their contemporaries from the European mainland, especially Guillaume de Machaut (b. ?1300, d. 1377), Eustache Deschamps (b. ?1346, d. ?1407), Jean Froissart (b. ?1337, d. ?1410), and Oton de Granson (d. 1397). Some ambitious Englishmen tried to emulate these poets by composing in Francien, the language of the noble courts, and Chaucer may have been among them. Fifteen of the poems in one manuscript collection of such verse have the letters 'Ch' written against them (MS French 15, edited by Wimsatt 1982). These poems date from the third quarter of the fourteenth century, and no other courtier or poet has been identified to whom these letters could refer. They are typical of the Francien verse of this period in every respect, including their metre.

Fourteenth-century Francien poets, unlike their Insular equivalents, counted syllables strictly, including all final schwas that could not be elided before a vowel or diphthong, and took no account of word stress within the line or hemistich.[14] The two most popular metres were the *octosyllabe* and the *vers de dix*: the former had remained virtually unchanged from the twelfth century, but the latter now avoided epic caesura, making it a line of 4 + 6M/F syllables. The most common type of line in *vers de dix* was that with masculine caesura (4M + 6M/F): it represents more than three-quarters of all lines in the *Poems of 'Ch'*.[15] The other common line types are the line with lyric caesura (3F + 6M/F) and the line in which an *e-atone* closing the first hemistich is elided before a vowel or diphthong opening the second (4E + 6M/F). In the *Poems of 'Ch'* these two types of line account for 12 and 9 per cent of total, respectively, and other types of line are extremely rare: my sample contains only one epic caesura (4F + 6M/F), one line with an irregular caesura dividing it into 7 + 3 syllables, and two examples of the foreign caesura (*coupe italienne*) that divides the line 5 + 5.

All these proportions are very similar to those found in the verse of Froissart (see Billy 1999), and these poems give only a few clues that 'Ch' could have been other than an L1 Francien speaker. These include a few clumsy examples of hiatus, a few of incorrect gender, and a somewhat higher proportion of lines with accents on syllables 4, 7, and 10 than in most French *vers de dix*.[16] But these peculiar features of the *Poems of 'Ch'* are relatively minor divergences from the norms of mainland verse; if Chaucer was the author, it is clear that he was not yet ready to engage in radical experiments with line structure, or at least not in French.

Chaucer's verse design and final schwa

The systematic syllabification of word-final schwas not elidable before a vowel or diphthong seems to have been a feature of all Chaucer's verse designs. Such elision was the invariable rule in mainland French verse and in his friend Gower's poetry, both in French and in English.[17] We cannot be certain that Chaucer was this systematic in his earlier short line, because this device still leaves many lines irregular in syllable count and an inconsistent treatment would render some lines more regular. In Chaucer's long line, however, syllabification of unelided word-final schwas makes close to 100 per cent of lines decasyllabic, and the chances of such regularity occurring by chance are negligible. Chaucer may have been led to make his syllable count more regular, or his treatment of final schwa more systematic, by Gower's *Mirour de l'omme*, which reintroduced syllabic regularity to Insular French verse in 1376. But it is more likely that Chaucer was imitating conspicuous features of the Italian texts he knew: the profusion of word-final vowels and the skilful use of synaloepha to regularize the number of syllables in the line.[18] Frequent elision undoubtedly helped Chaucer solve the English problem of whether readers would pronounce final schwa, and it also increased the proportion of lines with his preferred iambic rhythm. The downside, however, was that the regularities of his metre depended on the pronunciation of final schwa before a consonant, a feature of the language that was already archaic (see Windeatt 1977).

The readers of subsequent centuries deleted all final schwas in Chaucer's lines, as in their normal speech, and consequently they found them rude and rough, irregular in both syllable count and accentuation. But in 1863 F. J. Child argued that Chaucer's metrical intention was syllabic (and rhythmic) regularity, and that he syllabified word-final schwa before a consonant. This hypothesis was contested for more than a century, but modern advances in informatics have proved that Child was almost certainly correct.[19] The question was effectively settled by Charles and Nicholas Barber's massive computer exercise (1990–91), which showed that the number of syllables per line in the Hengwrt MS of *CT* correlates very closely with the number of word-final schwas that cannot be elided.

Chaucer's short line

The earliest poems that can safely be ascribed to Chaucer are predominantly octosyllabic, like most Middle English and Insular French verse. They are more regular in syllable count than any English verse that preceded them, providing unelidable word-final schwas are included in the syllable count, but this still fails to make them regular by French or Italian standards. As Tarlinskaja notes, *BD* is the earliest English poem in which more than three-quarters of the lines in the surviving witnesses have exactly eight syllables (1976: 88). She shows that 84 per cent of its lines have eight, 11 per cent have seven, and 5 per cent have nine syllables (1976: 256); the design's greatest regularity, however, is shown in another table: 100 per cent of lines have four ictuses (1976: 257). This makes Chaucer's line not an iambic tetrameter, nor an octosyllable, but a four-ictic dolnik with a transitionally iambic rhythm, like its predecessors. In most of the lines that appear to have nine syllables a word-final schwa contributes to the count; the presence of hypermetric lines in Chaucer's short metre therefore partly depends on whether his treatment of final schwa was already fully consistent.[20]

Chaucer gave a clear indication in *HF* that he sometimes consciously deviated from a strict syllable count:

(15)   Yit **mak**[e] hyt **sum**-what <u>a</u>-gre-able   (1097)
(16)   Though <u>som</u> vers **fayl**[e] in <u>a</u> sil-lable   (1098)

The editors of Benson et al. 1988 give this reading of (16), but in some manuscripts the word 'in' is missing, either because of a copyist's error or because Chaucer left position 5 void to illustrate his point. Certainly, my analysis shows that Chaucer's short-line metre did not complete the transition to *canonical iamb* between *BD* and *HF*, where 12 per cent of lines were still hypometric in 1378.

The frequency of initial inversion in English short-line verse is usually lower than in long-line, and Chaucer's short-line metre is no exception: he employed initial inversion in barely 1 per cent of lines in *HF*. When he wished to open a line with a trochaic word, Chaucer usually applied the anacrusic principle, and opened with a void position, rather than an inversion, as in the following lines:

> (17) [V] **Cre**-sus, <u>that</u> was <u>kyng</u> of <u>Lyde</u>   (105)
> (18) [V] **Pip**-ers <u>of</u> the **Du**-che **tonge**   (1234)

These are all *headless* lines (with a void in the first position), and the overwhelming majority of Chaucer's seven-syllable lines have this trochaic structure, indicating that the missing syllable is the first. This is a richer source of variety than later poets found in initial inversion, which rarely exceeds 4 per cent of lines in the iambic tetrameter (see Tables E and K). On the other hand, the frequency with which non-final ictuses are eroded in the *HF* (on average, 9 per cent) is very similar to that found in the canonical metre. Chaucer also sometimes erodes the first ictus in his four-beat line, delaying the impact of the trochaic rhythm, as in:

> (19) [V] <u>To</u> my <u>wyt</u>, what **cau**-seth **swe**venes   (3)
> (20) [V] <u>And</u> hir <u>comb</u> to **kemb**ᵉ hyr <u>hed</u>   (136)

Chaucer's short-line verse design did not complete the transition from dolnik to iambic tetrameter, and I would argue that this served an aesthetic purpose. Chaucer guarded his verse from the potential monotony inherent in a line of four (2 + 2) beats with iambic (w s) rhythm. In his lines, erosion reduced the volume of the right-strong pulse, anacrusis offered variety in the form of trochaic lines, and the occasional resolution provided a final frisson. Chaucer thus left it to Gower to invent the iambic tetrameter, and to later centuries of poets to solve the problems of its potential monotony; he himself merely polished the traditional Middle English short line.

Chaucer's farewell to the short line can be found in his *Tale of Sir Thopas*, which parodies contemporary minstrel romances composed in dolniks. The lines of this poem are remarkably regular in rhythm: only 3 per cent of his four-beat lines are headless and there are few departures from an iambic rhythm. Chaucer avoids monotony by combining four-beat and three-beat lines in strophes rhymed aab ccb (*tail-rhyme*). When Harry Bailey dismisses this verse as 'doggerel' and says 'namore of this', he may be reflecting Chaucer's own opinion of its acoustic effects (too many iambs, too many rhymes).[21] After this aborted tale he deserted the short line: both the remainder of *CT* and his 'Complaint to his Purse', which he composed in the year of his death, are in the long line of his own invention.

Italian influence on Chaucer's English long line

Since Chaucer had Italian friends from childhood, and had made an earlier trip to Italy, it is likely that he had read decasyllabic verse in Italian long before his second visit in 1378. But this trip lasted several months, and when he returned he had a copy of Boccaccio's *Filostrato* in his saddlebag, the inspiration for *TC*. As Windeatt 1984 notes, Chaucer translated many of Boccaccio's lines not only word for word, but also stress for stress.[22] As noted above, one of the features that distinguishes the Italian *endecasillabo* from the *vers de dix* is a profusion of synaloepha.[23] Another is its mobile caesura: it freely mixes lines with their principal mid-line stress in position 4 (*a minore*) with lines having this stress in position 6 (*a maiore*). The first hemistichs of both types may be either masculine or feminine, and second hemistichs are almost always feminine, making the *endecasillabo* a line of 10F syllables, variously divided.[24] This variety includes lines where a feminine word adds a post-tonic syllable to the first hemistich, and is compensated by reducing the second by one syllable. This is a principle so alien to French metrics that it was termed *coupe italienne*, and it gave the Italian metre four possible syllabic configurations: 4M + 6, 4F + 5, 6M + 4, or 6F + 3.

Finally, Italian poets harnessed their language's word stress to produce a very different rhythm from that found in the French or Occitan lines. The *endecasillabo*'s mobile caesura prevented phrasal stresses from occurring at regular intervals (of 4 and 6 syllables) in delivery. And the irregular placement of phrasal stresses combined with the strength of word stress in Italian to foreground the secondary rhythms offered by the mid-line stresses. Because stress is mandatory in position 4 or 6, and many lines have it in both, the majority of *endecasillabi* have an iambic rhythm, with their strong syllables and stressed monosyllables falling in even-numbered positions. Italian poets, however, gave their verse rhythmic variety by including lines with non-iambic rhythms; the following examples are from the first book of the *Filostrato*:

(21)	**gui**-da la **nos**-tra **man**, || **re**-ggi lo 'ngegno	(31)
(22)	de' Tro-**ian**[i] o de **Grec**[i] || il **grand**[e] ar-**di**re	(62)
(23)	io̲ de Par-**na**-so || le **Mu**-se pre-**ga**re	(40)

[Guide our hand, rule our mind, | the great burning of Trojans or of Greeks | I to entreat the Muses from Parnassus]

Instances (21) and (22) are *a maiore lines*, with their principal mid-line stress in position 6 (formula 6M + 4F), while (23) is *a minore*, with its principal mid-line stress in position 4 (formula 4F + 5F), and is an example of *coupe italienne*. All three lines vary from the normal iambic rhythm; (21) has clashing stressed syllables in positions 6 and 7, producing a triple-time (adonic) close;[25] (22) has stressed syllables in positions 3 and 6, giving it an anapaestic opening;[26] and (23) has stresses in positions 4 and 7, making the rhythm triple-time almost throughout.[27]

Although the great majority of lines in Boccaccio's and his contemporaries' *endecasillabi* meet the definition of the iambic pentameter, a substantial minority do not because of these rhythmic variants.[28] But Chaucer decided to make very little use of this source of variety in his own English long-line metre, and subsequent generations of English poets have reserved the Italians' deviant rhythms for special effects (as in the examples quoted in nn25–26).

Chaucer's English pentameter

In his early long-line poems Chaucer had employed the same strophe designs as Gower had in French, rhyme royal and the eight-line ballad stanza. In *CT*, however, he reverted to the Insular favourite, the rhymed couplet, which he had used in his most important short-line poems. His long-line verse design, on the other hand, was quite unlike that of any existing English or French poem, and its only possible models were Italian. Chaucer developed the *endecasillabo* into a metre that would meet the aesthetic demands of both syllabic regularity and English linguistic rhythm. It was also a metre that replaced the rhythmic monotony of 2 + 2 stresses with the variety obtained by mixing 2 + 3 with 3 + 2, in any order and in varying proportions. Like the *endecasillabo*, Chaucer's metre produces many lines that would pass as *vers de dix*; for example:

(24)   The lyf so short, || the craft so long to lerne   (*PF*, 1)
(25)   And cer-tes yf || ye wan-ten in thes^e tweyne   (*CP*, 76)
(26)   Thou art lar-gess^e || of pleyn fe-li-ci-tee   (*ABC*, 13)

Instance (24) is analogous to the staple French line of 4M + 6 syllables; (25) to the rarer variant in which position 4 contains an atonic monosyllable (a form of erosion); and (26) has a paroxytonic word at the caesura, with its final schwa elided (4E + 6). But Chaucer's line is not merely an English version of the *vers de dix*, because it eschews both lyric and epic caesura: the very few apparent examples of such lines have an alternative, and I believe better, explanation.[29]

Chaucer also employs many lines that the *endecasillabo* allows but the *vers de dix* does not; for example:

(27)   Up by the bri-dil, at the sta-ves ende   (*AA*, 184)
(28)   U-pon the cru-el-te^e and ti-ra-nnye   (*CP*, 6)
(29)   To herk-nen of Pa-lla-dion the ser-uyce   (*TC*, 1. 164)

All three of these lines would be considered deviant in French verse, but are very common in Italian: (27) is analogous to the *a minore* line with *coupe italienne* and comprises 4F + 5 syllables; (28) subdivides 6M + 4 (as a result of the elision of final schwa), and (29) subdivides 6F + 3; both (28) and (29) are analogous to Italian *a maiore* lines. Chaucer's model was, clearly, the Italian *endecasillabo* of Boccaccio and Petrarch, and not the *vers de dix* of Machaut and Froissart.

Chaucer's great innovation, however, was to elevate the iambic rhythm he found in an overwhelming majority of *endecasillabi* to a structural principal, and he did this by not placing lexically strong syllables in odd-numbered positions, and by placing stresses in most even-numbered ones. These rules are observed meticulously in instances (24) to (29) and in over 96 per cent of his lines: these are the first true iambic pentameters in any European language. The design's greatest potential weakness was monotony, because it lacked the alternative rhythms found in Chaucer's Italian models: and the human mind craves variety as well as regularity.

To meet the former demand, Chaucer employed the various types of tension, particularly erosion. Atonic monosyllables that bear no stress in normal speech occupy a number of strong (even-numbered) positions in the examples above: 'yf' and 'in' (25), 'by' and 'at' (27), and 'of' and 'the' (29). On average Chaucer eroded 12 per cent of non-final ictuses in this way, a figure similar to that found in the iambic pentameters of later poets (see Tables A and J).

Chaucer also employed initial polysyllabic inversion as a source of rhythmic variety in either hemistich, as the following examples show:

> (30) **Re**-<u>dy</u> to **wen**-den <u>on</u> my **pil**-gry-**mage**   (*CT: GP*, 21)
> (31) And <u>ek</u> for <u>me</u> **pre**-<u>ieth</u> to <u>God</u> so **dere**   (*TC*, 32)

On average he employed initial inversion, as in (30), in 3 per cent of first hemistichs and 2 per cent of second. There was, however, another device that had long been used by English poets for obtaining rhythmic variety in these positions, and Chaucer seems to have employed it in a few of lines. This was the void initial position, a relic of the anacrusic principle; used in the first hemistich, it produces a *headless* line; used in the second, it produces a *broken-backed* line, as the following examples show:

> (32) [V] <u>Whan</u> that A-**prill** <u>with</u> his **shou**-res **soote**   (*CT: GP*, 1)
> (33) **Ha**-<u>vynge</u> re-**ward on**-<u>ly</u> [V] to my **trouth**e   (*PF*, 426)

Instance (33) is a very unusual line: since few editors have proposed 'hevinge' as a trisyllable, the line seems to have an initial inversion, a medial inversion, and a void position. Hammond points out that, although a single manuscript may make 4.9 per cent of *CT*'s lines headless and 2.7 per cent broken-backed, both figures fall to under 1 per cent if the editor makes emendations based on alternative readings in other witnesses (1925: 134–37). Headless and broken-backed lines are thus even rarer than non-iambic lines in Chaucer, but many of his successors were much less disciplined and their verse is considerably less smooth as a result, as I shall show in the next chapter.

Erosion, inversion, and void positions gave Chaucer's lines some rhythmic variety, but significantly less than that found in his Italian models. He seems to have decided, therefore, to emulate the subtle mixing of *a minore* and *a maiore* lines in the *endecasillabo*. English, unlike Italian, has no shortage of oxytonic words and stressed monosyllables, thus facilitating the composition of lines that have a word boundary immediately after position 4 (as in (24) to (26) above); but English also has no shortage of paroxytons, thus providing words to place in positions 4 and 5, denying a boundary (as in (27) to (29) above). Chaucer sensed that the contrast between the two types could provide a source of variety in his verse, and he did not leave their proportions to chance. These two types of iambic pentameter may be termed 'French' and 'Italian' lines, and in his early works in this metre Chaucer consistently employed around 24 per cent of 'Italian' lines, significantly more than the actual word configurations he uses would lead us to expect.[30] In *CT* he increased the percentage of such lines to more than 30, and in subsequent centuries English poets developed this trend, culminating in an almost perfect balance between the two types of line (see Duffell 2002b: 305).

Gower's Metrics

Gower completed his French short-line poem *Mirour de l'omme* (hereafter *MO*) in 1376, and worked on his Latin poem in elegiac couplets *Vox clamantis* (*VC*) between 1377 and 1381. Gower's earliest surviving verse in English, *Confessio Amantis* (*CA*), was composed between 1386 and 1390 and, apart from one passage, is in short lines. His long-line work in French that can be most securely dated is the *Traitié*, which clearly relates to his marriage in 1398, and was probably composed in the previous year. His English long-line poem *In Praise of Peace* (*PP*) was completed in 1399, although parts of it may have been composed earlier. Finally, although his French long-line *Cinkante Balades* (*CB*) may have been composed at any time between 1377 and 1399, their novel versification suggests that they were composed only after he had seen Chaucer's copy of the *Filostrato* and/or some attempts to imitate its metre in English.[31]

Gower's French metres

As noted, most Insular French verse contained not the primary rhythms of the mainland French poets, based on regular phrasal stress, but the secondary rhythms created by strong word stress. Most Insular poets, who could not depend on their readers' syllable-timing or syllabifying word-final schwas, thus neglected syllable count.[32] Gower decided to reintroduce the rigour of the mainland tradition, by including all unelidable word-final schwas in his own strictly counted lines: his shorter line has a consistent 8M/F syllables and his longer 10M/F.[33] In his French verse Gower employed fixed strophe forms borrowed from the mainland: a twelve-line strophe (rhymed aab aab bba bba) for *MO* and either seven- or eight-line strophes for his two groups of *balades*. For these sixty-nine poems he used only four rhyme schemes (each with only two or, at most, three rhymes) and, unlike many mainland ballade-writers, employed the *vers de dix* exclusively. Gower was a poet who took metre, like all life's obligations, very seriously indeed.

Some other features of Gower's French versifying, however, were revolutionary, and the first was harnessing the strong word stress of the Insular variety, as can be seen from the following *octosyllabes* from *MO*:

(34)	Pri-**mer** quant <u>dieus</u> ot <u>fait</u> les <u>cieux</u>	(61)
(35)	Mais <u>du</u> pe-**cché** q'es-**toit** mor-**tieux**	(64)

[When god first created the heavens | But sin, which may be mortal]

Most lines in the poem resemble these in having a word boundary after four syllables and no strong syllables in weak positions; as Macaulay pointed out, *MO* is predominantly iambic (1899: xliii–xlvi), and is thus reminiscent of the earliest (eleventh-century) French octosyllables. Only about 13 per cent of the poem's lines contain a strong syllable in a weak position, making it as close to an iambic tetrameter as Chaucer's *HF*, where 12 per cent of lines have the wrong number of syllables. In the late 1370s, at least, the two poets seem to have desired a similar level of rhythmic variety in their shorter line.

Gower's *vers de dix* share the preponderantly iambic rhythm of his *octosyllabes* but contain another striking innovation: they have no fixed caesura. Although the majority of his lines are of the canonical types, a substantial minority differ from those of any mainland poet.[34] He uses lyric caesura much less often, preferring to accommodate a feminine word mid-line by elision at the caesura (the line of 4E + 6). But, most radically, he employs lines of a type extremely common in *endecasillabi*, but almost unknown in *vers de dix*, as the following examples from *CB* demonstrate:

(36)	Du pro-vi-**den**-ce || q'est ce-<u>les</u>-ti-**al**	(1. 6)
(37)	En **tout**^e hu-<u>mi</u>-li-té || sanz <u>mes</u>-pri-**sure**	(12. 25)
(38)	Qe **nu**-lle <u>me</u>-di-**ci**-ne || <u>m'est</u> ve-**rraie**	(27. 4)

[Of providence that is celestial | in all humility and sincerity | of which no medicine may rid me]

Instance (36) subdivides 4F + 5M (*coupe italienne*); (37) subdivides 6M + 4F and (38) 6F + 3F (*endecasillabi a maiore*). In these poems almost 9 per cent of lines have *coupe italienne*, while 10 per cent are *a maiore*, with their principal mid-line stress in position 6; a further 3 per cent of lines have accents in both positions 4 and 6 with no clear hierarchy between the two. This lack of a fixed caesura, combined with a preponderantly iambic rhythm, makes Gower's lines *endecasillabi* in French.[35] Since, as far as we know, he had no Italian, this points to some form of collaboration with Chaucer in developing the metre, and to the dating of the first *Balade* soon after 1378 (see n31). Like its Italian precursor, Gower's metre was intermediate between syllabic and stress-syllabic, but, while the *endecasillabo* endured as the Italian long-line canon, Gower's *vers de dix* found no imitators because of the demise of Insular French and the loss of word stress in the mainland varieties of the language.

Gower's English tetrameter

Gower began *CA* at about the time that Chaucer completed *TC* in 1386; it took him four years to complete the first version, and he spent another three years producing two further versions. Gower probably ventured into English only because of Chaucer's example: lines 22–24 of *CA* note that few men (that is, educated men) composed in English at the time and Gower claims to have chosen the language 'for Engelondes sake', signalling an emergent nationalism that was to prove fatal to Insular French. Except for a short 'Complaint' (VIII. 2217–2300), all the lines of Gower's poem are octosyllables providing unelided final schwas are counted (see n17). They are also regularly iambic, as can be seen from the following lines from Book III OF *CA* (Peck 1980):

(39)	This <u>o</u> lord **hadd**^e in spe-ci-<u>al</u>	(1342)
(40)	A **Son**^e, a **lus**-ti **Ba**-che-<u>ler</u>	(1343)
(41)	In <u>al</u> the <u>toun</u> was <u>non</u> his <u>pier</u>:	(1344)
(42)	That **o**-ther **hadd**^e a **dowh**-ter eke	(1345)

Fewer than 4 per cent of Gower's lines in this poem have a strong syllable in an odd-numbered position, making it the first true iambic tetrameter in English.

Since barely 1 per cent of lines contain initial inversion, the poem's main source of rhythmic variety is erosion: atonic monosyllables provide almost 9 per cent of the poem's non-final ictuses, a figure comparable to that found in later iambic tetrameters (see Tables E and K). Examples of erosion in Book 1 of *CA* INCLUDE:

(43) That <u>of</u> to-**much**^e or <u>of</u> to-**lite** (19)
(44) And **wry**-ten <u>of</u> my **wo**-ful <u>care</u> (74)

The preposition 'of' represents an erosion of the first and third ictuses in (43) and the second ictus in (44). Lines, like (43), with two erosions are rare in Gower, who refrained from eroding consecutive ictuses, as did most subsequent poets who employed the iambic tetrameter. It says much for Gower's storytelling skill that he can hold our attention for substantial passages of the poem's 33,000 lines in this metre, but the risk of rhythmic monotony in the future English short-line canon is already apparent.

Gower's English pentameter

As well as inserting a decasyllabic 'Complaint' (hereafter *C*) in *CA*, Gower also employed 385 decasyllabic lines in *PP*, which was presented to the new King Henry IV in 1399 or 1400; their metre has attracted little critical attention until recently.[36] Gower's English long line, like his French, is a very strictly counted decasyllable, and many of his English lines meet the definition of the traditional French *vers de dix*, including the following:

(45) The **lon**-des <u>folk</u> || hath <u>ek</u> thy <u>riht</u> a-**ffer**med   (*PP* 13)
(46) The **wor**-schip^e <u>of</u> this <u>lond</u> || which <u>was</u> doun **fall**e   (*PP* 5)
(47) The **wo**-full **pein**^e || of **lo**-ves <u>ma</u>-la-**die**   (*C* 2217)

Instance (45) subdivides 4M + 6, (46) also subdivides 4 + 6, but with an atonic monosyllable in position 4, and (47) subdivides 4E + 6. That the metre is something other than an English *vers de dix* is proved by the presence of three types of line used by Chaucer in English, but only by Gower in French; for example:

(48) Wher **pite** dwe-lleth, || <u>in</u> the **sa**-me **pla**ce   (*PP* 334)
(49) To **ev**^ery <u>cre</u>-a-**tur**^e || **un**-<u>dir</u> the **son**ne   (*PP* 215)
(50) And <u>thus</u> whan **con**-sci-enc^e is **trew**-ly **wei**e   (*PP* 320)

These are what I call 'Italian' lines: (48) subdivides 4F + 5 (*coupe italienne*), and (49) and (50) are *a maiore* lines with elision at the caesura (6E + 4). Gower, like Chaucer, mixed such lines freely with 'French' lines like (45) to (47): in Gower's verse 'Italian' lines, those with no word boundary between positions 4 and 5, represent 23 per cent of total, as compared with 24 per cent in Chaucer's *TC* and 31 in Chaucer's *GP*.

   The examples given show that Gower's lines are as regular in rhythm as in syllable count: he places the strong syllable of a polysyllabic word in an odd-numbered position in barely 3 per cent of lines (mostly at the opening of hemistichs). Moreover, the majority of these inversions involve grammatical disyllables, such as 'undir' in (49), and only six of the medial inversions involve a lexical word, as in the following line:[37]

(51) Of <u>god</u> what <u>thing</u> him <u>was</u> **le**-<u>vest</u> to crave   (*PP* 30)

Note that this inversion meets parametric theory's bracketing condition: the word 'levest' coincides with the fourth foot (the iambic contrast expected in positions 7–8). Compared with other iambic pentameter poets, Gower employed very few initial inversions, which appear in under 1 per cent of lines, including the following:

> (52)   **Plein**-<u>ly</u> thurgh-**soght** my **wit**-tes **all**ᵉ I <u>have</u>   (C 2247)

Gower employed erosion more frequently than inversion: on average 6 per cent of his non-final ictuses are eroded; but this is very significantly less frequently than Chaucer used the device (12 per cent). There has historically been some debate on how iambic Gower's decasyllables were: Schipper argued that they were not as iambically smooth as his octosyllables (1896: 483–86), but Macaulay disagreed (1901: cxxi–cxxii). My analysis shows that Gower's iambic pentameter, like his tetrameter, was almost excessively regular. But, while his longer line is merely a slightly more regular version of Chaucer's, his shorter line must be recognized as the first true iambic tetrameter in English.

Conclusion

For more than three hundred years much of the population of England was bilingual, and the two languages naturally exerted considerable influence on one another. Poets versifying in this period inherited two very different metrical traditions, which were based on counting syllables in one case, and beats in the other. While the verse texts that they read reinforced the former (at least initially), oral texts such as nursery rhymes and proverbs entrenched the latter. Social pressures favoured syllables: French had much higher prestige, and it also had an established syllabic metrical system. But linguistic factors favoured beats: the English tendency towards stress-timing strengthened, and syncope and schwa deletion created a vast stock of new monosyllables. Insular French, which already had word stress, absorbed something of these features, while English gained many right-strong words and relocated phrasal stress so as to give rhyme precedence over alliteration. Most of these changes, however, made it easier to count beats than syllables, since many weak, unstressed syllables became variables in ordinary speech. Thus, by the thirteenth century, poets of both languages were composing four-beat verse that hovered on the margins of the iambic.

In the late fourteenth century two major poets learned from Italian models how to count beats in such a way as to produce a regular number of syllables. But two disasters hit their enterprise: the first was that their regularity depended on what was already an archaism, and their meticulous syllable count was lost with the eventual disappearance of word-final schwa. The second blow was the defeat of the Plantagenets in the Hundred Years War, which doomed the Insular variety of French, and with it any prospect of a French metrics based on the regularity of word stress. One of Gower's most important metrical innovations was thus lost for ever; but his English iambic tetrameter and Chaucer's pentameter were recovered in the sixteenth century, and became the canonical metres of subsequent English verse. The story of the development of these canons, and of the challenges they met from other types of metre, will occupy much of the remainder of the present volume.

Notes to Chapter 4

1. Chaucer's name shows that one of his ancestors made shoes in France; the conquest clearly brought new service industries to London, but they did not rival the scale of the massive construction programme of castles and cathedrals, for which the Normans used Anglo-Danish slave labour.

2. This duality is commemorated in modern English spelling: Norman judges sent 'Geoffrey' to 'gaol', but Plantagenet judges sent 'Jeffrey' to 'jail'.

3. Henry IV (r. 1399–1409) had just murdered his predecessor and seized the throne, and so had an urgent need to win the widest possible support in the two chambers; the change in the language of the personal correspondence of Henry V (r. 1413–22) is an important landmark in the advance of English; its exact date was pointed out to me by Herbert Schendl of the University of Vienna.

4. Among its abbesses this august institution numbered two queens, a princess, and the sister of a saint (see Legge 1963: 62). Differences in dialect did not prevent Insular French poets from finding a market for their works on the mainland, where copyists sometimes emended them in accordance with the orthographical norms of their own region (Legge 1963: 70).

5. As noted in Chapter 2, anti-rhythmic counting was also a feature of early syllabic verse in Galician-Portuguese and Spanish, which both have strong word stress; it may therefore be taken as evidence of strong word stress in Insular French.

6. The accuracy of mainland French copyists is also examined in detail in Duffell 2003: 113–14, which concludes that barely 1 per cent of the copying errors found in nine manuscripts of the same poem (the *Chanson d'Antioche*, Duparc-Quioc 1976) change the number of syllables in the line. Such syllabic accuracy doubtless occurs because metre is an important memory aid, and any copyist who understands the metre will tend to make only errors that conform to it.

7. The very few surviving lines in Insular French metre that contain only six syllables offer a test of whether four beats were part of the poet's metrical intention. In theory, this length of line could consist of three disyllables and thus provide only three beats; but I can find no example of such a line.

8. A further 14 per cent of lines can be regularized by counting word-final schwas facultatively (and inconsistently) in order to produce eight syllables. This figure also varies between poems, which suggests considerable variation between individual Insular French poets (and speakers) in the treatment of such schwas. Since most medieval poetry was composed for reading aloud (see Garcia 1978: 45), such inconsistent schwa deletion renders a fluent delivery in the French manner almost impossible.

9. Vising poured scorn on the idea that a higher-status group might surrender to the rhythms of a lower-status group (1884: 12); we don't know whether the arrival of the jazz age changed his view, but in his later work he cites a poem that is syllabically regular only in the second half, and assumes that the only possible explanation is that the writer got smart in the interval (1923: 81).

10. The statistics given in this section are taken from the tables of Tarlinskaja 1976, supplemented by my own analysis of the first three hundred lines of each poem in the editions I have cited in this section.

11. Examples of grammatical words representing beats include *wiþþ* (20), *forr* (33), and *onn* (67).

12. In choosing examples of Middle English texts I shall, as far as possible, avoid lines containing words that have not survived in the modern language, and I shall gloss them when they are inevitable.

13. My chronology of Chaucer's and Gower's work is based on Pearsall 1992 and Peck 1980, but also takes into account some dates proposed by Macaulay 1901 and Cressman 1983.

14. At this time final *e-atone* was syllabified in normal mainland speech.

15. The figures I quote are based on my own analysis of 300 lines chosen randomly from Wimsatt's text (they first appeared in Duffell 2000a). Note that a small percentage of 4M + 6 lines have an atonic monosyllable in position 4; this can be compared with erosion in metres that employ word stress.

16. The figure for lines accented in this way (45 per cent) is significantly higher than that found in the *vers de dix* of most French poets (see Duffell 1996: 217). Moreover such triple-time lines often occur in a series in the *Poems of 'Ch'*, as in 3. 4–10, 6. 12–16, and 7. 12–14 & 16–18.

17. Gower elides word-final schwa before an *h*, regardless of whether it opens a word of Romance or Germanic origin, but he does not syllabify the schwas of certain common words, probably because they were invariably monosyllables in contemporary speech; for example, 'thes^e' (*P* 261), 'whann^e' (*P* 173), 'mor^e' (*P* 218), and 'her^e' (*P* 228).

18. The frequency of elision in Medieval French verse varies from 9 to 14 per 100 lines; its Italian metrical equivalent is *synaloepha*, in which a final vowel is merged with a following initial vowel or diphthong. In Boccaccio's *endecasillabi* synaloepha occurs 87 times in every 100 lines (of which 34 are at the caesura), and in Petrarch's 121 times (45 at the caesura); see Duffell 1991: 312–13.

19. W. W. Skeat made Child's hypothesis the new orthodoxy by supporting it in his great edition of Chaucer's complete works (1894–97). But in the course of the twentieth century scholars realized that word-final schwa deletion had begun two centuries earlier than Chaucer (see Minkova 1987), and some began to have doubts about Child's hypothesis: two who attacked it were James Southworth (1957 & 1962) and Ian Robinson (1971). The alternative hypothesis is that Chaucer's lines are anisosyllabic and their verse design is based on four beats, like so much other English verse. But word-final schwa did not disappear entirely in Chaucer's dialect until the fifteenth century (see Minkova 1990), and other scholars sprang to Child's defence, including E. Talbot Donaldson (1948 & 1974) and M. L. Samuels (1972). For discussion of the use of computers in the study of Chaucer's metre see Solopova 2000.

20. Derek Pearsall has shown that two decades later Chaucer was grammatically very precise in the way he used word-final schwa to achieve metrical regularity in *CT* and that this precision was respected by the copyists of the earliest manuscripts (1999: 185–86).

21. The defects that Chaucer expected his audience to find in *The Tale of Sir Thopas* did not end with its lowly (and monotonous) metre: the narrative is slowed by excessive mundane descriptions.

22. Since earlier candidates for the first *endecasillabi* have proved to be seventeenth-century forgeries (Monteverdi 1939 & 1963), this distinction belongs to the lines of Giacomo de Lentini's sonnets (Sanguineti 1965: 15–44), which date from around 1250. The earliest sonnets include some with exclusively *bruschi* or *sdruccioli* rhymes (see Biadene 1899).

23. In the preceding century a number of Italians had become troubadours, but they had written in Occitan, like Boccaccio's Catalan contemporaries (see Billy 2000b: 4–11). For the differences between French and Occitan *vers de dix* and the influence of the latter on the *endecasillabo* see Duffell 2001.

24. As Menichetti 1993 and Billy 2000a point out, the French line, which normally has a first hemistich of 4M, was a bad fit for Italian phonology because of the preponderance of paroxytonic (feminine) words in the language. The mobile caesura and high frequency of synaloepha in the Italian metre make it much easier to accommodate paroxytons in the middle of the line. In the Italian metre lines of 4M + 6 syllables make up less than 20 per cent of total.

25. Lines like (21) are termed *fragmentos adónicos* in Spanish (Ferguson 1981); in English they are regarded as iambic pentameters with an initial inversion in the second hemistich. They are relatively rare; examples are Hamlet's famous line 'To be or not to be; that is the question' (Alexander 1958), which inverts phrasal stress, and Tennyson's 'Much have I seen and known; cities of men' (Ricks 1987), where the inversion involves lexical stress.

26. In Spanish, lines with an anapaestic opening like (22) are termed *melódicos*, and triple-time lines like (23) are termed *endecasílabos de gaita gallega* ('Galician bagpipe lines'). Both are very rare in English; Keats's line 'How many bards gild the lapses of time' (Barnard 1977) is an example of the latter.

27. A very small number of *endecasillabi* have none of these rhythms, and have their stressed syllables (and sometimes their caesurae) in other positions; they are usually classified as *endecasillabi con accenti non canonici* (see Menichetti 1993: 406–16).

28. Of Petrarch's lines, 79 per cent have a duple-time (iambic) close, while triple-time lines like (29) make up just 5 per cent of his total. Of Boccaccio's, 70 per cent have duple-time closes and 15 per cent are triple-time lines. If we accept lines like instance (27) as being iambic with initial inversion in their second hemistichs, Petrarch's proportion of pentameter-like closes rises further to 94 per cent, showing that his verse design is transitional between Boccaccio's and Chaucer's (see Duffell 1991: 305–38). Note that my scansion identifies even positions as ictic only in English instances with iambic (w s) templates.

29. Most candidates for an epic caesura involve words of doubtful syllabification, and most for a lyric caesura words with an alternative accentuation (see Duffell 2000b: 274–76).

30. This expectation is based upon the technique of probability modelling, which can be applied by calculating how often an Italian line would occur in a random mixture of the words in a specific sample of lines (see Duffell 2002b). The difference between expectation and actual in the case of Chaucer's 'Italian' lines equals 4σ for the earlier poems and 6σ for the *GP*; the chances that these differences are the result of sampling error are negligible (for how to calculate σ see the note following Table T).

31. Cressman 1983 argues that these poems were composed over a long period of time and opines that the earliest were completed soon after Gower's arrival in St Mary Overeys in 1377. Cressman assumes that Gower continued writing in French after completing *MO*, but in the years 1377–81 Gower was busy writing and revising the *VC* in Latin, the language of the Priory.

32. Note that the only exceptions to Gower's syllabification of word-final schwa are a few words like *comme* and *Dame*, which were exceedingly common in Insular French poetry, and were probably never pronounced as disyllables in normal speech (see Macaulay 1899: xlv). This may be compared with his treatment of common English words with the same configuration (see n17 above).

33. Gower anticipated French poets of the sixteenth century in ignoring contemporary speech norms and requiring an artificial delivery by his readers. The archaic convention of pronouncing *e-atone* has survived in modern French song and drama.

34. If we classify Gower's lines according to French norms, we can compare the figures with those for poems by Froissart (see Billy 1999 and Billy & Duffell 2005). In Gower 75% of lines subdivide 4M + 6, 13% subdivide 4E + 6, and <1% subdivide 3F + 6 (lyric caesura); the corresponding figures for Froissart are 85%, 6%, and 6%. Both poets occasionally employ erosion in position 4 (see n15 above).

35. Some 78% of Gower's *vers de dix* have no strong syllable in an odd-numbered position compared with 70% of Boccaccio's *endecasillabi*. In a further 10% of Gower's lines a strong syllable in an odd-numbered position is prevented from becoming prominent in delivery by a phrasal stress that immediately follows it; Gower's French long line could therefore be described as 88% iambic.

36. Macaulay's text of *PP* was based on the Trentham MS owned by the Duke of Sutherland. The texts of Gower's work that have survived are remarkable in that they were produced under the poet's supervision. Macaulay 1901: II, xxi–xxvii discusses this metre briefly, Owen 1994: 412 mentions it in a footnote, and Duffell & Billy 2004 offers a detailed analysis. The evidence of these poems should have proved decisive in the twentieth-century dispute over Chaucer's metre (see n. 19 above), because there can be little doubt that Gower counted unelided final schwas so as to make his lines perfectly decasyllabic.

37. Other possible inversions in Gower's text, including some that might be argued to be lyric caesurae, have a better explanation. Just over 10 per cent of Gower's lines contain a word of French origin that it is reasonable to assume should be given its original accentuation, this is particularly the case with words like 'courage' (*P* 160), which also occur in position 10 with rhyme. There are three paroxytons of Germanic origin that offer candidates for lyric caesura: 'wisdom' (*P* 31), 'whilom' (*P* 100), and 'ladi' (*C* 2286), but the final (full) syllable of these words should probably be stressed.

CHAPTER 5

Versifying in
Late Medieval Scotland and England

Politics and Language in Scotland

The kingdom of Scotland was founded in AD 844 when one ruler united the crown of the Scots, who had emigrated from Ireland, with that of the Picts, who had held the land in Roman times. The kingdom initially consisted of Scotland north of the Clyde and Forth, but subsequent kings added the lands to the south. The most fertile area of the country, Lothian, had been part of the kingdom of Northumbria and was populated by Germanic settlers; their tongue (known in Scotland as *Ynglis*) became that of the majority of the population and of the Scottish court. The languages of the Picts and of the Strathclyde Welsh died out, and Scots became the mother tongue only of the clans who inhabited the remote highlands. By the end of the fifteenth century Ynglis had stolen even the name *Scots*, which was thenceforth referred to as *Gaelic*. A number of Scottish kings were raised at their southern neighbour's court (where they were best protected from their relatives) and the two nations' barons often held lands on both sides of the border. English kings, with their greater military resources, often interfered in Scottish affairs and at the end of the thirteenth century one came close to conquest, but Scotland's independence was eventually ensured by the English defeat at Bannockburn in 1314. In 1503 the first Welsh king of England, Henry VII (r. 1485–1509), married his thirteen-year-old daughter Margaret to James IV of Scotland (r. 1488–1513). Although their descendants united the two crowns in 1603 it was not until 1707 that there was a formal union between the two nations.

Medieval Scottish Versification

The language that usurped the name *Scots* was the English of Northumbria, which had acquired numerous French loan words but had not undergone the same vowel changes as southern varieties. Another important difference was that the deletion of word-final schwa, which began as early as the twelfth century, was complete in Scots by the fourteenth. Nevertheless the two varieties of English, like the Insular and mainland varieties of French, remained mutually intelligible, particularly to the educated and the well read. The 'auld alliance' between the Scottish and Valois monarchs ensured that French influence in medieval Scotland was considerable, and both the subject matter and the form of medieval Scottish poetry are witnesses to that influence. As Fitzroy Pyle first pointed out, Scottish poets were schooled not in Insular, but in mainland French (1935: 40–41n14), and consequently their French models were syllabically regular. This is reflected in the way that Scottish poets versified in English, even though they had a similar regard for the number of beats or stresses in their lines as their southern contemporaries. The earliest verse text that has survived in Scots is attributed to a man called Thomas (a very popular name for rhymers), but the earliest major poem in the language is the *Brus* (Gray 1935) by John Barbour (b. ?1320, d. 1390).

The fourteenth-century Scottish short line

Barbour, who had probably studied in both Oxford and Paris, was an archdeacon in Aberdeen; he composed his poem on Robert the Bruce in 1376. The brilliant, spare narrative of the 13,000-line poem is very much to modern tastes; its author's learning sits lightly on him, and he is less prone than his contemporaries to digression or ornamentation for its own sake. Many of the sentiments Barbour expresses also seem incredibly modern: some of his words anticipate the American Declaration of Independence and at times his text sounds like a Hollywood film script, as in the following passage (I. 233–40) on freedom:

(1)   Na <u>he</u>, that <u>ay</u> has **li**-vit <u>free</u>,
(2)   May <u>nocht</u> knaw <u>weill</u> the <u>pro</u>-per-**tie**,
(3)   The <u>an</u>-ger, <u>na</u> the **wre**-chit <u>doom</u>,
(4)   That <u>is</u> **cou**-<u>plit</u> to <u>foul</u> **thrall**-<u>dom</u>.
(5)   But <u>gif</u> he <u>had</u> a-**ssay**-it <u>it</u>,
(6)   Than <u>all</u> per-**quer** he <u>suld</u> it <u>wit</u>;
(7)   And <u>suld</u> think **fre**-dome <u>mair</u> to <u>prize</u>
(8)   Than <u>all</u> the <u>gold</u> in <u>warld</u> that <u>is</u>.

Barbour's short line is octosyllabic, and word-final schwa is not syllabified in the archaic southern manner of Chaucer. The rough octosyllable was the short line favoured by most poets composing in the British Isles at that time, but Barbour's syllable count is exceptionally regular. The lines quoted above all have exactly eight syllables, as do 94 per cent of all lines in the poem, a figure significantly higher than that found in any short-line poem by Chaucer. The irregular lines in Barbour are evenly divided between those with one syllable too few (almost all headless lines), and those with one too many, as in the following examples:

(9)   [V] <u>Fand</u> a **li**-ttle **sun**-ken <u>boat</u>   (III. 47)
(10)   [V] <u>Read</u> to <u>them</u> that <u>were</u> him <u>by</u>   (III. 436)
(11)   And <u>als</u> u-**pon** the **to**-thir **par**-<u>ty</u>   (X. 65)
(12)   Of **si**-ccar **coun**-te-<u>nans</u> and **har**-<u>dy</u>   (XI. 249)

It is clear from the rhyme of these last two lines that 'party' and 'hardy' should be delivered with stress on the final syllable, and there are many similar words in the rhyme position; for example, 'battail' (I. 24), 'Scotland' (I. 27), 'Douglas' (I. 29), 'manere' (III. 410), 'mountain' (X. 27), 'power' (XI. 85), 'menye' (XI. 199), and verb forms in –ing such as 'ending' (I. 34). This stressing appears to have been optional, since many of these words appear elsewhere in the text in positions that suggest a strong–weak accentuation. There are also some inconsistencies in the syllabification of the inflexions '-it' and '-is': for example, 'couplit' in (4) above counts as two syllables, but 'rowit' (III. 27) and 'ruschit' (X. 71) count as one. Similarly 'lochis' (II. 414) counts as two syllables but 'landis' (XI. 147) counts as one, and 'landis renownit' (I. 31) counts as only four syllables in total, while 'hillis' may be either one syllable (XI. 185) or two (X. 20).

Barbour's lines are as iambic as they are octosyllabic: taking into account the ambiguities in stress noted above, some 94 per cent of lines have no strong syllables in a weak position other than the first. In the lines quoted above, 'couplit' in (4) is the only such inversion; other examples of position 3–4 inversion are 'angeris' (X. 101), 'hertis' (X. 102), and 'assemblit' (XI. 84). Judged as iambic tetrameters, Barbour's lines may not be as regular as Gower's, but they are more than a match for Chaucer's. Barbour was clearly developing stress-syllabic verse independently of his English contemporaries; that he mastered such metrics only in the short line is not surprising, since he almost certainly had neither Italian nor knowledge of the *endecasillabo*. On the other hand, he must have encountered the *vers de dix* in the work of mainland French poets; his choice of the octosyllable was therefore a decision to work in units of eight syllables rather than four and six. It was also a rejection of another option: the prevailing Scottish long-line metre of his day.

The fourteenth-century Scottish long line

The long-line metre of Barbour's Scotttish contemporaries was very similar to the alliterative metre of *Sir Gawain and the Green Knight*, as the opening lines of the fifteenth-century poem 'The Knightly Tale of Golagros and Gawane' (Amours 1897) show:

(13)   In the <u>tyme</u> of Ar-**thur**, || as <u>trew</u> men me <u>tald</u>
(14)   The king **tur**-nit on ane <u>tyde</u> || to-**ward** Tus-**kane**,
(15)   Hym to <u>seik</u> our the <u>sey</u>, || that **saik**-lese wes <u>sald</u>,
(16)   The <u>syre</u> that **sen**-dis all seill, || **suth**-ly to <u>sane</u>

The strophe design of this poem comprises thirteen lines that subdivide 8 + 5, contrasting with the contemporary French *treizain*, which subdivided 6 + 7, 5 + 8, or 4 + 9. Strophes of 8 + 5 lines or 8 + 6 are employed in a number of English and Scottish alliterative poems of the fourteenth and fifteenth centuries (see Fein 2000 and Kennedy 2000a). Both strophe forms are constructed on the same principle: an octave of four-beat lines precedes a bob and wheel containing shorter lines with fewer beats. The octave of 'Golagros and Gawane' has the most common rhyme scheme, ab ab ab ab, and its lines are typical of alliterative metre, comprising two hemistichs, each with either two or (occasionally) three beats marked by stress and alliteration. The five lines that follow could be described as a wheel without a bob, as can be seen from the close of the first strophe:

(17)   **Du**-kis and <u>digne</u> **lor**-dis, **douch**-ty and <u>deir</u>,
(18)   **Sem**-bi-llit <u>to</u> his **su**-mmovne,
(19)   **Ren**-kis of <u>grete</u> re-**nov**ne,

(20) **Cum**-ly **kin**-gis with <u>crovne</u>
(21) Of **gold** that was **cleir**

The transition from the octave is not marked by a single-beat line, but by a normal four-beat line with a new rhyme; then follow three lines each with three beats, and a final line of two beats. The rhyme scheme of the last five lines is cdddc, and both line length and rhymes can be described in the strophe by using subscript digits in the formula $abababab_4 \, c_4eee_3c_2$.

A number of the lines in the strophe quoted above are in triple time, or would be if the inflexions -*it* and -*is* were desyllabified (and we have seen from Barbour's poem that they probably often were). But many lines of this poem are in even clearer triple time, for example, the following:

(22) Of **sil**-uer and **sa**-phir || **schir**-ly thai <u>schane</u>   (22)
(23) **Moun**-tains an **ma**-rresse, || with **mo**-ny rank <u>myre</u>   (30)
(24) With **to**-rris and **tu**-ra-tis || **teir**-full to <u>tell</u>   (42)

As Scottish (and English) alliterative poets increasingly favoured such lines with a triple-time rhythm, so their long-line metre became indistinguishable from tumbling verse, which retained its popularity until late in the sixteenth century.

Chaucer's English Heirs

In the year 1400, which marks the end of the metrical careers of both Chaucer and Gower, Thomas Hoccleve (d. 1426) and John Lydgate (d. 1449) were both almost exactly thirty years old. They remained rivals for the favours of their Lancastrian rulers until Hoccleve's death, but in his own time Lydgate was by far the more famous and successful. Both are sometimes regarded as Chaucer's followers or successors, but that relationship is an oversimplification. Hoccleve may have known both the great poets of the previous generation: in *The Regiment of Princes* (hereafter *RP*) he addresses Chaucer as 'mayster dere and fadir reuerent' (line 1962) and Gower as 'my mayster Gower' (line 1975). On the other hand, although Lydgate borrowed some of his subject matter from Chaucer and made many references to his greatness, we cannot be sure that he even met him (see Renoir 1967: 56).

Hoccleve worked for nearly forty years as a clerk in the office of the Privy Seal, and seems to have dissipated most of the income from his modest salary, late-paid pension, and the occasional windfall. He repeatedly sought patronage and benefices, but with meagre success, and he frequently complains of his cash-flow problem in his work. Hoccleve wrote only one really long poem, *RP*, a translation and adaptation of three different Latin works for the benefit of the young Prince Henry which amounted to five and a half thousand lines. His best poetry is contained in a number of relatively short poems that tell us about his personal life: his impoverished marriage, his mental illness, and much else.

Hoccleve is a more attractive poet than Lydgate in many ways: his narrative gifts, modesty, humour, and sensitivity enliven his work. In his lifetime his reputation was eclipsed because of Lydgate's greater industry, and posterity has always viewed Hoccleve as a diminutive talent in Chaucer's shadow. Hoccleve is important to the history of English metrics because his work shows clearly that he understood the revolutionary new metrics of the poets he calls his masters, and that he could often use it to produce effective poetry.

Lydgate outlived Hoccleve and became the most famous English poet of his century, but he outshone his rival for royal and public esteem by quantity rather than quality; he composed ten times as many lines as Hoccleve. Lydgate's work was in great demand: whether you were a Lancastrian spin doctor wanting a translation of a French bestseller, or a local government boss needing some verse for a pageant, John Lydgate was the man. Starting life as a Suffolk ploughboy, Lydgate showed an early talent for Latin and was welcomed into the monastic life. He then translated and versified his way to fame and became the trusted servant of princes; although the latter invariably paid late, Lydgate never experienced the hardship that plagued Hoccleve. But he also seems to have missed out on the pleasure, being devoted to one Lady only, the Queen of Heaven, and he wrote best when he wrote for her. Lydgate composed a number of poems of immense length, based on French or Latin originals: 30,000 lines of *The Troy Book* between 1412 and 1420, 24,000 of *The Pilgrimage of Man* between 1426 and 1430, and 36,000 of *The Fall of Princes* between 1431 and 1438. In between he undertook numerous smaller commissions, so that in total well over 100,000 lines of his verse have survived.

Lydgate's poetry bores modern readers because he had no narrative gift and overused the devices that were the stock-in-trade of medieval writers: he embellished his work with numerous references to scripture, literature, and legend, and he missed no opportunity to moralize or preach a sermon. But his work is full of what in the Middle Ages passed for wisdom; it enhanced its readers' intellectual and moral status, and its bulk must have helped fill long rainy days in court and cloister.

Hoccleve's decasyllabic long line

The most incisive modern metrical analysis of Hoccleve's long-line verse can be found in two articles by Judith Jefferson, the first focusing on the syllable count of the long-line verse in the holograph (1987) and the second on its accentuation (2000). I shall draw heavily on her observations here and attempt to relate them to Hanson & Kiparsky's parametric theory (1996) and to my own study of Hoccleve's verse (Duffell 1991: 483–88). The texts Jefferson analysed are 'The Letter to Cupid' and 'The Series' in the Hoccleve holographs, and, in particular, all the metrically unambiguous lines (those with no words of doubtful syllable count or accentuation).[1] My statistical analysis was of the 'Complaint of the Virgin' and a 300-line sample from *RP* (Seymour 1981).

Hoccleve's strophe forms are those established by Chaucer, in particular the rhyme royal of *Troilus and Criseyde*, and he employed the long line for both *RP* and his less formal verse. The similarities between Hoccleve's long line and Chaucer's can be seen from this example of the modesty topos in lines 2078–79:

> (25) And **fa**-dir, **Chau**-cer <u>fayn</u> wold^e <u>han</u> me <u>taght</u>
> (26) But <u>I</u> was <u>dul</u> and **ler**-ned <u>lyt</u>^e or <u>naght</u>

These lines are clearly iambic pentameters if word-final schwa is elided before a vowel or letter 'h'. Before a consonant such schwas contribute to the syllable count as in the following line:

> (27) Re-**cor**-dyng <u>in</u> my **myn**-de <u>the</u> le-**sson**   (2010)

A few common words ending in schwa, however, are always treated by Hoccleve as monosyllables; examples include *swiche* (990), *sothe* (1898), *where* (1918), and *whyche* (1936).

Jefferson's analysis is of the poems in the holograph, where the syllable count adheres more closely to 10M/F syllables, but the surviving manuscripts of other poems contain many lines with at least one syllable missing, for example:

> (28) Con-**sy**-de-<u>ring</u> [V] <u>how</u> that <u>I</u> am <u>nouȝt</u>   (976)
> (29) [V] <u>thys</u> fals **tre**-son **co**-men <u>ys</u> and <u>ryf</u>   (1941)

These lines are possibly the result of copyists' errors, but I have scanned them with voids in position 5 and 1, because broken-backed and headless lines also occur in Chaucer, and we have no good reason to believe that Hoccleve would have censored them in his own verse. In my sample from *RP* 94 per cent of lines have 10M/F syllables and the remainder may be regarded as deviations of a type that Chaucer had also employed on occasion.

Some earlier writers were prepared to accept that Hoccleve's long line is a pentameter, in the sense that its verse design is decasyllabic, but argued that it fails to be iambic (see, for example, Furnivall 1897: xli, Saintsbury 1906: I, 232, and Hammond 1925: 55). Jefferson, however, shows that Hoccleve's choice of language and word order strongly favours an iambic rhythm and that many of the departures from that rhythm in the manuscripts could be simple scribal errors (2000: 212–22). My statistics for *RP* indicate that approximately 93 per cent of Hoccleve's lines are consistent with a constraint against strong syllables in weak positions; among the remaining 7 per cent are:

> (30) The <u>moost</u> **la**-<u>kke</u> that <u>han</u> the **lor**-des **grete**   (1926)
> (31) Of <u>my</u> **sim**-<u>ple</u> con-**ceyt** wol <u>I</u> the <u>clasp</u>   (1956)

A further 7 per cent of lines have a stressed monosyllable in a weak position like the following line:

> (32) But <u>syn</u> our^e <u>lord</u> Cryst <u>was</u> o-**be**-di-<u>ent</u>   (1979)

In normal speech the monosyllable 'Cryst' in position 5 would receive strong phrasal stress; this apparent inversion can be regarded as an example of *demotion* (Attridge 1982: 168–72), or as evidence that only lexically strong syllables are constrained by the verse design.

There can be no doubt that Hoccleve's verse is predominantly iambic as well as decasyllabic, and Jefferson concludes that Hoccleve's metre is best described in terms of 'avoidance strategies' rather than of adherence to an iambic template (2000: 223–25). She argues that he intended his lines to be decasyllables and imposed Chaucer's five-beat norm on most of them, and he avoided a succession of lines with triple-time rhythm and only four beats. The result is another type of what Tarlinskaja calls the transitional iamb (1976: 128), one that, unlike ictic verse, gives primacy to syllable count. In any account of the progress of the iambic pentameter, Hoccleve's metre must appear as a clear step backwards from that of his masters.

The metre of Lydgate's short and long lines

The main features of Lydgate's metrics can be seen from the statistics that follow, which first appeared in Duffell 2000a. My figures were based on an analysis of Lydgate's poem 'Mumming at London' (hereafter *ML*; MacCracken 1911), composed *c.* 1427, and of a random sample of lines from his *Life of Our Lady* (hereafter *LOL*; Norton-Smith 1966), composed *c.* 1434; the chief findings were then verified by a study of *The Troy Book* (Edwards 1998), completed *c.* 1420.

The most obvious of feature of Lydgate's short and long lines is their irregular syllable count: even under the most favourable assumption more than a quarter do not contain the mode number of syllables (eight and ten respectively).[2] Josef Schick attempted to categorize the irregularities of the long line in his study of Lydgate's *Temple of Glas* (1891), and he showed that most of the syllabic irregularity stems from Lydgate's omission or addition of an unstressed syllable at the beginning of the line or after the caesura. This feature can be seen clearly in the following lines from *LOL*:

> (33)   For <u>she</u> is the <u>tour</u> || wi-**thou**-tyn **wor**-des <u>moo</u>   (26)
> (34)   That **ne**-uer <u>man</u> || [V] **en**-tre <u>shall</u> ne <u>pace</u>   (55)
> (35)   [V] **Cau**-seth <u>all</u> || no **won**-dre þat I <u>sayde</u>   (174)

Instance (33) has an extra syllable in the first hemistich, (34) is broken-backed, and (35) is headless; all these irregularities occur in Chaucer's verse, but they are much more common in Lydgate's: they make up more than one-third of total in both his short and long lines. In just over 2 per cent of lines two syllables are missing, usually because both hemistichs lack an initial syllable, but sometimes because one hemistich lacks both, as in the following line:

> (36)   That **ne**-uer <u>man</u> || [V] <u>myght</u> [V] <u>yet</u> vn-**close**   (30)

Such lines led MacCracken to consider the possibility that Lydgate is mixing four- and five-beat lines in the same poem (1911: viii), but this is contra-indicated by the fact that lines that are unambiguously four-beat never appear in Lydgate's long-line poems. My scansion of (36) also makes this line mimetic: the second hemistich's close-packed stresses make it unusually 'tight' and virginal/vaginal. Other examples of possible four-beat lines in Lydgate's long-line poems have a better explanation, namely that Lydgate intended some word-final schwas to be syllabified; for example:

> (37)   The **lar**-ge **mo**-ne || <u>bryght</u> and **no**-thyng <u>pale</u>   (114)

Pearsall 1999 shows that Chaucer invariably syllabified adjectival final schwas like that in *newe* before a consonant, and this practice seems to have endured into the next century.[3] Minkova notes that such schwas were the last to survive and points out that their syllabification was eurhythmic (1990: 321–30). Syllabifying the final schwa of *mone* in (37) is equally important to its rhythm, and my statistical analysis shows that the average syllable count of Lydgate's lines with word-final schwas is closest to that of his schwa-less lines if word-final schwa is syllabified thus between two stressed syllables.

As a result of the omission and insertion of unstressed syllables in Lydgate's verse, barely 80 per cent of his lines in either metre are iambic, and this 'roughness' of rhythm offended critics of Saintsbury's generation (who had recently rediscovered the regularity of Chaucer and Gower) and of the generation that followed. They heaped scorn on Lydgate and his lack of skill as a versifier; thus Saintsbury described him as 'a doggerel poet with an insensitive ear' (1906: 1, 223), and Hammond went further, accusing him of intellectual mediocrity as well as lack of talent (1927: 152). Subsequent critics were kinder: Pyle 1937 and Lewis 1938 thought that Lydgate might not have been trying to compose decasyllables at all, and Pearsall 1970 was also convinced that Lydgate's deviations in syllable count were part of his verse design. Pearsall also pointed out that Saintsbury's generation had only poorly edited texts of a corpus that was not entirely Lydgate's (1970: 60). In the same year Hascall offered a linguistic description of Lydgate's long-line verse design accompanied by a call for justice, if not enthusiasm, when judging Lydgate's verse (1970: 145). Hascall concluded that Lydgate's verse design allowed weak positions to contain not only one syllable but also either a void or the two syllables of a phonological word (1970: 140–41). He also pointed out that reading Chaucer's verse without syllabifying word-final schwa (as became the practice between the fifteenth and nineteenth centuries) must have made his lines sound exactly like Lydgate's (1970: 142). Thus Lydgate, it might be argued, was simply bringing Chaucer's metre up to date, but in a different way from later poets.

Lydgate's updating of the iambic pentameter consisted of sacrificing the weak-position size of one syllable, perfected by Gower, in deference to the unpredictability of his readers' pronunciation of words ending in schwa. In the fifteenth century such a sacrifice was feasible because iambic verse was a recent development, and depended on a delivery that was already archaic at the end of the fourteenth century. Lydgate's short line is a line of four beats and his long line one of five; a five-beat line preserved one of Chaucer's most important innovations, but Lydgate rejected others: as well as the position size of one syllable, he abandoned the freely variable caesura that Chaucer had borrowed from Italy. As Pyle points out, almost all of Lydgate's long lines have a word boundary between the second and third strong positions, making the line one of 2 + 3 beats. Lydgate's choices of a four-beat line with no caesura and a five-beat line divided 2 + 3 are likely to have been influenced by his familiarity with French verse, of which he translated many thousands of lines. The lack of caesura in his shorter metre allows lines like the following line from *ML*:

(38) Hir <u>pompe</u>, her **sur-quy-<u>dye</u>**, hir <u>pride</u>   (121)

Here the second and third beats are provided by the same word.

The hypothesis that Lydgate's long-line verse design has a caesura between the second and third beats is supported by 97.5 per cent of his lines; such a formula allows both lines of 4 + 6, like the *vers de dix*, and lines of 4F + 5M (*coupe italienne*); an example of the latter is the following line from *LOL*:

(39) She <u>was</u> the **cas**-tell <u>of</u> the **cris**-tall <u>wall</u>   (29)

Many of the 2.5 per cent of lines in *LOL* where beats 2 and 3 appear to be in the same word have a more consistent alternative scansion; for example, the following line:

(40)a   And <u>hathe</u> no **che**-ry-<u>shyng</u> || but <u>the</u> sonne <u>shene</u>   (45)

But this line reads far better if we assume that 'cheryshyng' should be subject to syncope and that the schwa between the last two stresses should be syllabified, thus:

(40)b   And <u>hathe</u> no **che**-r^yshyng || <u>but</u> the **son**-ne <u>shene</u>   (45)

Lydgate's verse design not only has a mandatory word boundary between its second and third beats, it allows lines like the following, which in the *vers de dix* would be described as having epic caesura:

(41)   With **sil**-uer **dro**-pes || v-**pon** the **le**-ves <u>fayre</u>   (34)

Many other lines in *LOL* are analogous to *vers de dix* with lyric caesura, with positions 3 and 4 occupied by a paroxytonic word, for example, 'starres' (110) or 'increseth' (159).

   Although Lydgate's verse designs seem to be influenced by French metres, his setting weak-position size at between zero and two syllables produces ictic verse, both four-beat and five-beat. Lewis 1938 notes that Lydgate's metrics is thus a reversion to a much earlier English tradition, and Hammond 1927 records that Lydgate's mode of versifying was followed by every poet writing in the period between Hoccleve and Surrey. But Chaucer's influence was not entirely lost: he gave fifteenth-century English poets the five-beat line, and he gave them a taste for the line we call the iambic pentameter. As Chaucer's lines were robbed of final schwas, however, his readers perceived the lines that remained iambic as the poet's preference rather than his norm; they also lost the distinction between Chaucer's metre and Lydgate's. The iambic pentameter continued to be cultivated in the fifteenth century, but it was one, not the only, realization of the late Middle English long-line verse design, the five-beat ictic metre.

Post-Chaucerian Iambic Verse: Two Royal Prisoners

In 1405 one of Scotland's many child-kings fell into English hands while fleeing from a murderous uncle. James I (r. 1424–70) of Scotland was eleven years old when he first arrived in London in 1405, and he remained a prisoner until 1424, when the Scottish lords ransomed him and set him on his ancestors' throne. The terms of James's captivity were not so onerous as to prevent him writing poetry and finding an English consort. His love poem, *The Kingis Quair* (Mackenzie 1939), was composed in the latter part of that period, by which time the king of England had another royal prisoner. Charles Duc d'Orléans, brother of the French king, was captured at Agincourt in 1415; he remained a prisoner in England until his return to France in 1440, and remained politically influential until his death in 1465. Charles composed a considerable body of poems in French (Champion 1907), mostly in *octosyllabes* and *vers de dix*, which were technically very polished. In the twenty-five years of his captivity he became fluent in English, and he also composed a large body of verse in that language (Steele 1941). He was a master of the most popular contemporary French forms, the *ballade* and *rondel*, and he composed both French and English versions of some poems. Most of Charles's English lines are also either octosyllabic or decasyllabic, but their versification is very different from that of his French poetry.

James I's long line

The metre of *The Kingis Quair* ('The King's Book', hereafter *KQ*) resembles the long line of Chaucer more closely than that of either Hoccleve or Lydgate. This can be seen from the following lines (11–14) from 'Cantus' (Mackenzie's text, given in Scott 1967):

> (42) From <u>beugh</u> to <u>beugh</u> they **hip**-pit <u>and</u> thai <u>plaid</u>,
> (43) And **fresch**-ly <u>in</u> thair **bir**-dis <u>kynd</u> a-**rraid**
> (44) Thair **fe**-th^eris <u>new</u>, and <u>fret</u> thame <u>in</u> the <u>sonne</u>,
> (45) And **than**-kit <u>lufe</u>, that <u>had</u> thair **ma**-kis <u>wonne</u>.

These instances clearly meet the definition of iambic pentameter. They also have a word boundary after position 4, but James's metre cannot be considered a *vers de dix* because many of his lines have no such caesura; for example, the following lines from 'Stanzas':

> (46) Quhare, <u>throu</u> the **gra**-vel, <u>bryght</u> as **o**-ny <u>gold</u>   (4)
> (47) The **cris**-tall **wa**-ter <u>ran</u> so <u>clere</u> and <u>cold</u>   (5)

These lines are of the type I have termed 'Italian' (4F + 5), and they constitute approximately 17 per cent of total; this is far short of the 31 per cent found in *The Canterbury Tales*. Thus James's imitation of Chaucer's metre does not stretch to the finer point of using such lines as a contrast with ones subdivided 4 + 6, and unbroken sequences of twenty of the latter are common in *KQ*.

James's treatment of word-final schwa is very different from Chaucer's and Gower's: it follows the normal speech practice of the 1420s rather than an artificial convention based on archaism and foreign metrics. Counting word-final schwas before a consonant makes James's lines much less regular both syllabically and accentually. In the above examples 'thame' (44), 'lufe' (45), 'quhare' (46), and 'clere' (47) must all be monosyllables, as must 'sonne' (44) and 'wonne' (45), because such words are rhymed freely elsewhere in James's work with words not ending in schwa. It greatly increases the regularity of James's verse, however, if adjectival word-final schwa is syllabified for eurhythmic reasons between adjacent stresses, as in Lydgate's instance (40) above. For example, we find the following lines in *KQ* (the first from 'Cantus', the second and third from 'Stanzas'):

> (48) There <u>was</u> no **ta**-kyn <u>in</u> her **sue**-te <u>face</u>   (56)
> (49) The **sla**-we <u>as</u>, the **drug**-gar <u>beste</u> of <u>pyne</u>   (25)
> (50) The **ny**-ce <u>ape</u>; the **wer**^e-ly **por**-pa-<u>pyne</u>   (26)

At first sight 18 per cent of James's lines appear not to have 10M/F syllables, but this figure is reduced to 3 per cent if we syllabify adjectival final schwas for eurhythmic reasons as in my scansion of 'suete' (48), 'slawe' (49), and 'nyce' (50). The remaining 3 per cent can almost all be classified as headless or broken-backed lines; this figure is not dissimilar to that we find in Chaucer. Both a headless and a broken-backed line are found in 'Stanzas':

> (51) [V] <u>Sche</u> held <u>not</u>, bot <u>ay</u> in **va**-ri-<u>ance</u>   (70)
> (52) An **ug**-ly <u>pit</u> [V] <u>depe</u> as **o**-ny <u>helle</u>   (72)

James's verse is also as iambic as Chaucer's (or Gower's): only 4 per cent of lines in *KQ* have a strong syllable in a weak position, as in the following line from 'Cantus', where an inversion in positions 7–8 makes it a *fragmento adónico*:

> (53) And <u>sing</u> with <u>me</u>, a-**way**, **win**-<u>ter</u> a-**way**!   (3)

From these statistics and examples we can see that James's metre can be classified as iambic pentameter. The orthography of *KQ* shows that James wrote in the Scots variety of English, which had long completed the deletion of word-final schwas. His rules for syllabifying final schwas seem to be very similar to Lydgate's, but his metre is that of Chaucer and Gower. James's long line differs from Hoccleve's in that iambic rhythm is the Scottish king's chief priority, while syllable count is the Englishman's.

Charles d'Orléans's short line

Charles's English short line resembles Chaucer's in that, among his octosyllables, we find lines with a syllable too many or too few; they are, however, relatively rare. Both types of deviation from an 8M/F norm can be seen in the following lines (3639–42; I follow the text and numbering of Steele 1941):

> (54) My **gost**-ly **fa**-dir y <u>me</u> con-**fesse**
> (55) [V] <u>First</u> to <u>god</u> and <u>then</u> to <u>yow</u>
> (56) That <u>at</u> a **win**-dow <u>wot</u> ye <u>how</u>
> (57) I <u>stale</u> a <u>cosse</u> of <u>gret</u> swet-**nes**

Instance (55) is headless, after the established English fashion, and (54) has something like an epic caesura, producing a disyllabic weak position of the type sanctioned by Lydgate's verse design. Charles's English short lines differ from his French *octosyllabes* in this occasional variation of syllable count and, even more radically, in their rhythm. His English verse also differs greatly from Lydgate's: more than 95 per cent of the Charles's lines are not only octosyllabic, they are also regularly iambic, with no strong syllable of a polysyllabic word in a weak position (other than the first). Charles's short line may not be as regular an iambic tetrameter as Gower's, but it is more regular than Chaucer's. This suggests that Chaucer's and Gower's innovations were well understood by some poets in the second quarter of the fifteenth century, even though the two pioneers' treatment of word-final schwa was no longer viable.

Charles d'Orléans's long line

Charles's long line is as iambic and as regular in syllable count as his short; the following lines (4089–92) have all the features of the canonical iambic pentameter:

> (58) For **vn**-to **way**-lyng **we**-pyng <u>and</u> dis-**tres**
> (59) From <u>this</u> tyme <u>forth</u> bi-**co**-men <u>must</u> y <u>thral</u>
> (60) Syn <u>that</u> y <u>may</u> not <u>stroke</u> the **si**-dis <u>smal</u>
> (61) Of <u>yowre</u> swete **bo**-dy <u>ful</u> of <u>lus</u>-ty-<u>nes</u>

Note that the first and last of these are 'Italian' lines of 4F + 5; Charles, however, used relatively few of them, and they represent just over 6 per cent of his total. The verse design of the French 4 + 6 metre seems to have been in the back of his mind when he composed in English, yet he mastered the nuances of the English metre: he avoided strong syllables in weak positions (at least in 98 per cent of his lines); he used alliteration to great effect, as in (58) and (60); and he made the new monosyllables serve his metre. In the long term, English poets solved the metrical problem of a glut of stressed monosyllables by demotion, the subordination of their stress to a neighbouring one, not the eurhythmic syllabification of word-final schwas. Charles employs demotion here to achieve an iambic rhythm in 'this tyme forth' (59) and 'yowre swete body' (61). But, while Charles (like Lydgate) tended to demote the second of three stressed syllables, he often syllabified adjectival final schwa when only two clashing stresses were concerned, as in the following lines:

> (62) As **al**-le **de**-dis <u>of</u> my **la**-dy <u>dere</u>   (421)
> (63) If <u>hit</u> plese <u>yow</u> of **yow**-re **cur**-te-<u>sy</u>   (556)

If we disallow this treatment of word-final schwa, then 6 per cent of Charles's lines lack a syllable; but if we accept it as the early-fifteenth-century norm, his deviation from 10M/F syllables is negligible, reduced to a handful of headless lines, like the following:

> (64) [V] <u>Ne</u>-uyr-**more** to <u>loue</u> oft <u>have</u> I <u>thought</u>   (381)

The examples above show that Charles's long line is very strongly iambic: possible inversions are nearly all of words of French origin and ambiguous accentuation, such as 'servaunt' (oxytonic in line 213 of Steele's text, but paroxytonic in 217) and 'plesaunce'/'plesaunt' (oxytonic in line 404, but paroxytonic in 249). Only a small proportion of lines (just over 2 per cent of total) contain inversions of Germanic words, and these are often grammatical words with little stress, as in:

> (65) Of <u>alle</u> that <u>lyue</u> god <u>wot</u> **vn**-<u>dir</u> the <u>sky</u>   (464)

The rhythm of this line is very like that of Gower's instance (49) in Chapter 4: it is a *fragmento adónico*, and the stress in position 6 prevents the strong syllable in 7 from becoming prominent in delivery.

It is clear that the verse of both James I and Charles d'Orléans is more regularly iambic than that of the two native poets, Hoccleve and Lydgate. But James spoke a schwa-deleted language from infancy, and Charles had mastered syllabic versifying in French and was unencumbered by an alternative tradition of counting beats. The metrics of the two royal prisoners is sufficiently remarkable to deserve a place in the history of versifying in English: their stress–syllabic verse was smoother and more skilful than any composed in England for the next eighty years.

Chaucer's Scottish Heirs

When James I returned to Scotland, he had more urgent things to do than write poetry, but he did manage to re-establish the Scottish royal court as a place of international culture. The hundred years from 1420 to 1520 have left us the work of four major Scottish poets, each representing a different generation: James I himself, Robert Henryson (b. ?1424, d. ?1506), William Dunbar (b. ?1456, d. ?1513), and Gavin Douglas (b. ?1475, d. 1522). The last three were educated men of differing family backgrounds; they all attended university and received a theological training (although only the last two were ordained), but Henryson became a Dunfermline schoolmaster, while the young aristocrat Douglas became Bishop of Dunkeld. Dunbar, whose family ranked somewhere between those of the other two, spent much of his life at court, where he became a great favourite of the queen, but he failed to obtain the sort of preferment that Douglas achieved.

The poets of fifteenth-century Scotland, as Scott 1967: 13–18 notes, were closely in touch with the literary fashions of France and Italy; the work of Dante, Boccaccio, and Petrarch was read and admired, and Scots poets were greatly influenced by the group of French poets known as the *rhétoriqueurs*, which included Froissart, Granson, and Alain Chartier (b. ?1390, d. ?1440). The work of the four Scottish poets discussed here is clearly linked: Henryson was probably familiar with *KQ*, and Dunbar paid tribute to Henryson in one of his poems, while Douglas, who began his career at the time when Dunbar was unofficial court poet, must have known the latter's work. The most visible link between their poetry, however, is in its versification, which was more strongly influenced by Chaucer and by traditional Scots verse than by any continental model. Collectively the four poets have been called the 'Scottish Chaucerians', and Henryson's debt to Chaucer is apparent in several of his poems. *The Testament of Cresseid* begins with Henryson's reading *Troilus and Criseyde*, and the rest of the poem is what these days we would call a 'spin-off', although Henryson attributes it to another source.

The analysis of Henryson's and Dunbar's metrics that follows is based on the text of Bawcutt & Riddy 1992, and that of Douglas's on the text of Coldwell 1957, and all the verse instances quoted are from those editions. Before proceeding with that analysis, however, it is worth reflecting on the relationship between the metre and the language of fifteenth-century Scottish poetry. These poets composed in a dialect in which word-final schwa had long ceased to be pronounced, and the syllable count and rhythm of their verse shows this clearly. All four employed a long line that was both decasyllabic and iambic, and there is little doubt that its model was Chaucer's iambic pentameter.

Henryson's short and long lines

Although Henryson employed the long line he derived from Chaucer in most of his verse, he chose traditional native metres for two of his poems. His humorous poem

'Sum Practysis of Medecyne' is in the same alliterative metre and thirteen-line strophe as 'Gologros and Gawane', and his short tale of rural romance 'Robene and Makyne' is in common measure. The design of Henryson's short lines specifies four and three beats, not eight and six syllables, as the following lines show clearly:

(66) **Ro**-bene <u>sat</u> on <u>gud</u> grene <u>hill</u>   (1)
(67) **Ke**-pand a <u>flok</u> of <u>fe</u>   (2)
(68) '**Ma**-kyne, the <u>nicht</u> is <u>soft</u> and <u>dry</u>   (98)
(69) The **wed**-der is <u>warme</u> and <u>fair</u>   (99)

[fe: 'sheep']

Such a metre is, of course, entirely appropriate to the subject and, together with the alliterative poem, it establishes Henryson's metrical versatility.

Henryson, however, employed the same long-line metre for most of his verse, including his long poems, *The Testament of Cresseid* and the *Fables* (both in rhyme royal), and *Orpheus and Eurydice*, which begins in rhyme royal and closes in rhymed couplets. Henryson's long line is a strictly counted decasyllable, and its iambic rhythm is obvious to modern readers, because word-final schwa is not included in the count. But it is only marginally more iambic than Hoccleve's long line — 15 per cent of Henryson's lines contain a non-initial inversion, and 89 per cent have an iambic second hemistich (the corresponding figures for Hoccleve are 14 per cent and 86 per cent). But a clear iambic pulse runs through the vast majority of lines, as is illustrated by the following from *The Testament of Cresseid* (hereafter *TC*):

(70) To <u>cut</u> the **win**-ter <u>nicht</u> and <u>mak</u> it <u>schort</u>   (39)
(71) I <u>tuik</u> ane <u>quair</u> — and <u>left</u> all **u**-ther <u>sport</u>   (40)

These examples show that Henryson mixed 'Italian' lines with no word boundary between positions 4 and 5 (70) with lines that subdivide 4 + 6 like the French *vers de dix* (71). But 'Italian' lines represent only 14 per cent of Henryson's total, compared with 24 per cent in *Troilus and Criseyde* and 31 per cent in *The Canterbury Tales*. Henryson not only failed to follow Chaucer in boosting the proportion of Italian lines in the interests of rhythmic variety, he seems to have preferred to avoid them.[4] Moreover, a preference for lines dividing 4 + 6 is not the only way in which Henryson's line is more like the *vers de dix* than Chaucer's: the Scots poet employs lyric caesura in 7 per cent of the lines of *TC*, including the following:[5]

(72) For <u>I</u> **trais**-<u>tit</u> || that **Ve**-nus, **lui**-fis <u>quene</u>   (22)
(73) To <u>all</u> **god**-<u>dis</u> || he <u>dois</u> baith <u>lak</u> and <u>schame</u>   (276)

Henryson also employs epic caesura on a number of occasions, but we cannot be sure how frequently; for example, we find the following lines:

(74) **Doc**-tour in **phi**-sick, || cled <u>in</u> ane **skar**-lot <u>goun</u>   (250)
(75) **Wrin**-<u>gand</u> his **han**-dis || of-**tymes** he <u>said</u> a-**llace**   (374)
(76) That <u>he</u> had **le**-vit || to <u>se</u> that **wo**-full <u>hour</u>   (375)

Instance (74) is the clearest epic caesura here; we cannot be absolutely sure about (75) and (76), because Henryson may have intended the inflexions *-is* and *-it* to be desyllabified — in some of his lines they do not seem to contribute to the syllable count. But the existence of lines such as (74) makes it much more likely that 'handis' and 'levit' are meant to be disyllabic (like 'traistit' and 'goddis' in (72) and (73) above), and that all the lines like these have epic caesurae.

As I have noted, French influence on Scottish culture was strong throughout the fifteenth century, and we should therefore not be surprised when we find French metrical features creeping into Henryson's long-line verse. While Chaucer's line was undoubtedly the chief model for Henryson's metre, the *vers de dix* of his French contemporaries provided an alternative design for a decasyllable, and the Scottish poet seems to have made more than occasional use of it. It could be argued that Henryson's use of epic and lyric caesurae helps provide his verse with a similar variety in line structure to that which Chaucer achieved by boosting his proportion of 'Italian' lines. In summary, we can say that Henryson's long line is almost iambic pentameter, but that it admits features of the *vers de dix* that the canonical English metre does not.

Dunbar's short and long lines

Dunbar's reputation as a very accomplished metrist is fully justified (see Bawcutt & Riddy 1992: xiii); he employed a variety of different strophe designs and verse designs with great skill. His strophe designs include the rhyme royal of *The Thrissill and the Rois*, the elaborate nine-line stanza (rhymed aab aab bab) of *The Goldyn Targe*, monorhyme quatrains and quintains, strophes with Latin heads and tails, and a variety of ballad metres (rhyming ab, aab, or aaab). Among his various verse designs he employed a variety of short- and long-line metres, both stress-syllabic (the tetrameter and pentameter) and traditional (the alliterative long line and ictic short line). In his eighty surviving poems Dunbar always seems to choose the most appropriate form for his subject. For example, his four-beat line, which is very close to iambic tetrameter in his formal religious poems, becomes ictic in his fun poems. Thus in 'Rorate, celi, desuper' we find syllabic regularity and a prevailing iambic rhythm in both the English and the Latin lines:

(77)	He-<u>vins</u> dis-**till** your **bal**-my **schou**ris	(2)
(78)	For <u>now</u> is **ris**^{sin} the <u>brycht</u> day <u>ster</u>	(3)
(79)	Fro <u>the</u> ros, **Ma**-ry, <u>flour</u> of **flou**ris.	(4)
(80)	*Et **no**-bis **pu**-er **na**-tus <u>est</u>*	(8)

There is a constraint against strong syllables in weak positions in this poem, with an initial inversion in (77), and erosion of the first ictus in (79) and the third in (78) by the article 'the'. In contrast to this poem's prevailing iambic rhythm, Dunbar's humorous poem 'Sir John Sinclair Begowthe the Dance' is in an ictic metre that allows both void and disyllabic weak positions, as can be seen from the following lines:

(81)	[V] <u>Then</u> cam <u>in</u> [V] **Dun**-bar the **mac**kar	(22)
(82)	And <u>to</u> the **dan**-ceing <u>soin</u> he him <u>med</u>	(46)

When Dunbar composed his 'Now Lythis of Ane Gentill Knycht', his tale of Sir Thomas Norny, he appositely employed the strophe and metre of Chaucer's *Sir Thopas*; but the Scots poet knew when to say 'namore': he limited the poem to nine strophes.

Dunbar's metrical skill is just as evident in his long-line verse: his iambic pentameters are a match for Gower's and Chaucer's, as is shown by the following lines from one of his shorter poems:

(83) Sweit <u>rois</u> of **ver**-tew || <u>and</u> of **gen**-til-<u>nes</u>   (1)
(84) De-**lyt**-sum **lyll**^{ie} || of e-verie **lus**-ty-<u>nes</u>   (2)
(85) In <u>to</u> your <u>garthe</u> || this <u>day</u> I <u>did</u> per-**sew**   (5)
(86) Thair <u>saw</u> I **flow**-ris || <u>that</u> fresche <u>wer</u> of <u>hew</u>   (6)

The proportion of 'Italian' lines like (83) and (86) in Dunbar's verse is 27 per cent, halfway between the proportions in Chaucer's early and late pentameters. One of the ways he achieves this is by placing the inflexions *-is* and *-it* in position 5, as in (86), which contrasts with Henryson's accommodating them with the aid of lyric and epic caesurae. Dunbar's metre is unquestionably the canonical iambic pentameter, and the first example of it in the English language that does not rely on the use of word-final schwa to produce its regularities.

Dunbar also composed a long-line poem in the alliterative metre, *The Twa Marriit Wemen and the Wedo*, and it is of considerable metrical interest, as the following lines show:

(87) For <u>thocht</u> I <u>say</u> it my <u>self</u>, || the **se**-v^erance was **me**-kle   (311)
(88) Be-**twix** his **bas**-tard <u>blude</u> || and <u>my</u> birth **no**-ble   (312)

In this poem Dunbar never rhymes the last stressed syllable (Bawcutt & Riddy 1992: xiii describe it as unrhymed), but he frequently rhymes the hypermetric syllable (weak rhyme, double-underlined here). Instance (87) alliterates in the traditional fashion on its sibilants, but (88) combines the stress pattern of an iambic pentameter with alliteration on both stressed and unstressed syllables. Dunbar's use of alternatives to full rhyme here anticipates the experiments of a number of twentieth-century poets, which I shall discuss in Chapter 10.

In summary, it is fair to say that Dunbar was as skilful a metrical craftsman as Chaucer, and almost as important a figure in the history of Insular versifying; and, although he left no French verse of the quality of Gower's, his macaronic Latin and English poems are a remarkable achievement.

Douglas's long line

Gavin Douglas is remembered for his *Translation of Vergil's 'Aeneid'*, which manages to be both scholarly and lively. Its sea scenes and battles convey the feeling of real spray and real steel, in a sinewy, striking, and monosyllabic language. The poem is a fitting complement to Barbour's *Brus* in an earlier century, but Douglas makes his narrative task easier by employing the long line as well as the rhymed couplet. Douglas's metre is predominantly both decasyllabic and iambic, but 10 per cent of his lines contain inversions, including the following:

(89) Our <u>land</u> and <u>sey</u> **ka**-<u>tchit</u> with **me**-kil <u>pyne</u>   (1. 1. 4)
(90) Sche <u>with</u> a <u>thud</u> **sti**-<u>kkit</u> on <u>a</u> scharp <u>roke</u>   (1. 1. 80)

Douglas's syllabic regularity is also affected by his use of epic caesura, as in the following lines:

(91)   As <u>to</u> hir **spe**-cial || a-**buf** all o-ther's <u>maid</u>   (I. I. 26)
(92)   Am <u>I</u> a-**ban**-don^yt || with <u>sa</u> hard **des**-ta-<u>ny</u>   (I. I. 72)

And his rhythmic regularity is reduced by his occasional use of lyric caesura, as in:

(93)   Sa <u>feil</u> **dan**-gerⁱs || sik **tra**-vell <u>mai</u> sus-**teyn**   (I. I. 16)
(94)   To <u>all</u> **lan**-<u>dis</u>, || but **cer**-tis <u>ne</u>-the-**lefs**   (I. I. 32)

A small number of Douglas's lines lack a syllable: this is usually either initially or at the caesura, but on a few occasions the eurhythmic syllabification of a word-final schwa would restore regularity to both syllable count and accentuation, as for example in the following line, where I have double-underlined the schwa concerned:

(95)   The **hu**-<u>ge</u> **wa**-llis **we**-tris <u>a</u>-pon <u>hie</u>   (I. 2. 55)

Douglas seems neither to have cultivated nor avoided the Italian line: 21 per cent of his lines have no word boundary between positions 4 and 5, including the following:

(96)   Gret <u>pane</u> in **ba**-tail **suf**-f^erit <u>he</u> als-**so**   (I. I. 7)
(97)   Or <u>he</u> his **god**-dis <u>brocht</u> in **La**-ti-<u>o</u>   (I. I. 8)

In summary, we can see that Douglas's long-line verse design is closer to Henryson's than to Dunbar's iambic pentameter. It continues the decasyllabic and mainly iambic tradition derived from Chaucer, but allows both the English licence of the void or disyllabic weak position and the French one of lyric caesura. Although Douglas's metre, like his diction, seems well suited to his subject matter, his versifying lacks the variety, artistry, and sophistication that we find in Dunbar.

Versifying in Early Tudor England

The most acclaimed poet in England in the early years of the sixteenth century was John Skelton (b. ?1460, d. 1529). Like Lydgate, he was an East Anglian and a Latin scholar, and his career culminated in his being acclaimed 'laureate' at the Universities of Oxford, Cambridge, and Louvain. Skelton's scholarly reputation led to his appointment as tutor to the young Henry VIII (b. 1491, d. 1547), and he spent the latter part of his life at court, where his talents for verbal abuse and self-publicizing made him powerful enemies, most of whom he outlived. His surviving English poems (Henderson 1931) were composed over a period of more than forty years and contain some of both the best and the worst versifying of the period. Since his short line was highly innovative, and merits more detailed discussion, I shall deal first with his conservative long line.

Skelton's long line

Skelton's use of the long line changed little in the course of his career; thus, for example, his early poem 'Elegy for Edward IV' is metrically indistinguishable from the much later 'Speak Parrot'. The following lines (9–12) from his short poem 'To the Second Person' (Henderson 1931: 15) demonstrate his verse design:

(98)   O **peer**-less <u>Prince</u>, || [V] **pai**-néd <u>to</u> the <u>death</u>,
(99)   **Rue**-<u>ful</u>-ly <u>rent</u>, || thy **bo**-dy <u>wan</u> and <u>blo</u>,   [blo: 'livid']
(100) For <u>my</u> re-**demp**-tion || gave <u>up</u> thy **vi**-tal <u>breath</u>,
(101) Was **ne**-ver **sor**-row || like <u>to</u> thy **dead**-ly <u>woe</u>!

The metre is unmistakably Lydgate's five-beat (2 + 3) line: only (99) clearly has the structure of a canonical iambic pentameter, although this would also be true of (98) if the final schwa of 'Prince' were syllabified for eurhythmic purposes. Henderson, who marks some word-final schwas in his text as being syllabified in this way, ignores this example. In terms of parametric theory, Skelton's verse design, like Lydgate's, has ten right-strong positions, sets weak-position size at between zero and two syllables, and constrains the unstressed syllables of polysyllabic words that are adjacent to the primary stress from appearing in strong positions. While lines may be decasyllabic, iambic, or both, these are only options within a broader range of structures that can be generated by such a verse design. The strophe designs of Skelton's long-line poems are sometimes conservative (for example, the rhyme royal of 'Speak, Parrot'), but he could also innovate: 'To the Second Person' is one of a sequence of short poems composed in double octaves rhymed abab bcbc dede ecec, a complex and ingenious scheme that he seems to have invented. From Skelton's long-line verse, however, we would not be able to guess how daring an innovator he could be.

Skelton's short line

In some poems Skelton employed four-beat lines similar in design to his five-beat ones; an example is the opening lines of his chauvinistic poem 'Against the Scots':

(102) A-**gainst** the <u>proud</u> Scots **clat**-te-<u>ring</u>,
(103) That **ne**-ver <u>will</u> leave <u>their</u> **trat**-<u>ling</u>:
(104) <u>Won</u> they the <u>field</u>, and <u>lost</u> their <u>king</u>?
(105) They may <u>well</u> say, <u>Fie</u> on <u>that</u> **win**-<u>ning</u>!

This metre also resembles Lydgate's; it produces apparent iambic tetrameters, as in (102) and (103), but also allows many lines that are ugly and ragged to the modern ear. Note that in the early sixteenth century, as in the fifteenth, poets happily rhymed the secondary stressed syllables in word like 'tratling' and 'winning', thus ensuring that what today is a strong syllable occupies the last weak position in the line; this suggests that syllable weight, as well as stress, entered into their corres-pondence rules.

   Skelton thus inherited an English metrics that lacked regularity in either syllable count or quantity, and he must have been acutely aware of this from his familiarity with Latin and French. The constants of fifteenth-century English verse were a regular number of beats and rhyme, only the second of which was shared with the versification of the other languages that Skelton wished to use in his verse. Like Dunbar, Skelton composed macaronic verse that mixed Latin lines with English: in some of Skelton's long-line poems five-beat lines are mixed with quantitative hexameters. Unlike Dunbar, he lacked the skill to use the same metre for the Latin lines as for the English ones in which they were set, and his shifting from one rhythm to the other in such poems disrupts their flow. Skelton's short-line innovation solved this problem by allowing him to compose in two languages in the same metre. He invented what we term *Skeltonics*, very short lines in which rhyme is the only organizing principle.

Skeltonics have no fixed rhyme scheme and vary in length from two beats to four. Lines are most likely to be regular in rhythm and syllable count when they have two beats, as in the following lines (5–8) of 'Against the Scots':

    (106) Lo, these fond sots
    (107) And **trat**-ling Scots,
    (108) How they are blind
    (109) In their own mind

Many passages of Skeltonics are in couplets like this but, if Skelton could find a third or fourth rhyme, he did not resist it. His favourite line length was three beats, but he did not hesitate to mix lines with different numbers of beats, as in the following lines (298–302) from his elaborate parody of a Latin poem by Catullus, *Philip Sparrow* (Henderson 1931: 68):

    (110) Me-**lan**-chæ-tes, that hound
    (111) That plucked Ac-te-on to the ground,
    (112) Gave him his **mor**-tal wound,
    (113) Changed to a deer,
    (114) The **sto**-ry doth ap-**pear**
    (115) Was **chan**-géd to an hart

If we challenge Henderson's decision to scan 'changed' differently in (113) and (115), these lines become a little more regular in rhythm, but the lines that precede and follow these make no case for assuming regularity. They show that Skelton's verse design generated no regularity of syllable, accent, or beat, and verse instances based on it contain only one type of structure. Skeltonic lines comprise either one or two phonological phrases, linked by rhyme, and they are thus very similar to those of the phrasal metres found in the ancient languages of the Middle East. Since Skelton was composing at a time when scholars all over Europe were busy translating the Old Testament, it is easy to envisage that this activity might have influenced him. Another influence may have been the traditional nursery rhyme, the lines of which have rhyme and an irregular number of syllables. Certainly, the banality and repetition in lines like (113) to (115) give some of Skelton's verse a juvenile ring.[6] In any event, subsequent English versifiers writing for sophisticated audiences largely ignored Skeltonics, at least until the twentieth century, when Robert Graves attempted to restore their author's reputation and William Carlos Williams developed a new ultra-short line, as I shall show in Chapter 10.

Conclusions

In the fourteenth century the modes of versifying employed by Scottish poets were similar to some of those found south of the border. Barbour's short line is as regularly iambic and octosyllabic as Chaucer's, and the alliterative metre (which was still employed in Scotland in the following century) resembled that of poems in the *Pearl* manuscript or of *Piers the Plowman*. The most striking difference was that word-final schwa had ceased to be syllabified in Scots, which had thus acquired a new stock of stressed monosyllables. In the fifteenth century, however, the most important versifiers in the two nations went separate ways. In England Hoccleve tried to maintain Chaucer's and Gower's archaic deployment of word-final schwa (although most fifteenth-century readers probably ignored it), while Lydgate reverted to an older metrical system based on beats rather than syllables. Lydgate preferred Chaucer's five-unit line to the traditional four-unit one, but he imposed on it a 2 + 3 structure that seems to have come from the French *vers de dix*. Since he relaxes the size of weak positions, Lydgate's metres are ictic, but his long-line verse contains many iambic pentameters, because five-beat ictic lines often do. When combined with the new schwa-deleted delivery accorded Chaucer and Gower's verse, Lydgate's apostasy ensured that the strict iambic pentameter verse design was temporarily lost to English poets and audiences.

In Scotland, on the other hand, James I, Henryson, and Douglas kept both ten syllables and iambic rhythm as their governing principles. From there it was only a short step to the canonical iambic metres, and Dunbar, who was as nimble in verse as on the dance-floor, took that step whenever he wished. Dunbar spent a year in London (1500–01), but seems to have made no disciples among its versifiers; his name disappears from the surviving records after the Battle of Flodden (1513). Versifying in England at this time was where Lydgate had left it, except for the short-line experiments of Skelton, which found no imitators. In the period that followed, the Scots lords largely spent their energies on domestic quarrels, while the English, relieved of the burden of two long wars, enjoyed an economic and cultural renaissance. And, just as fifteenth-century Scots poets had absorbed the latest ideas from the courts of mainland Europe, so sixteenth-century English poets looked across the seas for inspiration.

Notes to Chapter 5

1. MS Cosin v.iii.9 in the Durham University Library and MSS HM 111 and HM 744 in the Huntington Library.

2. The most favourable assumption is that word-final schwas count only when they make the line conform to the eight- or ten-syllable norm, but this requires the reader to read every line twice before delivering it. Note that counting either all or none of Lydgate's word-final schwas reduces the number of lines that are regular in syllable count and rhythm.

3. Hammond argues that by 1422 ordinary speakers had ceased to syllabify final schwas (1925: 131), but Pearsall states that Lydgate often treated word-final schwa in much the same way as Chaucer (1970: 61). Note that counting all unelided word-final schwas in Chaucer's lines greatly increases the proportion with the mode number of syllables, but counting them all in Lydgate's does not.

4. Duffell 2002b: 305 shows that Henryson employed 'Italian' lines significantly less often than his lexicon would lead us to expect; this is the antithesis of the situation in Chaucer, Gower, and Dunbar.

5. Note that Henryson in this predilection for lyric caesura differs from Hoccleve as well as Chaucer; one of the reasons why the Scots poet's line seems so clearly iambic to modern ears is that his inversions tend to occur early in the line, allowing the rhythm to reassert itself by the close.

6. Thus the homicidal avian in 'Who Killed Cock Robin' (who confesses 'I, said the Sparrow | with my bow and arrow') sounds more like an ancestor of Skelton's Philip than does Catullus's *passer deliciae meae puellae*.

CHAPTER 6

The Emergence of
English Metrical Canons

Petrarchism in Europe AD 1520–1580

In 1500 England's versifiers were a century behind their Scottish equivalents, and it took them much of the sixteenth century to catch up; literary events in mainland Europe played a key role in their progress. Most of Skelton's poetry is separated from that of the generation of English poets that followed by the advent of *l'art de pétrarquiser*, or Petrarchism, a style of discourse that produced love poetry of great psychological subtlety and verbal precision. The language of this poetry was that of elegant but personal conversation, and was used to display the poet's wit, knowledge, and refinement of both taste and feeling. The ability to compose in the new style was as desirable among courtiers as the ability to handle a sword, and of far more practical use: it could be exercised in the royal presence (where swords had to remain sheathed), or at the dining table, or in bed. Petrarchism characterizes the work of Skelton's two most important successors, Sir Thomas Wyatt (b. 1503, d. 1542) and Henry Howard, Earl of Surrey (b. ?1517, d. 1547), and the following brief synopsis traces the history of Petrarchism as it spread to England through the courts of Europe.

Italy

Following Petrarch's death in 1375, Italy experienced what writers have called the 'secolo senza poesia', when there was a vigorous revival of Latin scholarship and no significant poet composed in Italian. This state of affairs was changed by the multi-talented Pietro Bembo (b. 1470, d. 1547), who complemented his Latin scholarship by composing sonnets in the Petrarchan manner. In 1520 his sonnets, composed over the previous thirty years, were published in Rome, where Bembo was secretary to Pope Leo X. After the latter's death in 1521, Bembo left Rome for Padua to devote himself to literature. In 1539 he returned to Rome to become a cardinal, and he spent his last years on the affairs and writings of the Church. Bembo's Petrarchism inspired numerous Italian imitators, perhaps the most important of whom was Annibale Caro (b. 1507, d. 1576).

The Iberian peninsula

Bembo's Padua years saw the spread of *l'art de pétrarquiser* to Spain and Portugal, where linguistic similarity to Italian favoured the import, and to France and England where it did not. Petrarchism was introduced into Spain by Juan Boscán (b. 1490, d. 1542), whose friends included the Venetian ambassador, and Garcilaso de la Vega (b. 1501, d. 1536), a courtier who had fought in Italy. These two poets were unaware that several Castilian poets, including the Marqués de Santillana (b. 1398, d. 1458), had attempted to compose sonnets 'al itálico modo' much earlier (see Duffell 1987). Boscán's and Garcilaso's poems, published together by the former's widow in 1543, ushered in a long period of dominance for Italianate verse in Spain. Garcilaso, who was arguably the finest poet in Europe between Chaucer and Shakespeare, also influenced two generations of Portuguese poets, in particular, Francisco de Sá de Miranda (b. 1485, d. 1558) and Luis Vaz de Camões (b. 1524, d. 1580); Petrarch's and Bembo's influence thus spread westward.

France

Petrarchism's expansion to the north was no less rapid; two poets at the court of the French King Francis I (r. 1515–47) were influential in this: Mellin de Saint-Gelais (b. 1487, d. 1558) and Clément Marot (b. 1497, d. 1554). After an extensive education in Italy, Saint-Gelais became court poet to Francis soon after his accession; Marot became the King's valet on his return from Italy in 1527 but, as an attendant on the King's sister, he had had a long acquaintance with the royal court. Although Wyatt arrived at the Emperor Charles V's court too late (1537) to have met Garcilaso, the English poet must have known the work of Marot well, because he adapted one of the latter's poems. Surrey spent a year at the French court as a hostage and probably met both Saint-Gelais and Marot. There may be more than coincidence in the fact that Marot, Wyatt, and Surrey all translated the poetry of the Old Testament as well as Petrarch into their mother tongues. Wyatt also spent a considerable proportion of his career in France and chose a French form, the rondeau, for his first adaptations of Petrarch.

Petrarchan poem design: the sonnet

The principal metrical vehicle for Petrarchism was the sonnet, a fourteen-line poem usually subdivided 8 + 6, and sonnets were composed both individually and in sequences of varying lengths (which made them indistinguishable from longer poems with fourteen-line stanzas). The sonnet had been invented by Giacomo de Lentini (*fl.* Palermo, 1250), who employed an octave rhymed abababab plus a sestet rhymed cdcdcd (see Sanguineti 1965).[1] Subsequent Italian poets refined this simple design, and Petrarch's and Bembo's sonnets comprised an octave rhymed abba abba, followed by any of a variety of sestets (including cd_3 and cde_2). Saint-Gelais, Marot, and subsequent generations of French poets retained the octave of $abba_2$ of Petrarch and Bembo, but tried new alternatives in the sestet: the most common began with a couplet, c_2 + deed, which became canonical in French (the *sonnet régulier*).[2]

When the sonnet was introduced into England, Wyatt retained Petrarch's octave of $abba_2$, but frequently added a sestet ending in a couplet, $cddc + e_2$. Surrey also favoured a final couplet, but his departure from Petrarch's norm was even more radical: he used alternating rhymes (like Lentini's original design), but he also allowed a change of rhyme in the octave (ab_2+cd_2), and repeated this configuration in the sestet (ef_2), before closing with a couplet (g_2). This design became known, rather unjustly, as the *English* or *Shakespearean sonnet*, and it increased the number of rhymes to seven, compared with four or five in Italian and French. This change can be argued to be language-related: a comparison of rhyming dictionaries in different languages (for example, Casas Homs 1956 with Stillman 1966) suggests that English has fewer exact rhymes available, particularly for key words like *love* and *death*. Having to find only one rhyme for each of seven words (rather than three rhymes for the first two of five) helps solve a potential problem for English poets.[3]

Petrarchan verse design: the decasyllabic long line

The Italian poets' strophe design thus passed into the poetic traditions of the other major languages of south-west Europe with only minor alterations. The verse design of the Italian poets had a much more bumpy passage: the *endecasillabo* was a very subtle line that depended on stress patterns for its rhythmic effects. Similarities in the phonology of the three languages helped it become the Spanish *endecasílabo* and the Portuguese *decassílabo,* but in France, where word stress had long been weak and soon disappeared altogether, the subtleties of the *endecasillabo* were not appreciated. The first French sonnets employed the native *vers de dix*, and no subsequent French poet was tempted to compose the French equivalent of the *endecasillabo* with a variable caesura. Even when the first French translation of part of the *Canzoniere* appeared in Paris in 1548 its metre was the French line of 4 + 6 syllables with phrasal stress in the last position of each hemistich (see Jasinski 1903: 50). Later in the sixteenth century the *alexandrin*, which had become established as the metre of dramatic verse, displaced the *vers de dix* in French sonnets. When the first sonnets were composed in English in the 1520s, the obvious metrical alternatives were thus imitations of the *endecasillabo* or the *vers de dix* and the home-grown line that had been in use from Lydgate to Skelton. As I shall demonstrate, Wyatt and Surrey made rather different choices.

Wyatt and Surrey

Sir Thomas Wyatt was a Yorkshireman who studied at Cambridge, and who served in what is now the diplomatic service. This meant that, like Chaucer, he travelled widely on the European mainland; Wyatt's journeys took him to France, the Netherlands, Italy, and Spain. Wyatt numbered among the lovers of Henry VIII's second bride Ann Boleyn, most of whom lost their heads, and Wyatt himself served time in the Tower under sentence of death. It is difficult to believe that Wyatt would have survived if Henry had known of his relationship with Ann, but he was pardoned and lived to die of overwork in the royal service. Henry Howard, Earl of Surrey, was an aristocrat with a better claim to the throne than his king's, and added to royal resentment by becoming a national military hero. Henry had Surrey imprisoned in the Tower for doing what every other noble did, bearing the arms of his ancestors: the fact that Surrey's ancestor was Edward the Confessor was fatal to him. In a typical gesture Surrey offered single combat 'in his shirt' against his accuser (in full armour), but Henry was taking no chances and had Surrey beheaded.

Wyatt's travels meant that he was familiar with a number of metres in a number of languages and with some of the poets who used them. In his own poetry (Rebholz 1978) he developed both a short- and a long-line metre, neither of which conformed precisely to mainland models. Instead he preserved some of the features introduced by Gower in the English short line and by Lydgate in the long. Surrey was also a significant metrical innovator and helped establish the sonnet at the court of Henry VIII. Surrey reproduced the short line of Wyatt, the iambic tetrameter, with skill and ease, but appears to have been critical of Wyatt's long line, since he parodied it in Poem XXX (Keene 1985), which is dedicated to the older poet. Surrey spent a year in France and was much more familiar with French verse than Italian; as a result, when he chose a long line for his own sonnets, it was rather different from Wyatt's.

Wyatt's stress-syllabic short line

Wyatt employed an updated form of Gower's short English line in which word-final schwa was deleted, as in fifteenth-century Scots or modern English. Wyatt's wit, as well as his mastery of this line, can be see from the following *Epigram* (Poem LIV; Rebholz 1978: 76):

(1)   What <u>word</u> is <u>that</u> that **chan**-geth <u>not</u>,
(2)   Though <u>it</u> be <u>turned</u> and <u>made</u> in <u>twain</u>?
(3)   It <u>is</u> my **an**-swer, <u>God</u> it <u>wot</u>,
(4)   And <u>eke</u> the **cau**-ser <u>of</u> my <u>pain</u>.
(5)   It <u>love</u> re-**war**-deth <u>with</u> dis-**dain**,
(6)   Yet <u>it</u> is <u>loved</u>. || What <u>would</u> ye <u>more</u>?
(7)   It <u>is</u> my <u>health</u> eke <u>and</u> my <u>sore</u>.

The lines of this poem are both perfectly octosyllabic and perfectly iambic; the poem's wit consists in concealing and revealing the identity of its subject at the same time. The palindrome referred to in (2) is 'Anna', and the name is repeated in the pun 'my answer' ('Ann, sir') in (3), a trick reprised in 'the causer' ('the cause, sir') in (4). Wyatt's metre here is no longer defined by beats; a weak-position size of exactly one syllable produces a line of four iambic feet (*iambic tetrameter*), and he makes skilful use of the plethora of monosyllables in early modern English, both tonic and atonic. The former usually occupy even positions and the latter odd, but note the erosions of the third ictus in many lines, as in (5) 'of', (6) 'with', and (7) 'and', above.

The iambic tetrameter rapidly became established as the canonical English short line, but a long-line canon took far longer to emerge. The iambic pentameter lay waiting in Chaucer's and in Gower's verse, obscured by the loss of word-final schwa, and also in Dunbar's, of which Wyatt was probably unaware. But in the sixteenth century there were strong rival candidates for the position of English long-line canon.

Wyatt's experimental long line

Wyatt chose for his sonnets a long line that differed significantly from those of Italy, Spain, and France; his metre clearly allows some lines that meet the definition of iambic pentameter and others that do not. Although it seems that he was well able to compose regular iambic decasyllables, he often chose to do something else, as the following lines from his sonnets (Rebholz 1978) illustrate:[4]

(8)	The **li**-vely <u>sparks</u> that <u>is</u>-sue from those <u>eyes</u>	(XXV. 1)
(9)	<u>Like</u> to <u>these</u> im-**mea**-su-ra-ble **moun**tains	(XXIV. 1)
(10)	But of **ha**-ting my-**self** ‖ that <u>date</u> is <u>past</u>	(XII. 3)
(11)	**En**-vy <u>them</u> ‖ be-**yond** all **measure**	(XXII. 4)
(12)	With **fei**-gned **vi**-sage ‖ now <u>sad</u> now **merry**	(IX. 11)
(13)	**Who**-so <u>list</u> to <u>hunt</u>, ‖ I <u>know</u> where <u>is</u> an **hind**	(XI. 1)
(14)	I <u>fly</u> a-**bove** the <u>wind</u> ‖ yet <u>can</u> I not a-**rise**	(XVII. 3)

Instance (8) has both ten syllables to the final stress and an iambic rhythm, but the remainder are clearly not iambic pentameters: (9) has 9F syllables and is trochaic; (10) has 10M but is not in duple time; (11) has 7F syllables and is trochaic; (12) has 9F and is not iambic; (13) has 11F; and (14) has 12M, but at least is iambic. Full analysis of the twenty-two sonnets that are most certainly by Wyatt reveals the following distribution of line lengths (Duffell 1991: 549):[5]

>10M/F = 19%; 10M/F = 59%; 9F = 15% ; <9F = 6%.

Thus fewer than 60 per cent of Wyatt's lines are decasyllables when delivered with modern accentuation and, even if we accept that precedent allowed the re-stressing of words like 'merry' as weak–strong at line ends, that still leaves a quarter of Wyatt's lines with the wrong number of syllables.

Instance (13) above is the clearest indication that Wyatt sometimes intended other than ten syllables and/or an iambic rhythm, because it is repeated elsewhere in the poem converted into a perfect iambic pentameter by the omission of its second syllable '-so'. But (13) makes a more dramatic and effective opening: each hemistich has three prominent syllables, the falling rhythm of the first contrasting with the rising rhythm of the second, and this reinforces the semantic contrast in the image of predator and prey. The irregularity of this line is evidence not only of Wyatt's metrical intention but also of his craftsmanship. Clearly, the iambic pentameter is only one possible realization of his verse design, which can be deduced only from a close study of the lines that do not meet that definition. Annabel Endicott's dissertation is such a study, and she suggests that Wyatt's frequent switches into triple time may have been in imitation of the Italian *endecasillabo* with its variety of rhythms (1963: 108–09). But Wyatt employs twice as many triple-time lines as Petrarch when he adapts one of the latter's poems (Rebholz, Poem IX; see Duffell 1991: 556).

Rebholz argues that Wyatt's metrical intention was not the iambic pentameter as we know it, but a 'flexible pentameter', the term he uses for Lydgate's five-beat ictic line. But this is an inadequate description of Wyatt's long line: when his line has five beats, they do not always subdivide 2 + 3, because he observes no word-boundary constraint between the second and third ictus. Moreover, some of his lines have four beats, which subdivide 2 + 2, as in (11) and (12), and some have six, which subdivide 3 + 3, as in (14). Endicott accounts for these lines that contain other than five beats by quoting the conclusion of Baldi 1953, that Wyatt wished to mix flowing lines (iambic pentameters, with their 2 + 3 or 3 + 2 stresses) and balanced, or symmetrical ones, with 2 + 2 or 3 + 3 stresses (1963: 72). Wyatt's verse design is thus very flexible indeed: it allows from eight to twelve right-strong positions, and its weak positions may contain between zero and two syllables, but may not contain strong ones. Such a line is clearly in the tradition of the Middle English alliterative metre with its two hemistichs, each of which may contain either two or three beats. It allows four- and six-ictic lines as well as five-ictic ones and in modern Russian poetry would be termed a *free dolnik* (see, for example, Smith 2002). In any event, this design permitted Wyatt to compose a great many lines that were both decasyllabic and iambic, while granting him the freedom to include lines that were neither.

Wyatt's verse occupies a point in the history of English long-line metre where everything appears to have been in the melting pot: rhyme, rhythm, stress/strength, isosyllabism, all still have undecided futures, and all are available for experiment. In this state of flux Wyatt challenged the rules of Romance verse and often rebelled against the foreign practices of counting syllables and of rhyming only strong ones. He set out to create an English line that differed significantly from its continental equivalents, a line that had the smoothness of the iambic pentameter when he felt it appropriate, but which reverted to a traditional English pattern of beats when he felt it was not. Wyatt's template and correspondence rules are difficult to identify because he was building on a green-field site: the English metrical system was not yet fixed, and we do not know whether he was hovering between alternatives or simply trying to have the best of two worlds, the English and the French. In subsequent centuries his verse has been esteemed whenever diversity has been in fashion, and regularized or criticized when it was not; thus the present age prefers Wyatt's poetry to that of his friend and younger contemporary Surrey.

Surrey's iambic English 'vers de dix'

Surrey not only invented the English sonnet, he was the first English poet to realize that a pattern of five iambs is strong enough to be recognizable without the prop of either alliteration or rhyme. He pioneered *blank verse* in his translation of Books II and IV of Virgil's *Aeneid*, and his iambic English line, like the Latin hexameter, had sufficient internal structure to make rhyme unnecessary. Surrey's blank verse, however, was different in some important respects from the long line he employed in his rhymed verse. The long line of his sonnets can be illustrated by the following lines (5–9) from Poem 7 (Keene 1985):[6]

(15)   **Sum**-<u>mer</u> is <u>come</u>, || for **e**-very <u>spray</u> now <u>springs</u>;
(16)   The <u>hart</u> hath <u>hung</u> || his <u>old</u> head <u>on</u> the <u>pale</u>;
(17)   The <u>buck</u> in <u>brake</u> || his **win**-ter <u>coat</u> he <u>flings</u>;
(18)   The **fi**-shes <u>flete</u> || with <u>new</u> re-**pai**-rèd <u>scale</u>;

All the lines of this poem, and of most of Surrey's sonnets, are subdivided into 4 + 6 syllables by a mid-line word boundary: the formula of most is 4M + 6, but some lines are 3F + 6, with the lyric caesura that was beginning to be shunned in French poetry at this time. Lines 1 and 10 of this poem contain lyric caesurae:

(19)   The <u>soote</u> **sea**-<u>son</u>, || that <u>bud</u> and <u>bloom</u> forth <u>brings</u>
(20)   The <u>swift</u> **swal**-<u>low</u> || pur-**su**-eth the flies <u>small</u>;

It may be argued that Surrey intended 'season' in (19) to be pronounced like *saison* in French, but this is less likely to apply to 'swallow' in (20), and it is certainly not the case in many of the other examples in Surrey's sonnets, which involve words like 'people' (Poem 8. 4) and 'weather' (Poem 8. 6). This metre differs from iambic pentameter in two respects: it has a caesura immediately following position 4, and it does not entirely ban strong syllables from weak positions. Surrey's long line is almost as regularly iambic as it is decasyllabic, and it could well be described as an iambic *vers de dix*.

   This metre employs most types of tension found in the iambic pentameter: inversion (as in (15) above), erosion (for example, the two erosions in (24) below) and resolution. Although Surrey's syllable count is usually strict, he allowed a few licences: he even admits a void position in:

(21)   [V] <u>In</u> lost <u>youth</u> || or <u>when</u> my <u>hairs</u> be <u>grey</u>   (8. 8)

And he sometimes does not syllabify a final liquid, as with 'Windsor' in:

(22)   And **Winds**^or, a-**las**, || doth <u>chase</u> me <u>from</u> her <u>sight</u>   (19. 12)

Table A compares the frequency with which various forms of tension occur in Surrey's verse and that of poets who preceded or followed him. A possible indication that Surrey's metre was experimental and tentative is that his sonnets and other poems imitated from the Italian are composed in a very monosyllabic language: by my calculation 85 per cent of the words in Surrey's rhymed verse are monosyllables; and monosyllables make counting easy.[7]

   Many of Surrey's rhymed poems contain no 'Italian' lines, where positions 4 and 5 are occupied by syllables of the same word, an essential feature of Chaucer's and Gower's metre and of the subsequent English long-line canon. Some sonnets, however, do contain such a line (for example, Poems 10, 11, and 13), and in Poem 18 he employs both a lyric caesura and an 'Italian' line:

(23)   The <u>wild</u> **fo**-<u>rest</u> the **clo**-thèd <u>holts</u> with <u>green</u>   (29)
(24)   And <u>with</u> re-**mem**-brance <u>of</u> the **grea**-ter <u>grief</u>   (53)

Nevertheless, 'Italian' lines constitute only 4 per cent of total in Surrey's rhymed verse, the same proportion that Billy 1999 finds in the *décasyllabes* of Jean Froissart. Clearly, such lines were tolerated as exceptions in French, and the combination of caesura and rhythm, makes the metre of Surrey's rhymed verse transitional between the *vers de dix* and the iambic pentameter.

   In his translation of Virgil's *Aeneid*, however, Surrey employed fewer lyric caesurae and more 'Italian' lines; he also employed a little more inversion and erosion, as the following lines from Book 11 show:

(25)	**Shrou**-<u>ding</u> them-**selves** ||	**un**-<u>der</u> the **de**-sert **shore**	(33)
(26)	The <u>Greeks</u> are <u>lords</u> ||	**o**-<u>ver</u> this **fi**-red <u>town</u>	(419)
(27)	The <u>town</u> **rest**-<u>less</u> ||	with **fu**-ry <u>as</u> I <u>sought</u>	(1024)

The medial inversions in (25) and (26) involve grammatical words ('under' and 'over'), while the lyric caesura 'restless' in (27) disturbs the rhythm in a way that is wholly appropriate to the line's meaning. Almost 14 per cent of the lines in this poem contain an inversion, compared with less than 6 per cent in Chaucer's *CT* and just over 10 per cent in Surrey's rhymed verse, as Table A shows. But Surrey employs the 'Italian' line much more often than the lyric caesura in the *Aeneid*; for example, the following line from the same book:

(28)	And <u>some</u> with **wea**-pons || <u>walk</u> the **nar**-row <u>streets</u>	(425)

Instance (28) has a very pronounced iambic rhythm, again appropriate to the action, and also an elegant alliterative pattern. The proportion of monosyllables in the *Aeneid*, 76 per cent, is close to the average for English poetic texts, which indicates that Surrey's translation is a more assured piece of versifying than his rhymed poems. Nevertheless, the proportion of 'Italian' lines in the poem (12 per cent) is lower than the poem's lexicon would lead us to expect (see Duffell 2002b: 305).[8]

Surrey, like Wyatt, used the English long line as a field for experiment; and, apart from its lyric caesura, which the strong stress of English makes sounds clumsy, his iambic *vers de dix* was not a bad fit for the language. But, although it found a few imitators, it was doomed by its monotony of caesura, and the changes in his versifying of the *Aeneid* suggest that even Surrey realized its shortcomings.

Surrey's iambic nursery-rhyme metre

The lack of a single, dominant long-line metre in the first half of the sixteenth century is evidenced by Surrey's cultivation of a traditional alternative. Many of his poems are composed in couplets derived from traditional English folk-verse. Their metre was called *poulter's measure* (because poulterers allegedly compensated for bad eggs by giving an extra one with every dozen). Poulter's measure is a syllabically regularized version of an English nursery rhyme:

(29)	The <u>grand</u> old <u>Duke</u> of <u>York</u>, | He <u>had</u> ten **thou**-sand <u>men</u>;
(30)	He <u>marched</u> them <u>up</u> to the <u>top</u> of the <u>hill</u>, |
	And he <u>marched</u> them <u>down</u> a-**gain**.

Weak positions in this rhyme may contain two light syllables, which shows that, like most traditional English verse, it is based on feet, or beats/offbeats, and not syllable count. But poulter's measure, as cultivated by early-sixteenth-century poets, eschews this double-occupancy, and its hemistichs contain 3, 3, 4, and 3 iambic feet. For example, in Surrey's Poem 15 we find the lines (7–8):

(31)	Hot <u>gleams</u> of **bur**-ning <u>fire</u>	|| and **ea**-sy <u>sparks</u> of <u>flame</u>
(32)	In **ba**-lance <u>of</u> u-**ne**-qual <u>weight</u>	|| he **pon**-de-<u>reth</u> by <u>aim</u>.

In this metre Surrey erodes fewer than 5 per cent of ictuses, like the second in (32), but employs very little inversion (under 1 per cent of lines initially), and he is even more reluctant to relax his syllable count. The following lines (33–34) from Poem 22 are unusual in that the first contains an initial inversion and the second a disyllabic interval:

(33) '**Un**-der a **mul**-berry tree it was,' first said the one;
(34) The next named a **po**-me-gra-nate tree, ||

where-by the truth was known

The enjambment across the caesura of (33) offers the only relief from the metre's fixed but complex accentual structure (3 + 3 + 4 + 3), and the disyllabic interval in (34) is distracting rather than diverting. It is easy to surmise why this metre fell from use: it is rigid and monotonous, making it particularly unsuitable for long poems. But the demise of poulter's measure cannot be attributed to a bad fit for the phonology of the language; it represents an aesthetic choice by English poets and audiences.

Long-Line Verse between Surrey and Sidney

In the forty years after Surrey's death English poets continued to exercise their personal choice of long-line metre: tumbling verse, poulter's measure, or Surrey's iambic *vers de dix* that was almost, but not quite, iambic pentameter; and there were minor developments in all three. As Saintsbury notes, more or less iambic lines of 6 + 6 syllables, reminiscent of the alexandrine, began to creep into the tumbling verse of this period, making it what he called 'doggerel' (1906: 1, 336–43). Such lines are very like one of Wyatt's experimental variants, (14) above, but they formed a minority in tumbling verse where the majority of lines continued to be in triple time, with four rather than six prominence peaks. Another development was that the second, longer line of poulter's measure, with 4 + 3 stresses, was sometimes employed on its own, a sort of iambic common measure. Finally, the iambic *vers de dix* came to resemble the canonical iambic pentameter slightly more closely when poets followed the example of Surrey's *Aeneid* and increased the proportion of running, or 'Italian', lines to 12 per cent, or slightly higher. Most users of this metre, however, continued to employ lyric and, even more often, epic caesura, so their verse still seems very rough to ears accustomed to the canonical line.

The history of English long-line versification in this period is encapsulated in a remarkable work, the *Mirror for Magistrates* (Campbell 1938), which was suppressed in 1555, published in 1559, and expanded in 1563 and 1578, and which continued to grow well into the next century. This series of poems telling of the deaths of famous men was a compilation of work by at least ten authors, some of them established men of letters. Predictably, the first poem in the compilation is in tumbling verse, but the iambic *vers de dix* of Surrey soon takes over as the dominant metre. The metrically most important contributions were added in the version of 1563: the 'Induction' and 'The Complaynt of Henry Duke of Buckingham', by Thomas Sackville (b. 1536, d. 1608), a young nobleman whose long and successful career culminated in his becoming Earl of Dorset. Saintsbury calls these two poems 'the finest piece of versification in English between Chaucer and Spenser' (1906: 1, 333), because their language is direct and their metre iambically regular.

Sackville achieved this regularity by banishing both lyric and epic caesurae, and by employing very few inversions, even initially; and the frequency of erosion in his verse is similar to that in Sidney's or Spenser's more than a decade later (see Table A). Sackville's line is canonical in every respect except one: running, or 'Italian', lines are relatively few (they constitute 15 per cent of the total in the 'Induction' and 16 per cent in the 'Complaynt'). In this respect, the metre of the 'Induction' and 'Complaynt' is closer to that of Surrey's *Aeneid* than to the canonical iambic pentameter.[9] Sackville was one of the few contemporary poets whose work Sidney praised in his *Defence of Poetry* (Van Dorsten 1966), and this high estimation has been shared by Saintsbury and most modern critics (see Cunliffe 1912: lxxix).

Sidney and Spenser

Sir Philip Sidney (b. 1554, d. 1586) was the son of a socially prominent family with an estate in Kent, and his prospects were improved further when his sister married the influential Earl of Pembroke. After leaving Cambridge he travelled widely in Europe for several years, while his relatives lobbied on his behalf for an official appointment. In 1582 he was knighted and in 1584 given a command in the Netherlands, where he distinguished himself in battle but was wounded and died of the consequent infection. His life of leisure allowed plenty of time for writing, and he gathered a circle of friends with literary aspirations. By 1580 he had completed *Arcadia* and the *Defence of Poetry* and had begun *Astrophel and Stella*, all of which were published in the 1590s, when he was lionized as a national hero. His example triggered the publication of a large number of collections of sonnets, including those by Spenser and Shakespeare. Sidney was deeply interested in every aspect of poetics, including metre, and his quest for an English long line led him to experiment with quantitative verse on the Classical model (see Hanson 2001) as well as with metres modelled on those he found in France and Italy.

Edmund Spenser (b. 1552, d. 1599) was the son of middle-class parents and was born and brought up in London. After leaving Cambridge he worked as secretary first to the Bishop of Rochester and later to the Lord Deputy of Ireland. His years in that country he regarded as exile, but it helped him produce a large body of poetry that was widely admired. He established his poetic reputation at the end of the 1570s, but his longest and most important work, *The Faerie Queene*, was not published until 1591. His exile ended when Irish insurgents burned down his home and forced him to return to London, where he died destitute. Posterity was kinder to him than life had been: Spenser was buried in Westminster Abbey next to his hero Chaucer, and to subsequent generations he became known as the 'Prince of Poets' and the 'Poet's Poet'. Spenser's artistic relationship with Sidney parallels Chaucer's with Gower: the two sixteenth-century poets shared a deep interest in metre, just as their predecessors had done two hundred years earlier. But in the case of Sidney and Spenser, changes in the language did not obscure their achievements in this field from the generations that followed.

Sidney's alexandrine

Sidney was familiar with sonnets in French and Italian that were in two very different types of metre, one syllabic, the other transitional between syllabic and stress–syllabic. The closer of these two influences geographically was undoubtedly the French, but that language no longer enjoyed the privilege of being the official language of England, as it had been in Chaucer's and Gower's time. By 1580 French sonneteers had adopted the *alexandrin*, which gave the generation of poets active in England in 1580 another possible basis for an English long-line metre, and both Sidney and Spenser experimented with it. As when Surrey experimented with the *vers de dix*, both these poets seem to have realized instantly that English phonology favoured a stress–syllabic version of the French metre.[10]

Sidney employed the longer French metre for seven poems in *Astrophel and Stella* (Bullett 1947: 173), including the first of its 108 sonnets, from which the following lines (3–4) are taken:

(35) **Plea**-sure might <u>cause</u> her <u>read</u>, || **rea**-ding might <u>make</u> her <u>know</u>
(36) **Know**-ledge might **pi**-ty <u>win</u>, || and **pi**-ty <u>grace</u> ob-**tain**

All Sidney's alexandrines subdivide 6M + 6, like their French model, but Sidney employs only masculine lines, unlike contemporary French poets, who often alternated masculine and feminine rhymes. Sidney's metre is a double iambic trimeter rather than a hexameter, since the structure of the two hemistichs is identical and there is no metrical interaction between them. Sidney employs initial inversion in seven of the hemistichs (25 per cent) in this sonnet, including both of (35), but in his other alexandrines he averages only one inversion per sonnet. The overall rate is thus 4 per cent, significantly lower than in his pentameters (see Table A).

Sidney erodes 4 per cent of ictuses in this metre, in most cases the middle ictus of one hemistich, as in (38) below; only rarely does he erode the final ictus of the first hemistich, as in (37):

(37) Their <u>rays</u> to <u>me</u>, who <u>in</u> || their **te**-dious **ab**-sence <u>lay</u>
                                                                     (LXXVI. 2)
(38) Those <u>lips</u> which <u>make</u> death's <u>pay</u> || a <u>mean</u> price <u>for</u> a <u>kiss</u> (LXXVII. 6)

Note that the mid-line word boundary may be enjambed, as in (37), so that the syntax subdivides the line into 4 + 8 or 8 + 4 syllables rather than 6 + 6. Nevertheless, other than in the first sonnet with its many inversions, tension in Sidney's alexandrines is sparse, and the unvarying pattern of 3 + 3 stresses and regular iambic rhythm tend to monotony. By employing the alexandrine in his sonnets Sidney showed that he could follow the latest French fashion whenever he wished, but the fact that he composed so few in the metre suggests that he found some features of the Italian *endecasillabo* more aesthetically pleasing.[11]

Sidney's iambic pentameter

Hanson attributes the reinvention of the iambic pentameter to Sidney, and argues that he developed his line from the *endecasillabo* of Dante and Petrarch by introducing a constraint against strong syllables in weak positions that he had not found in the Italian metre (1996: 80). This overstates the scale of Sidney's innovation, first because he had Sackville's precedent, and secondly because the *endecasillabo* had acquired some accentual constraints by Sidney's time. Petrarch had severely limited triple-time rhythm in his lines (see Chapter 4, n29), and Torquato Tasso (b. 1544, d. 1595) composed *endecasillabi* in which some 89 per cent of second hemistichs are iambic (see Duffell 1991: 319). Sidney's verse design is certainly more Italianate than Sackville's in that it produces more of the running lines that are a distinguishing feature of the *endecasillabo*. The following lines, which open Sonnet IX of *Astrophel and Stella*, illustrate Sidney's metre:

(39)   Queen **Vir**-tue's <u>Court</u>, which <u>some</u> call **Ste**-lla's <u>face</u>
(40)   Pre-**par'd** by **Na**-ture's **choi**-cest **fur**-ni-<u>ture</u>

Sidney excelled his predecessors in fitting polysyllables of all configurations to an iambic template: in these lines we find 'stately' (s w), 'prepar'd' (w s), and 'furniture' (s w s), and in the line that follows 'alabaster' (s w s w). He also employed 24 per cent of 'Italian' lines, like (40), a similar proportion to that found in Chaucer's early pentameters (see Table A).

Sidney used initial inversion in his pentameters in over 9 per cent of lines, significantly more than Chaucer or Sackville, and his lady's name is one of his favourite initial inversions, as in:

(41)   **Stel**-<u>la</u> be-**hold**, and <u>then</u> be-**gin** t° en-**dite**   (xv. 14)

Sidney often employed vocalic glides to achieve a regular syllable count, as in 'to endite' in (41); this device, which resembles Italian synaloepha, became a staple of English versifying over the next two centuries. Sidney eroded just over 7 per cent of ictuses on average in his pentameters, fewer than Chaucer or Shakespeare, but in one line he approached the limits of erosion:

(42)   Not <u>at</u> the <u>first</u> sight, <u>nor</u> with <u>a</u> dribb'd <u>shot</u>   (II. 1)

An iambic delivery requires three erosions in this line ('at', 'nor', and 'a'), and the reader is stretched to recognize the metre because there are few clear candidates for prominence peaks: only one of the two monosyllables in positions 4 and 5 and another of those in 9 and 10. Subsequent poets avoided two consecutive erosions in a pentameter line, and eroded the first two ictuses only very rarely, but Sidney seems to have discovered these limits by trial and error.

Thompson (1961: 139–55) argues that Sidney occupies a pivotal position in the development of the iambic pentameter, because he adjusted the natural rhythms of English phrases to the iambic verse design more skilfully than any poet before him. One feature of the *endecasillabo* that Sidney did not imitate was its almost invariable feminine ending; all lines in the sonnets of *Astrophel and Stella* have either 10M or 12M syllables. Sidney appears to have regarded the 10F line as a separate metre, and he combines it with the alexandrine as readily as with the line of 10M (see Bullett 1947: 213 & 215).

Sidney's trochaic tetrameter

The poems that close *Astrophel and Stella* include six lyrics in trochaic tetrameter (totalling 313 different lines), and Sidney constructed his short line with a falling rhythm on similar principles to his longer iambic lines. Again he counted syllables strictly, but in this metre he gave 25 per cent of his lines 4F syllables (four full trochees).[12] He doubtless knew Latin poems in trochaic metres with many masculine (*catalectic*) lines, and he did not hesitate to make them the norm in his English tetrameters. Tension represents a problem in trochaic verse, where the inversion of polysyllabic words would mask the distinctive falling rhythm. Sidney avoids even initial inversion, but he erodes just over 11 per cent of non-final ictuses (see Table E).[13] The following lines from 'O Dear Life, When Shall it Be?' (Bullett 1947: 223–24) demonstrate the extremes of regularity in this metre:

(43)	Thy re-**mem**-brance to di-vorce	(5)
(44)	From the i-mage of thy lo-ver	(6)
(45)	En-ter brave-ly e-very-where	(20)
(46)	Beau-ty, mu-sic, sweet-ness, love	(34)

Instance (43) contains one erosion and (44) contains two, but (45) and (46) consist mostly of trochaic words that exaggerate the rhythm.

In the sixteenth and seventeenth centuries the trochaic tetrameter was often employed for musical settings, most notably in the *Book of Ayres* (Davis 1970) by Sidney's disciple Thomas Campion (b. 1567, d. 1620). Trochaic metres, however, have played a much slighter role in other genres of English poetry, and have rarely been employed for long poems; the reasons for this are probably linguistic: although English is a language of moraic trochees, grammatical words generally precede lexical, so that most English utterances and lines have an iambic rhythm.

Spenser's tumbling verse

Spenser employed native metres in his series of pastoral poems, or eclogues, *The Shepheardes Calender* (McCabe 1999), which was published in 1579. The structure of this work reveals how great was Spenser's interest in metre, and no two consecutive poems have the same verse design. 'Januarye', 'Aprill', 'June', 'August', 'October', and 'December' are in iambic pentameter; 'Februarie', 'Maye', and 'September' are in tumbling verse; 'March' and 'Julye' are in common measure (the former in *Sir Thopas*'s strophe), and 'November' is in what Russian metrists term *free iambs*: a mixture of iambic hexameters, pentameters, tetrameters, and dimeters (the last of which are also interwoven in 'Aprill'). The twelve poems thus exemplify six different types of line: four-beat and three-beat native lines, plus four iambic measures. They also exhibit eight different strophe designs, from the rhymed couplet to a very complex ten-line scheme. Spenser showed a mastery of all these forms, and effectively demonstrated all the principal options for future poets.

Although Spenser's tumbling verse has the same four beats, it employs alliteration much more sparingly, and differs from Tusser's in many important respects. First, Spenser uses atonic monosyllables to provide 3 per cent of non-final ictuses, and places disyllabic words in about 1 per cent of inter-ictic intervals; the following lines from 'Februarie' exemplify these two features:

(47)   As **do**-en high **To**-wers <u>in</u> an earth-**quake**   (6)
(48)   Or **sic**-ker thy <u>head</u> ve-ray **tot**-tie <u>is</u>   (55)

As these lines show, Spenser also fills about 50 per cent of inter-ictic intervals with a single syllable, and a whole line may be iambic, like the following from 'September':

(49)   For <u>it</u> had <u>been</u> an **aun**-cient <u>tree</u>   (207)

Spenser's employment of duple and triple time with about equal frequency is much closer to the rhythms of normal speech than is other tumbling verse. His metre meets Tarlinskaja's definition of a dolnik, but it is a dolnik with an artificially boosted proportion of triple time compared with English prose, where only one third of inter-ictic intervals are of two syllables.

As the lines quoted above demonstrate, Spenser's use of alliteration in this metre was not systematic and, since most of the new monosyllables in early modern English were stressed, he did not hesitate to alliterate them even when they were in weak positions, as in the case of 'cold' in the following line from 'Februarie':

(50)   The <u>kene</u> cold <u>blowes</u> || through my **bea**-ten <u>hyde</u>   (3)

Occasionally Spenser allows a third syllable to appear between ictuses and this produces rhythmic ambiguity; for example, in the following lines from 'Maye':

(51)   The <u>time</u> was <u>once</u> and may a-**gaine** re-**torne**   (103)
(52)   And <u>match</u> them-<u>selfe</u> with **migh**-ty po-ten-<u>tates</u>   (122)

Here the combination of duple time in one half of the line with an inter-ictic interval of three syllables in the other makes an alternative delivery possible: 'may' and 'po-' may be made prominent, producing five beats not four, and giving a perfect iambic pentameter. This ambiguity may have deterred subsequent poets from following Spenser's example, although, as Fabb 2002a: 108–22 shows, stress-syllabic metres can be equally ambiguous.

Spenser's alexandrine

Spenser, like Sidney, was attracted to the alexandrine: in *The Faerie Queene*, begun in 1580, he employed strophes rhymed abab bcbcc, each consisting of eight penta-meters followed by one hexameter. Spenser's alexandrine, however, has a striking innovation: it is no longer 6 + 6 syllables, but a unified line of 12 syllables in total. The following lines are from Canto 1 of the First Book of *The Faerie Queene* (Hamilton 1966: 80–100):

(53)   U-**pon** his <u>foe</u>, a **Dra**-gon, **hor**-ri-<u>ble</u> and <u>stearne</u>   (27)
(54)   And <u>by</u> her <u>in</u> a <u>linc</u> a <u>milke</u> white <u>lambe</u> she <u>lad</u>   (36)
(55)   And <u>this</u> faire **cou**-ple <u>eke</u> to <u>shroud</u> them-**selves** were <u>fain</u>   (54)
(56)   The **car**-ver <u>Holme</u>, the **Ma**-ple **seel**-dom **in**-ward <u>sound</u>   (81)

Spenser's line is a unified hexameter: instances (53) and (56) have first hemistichs of

6F syllables and this is compensated in their second, which contains only 5M, thus preserving the syllable count of 12M. This type of compensation, the equivalent of *coupe italienne* in the *vers de dix*, is unknown in either the French *alexandrin* or its Italian derivative. And this compensation is what converts Spenser's line into a true iambic hexameter, a unified dodecasyllable, with twelve syllables and six feet, in contrast to Sidney's alexandrine, which is a double trimeter (each hemistich has six syllables and three feet).

Note that (54) opens with two consecutive erosions and Spenser generally employs more tension than Sidney in this metre; but, although Spenser added a measure of variety to the alexandrine that his model lacked, this did little to reduce the accentual monotony (3 + 3) of an English stress-syllabic version. In *The Faerie Queene* Spenser offers a choice to subsequent English poets: pentameter or hexameter; and in his stanza the pentameter predominates (in the ratio 8:1) for a good aesthetic reason: the opposite ratio would have been much more monotonous. Had he reversed the proportions, it is doubtful whether the resulting poem would have been as popular or influential. Although both Sidney's divided and Spenser's unified variants have been employed right up to modern times, the alexandrine has never rivalled the pentameter in popularity, and the problem of its monotonous 3 + 3 structure, which seems to make the line heavier and slower than the shorter line, was solved only at the end of the nineteenth century, as I shall reveal in Chapter 8.

Spenser's iambic pentameter

Although Sidney may have underestimated the value that mid-line word-boundary variation gives the iambic pentameter, Spenser employed this device more skilfully than most of his predecessors. This can be seen from the following lines from Canto 1 of the First Book of *The Faerie Queene*: they illustrate the rhythmic subtlety of the iambic pentameter and every mid-line word configuration that can be accommodated within it:

(57) U-**pon** a <u>great</u> ad-**ven**-ture <u>he</u> was <u>bond</u>	(19)
(58) That **grea**-test <u>Glo</u>-ri-a-na <u>to</u> him <u>gave</u>	(20)
(59) That **grea**-test **glo**-rious <u>Queene</u> of *Fae-rie* <u>lond</u>	(21)
(60) To <u>prove</u> his **pu**-i-<u>ssance</u> in **bat**-tell <u>brave</u>	(25)

While (57) has a word boundary at position 4, (58) has a single word in positions 4–7, (59) one in 4–5, and (60) one in 4–6. According to my calculations, some 30 per cent of Spenser's lines have no word boundary immediately following syllable 4. This proportion had been employed by Chaucer in *The Canterbury Tales*, it also appears in the drama *Gorboduc* first performed in 1561, which I shall discuss in the next chapter.[14] But Spenser also employed other sources of variety in his pentameter: initial inversion in almost 7 per cent of lines and erosion of just over 7 per cent of ictuses (see Table A).

Spenser was undoubtedly a versifier of the highest order, and Saintsbury (1906: 1, 350–58) and Thompson (1961: 88–127) are correct to acknowledge the enormous contribution made by *The Shepheardes Calender* to the development of English stress-syllabic metrics.[15] The only feature of the canonical iambic pentameter that is missing from Spenser's *Faerie Queene* is the feminine line, and this he remedied more than a decade later, when he published his sonnet collection, the *Amoretti*. In Spenser's sonnets, as in Shakespeare's, more than 8 per cent of lines are feminine; in this the two poets were probably influenced by the stage practice, where a fair proportion of feminine lines helped dialogue sound more like normal speech. Shakespeare's earliest plays predate the publication of the *Amoretti* by several years and contain an even higher proportion of feminine lines (17 per cent, for example in *Richard III*, which was performed in the late 1580s).[16] Spenser's verse design could well be used to illustrate the detailed workings of the English long-line canon, but I shall use the iambic pentameters of Shakespeare's sonnets for this purpose since they have received far more critical attention (see, for example, Kiparsky 1977, Wright 1988, and Hanson 1995b).

Shakespeare and the English Long-Line Canon

Little is known and much has been written about the life of William Shakespeare (b. 1564, d. 1616), who hailed from Stratford in Warwickshire but spent most of his life in London, where he was active as a playwright between the late 1580s and 1613. His background is so ordinary, and his literary output so extraordinary, that many conspiracy theories have been entertained to explain the latter. But throughout Shakespeare's long public career nobody working with him doubted that he was the author, and after his death his friends had no hesitation in collecting his work as a tribute. Few contemporary critics back the conspiracy theories, but this is as much the result of the populist temper of our times as of any change in the balance of evidence.

In recent years a great deal of metrical research has focused on Shakespeare's long line, including some of the most important contributions to the study of the iambic pentameter in general. One of these, Hanson 1995b, reveals that Shakespeare had two different verse designs for the iambic pentameter: the first, which is very like Milton's, he employed for his sonnets, and the second, which is based on feet not syllables, he used in the blank verse of his plays. Many years earlier Tarlinskaja had demonstrated that dramatic and non-dramatic iambic pentameters in general have very different characteristics (1976: 138–75). I shall therefore separate the two types of iambic pentameter and postpone consideration of Shakespeare's, and other poets', dramatic verse until the next chapter.

Shakespeare's non-dramatic long line

If we set aside certain passages in his plays, the best-known iambic pentameters by Shakespeare are from his sonnets (Harrison 1949), which were probably composed between 1592 and 1598, when the form enjoyed a vogue following the posthumous publication of Sidney's *Astrophel and Stella*. Of Shakespeare's 154 sonnets only one (145) is in tetrameters, and, since one sonnet (126) lacks a final couplet, my sample of verse instances comprises 2140 lines in total. I shall infer the poet's verse design from these instances and compare it with the parametric description given by Hanson 1995b. Almost 9 per cent of the sonnets' lines are feminine, a lower proportion than that in Shakespeare's dramatic verse, and slightly higher than the level employed by Spenser in his *Amoretti*, which were published in 1595. Shakespeare used feminine lines for artistic effect: Sonnets 20 and 87 contain fourteen and twelve feminine lines respectively; in 20 they brilliantly reinforce the poem's meaning: the poet complains that the young man's penis is redundant, and an uncounted syllable, like a limp member, graces every line. In contrast, in Sonnet 87 the feminine line is used to express a sense of loss and resignation.

Unlike his own and his contemporaries' dramatic verse, Shakespeare's sonnets do not include occasional lines that are truncated (with six or eight positions) or extended (with twelve). The poet's template is thus uncontroversial and contains ten right-strong positions, but his correspondence rules are less clear and merit a more detailed examination.

Shakespeare's position-size parameter

The presence of feminine lines shows that final positions have a maximum size of more than one syllable: as in Romance metres, the final stress may be followed by one or more post-tonic syllables. Hanson, however, argues that Shakespeare's rules allow an extra syllable in other positions, because his maximum position size is one foot, or moraic trochee. Any position may thus contain (a) a heavy syllable, (b) a light syllable, (c) a stressed followed by an unstressed syllable, or (d) a series of unstressed light syllables (1995b: 67). Hanson cites Weissmiller 1989 in support of her hypothesis that Shakespeare's pentameter is foot-based, but admits that her case must rest on examples where the multiple occupancy of a position constitutes two different words (1995b: 73). The examples she gives, however, are all from Shakespeare's dramatic verse (for example, *King Lear*, v. 3. 274 and IV. 7. 83), and I can find little evidence for her hypothesis in the sonnets. The following lines from the *Sonnets* might be argued to be examples of disyllabic positions:

(61)	**Kno**-wing a **be**-tter **spirit** doth <u>use</u> your <u>name</u>	(80. 2)
(62)	And <u>trouble</u> deaf **hea**-ven <u>with</u> my **boot**-less <u>cries</u>	(29. 3)
(63)	Being <u>had</u>, to **tri**-umph, **be**-ing <u>lack'd</u>, to <u>hope</u>	(52. 14)
(64)	Weeds <u>a</u>-**mong** <u>weeds</u>, or **flow**ers with **flo**-wers gath^ered	(124. 4)

The word *spirit* (61) also ends the first colon in 86. 5 and 144. 4, and Hanson's hypothesis makes epic caesura a feature of this metre; but the only unequivocal example she gives is from *Hamlet*, I. 4. 5 (1995b: 74). I would argue that neither (61) nor (62) contains epic caesura, because the word in position 4 is syllabically ambivalent: thus 'spirit' counts as one syllable in 56. 8 and 98. 3, but two in 129. 1; and 'heaven' counts as one syllable in 93. 9 and 21. 3, but two in 21. 12 and 29. 3. Similarly, 'trouble' (62), 'being' (63), and 'flowers' (64) can be pronounced as two syllables or as one (London vendors sometimes even spell the last word 'flars').

There are many other syllabic ambiguities in the sonnets: *buried* can be pronounced as either two syllables (as in 31. 9) or three (as in 31. 4); *influence* can be three syllables, but in 15. 4 I would argue that it is two, as is also the case with *mightier* in 16. 1; and 'disabled' occupies the last four positions of 66. 8. The only line where extra syllables cannot be accounted for in this way is:

(65)   My sin-ful earth these rebel powers that thee a-rray   (146. 2)

But here the words 'my sinful earth' are repeated from the previous line and it is likely that they have been repeated in error in place of a disyllable (Harrison 1949: 126 suggests 'bearing' or 'feeding'; Alexander 1958 places 'My sinful earth' in brackets to indicate a lacuna).

Hanson states that Milton's iambic pentameter is syllable-based, because word-final l, m, n, and r do not always represent syllables, and because Milton sometimes counts sequences of two vowels as a syllable, even when they are in different words (1995b: 72). She also lists a number of words that are 'for all poets in the English tradition [...] optionally monosyllabic' (1995b: 73). But everything that Hanson says of Milton's iambic pentameter applies equally well to Shakespeare's non-dramatic long line. There is clear evidence that the poets of Shakespeare's time believed that the unit of their versifying was the number of syllables (see, for example, Van Dorsten 1966: 73), and Hanson acknowledges this (1995b: 71). I see no reason to doubt that belief in the case of Shakespeare's sonnets, and I would argue that this particular hypothesis of Hanson's (position size equals one foot) is, at best, unproven for his non-dramatic verse.

Shakespeare's prominence site and type

Hanson is more justified in regarding the metre of the sonnets and the plays as one in regard to the remaining parameters of Shakespeare's verse design. She argues that stressed and unstressed syllables may appear in any type of position in the sonnets, and the following instances illustrate this:

(66)   To be death's con-quest and make worms thy heir   (6. 14)
(67)   By ad-ding one thing to my pur-pose nothing   (20. 12)

In (66) the strong position 6 contains an unstressed syllable ('and'), while the weak positions 3 and 5 contain stressed ones ('death's' and 'make'); in (67) the strong position 6 contain an unstressed syllable ('to'), while the weak position 5 contains a stress ('thing'). Hanson therefore argues that Shakespeare's prominence type is strength, and his prominence site is weak positions: strong syllables (those with greater lexical stress than their neighbours) can appear in weak positions only under exceptional conditions. But she ignores the possibility of a constraint that prohibits unstressed syllables occupying consecutive strong positions (other than the first two in the line). Although Shakespeare crodes more than 10 per cent of ictuses, he observes this constraint throughout the sonnets.

Parametric theory is much more rigorous in its analysis of inversion, which it accounts for in three ways: *the rhythm rule* (Kiparsky 1977: 218–20), the *closure principle* (Hanson & Kiparsky 1996: 293), and the *bracketing condition* (Kiparsky 1977: 201–05). The rhythm rule, or 'move X', is a general one in English, whereby in normal utterances the stress of certain words shifts so as to avoid consecutive, or clashing stresses: thus we say 'sweet six-teen', but 'six-teen tons', giving both a [s w s] stress contour (see Hayes 1995: 35–36). In Shakespeare's sonnets we find such a stress shift in words such as 'there-by' (1. 2), 'un-thrift' (9. 9 and 13. 13), and 'un-us'd' (4. 13). It should be noted that, although the rhythm rule accounts for some of the mismatches between strong syllables and weak positions in the sonnets, it occurs in well under 1 per cent of lines. It could also be argued that the word 'therefore' is subject to rhythm rule in the following lines:

> (68) **Gen**-tle thou <u>art</u>, and **there**-fore <u>to</u> be <u>won</u>   (41. 5)
> (69) **Beau**-teous thou <u>art</u>, **there**-fore to <u>be</u> as-sailed   (41. 6)

But (69) can also be accounted for by the closure principle, whereby rules tend to be more relaxed at the beginning and stricter at the end of units (Smith 1968), because 'therefore' may represent a hemistich-initial inversion. The most common application of this principle in stress-syllabic verse is line-initially, as in both (68) and (69), and it occurs in just under 5 per cent of lines in Shakespeare's sonnets. Initial inversion in the second colon occurs in under 1 per cent of lines: a clearer example than (69) of initial inversion in both cola is the following:

> (70) **Ri**-<u>cher</u> than <u>wealth</u>, **prou**-<u>der</u> than **gar**-ments' <u>cost</u>   (91. 10)

The bracketing condition states that, as a rare exception, inversions may occur in other positions in the line providing the two syllables concerned are both in the same foot and the same word: such a condition also occurs in well under 1 per cent of the lines of Shakespeare's sonnets, including the following:

> (71) And <u>peace</u> pro-**claims** o-<u>lives</u> of **end**-less <u>age</u>   (107. 8)
> (72) Do <u>I</u> en-<u>vy</u> those <u>jacks</u> that **nim**-ble <u>leap</u>   (128. 5)

The inversions of 'olives' in (71) and 'envy' in (72) both meet the bracketing condition in that their foot and word boundaries coincide. Finally, as Hanson (1995b: 71) points out, there is one inversion in the sonnets that falls into none of the above categories: significantly, it involves a grammatical word, a type that is particularly susceptible to inversion, as has been shown in Chapter 4.

> (73) And <u>I</u> will **com**-ment <u>u</u>-**pon** that of-**fence**   (89. 2)

In total, inversion that is not line-initial occurs in just over 2 per cent of lines in Shakespeare's sonnets.

To summarize, my analysis confirms the description of Shakespeare's long-line verse design given by Hanson 1995b other than in one respect: her position-size parameter of one foot cannot be justified for his non-dramatic verse. This parameter is one of the distinguishing features of his and his successors' dramatic verse, as I shall show in the next chapter.

Non-parametric features of Shakespeare's long line

I have argued in detail elsewhere that the verse design of the English iambic pentameter has important features not identified by parametric theory (Duffell 2002b). These features include a constraint on unstressed syllables in strong positions (consecutive erosion) and caesura variation. Shakespeare's iambic pentameters combine what I call 'French' and 'Italian' lines, as the following examples show (a word boundary dividing the syllables in positions 4 and 5 is marked with double strokes):

> (74) Look <u>in</u> the <u>glass</u>, || and <u>tell</u> the <u>face</u> thou **view**est   (3. 1)
> (75) When **for**-ty **win**-ters <u>shall</u> be-**siege** thy <u>brow</u>   (2. 1)

In Shakespeare's non-dramatic pentameters 33 per cent of lines are of the 'Italian' type, whereas his lexicon would lead us to expect only 18 per cent (Duffell 2002b: 305). The difference between these two figures is very highly significant, being the equivalent of what statisticians term *six standard errors* (see the note following Table T). Thus Shakespeare, like Chaucer and Spenser, must either consciously or subconsciously have cultivated variety in the syntactic boundaries within his pentameter lines.

The distinctive features of Shakespeare's non-dramatic iambic pentameter are shown in Table A, and the remainder of his surviving verse is in a variety of short lines, found in the lyrics of his plays, or in the much freer long line (the dramatic pentameter) that makes up most of their dialogue. Since some of his best-known plays belong to the seventeenth century, and his verse technique still seems to have been developing in that period, I shall postpone consideration of his lyric metres and his dramatic pentameter until the next chapter, when the latter can be set in context and compared with the metre of his theatrical contemporaries.

Conclusions

Although the line we term iambic tetrameter became established as the English short-line canon early in the sixteenth century, a long-line canon took much longer to emerge. A number of other metres might have become the canon, some of them native, and others imported. Wyatt, like Lydgate before him, sought an English long line of which the iambic decasyllable would be one, but not the only, possible realization. Surrey employed poulter's measure, an iambic version of a traditional ictic metre, and an iambic metre modelled on the French syllabic *vers de dix*. Sidney developed trochaic verse, but wisely limited it to short-line lyrics, while Spenser updated tumbling verse and common measure, and these two poets developed different iambic versions of the French *alexandrin*. But it was Spenser who recaptured in modern English all the nuances of Chaucer's iambic pentameter as it appears in the *Canterbury Tales*. A generation of playwrights then brought this line to mass audiences, making it the accepted metrical stylization of dignified English speech, and poets of subsequent centuries endorsed this choice. The iambic pentameter's dominance was challenged only at the end of the nineteenth century, when the pan-European vogue for free verse swept over it and around it.

While French metrics remained a rock that survived intact for almost a thousand years, English versification changed beyond recognition between 1066 and 1580. During the latter part of this period native and foreign metres competed for popularity and esteem, and many poets experimented on the margins of the two. The iambic pentameter emerged as the English long-line canon for a mixture of reasons, linguistic, aesthetic, and sociological. It had in its favour that it was a good fit for the language, and that it offered a mixture of regularity and variety, appealing to the human desire for both security and stimulation. But it was also fortunate in attracting at an early stage in its development poets whose work would be read and reread by later generations.

Notes to Chapter 6

1. Wilkins 1959: 26–39 argues that, since no surviving Occitan or Italian poem has strophes with the same rhyme scheme as the earliest sonnets, Lentini must have invented the form by adding a six-line tail of his own devising to the Sicilian *strambotto* (see Biadene 1899: 11).

2. One of the few English poets to employ the *sonnet régulier* was Sir Philip Sidney, whom I shall discuss later in this chapter.

3. Some English poets, nevertheless, have risen to the challenge of the original Petrarchan design with its fewer rhymes, and Edmund Spenser, whom I shall discuss later in this chapter, always made a point of repeating one of the rhymes in the quatrains of his English sonnets.

4. My scansion identifies all even-numbered positions in English iambic pentameters as being ictic, but many of Wyatt's lines are not iambic pentameters.

5. These sonnets appear in the Egerton Manuscript (British Museum MS 2711) and have Wyatt's name written against them; some are believed to be written, or to have emendations, in his own hand. Together with other poems attributed to Wyatt, these twenty-two sonnets were published in 1557 by Richard Tottel in his *Songs and Sonnets* (usually known as *Tottel's Miscellany*; ed. Rollins 1928–29). Tottel regularized many of Wyatt's lines in his edition, but, since Wyatt's emendations in the Egerton MS often make a line's rhythm and/or syllable count less regular, there can be no doubt that Tottel's regularity was not the poet's metrical intention.

6. This poem is an imitation of Petrarch's *Canzoniere*, CCCXX: 'Zefiro torna e'l bel tempo rimena' (Vianello 1966). Surrey shows his rhyming skill by employing only two rhymes abab abab abab aa.

7. Strang 1980: 288 notes a significant increase in monosyllables between the eleventh century and the sixteenth; by my calculation early Modern English texts comprise ± 75% monosyllables, Old French texts ± 60%, and fourteenth-century Italian texts ± 50% (Duffell 2002b: 305).

8. The differences in Surrey's metrical style are probably not chronological: most poets' blank verse contains a higher proportion of 'Italian' lines than their rhymed verse.

9. He changed his metre significantly in his collaborative writing for the theatre, as I shall show in the next chapter.

10. Six-stress lines occur in Middle English alliterative metre and in Wyatt's sonnets, for example (13) and (14) above; these earlier lines, of course, are not regular in syllable count like those of Sidney and Spenser.

11. *Astrophel and Stella* contains, besides the 108 sonnets mentioned, two long-line poems that include lines of 10F syllables, and seven short-line poems, of which six are in trochaic tetrameter and one in iambic trimeter.

12. Carper & Attridge describe the rhythm of trochaic verse in which all the lines are masculine as 'simple' and 'chant-like' (2003: 131).

13. Note that confining inversion to monosyllables has also been a feature of iambic metres in some languages, including German and Russian (Bailey 1973b: 133).

14. Elizabethan dramatists are more likely to have followed *Gorboduc*'s example, but other English poets probably followed Spenser's.

15. Thompson devotes more than one third of *The Founding of English Metre* to Spenser and Sidney.

16. It is, of course, impossible to judge definitively whether Chaucer and Gower favoured feminine endings, since the vast majority of their lines end in word-final schwas. If we syllabify these schwas we make the lines sound more like their Italian models; if we don't we make them sound more like normal fourteenth-century English speech; I can think of no way of resolving this dilemma.

CHAPTER 7

Consolidating and Refining the Canons

This chapter chronicles English metrical developments between 1600 and 1750; by the earlier date Sidney and Spenser had developed the iambic pentameter that was to become the English long-line canon. I discussed Shakespeare's non-dramatic long line in the previous chapter because it so closely resembles theirs, and because his sonnets, although not published until 1620, were probably composed in the 1590s. But one of the chief reasons why this metre has become canonical is that many of England's greatest dramatists have employed it. The most influential of these was Shakespeare himself, but the long-line metre of his dramatic verse differs considerably from that of his sonnets. Since he composed his later plays only in the seventeenth century I have deferred discussion of Shakespeare's dramatic verse to this chapter, when I can present his dramatic long line in its historical context, noting how English playwrights versified before and after him. But first I shall say something of his employment of shorter lines in his plays.

Shakespeare's Short-Line Verse Designs

Shakespeare's shorter lines represent only a very small proportion of his total verse output, and they have survived almost entirely in the lyrics sung by characters in his plays. In the few of these for which he employed the short-line canon he avoided the initial inversion of polysyllabic words, but frequently inverted phrasal stress by placing an atonic monosyllable in an ictic position (erosion), as in this line from 'Winter' (*Love's Labour's Lost*, v. 2. 899–916):

(1)   When **roas**-ted **crabs** hiss <u>in</u> the <u>bowl</u>   (14)

Shakespeare employs Sidney's favourite, the trochaic tetrameter, more frequently than the iambic canon, as in the song in *Midsummer Night's Dream* (v. 1. 360–79):

(2)   <u>Now</u> the **hun**-gry **li**-on <u>roars</u>   (1)
(3)   <u>From</u> the **pre**-sence <u>of</u> the <u>sun</u>   (15)
(4)   **Foll**°-wing **dark**-ness <u>like</u> a <u>dream</u>   (16)

As noted, this metre allows erosion but not polysyllabic inversion: in (3) the first and third ictuses are eroded, and in (4) there is syllabic ambiguity, since 'following' may be two syllables or three.

Shakespeare is even fonder, however, of a variable tetrameter, in which iambic lines of eight syllables are mixed with trochaic lines of seven, as in the following lines from two other songs (*Twelfth Night*, II. 3. 36–43, and *Cymbeline*, IV. 2. 259–82):

(5)	O **mis**-tress <u>mine</u>, where <u>are</u> you **roa**-ming	(1)
(6)	[V] <u>Then</u> come <u>kiss</u> me, <u>sweet</u> and **twen**-ty	(11)
(7)	[V] <u>Youth's</u> a <u>stuff</u> will <u>not</u> en-**dure**	(12)
(8)	[V] <u>Fear</u> no <u>more</u> the <u>heat</u> o' the <u>sun</u>	(1)
(9)	[V] **Gol**-den <u>lads</u> and <u>girls</u> all <u>must</u>	(5)
(10)	As **chim**-ney-**swee**-pers, <u>come</u> to <u>dust</u>	(6)

Note that this metre has many other sources of rhythmic variety besides mixing feminine lines with masculine and trochaic lines with iambic: instance (5) has a monosyllabic initial inversion in its second hemistich; (7), (8), and (9) have void initial positions; and (8) has an ambiguous interval between its third and final ictuses: 'o' the' may be two syllables or one (it is sometimes spelled 'o' th'' in this period).

But some of Shakespeare's duple-time songs undoubtedly do contain disyllabic (and void) intervals, as is shown by the following lines from *As You Like It* (II. 7. 174–90) and *Winter's Tale* (IV. 3. 1–12):

(11)	[V] <u>Blow</u>, [V] <u>blow</u>, thou **win**-ter <u>wind</u>	(1)
(12)	Most **friend**-ship is **feig**-ning, most **lo**-ving mere **fol**-ly	(8)
(13)	When **daf**-fo-<u>dils</u> be-**gin** to <u>peer</u>	(1)
(14)	For the <u>red</u> blood <u>reigns</u> in the **win**-ter's <u>pale</u>	(4)

Instance (11) has two zero intervals / void positions in the first hemistich; (12) has only disyllabic intervals; (13) is a regular iambic tetrameter; (14) has an even mixture of triple and duple time. The metre of both songs is thus the four-ictic dolnik, and instances (12) and (14) are indistinguishable from lines of tumbling verse.

Shakespeare's songs demonstrate that the most influential of English poets continued to employ traditional modes of versifying as well as helping establish the long-line canon. This coexistence, which was also a feature of most subsequent periods, was based in human psychology: English poets and audiences continued to perceive lines of verse as a series of beats that under certain conditions produced a regular number of syllables, but under others did not.

English Dramatic Metres

Tarlinskaja argues that the dramatic iambic pentameter differs significantly from the non-dramatic (1976: 138–75), and this is confirmed by my comparison of the metre of Shakespeare's sonnets with that given for his plays by Hanson 1995b. The tradition of actors declaiming in verse is of considerable antiquity, and in English was established in the Middle Ages; the metrical history of dramatic verse in many ways parallels that of non-dramatic.

Medieval dramatic verse

The medieval Church allowed the human dramatic urge an outlet in pageant plays celebrating events in the Christian calendar. In a number of English towns trades guilds also competed in presenting religious dramas on the feast of Corpus Christi (the first Thursday after Trinity Sunday; it fell between 23 May and 24 June), and cycles of such plays have survived from the fourteenth and fifteenth centuries. The examples that follow are from a cycle of plays performed in York, perhaps from as early as 1376 until the 1560s. Since plays had propaganda value for the cult of the Virgin, their demise resulted as much from the Reformation as from a change in public taste. The cycle comprises fifty plays and some fourteen thousand lines of verse, and my quotations are from the selection with modernized spelling edited by Beadle & King (1984).

Most of the verse of the York plays is in the type of strophe employed for the long alliterative line in both Scotland and England: typically the strophe begins with a quatrain of four-beat lines rhymed abab, and closes with a series of shorter lines that have a more intricate rhyme scheme. The following lines from the Tapiters' and Couchers' play *The Dream of Pilate's Wife* (Beadle & King 1984: 154–74, lines 37–42) demonstrate the metre:

(15)   I am <u>dame</u> **pre**-cious **Pro**-cu-la, of **prin**-ces the <u>prize</u>,
(16)   <u>Wife</u> to Sir **Pi**-late here, <u>prince</u> wi-thout <u>peer</u>.
(17)   A <u>well</u> of all **wo**-man-hood I am, **wit**-ty and <u>wise</u>,
(18)   Con-**ceive** now my **coun**-te-nance so **come**-ly and <u>clear</u>.
(19)   The **co**-lour of my <u>corse</u> is full <u>clear</u>
(20)   And in **ri**-chesse of <u>robes</u> am **I rayed**

There are four mandatory beats in each of the first four lines; the pronoun 'I' in (17) supplies an optional fifth. Instances (19) and (20) open a 'wheel' of three-beat lines rhymed bcbbc.[1] The play's rhymes are not always as perfect as those in this strophe, nor is its alliteration as consistent. The maximum size of weak positions is four syllables, but an interval of two is very common, giving a triple-time rhythm to many lines.

Some of the York plays also contain lyrics in shorter lines of two or three beats, like the following from the Pewterers' and Founders' play *Joseph's Trouble about Mary* (Beadle & King 1984: 48–58, lines 163–66):

(21)   But **Ma**-ry, <u>all</u> that <u>see</u> thee
(22)   May <u>wit</u> thy <u>works</u> are <u>wan</u>.★
(23)   Thy <u>womb</u> it <u>al</u>-ways <u>wrays</u> thee
(24)   That <u>thou</u> hast <u>met</u> with <u>man</u>.
                    [★ 'can perceive your ways are wicked'; wrays: 'betrays']

All the inter-ictic intervals in this strophe contain one syllable, and the metre is a particularly regular and iambic version of a popular ballad metre that alternates 3F and 3M lines.

The metre of the York plays is thus typical of English verse before Chaucer and Gower; in these plays we can see the dolnik emerging from older accentual forms, and we can also see that shorter lines tend to have a predominantly iambic rhythm. The metrical skill involved in composing them was considerable, as was that required for staging them (see Beadle & King 1984: xvii): the poets' use of rhyme, alliteration, and strophe structure is as adroit as that of any of their contemporaries. We know nothing of the medieval plays' authors other than that celebrity poets sometimes wrote them when the money was right. 'Mumming at London' by John Lydgate, which I analysed in Chapter 5, belongs to the same tradition as the York plays, both in terms of seeking a mass audience, and of preserving an ancient mode of versifying.

Renaissance dramatic verse: the native tradition

Although their history was as violent and colourful as any other, C. S. Lewis (1954) called the reigns of the first four Tudor monarchs the 'Drab Period' of English literature (see Drabble 1985: 289); its foremost poets were Skelton, Wyatt, and Surrey. In this period Corpus Christi plays performed by guildsmen were gradually succeeded by mystery plays and dramas based on classical and foreign models, and performed by schoolboys or law students. Thus the anonymous mystery play, *Everyman* (1509–19), was imitated from a Dutch model, and its metre can be seen from its most famous lines (Cawley 1956):

> (25) E-v^ery-man, <u>I</u> will <u>go</u> || with <u>thee</u>, and <u>be</u> thy <u>guide</u>
> (26) In <u>thy</u> most <u>need</u>, || to <u>go</u> by thy <u>side</u>

Although (25) is scanned as an iambic hexameter with an irregular opening, (26) is neither an octosyllable nor a regular iambic tetrameter, and the metre of both is more accurately described as a dolnik with two to three ictuses in each hemistich.

Saintsbury calls this metre 'doggerel' and says its lines vary from octosyllable to alexandrine but have neither a regular syllable count nor a reliable accentual pattern (1906: 1, 336–43). It is clearly descended from the medieval alliterative measure, and Cunliffe describes it as a metre of the 'native tradition' (1912: lxxi–lxxvi). The earliest surviving English plays by known authors were in the same traditional metre: *King Johan* by John Bale (b. 1495, d. 1563); *Ralph Roister Doister* by Nicholas Udall (b. 1504, d. 1556), which was first acted in 1552; and *Gammer Gurton's Needle*, of disputed authorship, which was first acted ten years later. The metre of these 'doggerel' plays reminds us of Wyatt's verse: lines with five prominence peaks or beats occur alongside balanced lines of 2 + 2 or 3 + 3 beats. In contrast, one early Elizabethan drama employed a metre that was closely related to poulter's measure as used by Surrey: *Damon and Pithias* by Richard Edwards (b. ?1523, d. 1566) was probably composed shortly before 1567, and the lines of its rhymed couplets have a three- and four-beat structure reminiscent of poulter's measure, as can be seen from the following (Cunliffe 1912: lxxiv):

> (27) Loth <u>I</u> am <u>to</u> de-**parte** | sith <u>sobbes</u> my **trem**-bling <u>tounge</u> doth <u>stay</u>.
> (28) O **Mu**-sicke <u>sounde</u> my **dole**-full <u>playntes</u> | when <u>I</u> am <u>gone</u> my <u>way</u>!

The authors of these plays were educated men and some were also well travelled; this was important, because in the first half of the sixteenth century a new European drama based on Classical models was developing in Rome and Paris. This new drama began in Italy: Antonio Cammelli's *Filostrato e Panfila* was produced in 1499, and Galeotto del Carretto's *Sofonisba*, which was first produced in 1546, had been written in 1502 (see Cunliffe 1912: xxiv–xxx). In France, Étienne Jodelle's *Cleopâtra captive* appeared only in 1553, but French translations of Sophocles and Seneca in *alexandrins* and *hexasyllabes* date from 1537–44 (see Cunliffe 1912: lii–lvi). In both Italian and French, poets had employed for centuries the metre that became the language's long-line metrical canon, the *endecasillabo* and the *alexandrin*, and these metres established themselves effortlessly as the staples of dramatic verse. The theatre disseminated metre on a larger scale than any other medium of the time, and helped make the process of canon formation self-reinforcing: playwrights used the canon because everyone could recognize it, everyone could recognize it because they heard it constantly in the theatre. Drama played a similar role in the establishment of the iambic pentameter in England, but at the time of its introduction onto the Elizabethan stage the form of the English long-line canon was still undecided.

The advent of the iambic pentameter and blank verse

One play was decisive in establishing the metrical norms of English drama; it was a tale of ancient English royalty and its second performance took place before the young Queen Elizabeth in 1562. *Gorboduc* (Tydeman 1992) is a tragedy in the style of Seneca and was the work of two men: Thomas Norton (b. 1532, d. 1584) is credited with the first three acts and Thomas Sackville (b. 1536, d. 1608) with the last two. Since Sackville was an established poet who visited Italy and knew some Italian, he may have been the more influential in the choice of the play's metre, iambic pentameter, and its form, blank verse. Italian plays in blank verse (*sciolti*) predate French and English attempts to revive Classical drama (see Elwert 1973: 108–09), but *Gorboduc*'s authors also had other models for an unrhymed long line in Surrey's English translation of the *Aeneid* and in Seneca's Latin tragedies.

The metrical styles of the two parts of *Gorboduc* are remarkably similar, but the metre of the part attributed to Sackville differs in some respects from that of his 'Induction' and 'Complaynt', which I discussed in Chapter 6. The metrical styles of these works can be compared from the figures given in Tables B and C. One of the most striking similarities is between the proportion of 'Italian' lines in the two halves of the play: 30 per cent in Norton's part and 29 in Sackville's, which contrasts with 15 per cent in Sackville's 'Induction'.[2] Both parts share some of the distinguishing features of the 'Induction': a monopoly of masculine lines (with rare exceptions in Norton's part), and a strong iambic pulse, resulting from the avoidance of epic and lyric caesurae. Significant differences between the two poets' metrical styles in this play include medial inversion (more in Norton), third-ictus erosion (more in Sackville), and enjambment (marginally more in Sackville).

The following lines illustrate the two poets' use of tension:

(29)	My **fa**-ther? <u>Why</u>? I <u>know</u> **no**-<u>thing</u> at <u>all</u>	(I. 1. 19)
(30)	**Cause**-<u>less</u>, un-**kind**-ly, <u>and</u> in **wrong**-ful <u>wise</u>	(I. 1. 27)
(31)	The <u>realm</u> di-**vi**-ded **in**-to two **sun**-dry <u>parts</u>	(I. 2. 129)
(32)	Or <u>with</u> the **strang**-ling <u>cord</u> hang'd <u>on</u> the <u>trees</u>	(v. 2. 1569)
(33)	And <u>of</u> the **mur**-der <u>of</u> their **sac**-red <u>prince</u>	(v. 2. 1572)

Instance (29) contains one of Norton's fourth-foot inversions (note that the evidence from other plays suggests that 'nothing' was not invariably s w at this time); (30) has one of Norton's initial inversions, and easily slides into a dactylic rhythm if the wrong monosyllable ('in') is stressed in the latter part of the line; (31), again in Norton's part, contains one of the play's rare examples of a disyllabic inter-ictic interval, '-to two' (note that eliminating the '-to' weakens the line's grammar). Instance (32), by Sackville, combines first- and fourth-ictus erosions; and (33) combines Sackville's favourite third-ictus erosion with a first-ictus erosion. As these examples show, the metre of both parts of the play is syllable-based and not foot-based (Hanson 1995b), and the loosening of the weak position-size parameter in the dramatic pentameter was a later development (see Table B).

Saintsbury is very critical of *Gorboduc*: he deprecates its end-stopped lines, although it contains more enjambment than Marlowe's or Shakespeare's early plays (see Table C), and he says that *Gorboduc* 'fails to achieve sweetness or magnificence' (1906: 1, 347). But an objective analysis of the play's metre shows it to be very similar to that of Saintsbury's favourite, Spenser (see Table A); in particular, *Gorboduc* anticipates Spenser's cultivation of the 'Italian' line by some years, a subtlety that the playwrights who followed failed to capture. Thus, for example, there are only 14 per cent running lines in *Jocasta* (Cunliffe 1912), translated from the Italian in 1566, and only 13 per cent in *Gismond of Salerne* (also in Cunliffe 1912), which was first performed in 1567 or 1568. These figures are very similar to those found in Surrey's *Aeneid* three decades earlier, and in both plays barely 5 per cent of lines are enjambed. *Gismond of Salerne* also disregarded *Gorboduc*'s example in another way: it was in quatrains rhymed xaxa and was reworked in blank verse only in 1591.

The metre of Marlowe's and of Shakespeare's dramatic verse

By 1578 the first theatres had been constructed, and lawyers and schoolboys soon gave place to professional actors. The number of playwrights multiplied, and a few of their plays were clearly intended as enduring literary products since they appeared in print in their authors' lifetimes, and in versions too long for theatrical performance.[3] In the early part of Shakespeare's career his most significant rival was Christopher Marlowe (b. 1564, d. 1593), who seems to have begun writing plays in the early 1580s while still at Cambridge. Marlowe's first major work, however, was *Tamburlaine the Great*, the second part of which was completed in 1588, and his murder in 1594 ensured that his output was limited to seven plays (Steane 1969) plus some poems and translations. Saintsbury is as dismissive of Marlowe's blank verse as he is of *Gorboduc*'s, arguing that it is still largely end-stopped and cannot be compared to Shakespeare's (1906: 1, 346–48). But the frequent use of enjambment developed only in the course of Shakespeare's career, and the early *Richard III* is much more end-stopped. The most striking difference between the dramatic iambic pentameter of the two poets is that Marlowe eroded the fourth ictus more often and eschewed feminine lines, just as Sidney, the early Spenser, and the authors of *Gorboduc* had done (see Tables A and C). The following line, which, like all my examples, is from Part II of the play, illustrates two metrical features that Marlowe employed much more often than his predecessors, initial inversion and fourth-ictus erosion:

(34)   **Mar**-ching from **Cai**-ron **north**-ward with his camp   (I. 1. 47)

Marlowe's line, however, has many similarities to Shakespeare's: for example, although in Marlowe's earliest surviving play *Dido, Queen of Carthage* the proportion of 'Italian' lines is only 24 per cent, in Part II of *Tamburlaine the Great* this figure is 36 per cent, the average figure found in Shakespeare's blank verse. Marlowe's dramatic iambic pentameter also resembles that of *Richard III* in that he employs similar levels of inversion, resolution (disyllabic and void weak positions), and erosion of ictuses other than the fourth. Most candidates for disyllabic positions in Marlowe's verse involve syllabically ambiguous words, like *boisterous* (I. 2. 70), *lingering* (I. 3. 75), or *Barbary* (I. 6. 7), and in only a few examples (representing less than 1 per cent of total lines) are the two syllables in the inter-ictic interval from separate words, including the following lines (I. 3. 61–62):

(35)   I like that well. But tell me, my lord, if I
(36)   Should let you go, would you be as good as your word?

In (35) position 7 contains 'me, my', and in (36) there are two such positions: 7 contains 'be as' and 9 contains 'as your'. Note that such lines with two disyllabic positions are metrically ambiguous: Marlowe may have intended them to be hexameters, since he occasionally includes an iambic line of a different length (mostly the tetrameter) in his plays.

Both Marlowe and Shakespeare employed initial inversion in their plays slightly more frequently than their predecessors; but it was Shakespeare who greatly increased the number of disyllabic inter-ictic intervals to produce the foot-based metre described in Hanson 1995b. The following lines illustrate two metrical features that Shakespeare employed more often than Marlowe or his predecessors: inversion opening the second colon (exemplified by a line from *Richard III*), and polysyllabic weak positions (exemplified by a line from *Antony and Cleopatra*):

(37)   By **drun**-ken **pro**-phe-cies, **li**-bels, and dreams   (I. 1. 33)
(38)   Call **in** the **mes**-sen-gers. As I am E-gypt's queen   (I. 1. 29)

The development of both these features is quantified in Tables B and C, which compare the sources of variety in the metres of four plays and two non-dramatic works by the playwrights discussed here.[4] Table B compares the use of inversion and resolution (in this case the use of non-standard inter-ictic intervals), and of feminine and 'Italian' lines; Table C compares the use of erosion and enjambment.[5]

The tables demonstrate the chief sources of variety in this metre as employed in four plays and two non-dramatic works, Sackville's 'Induction' to the *Mirrour for Magistrates* and Shakespeare's *Sonnets*. Table B shows that Shakespeare was the only one of these poets to realize the variety that can be achieved by a mixture of masculine and feminine lines, and that he increased the feminine proportion in his plays, probably because it made his lines better resemble normal speech. Both tables also show that Sackville's dramatic line bears as strong a resemblance to Norton's as to his own verse in the 'Induction'. Table A shows, in addition, that Marlowe and Shakespeare significantly increased the proportion of 'Italian' lines in their dramatic verse from the levels found in *Gorboduc*, or in Spenser's *Faerie Queene*, or in Shakespeare's *Sonnets*. Table A also shows that Marlowe used initial inversion more often than the writers of *Gorboduc* and that in this he was followed by Shakespeare.

By the time he wrote his later plays, however, Shakespeare had found an even more powerful source of rhythmic variety: a more flexible position size, giving a significant proportion of the lines in *Antony and Cleopatra* an inter-ictic interval of two syllables. This is the foot-based pentameter of Hanson 1995b, and the figures in Table B suggest that, although Marlowe had used this feature tentatively, it was Shakespeare who set the example for Jacobean dramatic pentameters. The other poets in this analysis did not employ feminine lines or make much use of variable position size as sources of variety, but they continued to use erosion extensively and, in Marlowe's case, employed it significantly more frequently than any poet before him.

The dramatic pentameter of Marlowe and Shakespeare is foot-based, as described by Hanson 1995b, and their lines' constant is five feet or beats, rather than a fixed number of syllables. A metre of this type may be argued to fit better the nature of the language, with its tendencies towards stress-timing and syllabic ambiguity. The similarity between foot-based verse and normal speech was probably the factor that led one of Shakespeare's successors to take this mode of versifying to extravagant lengths.

Jacobean dramatic verse: Webster

The career of John Webster (b. ?1578, d. ?1632) began as Shakespeare's came to an end, and the younger poet took the foot-based pentameter to new extremes. Webster, like his father, was a London coach-maker, but the son managed to combine this profession with writing four plays, of which three have survived, and with collaborating on several others. His literary reputation rests chiefly on two plays (Lucas 1927), *The White Devil* (1611–12) and *The Duchess of Malfi* (1613–14).

Dramatic verse has clear differences from non-dramatic in a number of traditions, particularly those that demand drama be as realistic as possible, when part of the playwright's job becomes to suspend disbelief.[6] Abandoning verse for prose is, of course, one way of achieving this linguistically; but versifying makes language more easily memorable, and authors have continued to write plays in verse because they have wanted actors to remember their words and audiences to carry them away with them. Webster pursued realism by making his verse as much like the prose of normal speech as possible, and one way in which he did this was by freely employing paroxytons (and occasionally proparoxytons) at the line end. In my sample of Webster's lines more than one in five lines are feminine, as they are in Shakespeare's. Another prose-like characteristic of Webster's verse is his use of enjambment: my figures show that he enjambed more than a quarter of his lines, significantly more than Shakespeare. Webster also broke the monopoly of the pentameter in his plays: shorter iambic lines occur frequently in his characters' dialogue, and such lines constitute around a quarter of total (they have therefore been excluded from my figures). All these measures helped Webster disguise the fact that his language is made up of lines, but the remaining way he sought to pass off his verse as normal speech was the most radical: he greatly reduced the regularity of stress and non-stress. Like prose, his verse has unpredictable inter-ictic intervals.

Little over half of Webster's lines are canonical iambic pentameters, but when he wants to compose such lines he can do so as easily and elegantly as Shakespeare, as the following lines show (all my quotations are from Act IV of *The Duchess of Malfi*; Lucas 1927, II):

> (39)   You <u>may</u> dis-**cerne** the <u>shape</u> of **love**-li-<u>nesse</u>   (1. 8)
> (40)   More **per**-fect, <u>in</u> her <u>tears</u>, than <u>in</u> her <u>smiles</u>   (1. 9)

Instance (39) is strongly iambic and the erosion of the second and fourth ictuses in (40) presents a particularly effective contrast with it. But disyllabic and void weak positions abound in Webster's verse: in my sample together they represent 46 per cent of lines; Lucas, who uses a 500-line sample of *The Duchess of Malfi* (1927: IV, 251), states that there is one resolved foot for every two lines. Disyllabic weak positions may involve syllables in the same word or different words, as the following examples show:

> (41)   And the <u>hand</u> as <u>sure</u> as the <u>ring</u>; and <u>doe</u> not <u>doubt</u>   (1. 57)
> (42)   Ne-<u>ces</u>-si-ty <u>makes</u> me **suf**-fer **con**-stan-<u>tly</u>   (2. 31)

Many of Webster's lines contain more than one disyllabic weak position; the following contain three and five respectively:

> (43)   From <u>true</u> le-**gi**-ti-mate **is**-sue: com-**pas**-sio-nate **na**-ture   (1. 43)
> (44)   O, but <u>you</u> must re-**mem**-ber, my <u>curse</u> hath a <u>great</u> way to <u>goe</u>   (1. 121)

I have scanned (44) so that it becomes triple-time (anapaestic) throughout, a process that should perhaps be termed *dissolution* rather than *resolution* in otherwise iambic verse. But there is an alternative scansion of (44): 'must' rather than 'you' can be peaked in delivery, which would make the first weak position trisyllabic.

In addition to trisyllabic inter-ictic intervals in Webster's verse there are many zero intervals, and the following lines illustrate both:

> (45)   But <u>you</u> shall have the <u>heart</u> [V] <u>too</u>; when you <u>need</u> a <u>friend</u>   (1. 58)
> (46)   I <u>bad</u> thee, <u>when</u> I <u>was</u> dis-**trac**-ted of my <u>wits</u>   (2. 298)
> (47)   [V] <u>Looke</u> you: <u>here's</u> the <u>peece</u>, from <u>which</u> 'twas <u>ta'ne</u>   (1. 67)
> (48)   To <u>store</u> them <u>with</u> fresh **co**-lour: <u>who's</u> [V] <u>there</u>?   (2. 371)

Void positions as in (45) and (48) occur in almost 6 per cent of Webster's lines, and this is combined with a higher level of medial inversion (which can be interpreted as a zero balanced by a disyllabic interval). Webster's use of inversion differs from Shakespeare's in some ways, as the following lines show:

> (49)   To <u>re</u>-**move** <u>forth</u> the **com**-mon **Hos**-pi-<u>tall</u>   (1. 152)
> (50)   All <u>the</u> **mad**-<u>folke</u>, and <u>place</u> them <u>neere</u> her **lod**ging   (1. 153)

Instance (49) has a position 2–3 inversion that breaks the bracketing condition; (50) has a second-foot inversion, or lyric caesura, which is extremely rare in almost all other English poets' pentameters.

The combination of all Webster's flexibilities can produce metrical ambiguity: we have noted that one possible delivery of (44) makes it anapaestic, but the use of polysyllabic weak positions can also make a line metrically ambiguous in other ways. Thus (46) can be delivered as an alexandrine:

(46)a I <u>bad</u> thee, <u>when</u> I <u>was</u> dis-**trac**-ted <u>of</u> my <u>wits</u>   (2. 298)

Since lines of other lengths than five feet are employed frequently by Webster, it is impossible to be sure that an iambic hexameter was not his metrical intention. Clearly, increasing maximum position size can offer problems for the reader, something of great importance in dramatic verse. It seems likely that Webster recognized this problem: Lucas shows that his middle plays contain most resolved feet, and argues that Webster's lines reached a level of irregularity in the *Devil's Law Case* (1620) where he decided to beat a retreat in the direction of the canonical parameter (1927: IV, 250–56). Finally Lucas notes the similarity between Webster's metrics and older modes of versifying in English: 'There are times in the *Devil's Law Case* when he seems to revert in effect to the older English system of simply counting the accented syllables and ignoring the number of accented ones' (1927: IV, 251n1). The above examples from *The Duchess of Malfi* show that *The Devil's Law Case* may be extreme, but it is not unique: all Webster's lines are best described as five-ictic dolniks.

Subsequent dramatic verse

In the decades following Webster's death English playwrights were put out of business as a result of the closure of the theatres by the Civil War's Puritan victors. When the theatre resumed its central position in social life after the restoration of the monarchy in 1666, poets who composed for the stage strove to make their verse as polished as non-dramatic varieties. The long-line canon and the heroic couplet took over the stage; for more than a century, frills replaced armour, wigs covered hair, criminal dandies replaced ruffians, and elegance in verse was preferred to emotional power. This eventually resulted in the demise of dramatic verse; in the struggle to make dialogue sound natural and to find language that could convey even the most destructive human emotions, polished verse inevitably was eclipsed by prose (see Hobsbaum 1996: 31). In subsequent centuries many English poets attempted to revive blank-verse drama, and even today Elizabethan verse plays can still draw large audiences. But in modern drama prose, as the most naturalistic medium, is now unchallenged.

Subverting the Canons: John Donne

There is one major English poet whose verse often seems like very normal speech, even though it was not intended for a theatre audience. John Donne (b. 1572, d. 1631) was born into a devout Catholic family and his faith debarred him from taking his degree at the end of his studies in Oxford, although he later converted to Anglicanism and eventually obtained a DD from Cambridge. He travelled widely in the service of a number of very important men, and he was briefly imprisoned for marrying above his station, but resumed his peripatetic career. His wife died giving birth to their twelfth child shortly after he had been persuaded by lack of secular advancement to take holy orders. He was then very successful in obtaining various livings, and became Dean of St Paul's and the most famous preacher of his day.

Donne resembled the characters in Webster's plays by being larger than life in many ways.[7] Donne's aggression and self-assertiveness reveal themselves not only in his imagery and diction, but also in his subversive and highly individual metrics. His poems included lyrics, sonnets, elegies, epistles, satires, and sermons and, although it has been argued that his metrics differs according to the type of poem, I shall concentrate here on features of his versifying that were common to them all, and illustrate them by lines from different types of poem.

The verse designs of Donne's lyrics

In his *Songs and Sonnets* Donne makes extensive use of the two stress-syllabic canons: he skilfully interweaves iambic pentameters with shorter iambic lines to create the effect of a sung lyric with its refrain. He also opens some poems with a series of tetrameters or trimeters before settling to the pentameter line, and the shorter line often consists of a single attention-getting phrase. Like many of his contemporaries, Donne also sometimes employed the trochaic tetrameter for his lyric poems. Within poems he uses changes in line length for a similar purpose; for example, in 'The Anniversary' he combines the two stress-syllabic canons very effectively, as the following lines (7–8) show (all my quotations are from Smith 1971):

(51) **On**-ly our <u>love</u> hath <u>no</u> de-**cay**;
(52) This, <u>no</u> to-**mo**-rrow <u>hath</u>, nor **yes**-ter-<u>day</u>

In his iambic lyrics Donne brings rhythmic variety by the use of initial inversion, as in (51), or, more conspicuously, by filling weak positions with more linguistic material than we expect, as in (53), which opens 'A Valediction: Forbidding Mourning':

(53) As **vir**-tu-ous <u>men</u> pass **mild**-ly a-**way**

Note that both 'virtuous' and 'mildly' can be either two or three syllables, and this line could be interpreted as an iambic pentameter with a fourth-foot inversion. But such ambiguities are common in Donne's verse and his metrical intention was probably a four-ictic line, like all the others in the poem, with two disyllabic weak positions. In any event, this ambiguous opening line can be seen as a skilful device to seize the reader's attention for a poem that metrically is one of Donne's plainest, but in all other respects is one of his most brilliant.

Donne's long-line verse design

Donne's long-line metre differs from the canonical iambic pentameter in containing rather more medial inversion (nearly 5 per cent in his *Satires*, compared with just over 2 per cent in Shakespeare's sonnets), as the following lines from the *Satires* show:

(54) And **spy**-ing <u>heirs</u> **mel**-<u>ting</u> with **lu**-xu-<u>ry</u>   (2. 79)
(55) But <u>these</u> **pu**-<u>nish</u> them-**selves**: the **in**-so-<u>lence</u>   (2. 39)
(56) Seeks <u>her</u> at <u>Rome</u>, there, <u>be</u>-**cause** <u>he</u> doth <u>know</u>   (3. 45)
(57) That <u>wilt</u> con-**sort** none, <u>un</u>-**til** <u>thou</u> have <u>known</u>   (1. 33)

In (54) the inversion of 'melting' can be explained by the bracketing condition, as can 'punish' in (55); but in the latter example the inversion is in the second foot, which is very rare indeed in English iambic pentameters. The other two inversions do not meet the bracketing condition, because they involve syllables in positions 6–7; they do, however, invert grammatical words. Hanson 1995a is devoted to a study of such words in Donne's verse, and she concludes that they have a special status in his versifying, in that he does not recognize their strong syllables as such.[8]

Another way in which Donne's verse design differs from that of Shakespeare's sonnets makes his lines more like the blank verse of Shakespeare's plays.

> (58) Ill **spi**-rits <u>walk</u> in <u>white</u>, we **ea**-sil-y <u>know</u>   (*Elegy* 19. 22)
> (59) As <u>souls</u> un-**bo**-died, **bo**-dies un-**clothed** must <u>be</u>   (*Elegy* 19. 34)
> (60) Than <u>are</u> new **be**-ne-ficed **mi**-nis-<u>ters</u>, he <u>throws</u>   (*Satire* 2. 45)

Position 9 in (58) is syllabically ambiguous, but positions 7 in (59) and 5 in (60) are clearly disyllabic, and suggest that Donne's position-size parameter is greater than one syllable. The number of possibly disyllabic positions in Donne's *Satires* averages at least 12 per 100 lines; if adjacent vowels, as in 'the other', should be slurred or elided, as Smith argues (1971: 33), this proportion is considerably reduced; but, if we accept that Donne's metre is foot-based, this is unnecessary.

Although the frequency of disyllabic positions in Donne falls far short of that in Webster, their presence, like his different rules for inversion, makes Donne's lines seem very different from Shakespeare's non-dramatic pentameters. This difference is increased by another feature of Donne's verse: he frequently places monosyllables with strong phrasal stress in weak positions. This breaks no constraint in parametric theory, but perhaps one of the weaknesses in parametric theory is that it provides no explanation of why other poets so rarely do this. The following examples are chosen from many in Donne's verse:

> (61) For **bet**-ter <u>or</u> worse <u>take</u> me, <u>or</u> leave <u>me</u>   (*Satire* 1. 25)
> (62) Now <u>off</u> with <u>those</u> shoes, <u>and</u> then **safe**-ly <u>tread</u>   (*Elegy* 19. 17)
> (63) The <u>ends</u> crown <u>our</u> works, <u>but</u> thou <u>crown'st</u> our <u>ends</u>
>   (*Holy Sonnets* 1. 9)

Normal speech would place most of the phrasal stresses in these lines on syllables in weak positions: on 'worse' in position 9 of (61), 'shoes' in position 5 of (62), and 'works' in position 5 and 'thou' in position 7 of (63); this contrast between phrasal stress and the metrical template is common in Donne's verse. From this analysis we can see that Donne's metre is no less distinctive and idiosyncratic than other elements of his style: he often subverted the long-line canon rather than conformed to it.

Regularity and Variety: Milton and Marvell

Two of the seventeenth century's major poets served, in turn, as Foreign Languages (that is Latin, or Foreign) Secretary to the Lord Protector, Oliver Cromwell (b. 1599, d. 1658). They were John Milton (b. 1608, d. 1674) and Andrew Marvell (b. 1621, d. 1678), and both were metrists of the highest order: Marvell raised the short-line iambic canon to new levels of artistry, and Milton its long-line equivalent. Milton also perfected an alternative short-line metre, and their metrical achievements are preserved in works of sufficient length to merit detailed linguistic analysis. In this section, therefore, I shall employ statistical techniques to describe their verse designs and compare them with those of the poets who preceded and followed them.[9]

Milton was the son of a London scrivener and went up to Cambridge with the apparent intention of entering the clergy, and there began to compose poetry in English. On graduating he travelled on the European mainland, and continued writing, mostly in Latin, but also in Italian. Latin was the European language of academic debate and of diplomacy, and his fluency together with his debating skill soon drew him into politics, and into the Civil War (1643–46). Milton was married three times and, although he wrote much about the theory of divorce, was twice widowed and was outlived by his third wife. He become blind in 1651 and was briefly imprisoned on the Stuarts' Restoration; on his release, he published *Paradise Lost* (1667), which he had completed in 1663, *Paradise Regained*, and *Samson Agonistes* (both in 1671), before dying of a gout-related illness. Milton's poetic reputation suffered in the first half of the twentieth century, but has recovered since (see Leavis 1924: 42–61 and Eliot 1957: 138–61).

Marvell was the son of a Yorkshire clergyman; he was educated at Cambridge and, after his father's death, was able to miss the Civil War by travelling on the Continent and learning languages. He held important offices under the Commonwealth and sang its leader's praises, but he also cultivated Royalist friends, which served him (and Milton) well on the Restoration. He resumed his career as a diplomat, became a Dutch agent, served as MP for Hull, and continued campaigning against royal absolutism. None of his lyric poetry was printed in his lifetime and, when his poems were published in 1681, they attracted little attention for two centuries. His poetic reputation grew steadily in the USA in the course of the nineteenth century, and by the middle of the twentieth was firmly established in his own country.

Milton's iambic pentameter

Milton composed both short- and long-line verse in the period until 1637, but all three of his last poems are in blank verse; in a preface to *Paradise Lost* he found it necessary to explain his use of the latter in a non-dramatic work. Milton's lines have a resonance and a memorable quality that, for many readers, is enhanced rather than diminished by his alien syntax, and he contributed greatly to the establishment of the metre as the English long-line canon. The most important features of Milton's long-line verse design are discussed by Youmans 1989 and its parameters are defined by Hanson 1995b. Milton's metre is similar to that of Shakespeare's non-dramatic verse, but he employed very few feminine lines, reserving them mostly for special effects.[10] But Milton made two important innovations in the pentameter: he increased the variety in his lines by his use of initial inversion, erosion, and enjambment, and was thus able to hold his readers' attention in a very long poem.

The first way that Milton's verse is more varied than his predecessors' is in his greater use of line-initial polysyllabic inversion (see Table D): almost 7 per cent of lines in *Paradise Lost* have this feature.[11] The following line from Book 1 of *Paradise*

Lost (Leonard 1998) interrupts a series of lines with iambic openings and is an example of Milton's skilful use of this device for mimetic purposes:

>   (64)   **Brea**-king the **hor**-rid **si**-lence <u>thus</u> be-**gan**   (83)

Milton's lines show about the same frequency of mid-line polysyllabic inversion as his predecessors' verse (under 2.0 per cent), but his use of erosion differs greatly. Milton eroded significantly more first and third ictuses than his predecessors (14 and 20 per cent, respectively); the following lines from Book 1 of *Paradise Lost* exemplify Milton's use of erosion at each point in the line:

>   (65)   Here <u>in</u> the <u>heart</u> of <u>Hell</u> to <u>work</u> in <u>Fire</u>   (151)
>   (66)   Of **O**-reb, <u>or</u> of **Si**-nai, <u>didst</u> in-**spire**   (7)
>   (67)   If <u>he</u> op-**pos'd**; and <u>with</u> am-**bi**-tious <u>aim</u>   (41)
>   (68)   That **wit**-nessed <u>huge</u> af-**flic**-tion <u>and</u> dis-**may**   (57)
>   (69)   There <u>the</u> com-**pa**-nions <u>of</u> his <u>fall</u>, o'er-**whelmed**   (76)
>   (70)   He **trus**-ted <u>to</u> have **e**-qual'd <u>the</u> most <u>high</u>   (40)

Erosion of the first ictus in the line, as in (65), is part of a monosyllabic initial inversion, the result of inverting the normal stress accruing to two monosyllables; (66) has erosion of the second ictus, (67) of the third, and (68) of the fourth. Table D shows that Milton's preference for erosion of the third ictus was also a feature of the verse of the poets who followed him. Although Milton sometimes eroded more than one ictus in a line, for example, the first and third in (69) and the second and fourth in (70), he avoided eroding two consecutive ictuses, thus revealing a cumulative constraint on strong positions in his verse design. Varying the ictuses eroded in each line and contrasting more regular lines with those containing erosion or inversion combines to produce an almost symphonic effect in Milton's verse.[12]

The second feature that distinguishes Milton's iambic pentameter is his use of the *verse paragraph*, an unbroken series of enjambments followed by a strongly end-stopped line. *Paradise Lost* contains more enjambment (39.3 per cent of lines in my sample) than any Jacobean drama (see Table C), and in many long passages of *Paradise Lost* syntactic and metrical boundaries are at variance. This device propels the reader headlong, and the mutual orgasm of syntax and metre at the paragraph's close has the triumphant finality of the verb in a Latin or German sentence. The variety of Milton's verse paragraphs can be seen from the line-end punctuation, as the opening lines of *Paradise Lost* in Leonard's edition show.[13] If we insert the number of lines between punctuation marks and enclose periods in brackets, we can observe a series of structures: [3, 2, 3, 5, 3.] [2, 5; 2, 1.] [3, 3? 1?] [6, 1, 8, 1.]. Throughout the poem these structures form a long string that hardly ever repeats itself; and this variety, combined with the variety of stressing and caesura, nurses the reader through thousands of lines of the same metre.

Milton's variable tetrameter

For his short-line masterpieces 'L'Allegro' and 'Il Penseroso' (both *c.* 1630), Milton employed not the iambic canon but a mixed or variable tetrameter. The following lines (41–46) from 'L'Allegro' (Leonard 1998: 21) demonstrate this metre's variety:

(71)   To <u>hear</u> the <u>lark</u> be-**gin** his <u>flight</u>,
(72)   And **sin**-ging **star**-tle <u>the</u> dull <u>night</u>
(73)   [V] <u>From</u> his **watch**-towre <u>in</u> the <u>skies</u>,
(74)   [V] <u>Till</u> the **dap**-pled <u>dawn</u> doth <u>rise</u>;
(75)   [V] <u>Then</u> to <u>come</u> in <u>spight</u> of <u>sor</u>-row,
(76)   And <u>at</u> my **win**-dow <u>bid</u> good **mor**-row.

The syllable count of these lines is 8M, 8M, 7M, 7M, 7F, 8F, respectively: three of these lines are octosyllables and three heptasyllables; three are trochaic and three iambic tetrameters. Moreover, Milton adopted the high frequency of erosion found in trochaic tetrameter: thus the third ictus in (72), the first and third in (73), and the first in (76) are eroded. To add further variety, Milton occasionally employs initial polysyllabic inversion in his 8M/F (iambic) lines, as in the following line from 'Il Penseroso':

(77)   **O**-ver thy **de**-cent **shoul**-ders <u>drawn</u>   (36)

Milton's metre in these two poems thus offers many options: four different line lengths, rising or falling rhythm, erosion of any of its three ictuses, and initial inversion in 8M/F lines.

We can interpret such a verse design either as a trochaic tetrameter that allows anacrusis or as an iambic tetrameter that allows headless lines (see Kiparsky 1977: 216). Because Milton's two poems offer a substantial sample of instances from which to deduce his verse design, statistical analysis can help resolve this question. Although a line count supports the iambic hypothesis (80 per cent of the lines in 'L'Allegro' and 60 per cent in 'Il Penseroso' are octosyllables of 8M/F), a word count shows that the lexicon of both poems is heavily trochaic. Following Kiparsky 1977: 227–29, we can determine whether a poem is more or less trochaic than normal speech by calculating the ratio of trochaic to iambic disyllables in the poem, and comparing this with a control prose text. The relevant proportions here are Milton's prose introductions, 4:1, his iambic pentameters, 3:1, 'L'Allegro', 8:1, and 'Il Penseroso', 5:1. Milton thus employed an exceptionally trochaic language in both poems, but particularly in 'L'Allegro', where the plethora of trochees seems to give the poem more energy than 'Il Penseroso'.

Milton was not the first, nor the last, major English poet to employ the variable tetrameter, but few poets have employed it so effectively and in such a sustained fashion. Milton, who was precise and punctilious in most things, readily employed a line with an unreliable syllable count because he recognized that lines of English verse are perceived primarily as a series of beats not syllables. He thus ran no risk that readers would fail to appreciate the regularity of his metre, while gaining the maximum latitude for rhythmic variation.

Marvell's iambic tetrameter

Many of Marvell's poems (Margoliouth 1971) are in iambic pentameter and heroic couplets typical of the Restoration period, but his 'Horatian Ode upon Cromwell's Return from Ireland', which has been called 'perhaps the greatest political poem in English' (Drabble 1985: 625), combines iambic tetrameter and trimeter couplets.

Many of his shorter personal poems also employ couplets and iambic tetrameters, as does his long (776-line) poem 'Upon Appleton House', which offers a large enough sample of verse instances to justify quantified statements about its verse design. I shall therefore use this poem for my most detailed analysis of this metre.

Although the iambic tetrameter may (at least subconsciously) strike the reader as two pairs of beats, it has no caesura in the sense of a fixed mid-line word boundary, and any two consecutive ictuses may fall within the same word; in the following line it is the second and third:

> (78)   But <u>hedge</u> our **li**-ber-<u>ty</u> a-**bout**   (100)

Polysyllabic initial inversion occurs in fewer than 3 per cent of Marvell's lines, but this feature is usually slightly less common in the shorter line. Marvell uses even fewer medial inversions; examples of initial and medial inversion in this poem include:

> (79)   **Foun**-ded by **fol**-ly, <u>kept</u> by <u>wrong</u>   (218)
> (80)   Fair <u>be</u>-**yond mea**-sure, <u>and</u> an <u>heir</u>   (91)

In (80) the stress on the first syllable of 'measure' is undoubtedly greater than that on the second syllable of 'beyond'; but it is an example of a strong syllable in a weak position, and the resulting inversion in positions 2–3 violates the bracketing condition, albeit by the placement of a grammatical word that bears little stress in normal speech.

In (80) the third ictus is also eroded; other examples of erosion in this poem include the first ictus of (81), the second of (82), and the first and third of (83), below:

> (81)   Fly <u>from</u> their **vi**-ces. || 'Tis thy <u>state</u>   (221)
> (82)   One <u>stone</u> that <u>a</u> just <u>hand</u> had <u>laid</u>   (210)
> (83)   In <u>the</u> just **fi**-gure <u>of</u> a <u>fort</u>   (286)

Marvell rarely erodes two ictuses in the same line of this poem, probably because in the shorter line it hinders the reader's perception of the iambic rhythm. The frequency with which these features occur in Marvell's verse and in the tetrameters of other poets (discussed in this and the previous chapters) is shown in Table E, which reveals a number of differences, some statistically significant. Thus Milton erodes more first ictuses, and more ictuses in total, in his mixed tetrameter than Marvell in his iambic lines; Milton also erodes the second ictus slightly more often than Pope, or Swift; and Marvell erodes the third ictus significantly less often than any of the other poets.

This table confirms the intuition that Milton's short-line metre offers vastly more rhythmic variety than Marvell's; the iambic short-line canon has remained a much less varied metre than its long-line equivalent. The iambic pentameter has variety of caesura, subdividing some lines into 2 + 3 beats and others into 3 + 2; and this division offers another point at which initial inversion can be introduced.[14] The pentameter also accommodates line-initial inversion more easily, because the iambic rhythm has longer to reassert itself in the remainder of the line. It also has more places, and combinations of them, where erosion can be employed; and from

Milton onwards the third ictus (that equidistant from the line-boundaries, which the tetrameter lacks) became a particular favourite for this treatment. This greater potential for variety not only led to the longer iambic line's being employed far more often than the short, it also deterred poets from employing the shorter line in longer poems (see below). When Marvell chose to employ the short-line canon in 'Upon Appleton House', he denied himself even feminine lines as a source of metrical variety. Yet Marvell's short-line verse is undoubtedly read more often today than his iambic pentameters; this is largely because he kept most of his tetrameter poems short. But it is also partly the result of two properties of his poetry that Milton's lacks almost entirely: humility and humour. Perhaps nothing demonstrates better than the relative fame of these two men the importance of form and metre to the making of a great poet.

Conformity: Restoration and Augustan Metrics

Metrical variety was not the prime objective of most poets in the hundred years following Milton's death, and the majority of English lines they composed were stress-syllabic. Restoration and Augustan audiences rated elegance and wit more highly than the simple or the natural, and this was reflected in metrics, where syllables were strictly counted and rhythms varied only according to a well-established set of rules. In versifying, as in much else, this was a time of clarity, order, and conformity, as poets attempted to make metre the ideal vehicle for wit, 'What oft was thought but ne'er so well express'd'. Five poets represent the best of verse-craft in the second half of the period with which this chapter deals, roughly the years 1675 to 1750, and the first two may be described as Restoration poets. John Dryden (b. 1631, d. 1700), who had been schooled in London and graduated at Cambridge, was the most acclaimed poet of the last quarter of the seventeenth century. Although he had inherited a modest estate, he supported himself mostly by his writing; he was a prolific poet, critic, translator, and playwright. He had celebrated the King's return in a series of major poems between 1660 and 1667 and in the following year was duly rewarded with the Poet Laureateship. John Wilmot, Earl of Rochester (b. 1647, d. 1680), came from a family that had fought with distinction on the Royalist side in the Civil War and he rapidly established himself as one of the new monarch's court wits. He owes his current fame as much to his scandalous personal life as to his lyrics and satires, which are among the finest in the English language.

The other three poets' work belongs almost entirely to the eighteenth century. The first was Dryden's Irish cousin Jonathan Swift (b. 1667, d. 1745), who was a clergyman, political pamphleteer, and man of literature. He was at the heart of English and Irish politics and letters for the last fifty years of his long life. There he was joined by Alexander Pope (b. 1688, d. 1744), a largely self-educated man from Windsor, who came to public attention by the sheer brilliance of his writing with the publication of his *Essay on Criticism* in 1711. Pope was the son of a Catholic draper and had been crippled by a childhood disease, and he threw all his energy into literature, where he excelled as poet, critic, translator, and polemicist. Foremost among the next generation of English literary figures was Samuel Johnson (b. 1709, d. 1784), the great lexicographer. He came from Lichfield and was forced by poverty to abandon his education at Oxford. After trying his hand as a schoolmaster he found editorial work in London and soon won attention by his own prose and verse. His words, wit, generosity, and eccentricity became legend as a result of the famous life published by his Scottish friend James Boswell (b. 1740, d. 1795). Johnson's younger contemporary Thomas Gray (b. 1716, d. 1771) was educated at Eton and Cambridge, where he spent much of his life. Since he wrote well in Latin as well as English, he gained a considerable reputation in an age when all things Classical were in vogue. He refused the Laureateship in 1757 and in his last years became fascinated by folk-verse and the English countryside, two of the obsessions of the age that followed.

Restoration and Augustan verse-art

Lines 337–82 of Pope's *Essay on Criticism* are an exposition and demonstration of Augustan verse-craft, which begins as follows:

> (84)   But <u>most</u> by **num**-bers <u>judge</u> a **po**-et's <u>song</u>:   (337)
> (85)   And <u>smooth</u> or <u>rough</u>, with <u>them</u>, is <u>right</u> or <u>wrong</u>   (338)

The alternation of stress and non-stress in these lines is very clear, as is the contrast between a running ('Italian') and a pausing line. The second line is monosyllabic and, as Bradley 1929 pointed out, such lines are very common among English pentameters and have been employed by many major poets. Note that in (85) all the weak positions contain unstressed syllables, so there is no incursion and the parenthetic phrase 'with them' breaks up the syntax. These devices save the line from falling into the banality that monosyllables can produce, of which Pope warns us later:

> (86)   And <u>ten</u> low <u>words</u> oft <u>creep</u> in <u>one</u> dull <u>line</u>   (347)

Much of the dullness of the 'creeping' in this line is the result of eight of the words having some claim to stress. Pope also notes the danger of slowness in the alexandrine, where its central caesura and constant three-beat rhythm tend to monotony:

> (87)   A **need**-less <u>A</u>-le-**xan**-drine <u>ends</u> the <u>song</u>,   (356)
> (88)   That, <u>like</u> a **woun**-ded <u>snake</u>, drags <u>its</u> slow <u>length</u> a-**long**   (357)

Here the stressed monosyllables 'drags' and 'slow' represent incursion and they effectively perform the operation they describe. This is mimesis, or *expressivité*, at its best.

What is probably the best exposition of mimesis in the English language appears in the following passage (lines 362–73):

> (89)   True <u>ease</u> in **wri**-ting <u>comes</u> from <u>art</u>, not <u>chance</u>,
> (90)   As <u>those</u> move **ea**-siest <u>who</u> have <u>learn'd</u> to <u>dance</u>.
> (91)   'Tis <u>not</u> e-**nough** no **harsh**-ness <u>gives</u> of-**fence**,
> (92)   The <u>sound</u> must <u>seem</u> an **e**-cho <u>of</u> the <u>sense</u>:
> (93)   Soft <u>is</u> the <u>strain</u> when **Ze**-phyr **gent**-ly <u>blows</u>,

(94)   And the smooth stream in **smoo**-ther **num**-bers flows;
(95)   But when loud **bil**-lows lash the **soun**-ding shore,
(96)   The hoarse rough verse should like the **tor**-rent roar.
(97)   When A-jax strives some rock's vast weight to throw,
(98)   The line too **la**-bours, and the words move slow.
(99)   Not so when swift Ca-**mil**-la scours the plain,
(100) Flies o'er the un-**ben**-ding corn, and skims a-**long** the main.

Note that five of these twelve lines are running ('Italian') lines with no word boundary immediately after position 4; this is about the average for iambic pentameters in this period.

Pope's artistry is apparent in every line of this passage but some of his devices are of particular note. In (92) to (94) nine of the syllables open and four close with a sibilant, giving a softness and smoothness to the lines that is reinforced in (94) by what is sometimes called an 'ionic foot': a steady increase in stress is produced by following two unstressed syllables by two stressed ones. In (95) and (96) the sibilants suddenly become harsh by aspirating them ('lash', 'shore', 'should'), incursive stressed monosyllables appear ('loud', 'rough', 'should'), and the assonances of 'hoarse' and 'roar' straddle the second of these lines. The weight described in instances (97) and (98) is emphasized by filling an even higher proportion of weak positions with stressed or heavy syllables ('-jax', 'some', 'vast'), while (98) contains a striking alliteration ('line' and 'labours') followed by another steady increase in stress over five syllables to slow the line down ('and the words move slow'). In (99) and (100) Pope mimes the lightness of foot and grace of his subject by filling his weak positions with light syllables. He adds the further impression of speed by a monosyllabic initial inversion in (100), and fills the interval between the first two prominence peaks with three light syllables that may be reduced to two by rapid delivery ('Flies o'er the un-**ben**-ding'). Most impressive of all, this last line is an alexandrine: Pope has made the wounded snake fly.

The heroic couplet and iambic pentameter

Between 1675 and 1775 the canonical iambic pentameter accounted for almost all the long-line verse composed in England, and one strophe form, the *heroic couplet*, was employed in most long poems and in verse drama. The heroic couplet dates back to Chaucer and was employed sporadically in the earlier part of the seventeenth century, but Dryden ushered in its period of dominance. He used it for most of his long poems and plays, but in his prologue to *Aurengzebe* (1675) he attacked the use of rhyme in drama, and he wrote *All for Love* (1678) in blank verse. The heroic couplet reduces the versifier's effort, because it requires only two rhymes, but those rhymes are so close together that they can be obtrusive, and the couplet's structural unit of twenty syllables can easily become monotonous. Restoration and Augustan poets scorned most of the devices that save the iambic pentameter from monotony: thus they eschewed feminine lines and they preserved the level of enjambment they found in Shakespeare's sonnets, rather than that of Milton's epic verse.[15] These poets also employed inversion and erosion less often than Milton (see Table D); even Pope, who followed Milton in eroding around 15 of first ictuses and more than 20 per cent of third, avoided second-ictus erosion, and used fourth-ictus erosion sparingly.

Poets in this period relied for variety to a large extent upon mixing what I have called 'Italian' and 'French' lines; the proportion of 'Italian' lines, those lacking a word boundary following position 4, reached a new high level in the iambic pentameters of the eighteenth century. Chaucer, Spenser, and Shakespeare had boosted the proportion of Italian lines in their verse to over 30 per cent in the interests of rhythmic variety, and in Milton's blank verse this figure rose to 41 per cent. But Restoration and Augustan poets raised it further, and it finally reached the full 50 per cent in Johnson's *The Vanity of Human Wishes* and Gray's *Elegy Written in a Country Churchyard* (both poems are included in Pollard 1976). Nor was this increase in 'Italian' lines simply a product of differences in the poets' diction; these levels are very significantly higher than a random deployment of their individual lexicons could have produced (Duffell 2002b: 305).

Table D compares figures for 'Italian' lines in Dryden's and Pope's heroic couplets with those for Gray's *Elegy*, which is in quatrains rhymed abab. The even distribution of 'French' and 'Italian' provides Gray's chief source of metrical variety in this poem, and it is a feature of almost every strophe. Just two quatrains (the only pieces of direct speech by the villagers) contain four lines of the same structure (the 4 + 6 type). In all other respects Gray's metre is remarkably regular, as can be seen from Tables H and J, where it is compared with the iambic pentameters of subsequent poets: the *Elegy* contains no feminine lines or medial inversion, and very few initial inversions or enjambments. Gray's *Elegy* probably gains aesthetically from not being in heroic couplets, with their insistent rhymes. The heroic couplet had become the ideal vehicle for ideas, arguments, and racy narratives because, once its artificiality was accepted, its regularity allowed the reader to focus on the poet's clever diction, imagery, and jokes. But, at the eighteenth century's close there occurred events that gave the rich and privileged less to laugh about, and which stirred deeper and more violent emotions. When poets and audiences were sated by the combination of wit and elegance that the form had carried for more than a century, the heroic couplet fell from favour.

Short-line and lyric metres

Restoration and Augustan poets continued to employ the short-line canon, but most preferred the iambic pentameter for poems of any length; an exception was Swift's *Cadenus and Vanessa* (Pollard 1976: 8–28), which comprises 889 iambic tetrameters and was composed soon after 1708. Table E compares Swift's metre with the tetrameter of Pope, whose relatively few short-line poems included adaptations of Horace in iambic tetrameters (Dobrée 1924: 339–47). Both poets employed rhymed couplets with very few initial inversions (under 3 per cent), and they eroded between 8 and 10 per cent of non-final ictuses, but their use of enjambment differs significantly: in Swift's long poem, 14 per cent of lines are enjambed, while in Pope's much shorter pieces the figure is only 4 per cent.[16] Both poets avoided feminine lines, and the rare exceptions have unlikely and imperfect disyllabic rhymes, rather like the humorous trisyllabic rhymes of the limerick. Examples include the following couplets, of which the first is from Swift's *Cadenus and Vanessa* and the second from Pope's imitation of one of Horace's *Satires* (Book II. 6):

(101)	But <u>lest</u> he <u>shou'd</u> ne-**glect** his **Stu**dies	(222)
(102)	Like <u>a</u> young <u>Heir</u>, the **thrif**-ty **God**dess	(223)
(103)	The <u>beans</u> and **ba**-con <u>set</u> be-**fore** 'em,	(137)
(104)	The **grace**-cup <u>served</u> with <u>all</u> de-**corum**	(138)

An important difference between these poets' iambic tetrameters is that Swift avoids eroding two ictuses in the same line, while Pope does not, as the following examples from the same satire show:

| (105) | 'Tis <u>for</u> the **ser**-vice <u>of</u> the <u>crown</u> | (34) |
| (106) | 'Twas <u>on</u> the <u>night</u> of <u>a</u> de-**bate** | (185) |

As this analysis of Swift's verse shows, the canonical iambic tetrameter offers few sources of variety, and it is not surprising that poets who desired more of it in a short line looked elsewhere. The beneficiary in most cases was a stress-syllabic version of common measure, in which an iambic tetrameter was followed by a trimeter. Rochester was the seventeenth-century master of this metre and Pope was among the many poets who employed it in the eighteenth century, as in his poem 'A Farewell to London', which opens:

(107)	Dear, <u>damn'd</u>, dis-**trac**-ting <u>town</u>, fare-**well**!
(108)	Thy <u>fools</u> no <u>more</u> I'll <u>tease</u>:
(109)	This <u>year</u> in <u>peace</u>, ye **cri**-tics, <u>dwell</u>,
(110)	Ye **har**-lots, <u>sleep</u> at <u>ease</u>!

This metre is clearly more brisk and lively than the short-line canon and throughout this period was its closest rival.

Trochaic and triple-time metres continued to feature in the metrical repertoires of seventeenth-century poets: both Dryden and Rochester occasionally employed them, and Dryden also used dolniks in 'The Secular Mask' (Sharrock 1968), which was probably his very last poem. Another of his metrical experiments involved combining iambic and anapaestic lines in common-measure strophes, found in a song from his play *Marriage à la Mode*. In each of its two strophes an anapaestic quatrain follows an iambic one and the effect of blending the two rhythms can be seen from the following lines (11–14):

(111)	What <u>wrong</u> has <u>he</u> whose <u>joys</u> did <u>end</u>,
(112)	And <u>who</u> could <u>give</u> no <u>more</u>?
(113)	'Tis a **mad**-ness that <u>he</u> should be **jea**-lous of <u>me</u>,
(114)	Or that <u>I</u> should bar <u>him</u> of a-**no**ther

This period also saw the development of the *ode*, a poem in mixed line-lengths in imitation of the Greek poet Pindar. Milton in his youth had composed an 'Ode to the Morning of Christ's Nativity' in octaves of trimeters, tetrameters, and pentameters with 3, 3, 5, 3, 3, 5, 4, and 5 iambic feet; and Marvell had composed an ode on Cromwell's return from Ireland, using strophes of iambic lines. But Dryden's *Song for Saint Cecilia's Day* and *Alexander's Feast* are even more varied: they combine lines of between two and six feet in passages that vary in rhythm from iambic to trochaic to triple-time. In contrast to these two odes where there is no fixed pattern of line lengths or rhythms, Gray regularized the order in which lines of each length occurred in his odes: in some he employed the variable tetrameter of

Milton's 'L'Allegro', but with the headless, trochaic lines forming the minority and appearing in fixed positions in the strophe. Thus in 'Ode on Pleasure Arising from Vicissitude' two trochaic lines open each strophe, and in 'The Bard' lines 1 and 5 of each strophe are trochaic. Both these poems also contain lines of other lengths, trimeters in the case of the first, and pentameters in the second, and their trochaic openings often give them great vitality, as, for example, in 'The Bard' (Reeves 1973), which opens with the curse:

(115)   [V] **Ru**-in <u>seize</u> thee, **ruth**-less <u>king</u>!
(116)   Con-**fu**-sion <u>on</u> thy **ban**-ners <u>wait</u>

Gray also employed the four-ictic dolnik in one very short poem, 'Sketch of his Own Character'; he was a very skilful versifier in many metres, but nothing else he wrote matches his *Elegy* in its other poetic qualities.

The Pindaric ode was an attempt to give the Augustan lyric some of the elegance and Classicism of the heroic couplet, and to offer another fitting vehicle for the high style that the era's poets so valued. But this high style also demanded stately diction and pedigreed imagery, both of which gradually descended into the formulaic and cliché-ridden, and the next generation of English poets reacted strongly against it. By the eighteenth century's close a series of events had shattered society and changed literary tastes, and with them the modes of versifying employed in English.

Conclusions

This chapter began by observing the lyric metres found in Shakespeare's plays, in which he imitated popular songs by employing metres that were not always regularly iambic. It then traced the metrical history of English drama, and showed that the foot-based pentameter, which Hanson 1995b identified in Shakespeare's dramatic verse, had begun to emerge in Marlowe's, and was taken a step further in the Jacobean theatre. To replicate the variable rhythms of normal speech, Webster steadily increased the proportion of disyllabic positions / inter-ictic intervals in his verse to the point where he had to draw back lest he breach the boundaries between verse and prose. Donne adopted the dramatic, foot-based iambic pentameter for his highly personal non-dramatic poetry, but did not go to the extremes of Webster in syllabic irregularity. The poets who followed them, however, returned to a much more regular stress-syllabism.

Milton reaffirmed the syllable-based iambic pentameter as the long-line canon, further refining blank verse and the verse paragraph, and went a little farther in the process of balancing pausing and running lines in his pentameters. For two of his best-known short-line poems he employed a variable tetrameter with more variety than the short-line canon. The iambic tetrameter was, nevertheless, employed by his friend Marvell and, with few changes, by the poets of subsequent centuries. Dryden followed Milton in composing his long poems in syllable-based iambic pentameters; he also introduced the more syllabically regular form of the metre into his dramatic verse, along with the heroic couplet. The Augustan poets embraced Dryden's metre and his strophe form, and refined both, composing an even balance of pausing and running lines. In their lyrics some Restoration and Augustan poets favoured a mixture of iambic tetrameters and trimeters (often in ballad strophes), rather than the undiluted short-line canon or traditional ballad metres. Other poets cultivated the ode, which most often consisted of iambic lines of different lengths, as a method of giving more substantial short-line poems greater variety than the canon offered.

By the last quarter of the sixteenth century the foundations of the English metrical system had been laid, and by the last quarter of the eighteenth the shell of the edifice was in place. The tasks remaining for its completion will be the subject of the next chapter.

Notes to Chapter 7

1. I have scanned (19) and (20) with three beats per line because the corresponding lines in other strophes clearly have them. In another context, however, it would be tempting to deliver these lines with a fourth prominence peak.
2. Over all, the similarities between the two metrical styles are much greater than the differences; it may be that Sackville influenced Norton, but the latter was the prime mover in the cultivation of the 'Italian' line. It is just possible that Norton wrote the whole play and that Sackville's name in the credits helped get it on stage and before the Queen.
3. Erne 2004 demonstrates Shakespeare's literary ambitions and his preoccupation with lasting fame.
4. The samples analysed are: the first and last 300 lines of *Gorboduc*, the first 300 lines of the *Mirror for Magistrates*, *Tamburlaine the Great*, Part II, and Shakespeare's *Sonnets*; these samples are compared with the first 300 lines of one early play by Shakespeare, *Richard III* (*c.* 1588), and of one late play, *Antony and Cleopatra* (1606).
5. Because these figures are based on samples, a figure for two standard errors (2σ) is given at the foot of each column, expressed as a percentage; differences of more than 2σ are statistically significant.
6. Bailey 1973b: 131 notes that the iambic pentameters employed in Russian drama have greater rhythmic variety than those in other genres, and this is probably for the same reason.
7. His fascination with death was not confined to his sermons and poetry: wearing a shroud for the painting of his portrait was a theatrical gesture worthy of *The Duchess of Malfi*.
8. According to the theory of Derek Attridge (1982) the iambic pentameter is simply a five-beat line with some extra restrictions that Donne, in particular, did not always observe; this enables instance (56) to be scanned as follows:

    (56)a   <u>Seeks</u> her at Rome, there, be-cause he doth know.
            B   ŏ   B   ô B   ŏ   B   o   B

9. The hypothesis behind my quantified methodology is that a verse design is 'the common denominator of all possible verse instances based on it' (Chatman 1965: 96); since these represent what statisticians term a *universe*, their structure can be determined by using sampling theory.
10. Thus in Book I of *Paradise Lost* 'preferring' (102) describes a doomed choice, and 'thunder' (174) has an onomatopoeic resonance; words like 'power' (44) and 'heaven' (212) frequently close lines, but their use mid-line shows that they can be monosyllables and thus provide masculine endings.
11. Details of my samples are given below the tables; since two standard errors on this figure equals ± 1.5 per cent, the difference between Milton and other non-dramatic poets is statistically significant.
12. Hobsbaum notes that a unique feature of Milton's pentameter is that he employed stronger and weaker stresses, and heavier and lighter syllables, as aesthetic devices (1996: 11–13). But he describes this in terms of a four-level theory of English stress (Trager & Smith 1951) that has largely been superseded by hierarchical theories (Liberman & Prince 1977 and Hayes 1989 &1995), and he also offers no statistical evidence in support of his observations.

13. There are numerous gradations of enjambment, as discussed in Chapter 1, but the editor's punctuation is sufficient to illustrate Milton's paragraph structures.

14. As Pinsky notes, 'Keeping the pause [...] from falling monotonously in the middle of the line is a challenge in the tetrameter' (1998: 69). His examples of how such monotony may be avoided, however, are trochaic tetrameters, which he describes as iambic lines with an omitted initial syllable (1998: 63–70).

15. Hobsbaum points out, however, that some poets' heroic couplets contrasted metrical and syntactic structures in a new and complex way: they used parenthetic syntax to create a series of mid-line syntactic boundaries, which prevented the reader halting at each rhyme (1996: 26–29).

16. Table D also shows that Marvell enjambed a high proportion of lines in his long poem.

CHAPTER 8

Completing the Spectrum of English Metres

In this chapter I shall discuss all the most important developments in English metrics between 1750 and 1900 except that of free verse, which is the subject of Chapter 9. By 1755, when Samuel Johnson completed his great *Dictionary of the English Language*, the most important elements of the English metrical tradition were as well established as the language itself. The long-line canon, the iambic pentameter, had been polished to a new perfection, and the dearth of variety in the short-line canon, the iambic tetrameter, had been alleviated by the inclusion of other line lengths in the same strophe. In the 140 years that followed, the iambic canon dominated long-line verse and longer poems, and the iambic tetrameter continued in popularity, either used alone or combined with other line lengths. The most important new metrical developments in the period, however, lay in other directions. First, its poets returned to the traditional ballad to find alternative forms for their lyric verse, forms that would avoid the rhythmic monotony of the short-line canon and the elaborate artifice of the ode. In the course of this process the dolnik regained popularity as an alternative to stress-syllabic metres, and both dolniks and trochaic metres were tried in longer poems. Traditional verse was also responsible for renewed interest in triple-time metres, and the late-nineteenth-century fashion for metrical versatility led some poets to seek a longer line than the pentameter. Finally, a few poets began to chafe at the rules, not only of stress-syllabic verse, but of metre itself.

The story of this last development will be told in the next chapter, and the present one will be devoted to a number of other developments in this period: the revival of the ballad; the continuity of the long- and short-line canons; attempts to employ dolniks and trochaic tetrameters in longer poems; the differentiation of ternary metres; and some late-nineteenth-century experiments with a line longer than the iambic pentameter.

Lyric and Ballad Metres

In 1765 the poet and translator Thomas Percy (b. 1729, d. 1811) published his three-volume *Reliques of Ancient English Poetry* (Prichard 1892–93), which contained a large number of verse texts dating from the fourteenth century to the seventeenth. Alliterative metre, tumbling verse, and ballad measures were thus brought to a new audience, and modes of versifying previously associated with nursery rhymes and proverbs gained a new literary respectability. In the last quarter of the eighteenth century revolution was in the air and, not surprisingly, English poets wanted to lose their chains, too. The poets of the Romantic Movement reflected the political radicalism of the times in their content and reacted against their predecessors' forms. They aimed at a simpler, less artificial language and sought to introduce a range of new metres and strophes. Most poets continued to employ the long-line iambic canon extensively, but sought new forms to supplement the short-line canon and the classical ode. I shall illustrate some of the changes in metrics during the first half of this period by examining the short-line verse of three English and three Scottish poets.

William Blake (b. 1757, d. 1827) was the son of a London hosier, had little formal education, and in his youth was apprenticed as an engraver. He continued to work in that trade for the rest of his life and his engravings are as striking, and have become as famous, as his poetry. His early poetry extolled the virtues of poverty and simplicity and in 1803 his anti-monarchical views led him to be accused (but acquitted) of sedition. After the fall of the French republic and rise of Napoleon, Blake forsook politics for religion and, in a series of prophetic poems, preached his own heretical version of Christianity. Robert Burns (b. 1759, d. 1796) was the son of a literate but impoverished Ayrshire gardener, and Burns's early death is often attributed to the malnutrition and hard physical labour of his youth. He escaped manual drudgery by collecting taxes for a government in London that he hated, and in his spare time managed to compose a large number of songs and poems. Burns pre-empted the English Romantics in their efforts to compose in the language of the common man by employing the Scots dialect for his verse.

William Wordsworth (b. 1770, d. 1850) was the son of a Cumbrian attorney whose parents died when he was still a child. After graduating from Cambridge he visited France and Switzerland, where he became a supporter of the French Revolution. On his return he formed important friendships with Coleridge and with Robert Southey (b. 1774, d. 1843), who became Poet Laureate before him (see Hopkins 1973: 124–52). The three poets moved to the Lake District, where Wordsworth remained for the rest of his long life, composing pantheistic and moralizing verse and enjoying the fruits of his fame. Samuel Taylor Coleridge (b. 1772, d. 1834) was the youngest son of a Devon clergyman, who died while Samuel was still a child; the boy was sent away to school and was intended for the Church, but, although a brilliant Classicist, he managed to leave Cambridge without a degree. Although Coleridge was emotionally unstable, in poor health, and for many years a drug addict, his output of poetry, prose, and criticism was considerable. At his death, as for much of his life, he was dependent on long-suffering friends.

James Hogg (b. 1770, d. 1835) was a shepherd from the Scottish Borders whose poetic talent was discovered by Scott. Hogg then moved to Edinburgh, where he became one of the pillars of the capital's literary establishment, and his work won admirers on both sides of the border, including the foremost English poets of his day. In his later years he managed to combine farming in Yarrow with writing for an international audience. Sir Walter Scott (b. 1771, d. 1832) came from an

Edinburgh white-collar family and on graduating from the capital's university began to study law. Success in getting his poetry published soon led him to abandon this career, and he became a successful poet, novelist, and publisher, earning (and losing) enormous sums of money and gaining a baronetcy in the process.

Blake's songs

Margaret Drabble emphasizes the individuality of Blake's versification, noting his statement that he must 'Create a System, or be enslav'd by another Man's' (1985: 105). Jacob Bronowski, on the other hand, points out that Blake was a poet who wrote in two different manners (1958: 13), and that this dichotomy applies equally to his metrics. Most of the verse Blake composed before 1800 is in short-line metres that are not strictly stress-syllabic. Many poems are in the traditional metres revived by the publication of Percy's *Reliques*, common measure and dolniks of various lengths, while others are in the variable tetrameters of Milton's 'L'Allegro'. Blake's use of these metres, however, is unique in that he often includes an isolated line with a different rhythm or number of ictuses from its neighbours. The following lines (11, 14, & 15) of 'Earth's Answer' from *Songs of Experience* (1794; in Bronowski 1958) characterize the rhythmic variety of Blake's short-line verse:

(1)   [V] **Sel**-fish **fa**-ther of <u>men</u>
(2)   [V] <u>Chain'd</u> in <u>night</u>
(3)   The **vir**-gins of <u>youth</u> and **mor**-ning <u>bear</u>

The first two of these lines have a falling rhythm and the third a rising one; their weak positions contain between zero and two syllables and their number of ictuses varies between two and four; the metre is thus a heterogeneous dolnik.

In his prophetic poems Blake abandoned rhyme as well as isosyllabism and employed a much longer line, one that subdivided into parallel or contrasting phrases. This line is clearly a development of the phrasal verse used in biblical prophecy, and Blake thus anticipated the development of Whitman's metre, which I shall examine in the next chapter. In Blake's poetry this line seems to have evolved from a dolnik of 4 + 3 beats (rather like a couplet of common measure), as exemplified by the following line (2) of 'A Prophecy' from *America* (1793):

(4)   **Sul**-len <u>fires</u> a-**cross** the At-**lan**-tic || <u>glow</u> to A-**me**-ri-ca's <u>shore</u>

While almost all the lines in this poem have this structure of 4 + 3 beats, a few variant lines have 4 + 2 or 3 + 3. In his later and much longer poems, such as *Milton* (completed 1808) and *Jerusalem* (completed 1820), Blake employed a freer mixture of variants including three-part lines with two or three beats in each, just as Whitman was to do fifty years later. Since Blake's use of this long line found no immediate imitators, and Whitman's inspired much modern versifying, I shall defer more detailed discussion of it until Chapter 9. Nevertheless, Blake's achievement in both short- and long-line metres is considerable; he was a metrical innovator with an important place in the history of versifying in English.

Burns's songs

Although Burns's language could not have been more different from that of the Augustans, in matters of metre he was as fastidious as they had been. His favourite line was the short-line canon, which he used with great skill and rescued from its risk of rhythmic monotony in numerous ways. One was to include short lines, usually dimeters, in his strophes for pause or emphasis. The effect of this *Burns stanza*, as well as his dialect and individual poetic voice, can be seen in the opening of one of his most famous poems, 'To a Mouse' (Barke 1960):

(5)	Wee **slee**-kit, **cow**-rin, **tim**'-rous **beas**tie,
(6)	O, <u>what</u> a **pa**-nic's <u>in</u> thy **breas**tie!
(7)	Thou <u>need</u> na <u>start</u> a-**wa** sae **has**ty
(8)	Wi' **bic**-k^ering **bratt**le.
(9)	I <u>wad</u> be <u>laith</u> to <u>rin</u> an' <u>chase</u> thee
(10)	Wi' <u>mur</u>-d^ering **pat**tle!

The remaining strophes make it clear that Burns's metrical intention for the shorter lines was a count of 4M/F, giving an iambic movement throughout. His metre also seems to be syllable-based since almost all of his potentially disyllabic positions involve words of ambiguous syllabification like '<u>mur</u>-d^ering' in (10). It is the contrast between line lengths rather than the variability of inter-ictic intervals that gives this metre the effect of ordinary speech in informal conversation.

Although Burns composed many poems in this metre, he showed himself the master of many others; one of his metrical tours de force is the poem 'Love and Liberty', which contains iambic and trochaic tetrameters, three- and four-ictic dolniks, and a four-beat triple-time measure. His ode 'Despondency' is in tetrameters and trimeters with an intricate rhyme scheme (aab aab cdcd efef), and he employs the Spenserian stanza effectively in several poems. A favourite metre for his songs is tetrameters alternating with trimeters, but some of these are in duple time, some in triple. Although Burns's poetry usually has a colloquial feel, his verse is remarkably regular in syllable count: as noted above, he rarely expands position size beyond one syllable except line-initially as double anacrusis. He employs the dolnik rarely, but skilfully; thus 'Yon Wild Mossy Mountains' is a four-ictic dolnik with a preponderance of triple time that recalls the tumbling verse of earlier Scottish poets.

One of the reasons why Burns may have been content with syllabically regular lyrics for his songs is that they were actually set to music, and music more often achieves variety by changes in tone than by changes in rhythm. Burns's songs are sung the world over and there is no doubting his poetic achievement; we should equally recognize his great skill as a versifier, a crafter of language into structures that are rhythmic and pleasing in recitation as well as song.

Wordsworth's ballads

Wordsworth and Coleridge first published their *Lyrical Ballads* in 1798, and enlarged editions appeared in 1800, 1802, and 1805 (Brett & Jones 1991). The poems were accompanied by prefaces and appendices calling for an English poetry with more natural diction ('the real language of men') and less emotional restraint ('real passion'). So successful was this appeal that the Augustan poets fell from favour for more than a century, while most English poets composed, and most readers cherished, the type of *Romantic* poetry advocated by Wordsworth and Coleridge. What is perhaps surprising is that Wordworth's versification offered no such radical change. His ballads are almost all strictly stress-syllabic and iambic, and his favourite lines are the iambic tetrameter and trimeter; it is only the simplicity of their diction that separates them from the short lines of the Restoration and Augustan poets. The following lines (58–60) from *Peter Bell* typify both Wordsworth's diction and his lyric metre:

> (11)   My <u>heart</u> is <u>touched</u>, I <u>must</u> a-**vow**,
> (12)   Con-**si**-der <u>where</u> I've <u>been</u>, and <u>now</u>
> (13)   I <u>feel</u> I <u>am</u> a <u>man</u>

The lines of a few of Wordsworth's ballads are in the commensurate triple-time metres, anapaestic tetrameters and trimeters; for example, 'Poor Susan', 'The Convict', and 'The Two Thieves'. In some of these, as in his only poem in alexandrines, he departs from strict syllabic regularity, as the following lines from 'Poor Susan' (3–4) and 'The Pet Lamb' (1 & 10) show:

> (14)   Poor **Su**-san has <u>pass'd</u> by the <u>spot</u> and has <u>heard</u>
> (15)   In the **si**-lence of **mor**-ning the <u>song</u> of the <u>bird</u>
> (16)   The <u>dew</u> was **fal**-ling <u>fast</u>, the <u>stars</u> be-<u>gan</u> to <u>blink</u>
> (17)   Seem'd to <u>feast</u> with <u>head</u> and <u>ears</u>, and his <u>tail</u> with **plea**-sure <u>shook</u>

Instances (14) and (16) have a single syllable in position 1, (15) has two syllables in position 1 ('In the'), and (17) has two syllables in the first position of each hemistich ('Seem'd to' and 'and his'). But this is no more than a minor extension of the closure principle, which makes rules laxer at the opening than at the close of units. Disyllabic positions elsewhere in the line are rare in Wordsworth's poems and, although Tarlinskaja includes 'The Waggoner' in her analysis of the English dolnik, she notes that well under 1 per cent of its lines contain an inter-ictic interval of two syllables (1993: 213). This minimal presence shows that Wordsworth understood how dolniks worked, but chose not to employ them extensively.[1]

When, as in his ballads, Wordsworth's lines are not modelled on Milton's, his lines are often very poorly crafted; in (11) to (17), for example, his metrical structures correspond too closely with his syntactic ones: many feet consist of phrases like the anapaestic 'by the spot' or 'of the bird', and the iambic 'with head' or 'and ears'. Mercifully his triple-time poems are all short, and the best, 'Lines Written in Germany' and 'Rural Architecture', are mildly humorous. We can thus see that, although Wordsworth rejected the high style and inflated diction of the previous generation of poets, his metrics was extremely conservative. His claim to a place in English metrical history rests not on his lyric metres, but on his appreciation and revival of Milton's pentameter and sonnet, which I shall discuss later in this chapter.

Coleridge's rimes

Encouraged to write ballads by Wordsworth, Coleridge produced 'The Rime of the Ancient Mariner', which surpassed any his friend had written, and which has fascinated and haunted generations of readers. He followed it with another mystic poem, 'Christabel', and in both rebelled against the modes of versifying established by the Augustan poets. Like those of Wordsworth's ballads, Coleridge's lines have four or three beats, but they are not iambic tetrameters and trimeters; they are dolniks, as the following lines from 'The Rime of the Ancient Mariner' (Beer 1974) show:

(18)	The <u>ship</u> was <u>cheered</u>, the **har**-bour <u>cleared</u>	(21)
(19)	**Mer**-<u>ri</u>-ly <u>did</u> we <u>drop</u>	(22)
(20)	[V] **Wa**-ter, **wa**-ter, **ever**y <u>where</u>	(121)
(21)	Nor **a**-ny <u>drop</u> to <u>drink</u>	(122)
(22)	Nine **fa**-thom <u>deep</u> he had **fol**-lowed <u>us</u>	(133)
(23)	From the <u>land</u> of <u>mist</u> and <u>snow</u>	(134)
(24)	**Se**-ven <u>days</u>, **se**-ven <u>nights</u>, I <u>saw</u> that <u>curse</u>	(261)
(25)	And <u>yet</u> I <u>could</u> not <u>die</u>	(262)

Instance (18), (21), and (25) are iambic realizations of the two line lengths; (19) has an initial inversion; (20) has an initial void position, (22) has a disyllabic position 5, (23) a disyllabic position 1, and (24) opens with two disyllabic intervals that contain a trochaic word.

'The Rime of the Ancient Mariner' combines a distinctive metre with great rhythmic variety, and Coleridge's choice of diction is highly appropriate. His use of alliteration is also very effective and his lines have an irresistible music; this poem was one of Coleridge's finest metrical achievements, and in 'Christabel' he continued to exploit syllabic irregularity for his own purposes, as the following lines show:

(26)	[V] **Knee**-ling <u>in</u> the **moon**-light	(284)
(27)	To <u>make</u> her **gen**-tle <u>vows</u>	(285)
(28)	Bard **Bra**-cy! bard **Bra**-cy! your **hor**-ses are <u>fleet</u>	(498)

In (26) Coleridge uses an initial void to give a falling rhythm that is skilfully balanced by a rising one in the next line: she kneels, she vows, she rises. In (28) he makes the sound echo the sense: three weak positions are disyllabic, and the line is as fleet as the amphibrachic hooves that carry it. By employing four- and three-ictic dolniks in these two poems Coleridge produces a level of excitement and of reader-involvement that Wordsworth's syllabic regularity fails to capture.[2]

The metrical personae of Hogg and Scott

Hogg composed verse in two different styles: for the first he employed the Scottish dialect and traditional metres, including dolniks and triple-time measures: thus his ballad 'Bonny Prince Charlie' (Mack 1970) is in four-ictic dolniks, and contains a great deal of triple time, as the following lines of its refrain show:

(29)	**Char**-lie, **Char**-lie, <u>wha</u> wad-na **fol**-low thee,
(30)	<u>King</u> o' the **High**-land hearts, **bon**-ny Prince **Charlie**

Hogg's second style employed standard English and stress-syllabic metres, most often the short-line canon, but he did not consider this cultured metrics superior to the traditional one; he says of the thirteenth bard in 'The Queen's Wake' (51–55):

(31)   Loathed <u>his</u> firm <u>soul</u> the **mea**-sured <u>chime</u>
(32)   And <u>flo</u>-rid <u>films</u> of **mo**-dern <u>rhyme</u>;
(33)   No **o**-ther <u>lays</u> be-**came** his <u>tongue</u>
(34)   But <u>those</u> his <u>rude</u> fore-**fa**-thers <u>sung</u>

Here Hogg shows his skill in the 'measured chime', while noting that a 'firm soul' could prefer the 'rude lay'; he was certainly a master of both, although occasionally he took the rude lay to comic extremes, allowing the sound to dominate the sense, as in 'Lock the Door, Lariston' ('lion of Liddisdale').

Scott had been inspired by Percy's *Reliques* to collect Scottish ballads and to compose many of his own, but he employed standard English, with only the occasional dialect form, in order to maximize his audience. Like Hogg, Scott had two styles: when speaking in his own voice he is usually strictly stress-syllabic (employing both iambic canons very skilfully), but many of his songs and lays are in traditional metres. Scott's long poem 'Harold the Dauntless' (Palgrave 1906) demonstrates his metrical versatility: from canto to canto he moves effortlessly between dolniks and stress-syllabic Spenserian stanzas. Scott made the dolnik and ballad measure respectable in Victorian parlours and established these metres as essential items in the repertoire of every accomplished versifier in the English language.[3]

The Long-Line Canon and the Dolnik

Many poets composed and published long-line verse in this period but, for reasons of space, I shall focus my analysis on that of Wordsworth (whose short-line verse is discussed above), three of his younger contemporaries (Byron, Shelley, and Keats), and two poets who worked in the middle years of the century (Tennyson and Browning).

George Gordon, Lord Byron (b. 1788, d. 1824) was an impoverished aristocrat who, after leaving Cambridge, spent much of his time on the European mainland. In the course of his travels he seduced many women, fathered (and abandoned) several children, and wrote poems that became best sellers in many countries. He was a passionate supporter of the causes of Italian and Greek independence and died of a fever while fighting for the latter. Percy Bysshe Shelley (b. 1792, d. 1822) was a member of the minor nobility who showed his rebellious nature at an early age and was expelled from Oxford for distributing atheist literature. He wrote prolifically, and his iconoclastic verse shocked the conventional public but at least succeeded in gaining its attention. His private life was a disaster of failed marriages and lost children, but he made many friends, including Byron and Keats, and joined the former in Italy, where he lost his life in a boating accident. John Keats (b. 1795, d. 1821) was a middle-class Londoner who abandoned his medical studies for poetry, but his first published volume received a hostile critical reception. He fell in love and became engaged, and published a second volume of brilliant and sensuous poems that were greatly admired by the discerning. He too escaped to Italy, but died of his illness a few months after his arrival.

Alfred Tennyson (b. 1807, d. 1890) was the son of a Lincolnshire rector who, after graduating from Cambridge, soon established a poetic reputation and became the most successful British poet ever. His poetry won him wealth and fame, and became mass entertainment in the drawing rooms of the middle classes. Nor did Tennyson lack more important admirers, with whose help he gained a seat in the House of Lords and held the Poet Laureateship for forty years. Robert Browning (b. 1812, d. 1889) was the son of a London clerk, self-educated in his father's library, and left London University without a degree. He tried his hand as a dramatist, not very successfully, and went on to compose a great quantity of lively, rebellious, and often optimistic poetry. But it was never as popular as Tennyson's, which better reflected the age's curious mixture of melancholy and jingoism. After eloping with fellow poet Elizabeth Barrett (b. 1806, d. 1861), Browning lived for many years in Italy, returning to London only after her death. In old age he at last achieved acclaim, and in the twentieth century many people esteemed his poetry more highly than Tennyson's.

The nineteenth-century ode

In this period poets continued to employ the long-line canon for dramatic works (whether plays or monologues), long narratives, and philosophical works; they also continued to combine it with other line lengths in odes that no longer aspire to the metrical complexity of Pindar's Greek. Thus Wordsworth composed what is one of the finest English odes, 'Ode on the Intimations of Immortality' (Gill 1984), in iambic lines of different lengths, but some other poets composed odes almost entirely in iambic pentameters. In the work of Keats (Barnard 1977) the ode's strophe became little more than a sonnet with its octave reduced to a quatrain, rhymed abab (although the strophe of 'Ode to a Nightingale' contains one trimeter line, and that of 'To Autumn' an extra pentameter). In the work of Shelley (Bloom 1966) the ode remained a more elaborate form: thus his 'Ode to Liberty' has a rhyme scheme abab cddd eecedee, in which the sixth and seventh lines are iambic tetrameters and the remainder pentameters. But Shelley's 'Ode to the West Wind' is entirely in iambic pentameters, its fourteen-line strophe consisting of three units of *terza rima* followed by a couplet (aba bcb cdc ded ee), and the strophe of his 'Ode to Heaven' consists of iambic tetrameters rhymed aab cbc ddd.[4] Over all, however, odes represent a very small proportion of the major poems for which the long-line canon was employed; most long poems of the period were entirely in iambic pentameters.

The nineteenth-century iambic pentameter

In Chapter 7 we saw that the dramatic and non-dramatic pentameters of the sixteenth and early seventeenth centuries differed significantly, but that the rise of the heroic couplet brought the metres of the two genres back together in the late seventeenth and eighteenth. In the nineteenth century there remained some differences between the iambic pentameter of blank verse and that of rhymed verse, but these resulted as much from Milton's influence as from Shakespeare's. On the whole the iambic pentameters of this period show a large measure of uniformity in their metrics, and this is shown by the statistics in Tables F to J. My four blank verse samples come from Wordsworth's *The Prelude* (Gill 1984), Keats's *Fall of Hyperion* (Barnard 1977), Tennyson's four monologues 'The Lotos-Eaters', 'Ulysses', 'Tithonus', and 'Tiresias' (Ricks 1987), and Browning's dramatic monologue 'Fra Lippo Lippi' (Jack 1970). My rhymed samples are the sonnets of Wordsworth and Keats, and 300-line samples from Shelley's *Adonais* (Bloom 1966) and Byron's *Childe Harold's Pilgrimage* (McGann 1994).[5]

There are more similarities than differences between my nineteenth-century samples, although they were composed over a period of more than fifty years. All the poets concerned followed a number of conventions established in the previous periods; for example, that *proved* could rhyme with *loved*, although their stressed syllables have different nuclei, and that many words are syllabically ambivalent: thus *heaven*, *power*, and *being* could be one syllable or two, and *agony* and *virtuous* could be two syllables or three. This ambivalence applied even to two occurrences of the same word in one sentence, as the following lines (148–49) from Keats's *Fall of Hyperion* demonstrate:

(35)   But <u>those</u> to <u>whom</u> the **mi**-series <u>of</u> the <u>world</u>
(36)   Are **mi**-se-<u>ry</u>, and <u>will</u> not <u>let</u> them <u>rest</u>

Poets in this period also found it easier to rhyme words like 'mi-se-ries' with 'trees' than to find a feminine rhyme for their disyllabic syllabification. But it was not entirely a question of rhyme: even in blank verse Keats sometimes employed an archaic accentuation in order to avoid a feminine line, as in the following lines from *The Fall of Hyperion*:

(37)   **In**-<u>to</u> the **dwel**-ling, <u>through</u> the <u>door</u> **cran**-<u>nies</u>   (206)
(38)   Can <u>put</u> no <u>end</u> to; **death**-wards <u>pro</u>-**gres**-<u>sing</u>   (260)

The poets represented by my samples avoided feminine endings in blank verse, and only Browning employed more than 1 per cent (in a dramatic monologue). Most poets in this period found feminine rhymes too useful to ignore in their rhymed verse, and in Keats's sonnets we find a proportion of feminine lines close to Shakespeare's. Wordsworth, on the other hand, eschewed feminine lines in his sonnets; as in so much else, he seems to have followed Milton's example rather than Shakespeare's.[6]

In his early poems Keats followed the Augustan practice of using balanced proportions of 'French' and 'Italian' lines. Combining this variation of caesura with feminine rhymes has a languid effect that is particularly appropriate to the meaning of the following lines (13–14) from the sonnet that begins 'Happy is England!'

(39)   **Beau**-<u>ties</u> of **dee**-per <u>glance</u>, and <u>hear</u> their **sing**ing
(40)   And <u>float</u> with <u>them</u> a-**bout** the **sum**-mer **wa**ters

The proportion of 'Italian lines' in my Byron and my two Wordsworth samples is 40 per cent or more, a not dissimilar figure to that found in *Paradise Lost*, but in Shelley's *Adonais* and my two mid-century samples the proportion is closer to that of Shakespeare's sonnets (33 per cent). Nineteenth-century poets continued to use more 'Italian' lines than a random deployment of their lexicon would have produced, but they seem not to have sought the even balance typical of the eighteenth century.

The norm for initial inversion in my samples is between 4 and 8 per cent, a level more typical of Shakespeare's sonnets than of his dramatic verse or of Milton's epic. Only Keats exceeded this limit, and (39) above is one of several examples in the same sonnet. Medial inversion is even more rare in this period and involves mostly grammatical words like *after*, *beyond*, and *upon*, which traditionally had been susceptible to it. Shelley is the exception in including medial inversions of lexical words in *Adonais*, including the following:

> (41)   O **gen**-tle <u>child</u>, **beau**-<u>ti</u>-ful <u>as</u> thou <u>wert</u>   (235)
> (42)   The <u>weight</u> of the su-<u>per</u>-in-**cum**-bent <u>hour</u>   (283)

These inversions are far from elegant, and the erosions ('as' in (41) and 'the' in (42)) also require unnatural emphasis in delivery to distinguish these lines from prose.

In total, erosion affects close to 10 per cent of all ictuses in my samples, and there is no significant difference between many of the poets analysed. Wordsworth, however, achieves in his blank verse a comparable frequency of erosion (14+ per cent) to that found in *Paradise Lost*, and Byron comes close to it in *Childe Harold's Pilgrimage*, which contains many lines with double erosion. The following lines (174–75) from Canto IV of Byron's poem illustrate the very different rhythm produced by eroding ictuses 2 and 4 from that obtained by eroding 1 and 3:

> (43)   To **bat**-tle <u>with</u> the o-cean <u>and</u> the shocks
> (44)   Of <u>the</u> loud **brea**-kers <u>and</u> the **cease**-less <u>roar</u>

These lines capture Byron's personal obsession with swimming wild seas and producing shocks, and metrically they are what Russian metrists contrast as *symmetric* (stressing ictuses 1, 3, and 5) and *asymmetric* lines (stressing 2, 4, and 5). The poets of this period avoided eroding consecutive ictuses, but both mid-century poets admitted rare exceptions; thus there are consecutive erosions in the following lines from the 'Choric Song' of 'The Lotos-Eaters', and from Browning's poems 'Fra Lippo Lippi' and 'Childe Roland to the Dark Tower Came':

> (45)   All <u>things</u> are **ta**-ken <u>from</u> us, <u>and</u> be-**come**   (46)
> (46)   To <u>plant</u> a <u>flag</u> in, <u>or</u> tie <u>up</u> a <u>horse</u>   (230)
> (47)   Makes <u>a</u> thing <u>and</u> then <u>mars</u> it, <u>till</u> his <u>mood</u>   (148)

Readers perceive 'from' in (45) as a beat because of the weakness of the preceding syllable, but, although the preposition 'up' in (46) is used adverbially, there is a tempting alternative triple-time delivery, in which 'tie' is the only prominence peak between 'flag' and 'horse'. Instance (47) has a surfeit of erosion, but the collapse of the line's rhythm is highly appropriate to its meaning, and it is rescued rhythmically and aesthetically by the alliterations on *m*.

In some of the sampled poems the fourth ictus is eroded significantly more often than the others, and in some erosion of the third predominates (note that Shakespeare, Milton, and Gray had favoured the third ictus for erosion). The same poet, however, may favour erosion of the third ictus in one poem and the fourth in another:

thus Wordsworth erodes more third ictuses in his blank verse poem and more fourth ictuses in his sonnets, while Keats does the converse. In view of its pedigree, it is tempting to interpret the symmetrical erosion of ictus 3 as the more aesthetic and to conclude that Wordsworth moved towards it as his style matured; but, if this is so, then Keats immatured, as *The Fall of Hyperion* is a late work. Since this poem also exhibits a reduction in the proportion of 'Italian' lines from that in his first epic *Endymion* and in his sonnets, it may simply be a hurried and less crafted work.

As noted above, although most nineteenth-century poets made use of the conventional syllabic ambivalence of some words, they eschewed disyllabic intervals, and their iambic pentameters were strictly syllable-based. Browning's 'Fra Lippo Lippi' was an exception; he had early dramatic ambitions and his metre resembles Shakespeare's dramatic line in some ways, for example, in the frequency of initial inversion. The following lines from 'Fra Lippo Lippi' typify these Shakespearean features:

    (48)   On the <u>wall</u>, the <u>bench</u>, the <u>door</u>. The <u>monks</u> looked <u>black</u>   (135)
    (49)   **Si**-<u>gning</u> him-**self** with the **o**-ther be-**cause** of <u>Christ</u>   (155)

Instance (48) clearly has a disyllabic anacrusis; (49) has an initial inversion, what may be a conventional elision, and a disyllabic interval between the third and fourth ictuses. There is also one line in my Tennyson sample that departs form the stress-syllabic: in 'Tiresias' the poet wishes to describe the ineffable (the naked Athene) and descends into unmetricality to do so:

    (50)   In-**ef**-fa-ble **beau**-ty, <u>out</u> of <u>whom</u>, at a <u>glance</u>   (54)

My scansion of (50) treats 'out' and 'whom' as ictic, but an alternative meaningful delivery would stress 'at' instead of 'whom'; the twelve syllables of this metrically ambiguous line were perhaps meant to match Athene's ineffability.

To summarize, this analysis reveals a remarkable degree of homogeneity in the nineteenth-century iambic pentameter, which was a strictly counted line of ten syllables. Feminine lines were the exception and some poets avoided them almost entirely, especially in blank verse; inversion was employed at the beginning of 4 to 8 per cent of lines, but was very rare mid-line, and approximately 10 per cent of non-final ictuses were eroded. Some poets skilfully employed both inversion and erosion selectively to obtain special effects and, although they continued to use a high proportion of Italian lines, most did not cultivate the even balance found in Augustan pentameters. Enjambment served to provide any further variety that poets desired: almost all my samples have a similar level to the 21 per cent found in Shakespeare's dramatic verse; but Wordsworth employed 33 per cent enjambment in *The Prelude* (one of the many ways in which his versifying follows Milton's), and Browning used less than 7 per cent in 'Fra Lippo Lippi' (one of the few respects in which his verse is more like that of Shakepeare's sonnets than his plays).

Arnold's free iambs

Although the canonical iambic pentameter accounted for most of the long-line verse composed in the nineteenth century, three of the mid-century's most important poets experimented with alternatives. Tennyson and Browning extended the range of the dolnik beyond ballads and lyrics, employing different versions of it in major poems, while Matthew Arnold (b. 1822, d. 1888) exploited the flexibility of the iamb. Arnold, who was the son of a famous headmaster, abandoned an academic career at Oxford to become an inspector of schools, but nevertheless found time to compose a considerable body of poetry (Allott & Allott 1977). Arnold's moral earnestness and universal outlook (in a chauvinist age) prevented his poetry from becoming as popular as that of the other two poets, but its technical brilliance has always found admirers.

In several of his poems Arnold employed a combination of iambic lines of different lengths, not in a fixed (as in the ode) but in a random order. Russian metrists term the lines of such a metre *free iambs*, and in English precedents for this freedom include the lines of varying length that are found in dramatic blank verse, and the poem 'My Picture Left in Scotland' by Ben Jonson (b. 1572, d. 1637).[7] Fabb 2002b offers a detailed analysis of one of Arnold's poems in this metre, the 37-line 'Dover Beach'. Arnold laid out this poem as four strophes of 14, 6, 8, and 9 lines, but Fabb combines the middle two into one 'verse paragraph', and thus makes the poem a kind of *meta-sonnet*: the first two paragraphs have the correct number of lines, but un-sonnet-like rhyme schemes, while the final paragraph is a truncated sonnet rhymed abba cbbc c (the c rhyme is also that of the opening line of the poem). The poem contains four different lengths of iambic line, which can be exemplified by its opening lines:

(51)   The <u>sea</u> is <u>calm</u> to-**night**,
(52)   The <u>tide</u> is <u>full</u>, the <u>moon</u> lies <u>fair</u>
(53)   U-**pon** the <u>straits</u>; — on the French <u>coast</u>, the <u>light</u>
(54)   Gleams, <u>and</u> is <u>gone</u>; the <u>cliffs</u> of **Eng**-land <u>stand</u>

Instance (51) comprises three iambic feet, (52) comprises four, and (53) and (54) each comprise five; there is also one line in the poem that comprises just two feet ('The Sea of Faith' (21)). Exactly half of the first twenty-eight lines of the poem are pentameters, but in the final strophe only the first and last lines comprise fewer than five feet.

In Fabb's analysis, Arnold's verse design is an iambic pentameter that allows *non-maximal* lines, which are indicated by an absence of asterisks at level 1 in his grid and bracket system (2002b: 106). Arnold's line might also be described as a *meta-pentameter*, the most appropriate metre for his meta–sonnet, since Fabb points out that the line divisions of the poem could be adjusted to make any of its iambic material form part of a pentameter (2002b: 107). Thus, adding the first hemistich of (52) would make (51) a pentameter, and adding the first hemistich of (54) to the second of (53) would do likewise. The high level of enjambment in the poem (37.8 per cent of lines), almost as high as that found in *Paradise Lost*, makes such a reordering seem almost more natural than Arnold's actual line divisions. Fabb also notes that most of the poem's inversions are contained in lines 4–7, as if the poet were flaunting this typical feature of the iambic pentameter (2002b: 112). Fabb notes that the iambic pentameter 'seems to emerge and then submerge' in this poem and, regardless of whether we accept his conclusion that Arnold aimed to communicate his metre, this analysis reveals the brilliance of the verse-craft involved. Arnold's metre imitates not only the sea's fluidity and lack of firm boundaries, but the poet's confused mental state, made explicit in the closing lines, where he refers to vast forces beyond his control and expresses confidence in nothing but love (and perhaps poetic technique).

Arnold's innovation consisted of extending the range of the iamb; the long-line innovations of Tennyson and Browning were the converse: they diminished its role and compromised its rhythm.

Tennyson's heterogeneous dolniks

The binary rhythms of iambic metre arise from the size of the intervals between stresses, which contain one syllable, whereas in ternary rhythms all the intervals are disyllabic. English prose and normal speech contain a mixture of the two types of rhythm in which an average of 33 per cent of intervals between stresses are disyllabic (Tarlinskaja 1993: 213–17). According to Tarlinskaja's definition (1976: 128), Coleridge's 'Ancient Mariner' is 'transitionally iambic' because disyllabic intervals make up only 5 per cent of total (see n3). The alternative long lines of Tennyson and Browning, however, are true dolniks, because more than 20 per cent of their intervals are disyllabic. Tennyson's twelve-line poem 'Break, break, break' (Ricks 1987) demonstrates some of the most important features of dolnik verse in general, as the following lines show:

(55)	[V] <u>Break</u>, [V] <u>break</u>, [V] <u>break</u>	(1)
(56)	On thy <u>cold</u> gray <u>stones</u>, O <u>Sea</u>!	(2)
(57)	The <u>thoughts</u> that a-**rise** in <u>me</u>	(4)
(58)	But <u>O</u> for the <u>touch</u> of a **va**-nish'd <u>hand</u>	(15)

Both the inter-ictic intervals of (55) contain zero syllables, both those of (56) contain one, but in (57) and (58) intervals of one and two syllables are combined. In the English dolnik zero intervals are rare and mainly used for special effects, as in (55), where they echo the waves and are metaphors for the poet's emotional state. In this poem 56 per cent of intervals are disyllabic, a significantly higher proportion than that found in normal speech, a difference that may also be mimetic, since waves break irregularly, and at what sometimes seem relatively long intervals. Another typical dolnik feature discernible from the above examples is that lines vary in the number of syllables in anacrusis. Thus (55) has zero anacrusic syllables, (56) has two, and both (57) and (58) have a single syllable in anacrusis. As a further source of variety, (58) has four beats, so that this poem ends with the traditional *common measure* of English folk verse, a line of four beats followed by one of three. Disyllabic positions, the anacrusic principle, and the rhythmic compatibility of three- and four-ictic lines thus constitute the essence of the English dolnik.

Tennyson, however, took the dolnik into new territory when he employed it in *Maud*, a poem (described as a 'monodrama') of over fourteen hundred lines; the revised version (1856) is divided into three parts and twenty-eight sections, and combines dolniks of five different lengths (*heterogeneous dolniks*). The first four sections are in six-ictic lines, but those that follow may be in three- or four-ictic, or a mixture of the two; these sections also contain isolated two-ictic lines, and the lines of the final section are five-ictic. Instances (59) to (61), below, contain two, three, and four ictuses, respectively, while (62) and (63) contain five-ictic and (64) and (65) six-ictic lines:

(59)	[V] <u>Long</u> [V] <u>dead</u>!	(II. 5. 2)
(60)	A <u>voice</u> by the **ce**-dar <u>tree</u>	(I. 5. 1)
(61)	[V] **Mor**-ning a-**ri**-ses **stor**-my and <u>pale</u>	(I. 6. 1)
(62)	It is **bet**-ter to <u>fight</u> for the <u>good</u>, than to <u>rail</u> at the <u>ill</u>	(III. 6. 57)
(63)	I em-**brace** the **pur**-pose of <u>God</u>, and the <u>doom</u> as-**signed**	(III. 6. 59)
(64)	I <u>hate</u> the **dread**-ful **hol**-low be-**hind** the <u>lit</u>-tle <u>wood</u>	(I. 1. 1)
(65)	I will **bu**-ry my-**self** in my-**self** and the **De**-vil may <u>pipe</u> to his <u>own</u>	
		(I. 1. 76)

As these lines show, the anacrusic principle is an important feature of *Maud*'s versi-fication, and the poem's inter-ictic intervals may contain one or two syllables. Longer lines may be predominantly in duple time like (64), or in triple like (62) and (65), but most contain a mixture of rhythms like (60), (61), and (63). In total 46.3 per cent of the poem's inter-ictic intervals contain two syllables, a significantly higher proportion than the 33 per cent of English prose.

In all the line lengths he employs in *Maud* Tennyson takes great care to avoid the regular iambic line (although his opening line (64) comes perilously close). It is tempting to read into this poem a metaphor for the poet's innovative metrics, with instance (65) proclaiming a rebellion against the canonical English pentameter, and instance (63) accepting defeat at the poem's close. Nevertheless, even in the final section Tennyson eschews the iambic canon, and his poem's lines contain far more triple time than Webster's foot-based pentameters. In summary, *Maud* is a tour de force of syllabically irregular versifying, and it contains an impressive variety in line length, rhythm, and rhyme scheme. This poem is proof of Tennyson's range and skill as a versifier, but its high proportion of triple time makes its artifice conspicuous and possibly detracts from the delivery of the poet's message.

Browning's four-ictic dolnik

In 'The Statue and the Bust' Browning chose to tell his story and deliver his moral in lines of a single length, a four-ictic dolnik in the oldest English tradition. The following lines exemplify the poem's rhythmic variety:

(66)	She <u>leaned</u> forth, <u>one</u> on **ei**-ther <u>hand</u>	(8)
(67)	[V] **Hol**-low-<u>eyed</u> and **hag**-gard-<u>cheeked</u>	(162)
(68)	[V] <u>Nights</u> and <u>days</u> in the **nar**-row <u>room</u>	(216)
(69)	Suf-**fi**-cient to **vin**-di-<u>cate</u> it-**self**	(230)
(70)	The <u>true</u> has no **va**-lue be-**yond** the <u>sham</u>	(235)
(71)	[V] **Ven**-ture as **wa**-ri-ly, <u>use</u> the same <u>skill</u>	(239)

A statistical analysis of the poem's rhythms shows that Browning employed the anacrusic principle freely: just over half of his lines have a single syllable in anacrusis, while 16 per cent have a zero, and 28 per cent a disyllabic anacrusis. Almost exactly one third of the poem's inter-ictic intervals are disyllabic, but they are very unevenly distributed: they represent approximately 43 per cent of first intervals and

49 per cent of second, but only just over 9 per cent of third. Approximately one line in five is in duple time: thus (66) is iambic, while (67) is rendered trochaic by its zero anacrusis. Most lines combine duple and triple time, intervals of one or two syllables: 28 per cent have intervals of 1–2-1 syllables, as in (68), 22 per cent intervals of 2–1-1, as in (69), and 16 per cent intervals of 2–2-1, as in (70). Only 9 per cent of lines have a disyllabic third interval, like (71), which is the only line in the poem with intervals of 2–2-2 (offset by a zero anacrusis).

From this analysis it can be seen that Browning's poem is extremely varied in rhythm and thus has much in common with a normal speech narrative. The poem has almost exactly the same proportion of disyllabic intervals found in English prose, and more than 90 per cent of its lines contain a mixture of rhythms (either a disyllabic interval or a disyllabic/zero anacrusis). Its percentage of lines with a disyllabic interval is more than double that of Webster's dramatic pentameter, as is the percentage of intervals that are disyllabic. Tarlinskaja shows that the percentages of disyllabic intervals found in the English dolnik vary considerably, which confirms her hypothesis that metric typology is a continuum (1993: 11). Thus, if the rules of a binary metre are relaxed a little it becomes foot-based; if they are relaxed a little more it becomes a dolnik; and if triple time is made compulsory instead of optional it becomes a ternary metre, with a new set of rules.

The Short-Line Canon and Trochaic Metres

Nineteenth-century poets continued to employ the iambic tetrameter, either alone or combined with the trimeter, for lyric compositions, and what is probably the finest long poem in the English short-line canon was composed in this period: Tennyson's *In Memoriam*. As Table K shows, however, Tennyson's tetrameter is metrically almost indistinguishable from Swift's a century earlier. Browning, who employed this metre in a number of shorter poems, increased the frequency of initial inversion from the traditional level, but his line is otherwise very similar to Tennyson's. Although enjambment continued to provide the chief source of variety in this metre, the proportion of enjambed lines remained the 11 to 14 per cent found in Swift rather than the 20+ per cent of the contemporary pentameter. The iambic tetrameter continued in popularity for shorter poems throughout the period. Some of the most interesting developments, however, were in the trochaic tetrameter: Tennyson and Browning both used it for important poems, and Henry Wadsworth Longfellow (b. 1807, d. 1882) chose a version of the tetrameter for his American epic, which is the longest English poem ever composed in a trochaic metre.

Tennyson's trochaic tetrameter

Tennyson employed the trochaic tetrameter in his poem 'Locksley Hall' and in a later sequel to it; its odd-numbered lines are feminine and its even are masculine (catalectic), and F/M pairs of lines are laid out on the page as 194 compound lines. Since this metre does not admit inversions of polysyllabic words, in order to provide variety Tennyson increased the frequency of erosion from historical levels: as Table K shows, the 11.4 per cent non-final average in Sidney becomes 17.3 in Tennyson, and the corresponding figures for the most eroded first ictus are 18.8 and 25.7 per cent. Double erosion of ictuses 1 and 3 is also common, as in the first line of the following pair (which Russian metrists would describe as 'symmetric'):

(72)   With the **stan**-dards of the **peo**-ples
        plun-ging thro' the **thun**-der-storm   (126)

Tennyson also erodes 12.3 per cent of second ictuses in this metre, a much higher figure than other poets, as in both lines of the following pair:

(73)   Left me with the **pal**-sied heart, and
        left me with the **jaun**-diced eye   (132)

This line also illustrates another unusual feature of Tennyson's use of this metre: he enjambs the odd-numbered line by giving it a final unstressed syllable that belongs syntactically to the following line. This syntax renders the latter an iambic line of 4M syllables, a powerful source of tension in this metre, and the 10.3 per cent of lines in which he does this represent a much more frequent use of enjambment than is found in the trochaic tetrameters of his contemporaries. Tennyson also employs a medial inversion of a grammatical word ('upon') that also occurs in Shakespeare's sonnets:

(74)   What is that which I should turn to
        ligh-ting **up-on** days like this   (99)

From this summary it can be seen that Tennyson managed to bring more variety to the trochaic tetrameter than did his predecessors or any subsequent poet.

Browning's trochaic tetrameter

Browning composed two poems of moderate length in trochaic tetrameter, 'A Toccata of Galuppi's' (90 lines) and 'Soliloquy in a Spanish Cloister' (72 lines). In both he alternates feminine (7F) and masculine (7M) lines, but the same orthographic device employed by Tennyson masks their metrical similarity: 'A Toccata' is laid out on the page with two tetrameters to the line. Its strophes contain three of these double lines, rhymed aaa, while those of the 'Soliloquy' contain eight single lines, rhymed abab cdcd. Both the metrical similarity and the contrast in subject matter and tone can be seen from the following lines:

(75)   Death stepped **ta**-cit-ly and took them
(76)   where they **ne**-ver see the sun.   ('Toccata', 30)
(77)   If hate killed men, **Bro**-ther **Law**-rence,
(78)   God's blood, would not mine kill you!   ('Soliloquy', 3–4)

'A Toccata' is a serious poem and 'Soliloquy' a humorous piece; this is reflected in the metre of 'Soliloquy', where stress is wrenched to obtain a rhyme in line 37, and the trochaism is exaggerated throughout: its ratio of trochaic to iambic disyllables is 8:1 compared with the ratio in 'A Toccata' of just under 6:1. In neither trochaic poem by Browning is there as much metrical variety as Tennyson provides: Browning enjambs fewer lines than Sidney and the only ictus that he erodes almost as often as Tennyson is the first. Nevertheless, few critics would compare the poetic achievement of 'Locksley Hall' to that of 'A Toccata of Galuppi's': the first is a great piece of versifying, the second a great poem.

Longfellow's trochaic tetrameter

Longfellow came from a middle-class New England family, and his gift for languages was recognized early. He travelled to Europe to acquire more, and spent many years teaching as a professor at Harvard. Longfellow was an even more popular parlour poet than Tennyson, but beneath his Christian optimism he was an insomniac and a depressive who had experienced the tragic deaths of two wives. An energetic translator, as well as a scholar and a poet, he was much intrigued by foreign metres; thus, for example, he composed two longish poems in accentual verse modelled on Classical quantitative dactylic hexameter, 'Evangeline' and 'The Courtship of Miles Standish'. When he decided to compose a national epic for the Native Americans, whom the European settlers were in the process of exterminating, he chose his metre with scholarly logic. He modelled its metre on the ancient oral epic of the Finnish people, the *Kalevala*, which had been published for the first time in 1822 and is in trochaic tetrameter. Longfellow's *The Song of Hiawatha* (Byrom 1970) was published in 1855; and he followed his Finnish model in making all the poem's five thousand lines 7F syllables in length and eschewing rhyme.

To maintain this unrelenting trochaic rhythm Longfellow had to employ a highly unnatural vocabulary with a ratio of trochaic: iambic disyllables of 24:1. Bringing a measure of variety to such a metre was by no means easy: Longfellow employed enjambment sparingly and, since he was not composing pairs of lines, did not utilize Tennyson's device observed in (60) above. Longfellow was therefore forced to employ erosion on a massive scale: as Table K shows, he eroded 50 per cent of first ictuses and 31 per cent of third. In many lines he eroded both these ictuses, making these lines symmetric in the Russian sense, for example:

(79)   The mu-si-cian, the sweet **sing**-er   (Int. 20)
(80)   On the **sum**-mit of the moun-tains   (II. 18)

Like Browning, Longfellow eroded the second ictus in the line much less frequently, as in the following line:

(81)   Decked them with their **brigh**-test **fea**-thers   (I. 155)

Very occasionally he even eroded the final ictus in the line, as in:

(82)   Who shall toil and **suf**-fer with you   (I. 18)

Another form of tension employed by Longfellow involved desyllabifying word-final *l*, *n*, or *r*, as in:

(83)   **Writt**^e**n** with **lit**-tle **skill** of **song**-craft   (Int. 109)
(84)   He the **Mast**^e**r** of **Life**, des-**cen**-ding   (I. 4)

This device may be construed as a form of disyllabic substitution, and the extra syllable of (83) makes the line unmetrical, which is appropriate to the meaning. But such anomalies occur on average once in every hundred lines with no such justification, and they are therefore likely to be an indication that Longfellow himself felt he needed to relieve the syllabic and accentual regularity.

It requires a highly artificial, almost childlike, delivery to make this poem's metre manifest, and this has made Longfellow's epic probably the most parodied poem in English (see Drabble 1985: 460).[8] Longfellow's metrical experiment is an artistic failure: despite his efforts its rhythm remains monotonous and boring, and the poem also reveals the poet's other limitations. Although sympathetic to their plight, it portrays the Native Americans as having simple mental processes suited to a simple metre. Thomas Byrom, who finds much to praise in Longfellow's poetry, nevertheless concedes (1970: vi–vii) that he is not a poet of the same calibre as Poe, Dickinson, or Whitman, whose work is discussed in the next chapter. Both the content and the metre of *The Song of Hiawatha* support this judgment.

Ternary Metres

Ternary metres, those in which all the inter-ictic intervals contain two syllables, have received scant attention from modern metrists, and introductions to English metre for the general reader devote little space to them and usually simplify the issues they raise. Thus G. S. Fraser (1970: 38–40) and John Hollander (1981: 8) note that lines of verse may contain anapaests (w w s) or dactyls (s w w), but neither explores the differences between the two rhythms or mentions the possibility of amphibrachs (w s w). Writing more recently, Philip Hobsbaum fudges this issue by saying that 'lines made up of trisyllabic feet usually contain a mixture of patterns' (1996: 2), while Robert Pinsky goes one step further, reducing all ternary metres to anapaests (1998: 66). Stephen Fry is even more confusing: he identifies Matthew Prior (b. 1670, d. 1734) as an exponent of the amphibrach, and shows that a limerick's rhythm may be either amphibrachic or anapaestic, but concludes that amphibrachs have no place in English (2005: 88–90). Scholarly works also play their part in this neglect of ternary verse: generative metrists focus on the binary (w/s) contrast contained in all metres, and they usually test their hypotheses against the most obviously binary metres and pay only cursory attention to the structure of ternary feet. For example, Nigel Fabb divides ternary metres into anapaestic and dactylic, the latter defined by their occurrence in an exclusively left-strong context (2002a: 25).[9] Hanson & Kiparsky, on the other hand, state explicitly that they have not considered how ternary verse may fit into parametric theory (1996: 300n21).

Varieties of triple time in Browning

It may be argued, however, that there are three types of ternary verse, not two, and in this section I shall examine as evidence on this issue three triple-time poems by the same poet, but which seem to have very different rhythms. They are Browning's 'The Lost Leader' (hereafter *LL*), 'How They Brought the Good News from Ghent to Aix' (hereafter *HB*), and 'The Englishman in Italy' (hereafter *EI*).[10] All three poems share a number of features that distinguish their verse design from duple-time or binary verse, one of the most obvious of which is that their correspondence rules do not allow inversion. This applies to monosyllabic as well as polysyllabic inversion, since in the very few lines where atonic monosyllables provide ictuses they are never articles, and are usually prepositions, as in the following examples:[11]

(85) **Shake**-speare was <u>of</u> us, [V] **Mil**-ton was <u>for</u> us   (*LL*, 12)
(86) And be-**twixt** the great <u>walls</u> of loose **flint**-stone | Or <u>in</u> the thick <u>dust</u>
                                                                          (*EI*, 25–26)

The first of these lines is of particular interest because, at first sight, it appears to contain the only example of substitution (a single-syllable interval, notated by [V] above). But, since this poem's verse design allows anacrusis, the missing syllable probably results from subdividing the line into two hemistichs, like those of tumbling verse, and applying the anacrusic principle to both.[12]

The anacrusic principle clearly operates in all three poems, although none of them contains a mixture of zero, single-syllable, and disyllabic anacruses. Their rhythms also differ at the close of the line: almost half of *LL*'s lines are feminine, whereas most of *HB*'s and all of *EI*'s lines are masculine. The openings and closes of the poems, therefore, offer some support for the hypothesis that Browning's three poems are in different metres, *LL* dactylic, *EI* anapaestic, and *HB* amphibrachic. Thus the overwhelming majority of lines in *LL* have zero anacrusis, no line has disyllabic anacrusis, and one line ends in two post-tonic syllables (the first of the following examples):

(87) <u>Best</u> fight on <u>well</u>, for we <u>taught</u> him — strike **gal**-lant-ly   (*LL*, 29)
(88) Then <u>let</u> him re-**ceive** the new **know**-ledge and <u>wait</u> us   (*LL*, 31)

These lines support the hypothesis that Browning's template is left-strong (that is, dactylic), and that its correspondence rules allow up to one syllable in anacrusis; similarly, lines like the following support the hypothesis that the template of *EI* is right-strong (anapaestic), and that the anacrusic principle allows it to open with an iamb, as in the second of the following:[13]

(89) Let me <u>keep</u> you a-**mused** till he **va**-nish | In <u>black</u> from the <u>skies</u>
                                                                          (*EI*, 7–8)
(90) Your <u>eye</u> from the <u>life</u> to be <u>lived</u> | In the <u>blue</u> **so**-li-<u>tudes</u> (*EI*, 179–80)

Inferring the template of *HB* is more problematic: it too might be described as anapaestic, because all its lines are masculine and almost half have two syllables in anacrusis. But the majority of the poem's lines open with a single unstressed syllable, and many divide naturally into four units [w s w] followed by an iamb [w s]; for example, instance (91), which mimics the clatter of horses' hooves:

(91) I **gal**-loped, Dirck **gal**-loped, we **gal**-loped all <u>three</u>   (*HB*, 2)
(92) And a-**gainst** him the **cat**-tle stood <u>black</u> e-very <u>one</u>   (*HB*, 20)

Since iambic closes (masculine endings) are common in *amphibrachic* metres, where they are described by Classical metrics as *catalexis*, the template of the poem could equally well be classed as an *amphibrachic tetrameter* that allows one syllable in anacrusis. This has led some generative metrists to consider of the precise structure of ternary feet in the context of their hypothesis that the contrasts in metre are essentially binary.

The structure of ternary feet

Like Classical metrics, generative metrics admits amphibrachic feet, but the orientation of amphibrachic templates is problematic, since middle-strong templates would be anomalous. Elsewhere I have argued that such templates are right-strong (w s), and that their correspondence rules set the size of weak positions at one (unstressed) syllable and that of strong positions at one trochee (Duffell 1999b: 67–70). This trochee is usually syllabic initially and medially, but may be moraic (that is, a single heavy syllable) in the final foot. Carlos Piera first proposed such a structure for the amphibrach (1980: 122–27), and it is shown below as a tree diagram, and illustrated by two feet from *HB*, 2:

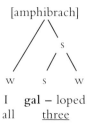

This may be compared with the structure that Paul Kiparsky proposed for the English anapaest (1977: 227–29), and which can be extrapolated to account for the dactyl: Kiparsky terms it a *falling* structure, and it is illustrated below by feet from *EI*, 2 and *LL*, 20:

Kiparsky supports such a falling structure by pointing out that the weak positions (or inter-ictic intervals) in one of Byron's triple-time poems contain trochaic, but not iambic, words.[14] This is not the case, however, in any of the three triple-time poems by Browning; thus, for example, iambic words occur in the inter-ictic intervals of all the following lines:

(93)   He a-**lone** breaks from the van and the **free**-men   (*LL*, 15)
(94)   Called my **Ro**-land his **pet**-name, my horse wi-**thout** peer   (*HB*, 52)
(95)   At all e-**vents** come — to the **gar**-den   (*EI*, 281)

From these examples it is clear that iambic words like 'alone' (93), 'without' (94), and 'events' (95) may appear in *HB*'s inter-ictic intervals; moreover, the dactylic *LL* contains trisyllables with a secondary stress on the final syllable, '**pros**-pe-ring' (*LL*, 17) and '**con**-fi-dent' (*LL*, 28), which exhibit a rising [S w s], rather than falling, dactyl [S s w]. Kiparsky's conclusion that there are no rising anapaests in English may well have been the result of sampling error, since Byron's poem is relatively short, but his insight that lexical structures in verse are clues to the poet's metrical intention may still be correct. I have already demonstrated that a poet seeking a strong trochaic effect uses a greatly enhanced proportion of trochaic words, and the same type of audit can be applied to Browning's lexicon in these three poems. The proportion of lexical trochees to lexical iambs in English prose is ± 4:1, and in iambic pentameters is ± 3:1; comparable figures for Browning's triple-time poems are: ± 3:1 (*LL*), 5:1 (*EI*), and 8:1 (*HB*). This suggests that in the last of these poems the poet consciously or unconsciously favoured trochaic words, which would support the above hypothesis that his template was amphibrachic and his strong-position size one trochee.[15]

The parameters of ternary verse

In the preceding sections I have argued the case for three distinct types of ternary rhythm, anapaestic, dactylic, and amphibrachic, and I have examined the foot structure of each. I shall conclude by attempting to summarize the parameters of each in terms of parametric theory, and by comparing them with those of binary metres. First, all metres, whether binary or ternary, share the same position-number options, and the majority of ternary designs, like the majority of binary, have between six and twelve positions in their template. The orientation of both binary and ternary metres is either left- or right-strong, but there are two types of right-strong ternary metre, distinguished by position size. In (right-strong) anapaestic, as in (left-strong) dactylic, metres strong-position size is one syllable and weak-position size two; but in amphibrachic metres the converse is the case: strong positions may contain two syllables (a syllabic trochee), while weak positions contain only one.[16] In English binary metres the prominence site is weak positions and the prominence type is strength, but in ternary metres these parameters are strong positions and stress. In anapaestic and dactylic metres this difference is dictated by the fact that weak positions may contain disyllabic words, and therefore strong syllables; and this in its turn ensures that strong positions must contain a measure of stress so as to become peaks of prominence. In amphibrachic metres, however, both types of position are constrained: a weak position may not contain a strong syllable, and a strong position must contain at least one stressed syllable.

The Quest for a Longer Line

A longer line has advantages: the *alexandrin* can convey more meaning in its 6 + 6 syllables than a line of only ten, and the French metre can achieve a statuesque symmetry that is beyond the English long-line canon. But the English equivalent is six iambs, subdivided into 3 + 3, and often seems slower and heavier than the French line. In Chapter 7 I examined this problem in the context of Pope's *Essay on Criticism* and showed how dramatic a difference he made to this metre by varying one inter-ictic interval. Earlier in this chapter I discussed Tennyson's six-ictic dolnik, a hexameter in which most of the intervals are disyllabic, but it has a rhythm that strikes the reader as highly artificial and it attracted few imitators. The strictly iambic hexameter, on the other hand, survived for centuries in the work of poets like Byron and Shelley in Spenserian stanzas where the intervening pentameters protected it from monotony. At the end of the nineteenth century there were a number of British poets who were admirers of French poetry, and still more who were schooled in Latin quantitative verse, in which the greatest achievement had been a line of six feet. Not surprisingly, therefore, some of the most ambitious versifiers of the period attempted a longer line. Two of the most notable were Algernon Charles Swinburne (b. 1837, d. 1909) and Ernest Dowson (b. 1867, d. 1900), who produced very different English hexameters.

Swinburne's six-ictic dolnik

Swinburne was born into the minor Northumbrian nobility, but spent much of his childhood in the Isle of Wight. When he left Oxford he lived by his writing, and after a dissolute life he meekly spent his old age in humiliating confinement. Swinburne shocked older Victorians and excited younger ones with the pagan message of his poetry, but astounded them all with its musicality. Swinburne was a versifier of exceptional skill; his use of rhythms, rhymes, and chimes is unsurpassed. He employed syllable-based and foot-based metres of every kind with equal facility, duple-time, triple-time, and dolnik, and he composed lines of every length, often in elaborately structured strophes. For a number of poems he sought a line longer than either his favourite four-ictic dolnik or the iambic pentameter (of which he invented some interesting variants, including one with an obligatory opening anapaest).

In 'Hymn to Proserpine', 'Hesperia', and 'A Song in Time of Revolution' (Binyon 1995) Swinburne developed a six-ictic dolnik, one with a less insistent triple-time rhythm than Browning's 'Abt Vogler', and with a less obvious division into 3 + 3 beats. In 'Hymn to Proserpine' he also used internal rhyme, as the opening lines illustrate:

> (96)   I have <u>lived</u> long e-**nough**, ha-ving <u>seen</u>
>   one <u>thing</u>, that <u>love</u> hath an <u>end</u>;
> (97)   **God**-dess and **mai**-den and <u>queen</u>,
>   be <u>near</u> me <u>now</u> and be-**friend**.
> (98)   Thou art <u>more</u> than the <u>day</u> or the **mor**-row,
>   the **sea**-sons that <u>laugh</u> or that <u>weep</u>;
> (99)   For <u>these</u> give <u>joy</u> and **sor**-row;
>   but <u>thou</u>, Pro-ser-**pi**-na, <u>sleep</u>.

The proportion of triple time in these lines (14 of their 24 weak positions are disyllabic) is typical of the poem, as is the contrast between the wholly triple-time (98) and the almost regularly iambic (99) that follows it. Such variety is the essence of Swinburne's metrical artistry, but his rhythms also often reflect the verse of Classical poets, whose civilization provided much of his content. Note that in (96) the six beats are subdivided 2 + 2 + 2 by the syntax, rather than 3 + 3; Swinburne was probably influenced in this by contemporary French poets, who were experimenting with a new *alexandrin* divided into 4 + 4 + 4 syllables (see Dominicy 1992: 169–72).

Laurence Binyon described Swinburne as 'a man of genius', and added that 'he conquered a new kingdom, but he left no heirs' (1995: v & vii). Many subsequent poets, however, rejected syllabic regularity and preferred a music that varied subtly from line to line, thus following Swinburne's precedent.

Dowson's free alexandrine

Ernest Dowson was a South Londoner from a prosperous but consumptive family; his passions included the Classics and French literature, but he left Oxford without a degree. His dissipation has been much exaggerated, but years spent trawling bars and brothels undoubtedly contributed to his early death. Most of his published work consisted of translations, but it included two volumes of his own poetry (Flower 1967). Unlike Swinburne, Dowson often employed deceptively simple rhythms, and he is best remembered today for two poems with long Latin titles: in the first, 'Vitae summa brevis spem nos vetat incohare longam', he combined canonical iambic pentameters with equally regular trimeters and dimeters; it begins:

> (100) They <u>are</u> not <u>long</u>, the **wee**-ping <u>and</u> the **laugh**ter,
> (101)   Love <u>and</u> de-**sire** and <u>hate</u>

The second poem, however, is metrically much more complex and interesting, and its metre is clearly derived from a recent innovation in French, where some poets were composing *alexandrins libérés*, lines of twelve syllables that ignored the rules for caesura in the canonical French long line (see Scott 1990: 74).

Dowson employed an English version of this 'liberated' or 'free' alexandrine in 'Non sum qualis eram bonae sub regno Cynarae' (a quotation from Horace, *Odes*, IV. 1), which comprises four six-line strophes rhymed aba cbc. The lines rhymed c are repeated with minor variations in every strophe, and the line rhymed b that separates them is an iambic pentameter, while the remaining lines are iambic hexameters. Of the four pentameters in the poem, two have their principal mid-line stress in position 4 and two in position 6 (of which one is a running, or 'Italian' line), and the twenty hexameters vary even more widely in structure, as can be seen from the following examples:

> (102) And <u>I</u> was **de**-so-<u>late</u> and <u>sick</u> of <u>an</u> old **pas**sion   (4)
> (103) I <u>have</u> been **faith**-ful <u>to</u> thee, Cy-**na**-ra! <u>in</u> my **fa**shion   (6)
> (104) **Sure**-<u>ly</u> the **kis**-ses <u>of</u> her <u>bought</u> red <u>mouth</u> were <u>sweet</u>   (9)
> (105) I <u>have</u> for-<u>got</u> much, <u>Cy</u>-**na**-<u>ra</u>! gone <u>with</u> the <u>wind</u>,   (13)
> (106) Flung **ro**-ses, **ro**-ses **ri**-o-tous-ly <u>with</u> the <u>throng</u>,   (14)
> (107) But <u>when</u> the <u>feast</u> is **fi**-nished <u>and</u> the <u>lamps</u> ex-**pire**   (20)

Instance (102) is a canonical *alexandrin* of 6M + 6F syllables with an iambic rhythm; half the longer lines in the poem are of this type, but the remainder are divided between three other types of line: the first has epic caesura and a count of 6F + 6F, like (103); the second has compensation at the caesura (the equivalent of the running, or 'Italian', iambic pentameter) and a count of 6F + 5M, like (107); and the third type does not subdivide 6 + 6 at all. Among this third type are (104), which subdivides 4F + 5M + 2M, and (105), which subdivides 5M + 2F + 4M and has strong phrasal stress on the monosyllables 'much' in position 5 and 'gone' in 9. Instance (106) is even more irregular: my tentative scansion shows 'ri-o-tous-ly' as four syllables for the sake of conformity, but making its third syllable any sort of a prominence peak goes against intuition. The line sounds most natural when 'rio-tou-sly' is pronounced as three syllables, even though this deprives it of a syllable and an ictus. From these examples it can be seen that Dowson's alexandrines offer great accentual variety, and his metre never sinks into a monotonous rhythm of 3 + 3 beats. Dowson is also very skilled in balancing repetition in one element of his language with variation in another, as in (106), which has four alliterations of *r* (if we include that in 'throng') and six different vowel sounds.

Their metrical complexity and variety undoubtedly contribute to making Dowson's alexandrines some of the most effective and memorable in the English language. With Swinburne's six-ictic dolnik and Dowson's free alexandrine the suite of metres that makes up the English metrical system can be seen to be complete. Stress-syllabic and dolnik lines had been developed of every length, from two feet to six, and all had been used successfully in major poems. The stress-syllabic repertoire now included a range of triple-time metres using the dactyl, anapaest, and amphibrach, as well those that employed the canonical iamb and the trochee. By the end of the nineteenth century English metre offered a highly complex system and a wide range of options; only the human desire to innovate ensured that it was not sufficient for the language's poets.

Conclusions

In the second half of the eighteenth century the publication of Percy's *Reliques* revived poets' interest in the ballad and the dolnik, and by the nineteenth some poets were employing the dolnik on an increasingly ambitious scale for other genres. Although the two iambic canons continued in popularity, there was also renewed interest in new and different rhythms: poets experimented with trochees and a variety of triple-time feet, and some substantial poems were composed in them. Swinburne's verse can be seen as the peak in the metrical ingenuity and versatility that characterized the poetry of this period. By the end of the nineteenth century almost every length of line, in every stress-syllabic rhythm and in the dolnik, had been attempted successfully. Twentieth-century poets thus had at their disposal a vast repertoire of metres, and some outstanding examples of how to employ them. But political and economic events in that century would threaten not only the parlour in which poetry was recited, but also the family gathered in it. Twentieth-century audiences had new expectations and writers naturally tried to meet them by new means, and for poets that meant exploiting some important metrical innovations that had appeared almost simultaneously in a number of languages and countries. To understand the next stage in the history of versifying in English, therefore, it is necessary to go back to the mid-nineteenth century and to look beyond the British Isles.

Notes to Chapter 8

1. Tarlinskaja shows that 'The White Hart at Rylston' also contains isolated lines with disyllabic intervals, but such lines are not the only peculiarity in 'The Waggoner', since a slightly higher proportion of its lines are not tetrameters at all. Wordsworth seems to have included these eccentric lines to add interest to an otherwise boring poem: in other respects its metre is the variable tetrameter of 'L'Allegro', but Wordsworth includes his headless/trochaic lines in blocks, rather than interweaving them in Milton's manner so as to create rhythmic variety.

2. Note that, according to Tarlinskaja's definitions, both 'The Rime of the Ancient Mariner' (5 per cent disyllabic intervals) and 'Christabel' (10 per cent) qualify as transitionally iambic (3–20 per cent), not as dolniks (1976: 128 & 1993: 213–14). Southey, however, composed poems that contain a higher proportion of disyllabic intervals, so that their metre meets the definition of a dolnik; see, for example, 'God's Judgement on a Wicked Bishop' (Grigson 1970: 52).

3. The poet and musician Thomas Moore (b. 1779, d. 1852) gave traditional metres the same respectability in Dublin parlours as Scott did in those of Edinburgh; where these two cities led, London and Boston soon followed.

4. Shelley employed lines with an irregular syllable count in 'The Cloud', where four-ictic dolniks with internal rhyme alternate with three-ictic dolniks. In this poem he demonstrated a metrical versatility and inventiveness that he otherwise confined to poem and strophe design.

5. In these tables I have included for the purposes of comparison the figures from Chapter 7 for Shakespeare's *Sonnets* and *Antony and Cleopatra*, Milton's *Paradise Lost*, and Gray's *Elegy*.

6. Milton employed feminine lines in only two sonnets: one, appropriately, is a tribute to Shakespeare, and the other has three rhymes for the paroxytonic Greek title of a book.

7. Pinsky argues that Jonson's poem has a 'show off' quality (1998: 27); it is certainly clever and self-conscious: the poet argues the superiority of hearing over sight and therefore makes the audible foot the basis of his versifying rather than the visible line. Thus the poem begins 'I now think Love is rather deaf than blind', and in line 8 Jonson refers to his poem's 'subtle feet' (Donaldson 1975: 145). Arnold's great achievement in 'Dover Beach', however, is that he leaves the reader who recognizes the metre's subtlety feeling 'how appropriate', not 'how clever'.

8. Such a delivery has become a feature of English media reporting, where correspondents often stress prepositions thus (my italics): 'This report comes *from* Chuck White, *of* NBC, *in* Rome, *on* Monday.'

9. He notes, however, that anapaestic metres may have a 'binary or unary initial foot'. This is consistent with his classification of Milton's *variable tetrameters* as iambic tetrameters that allow headless lines (or 'initial unary feet'). Two points in favour of this interpretation of binary metres are: (1) iambic metres reflect normal English speech, in which trochaic words are usually preceded by unstressed monosyllables such as articles or prepositions, and (2) while headless lines are allowed in right-strong (iambic) metres, left-strong (trochaic) metres do not admit anacrusis. But the first of these points is obviously irrelevant to ternary metres, and the second does not apply to dactylic metres, which contain a minority of lines with a single syllable in anacrusis (see instance (88) below).

10. Both 'The Lost Leader' and 'How They Brought the Good News from Ghent to Aix' are in tetrameters, while 'The Englishman in Italy' is in pentameters, disguised by the poet's orthography, which subdivides them into units containing three ictuses and two; this orthography represents the converse of that found in 'A Toccata of Galuppi's' where two four-beat units occupy the same line in the text.

11. Many modern writers on linguistics regard prepositions as lexical, not grammatical, words; see, for example, Getty 2002: 3.

12. There are many lines in Spenser's 'Februarie' that have a single-syllable interval mid-line, which divides the line into two-beat hemistichs; for example, 'so se-mest thou like [V] good fry-day to frowne' (30). Although tumbling verse allows other weak positions to contain a single syllable, mid-line exceptions to ternary rhythm are by far the most common.

13. Instance (90) is metrically very interesting because its three-beat hemistich is oxytonic, for which the two-beat hemistich that follows compensates by opening with two unstressed syllables. This emphasizes the anapaestic rhythm, which ensures that the primary stress of 'solitude' is subordinated to the preceding tonic monosyllable, while its secondary stress serves to provide the final peak and rhyme.

14. The appearance of stressed syllables in weak positions is a form of tension known traditionally as *incursion*, and in binary metres it is usually confined to stressed monosyllables, when it is known as *ictus demotion* (see Attridge 1982: 168–69), but in ternary metres incursion allows the strong syllables of polysyllabic words to appear in weak positions, or inter-ictic intervals.

15. Note that the extreme ratio of ± 24:1 in *Hiawatha* was the result of Longfellow's decision to make all its lines feminine; this decision doubled the number of lexical trochees required.

16. To employ Kiparsky's terminology, the structure I have described is a *rising amphibrach* (a w / s w contrast); its converse, a *falling amphibrach* (a w s / w contrast) would be anomalous, because it would include a right-strong element within a left-strong unit. Its rhythm would also need to be reinforced by the frequent use of iambic words, of which there are relatively few in English.

CHAPTER 9

The Advent of Free Verse

The term *free verse* (in French *vers libre*) was coined in the 1880s, and poets and critics have continued to employ it even though it has become increasingly clear that it is something of a misnomer. The term is, of course, an oxymoron: authors who want their language to be free write prose, and those who choose to versify are deliberately imposing upon theirs artificial structures called lines. The fact that the horizontal bars that free-verse poets prefer have no fixed length does not prevent them from being a form of confinement. Free-verse poets, like all others, versify, but in doing so they employ much more varied and less predictable structures than those to which poetry audiences had grown accustomed in the period from 1580 to 1880. Some metrists overstate the differences between free verse and traditional versification, in particular generative theorists from Halle & Keyser 1966 to Hanson & Kiparsky 1996. They define metre as a set of rules or constraints that will generate all the attested line structures in a poem; by this definition free verse is not metrical, since it has neither a template nor correspondence rules.[1] But other metrists, of whom I am one, have a broader definition of verse as *measured language* and metre as any form of *numerical regulation that is not found in prose*.

There are a number of ways of numerically regulating things: you can make all the numbers the same, or make them all different, or, indeed, combine both these forms of regulation. In traditional versifying the poet does the first, giving all the lines a predictable number of linguistic units (such as syllables, moras, or stresses); but free-verse poets do the third, making lines similar to or different from their predecessors depending upon the aesthetic effect they wish to produce. Thus the lines of traditional verse usually match, while those of free verse contain many contrasts as well as matches. In the preceding chapters I have shown that versifying meets the human need for security by its regularity and the need for surprise by its departures from the regular. The advent of free verse, therefore, gave poets the opportunity to shift the balance between security and surprise very much in favour of the latter.

As I hope to demonstrate, many of the elements of free verse can also be found in the versification of earlier centuries, but free verse became established only in the twentieth for a variety of reasons. First, the new balance between security and surprise that free verse offered appealed to Western audiences, who became increasingly familiar with change, shock, and surprise as the history of the period unfolded. Secondly, a number of important poets and influential critics espoused the cause of free verse at an early stage. Thirdly, the irregularity of free verse led many people to believe that it was easier to compose (when in fact the converse is the case). But bad publicity is still publicity, and vast quantities of bad free verse helped boost public awareness of the new mode of versifying.[2] Finally, the spread of free verse was aided by a dramatic change in poetry-reading habits: in the twentieth century most people experienced poetry by seeing it on the page rather than by hearing it in the parlour. As Derek Attridge showed in an important article (1987), the visual element in free verse can be as significant as the aural; indeed, it is often difficult to recognize the difference between free verse and prose by ear alone. The increased importance of the visual in versifying was signalled by the twentieth-century vogue for poems that formed a pattern on the page. The French poet Guillaume Apollinaire (b. 1880, d. 1918) exploited this potential in many of his poems (Bernard 1965), and M. L. Gasparov gives other examples of modern poems shaped like a fish and an apple (1996: 292). While relatively few poets cultivated these extreme examples of visual verse, many more used the fact that the audience could see their lines as an opportunity to add variety and to enhance their meaning. In particular, enjambment became an important way of linking and contrasting words and adding subtle extra layers of meaning to texts, and pararhyme, with its potential for new sound echoes, increased in popularity at the expense of the more obvious and obtrusive full rhyme.

The addition of free verse to the metrical resources, already considerable, available to poets writing in English greatly enriched the craft of versifying and made composition a more complex process. Meanwhile the general public found new diversions to distract it from poetry and, misled by the false belief that versifying was now so easy that anyone could do it, most people paid less attention to metre than in previous generations. Only the most serious and accomplished poets continued to study, discuss, and experiment with metre, and to perfect the techniques that were naively termed free verse. The great pioneers of free verse in English were born around or soon after the year 1880, and their innovations were largely a product of the first third of the twentieth century. But to understand all the types of verse that they developed it is first necessary to examine the earliest French *vers libre* and the verse of their precursors in English, who belonged to the previous generation.

Vers libre and the Antecedents of Free Verse in English

The development of free verse was a conscious decision by a number of poets as part of their programme to challenge the norms of their time (which they did in many respects other than their metre). They fervently desired a break with the past but, paradoxically, they achieved this largely by going back further than most of their contemporaries' memories. In the Germanic languages poets found their new freedom by returning to modes of versifying that existed before the absorption of syllabic regularity from Romance; and Romance poets first found it by introducing accentual patterns (in imitation of Classical quantitative ones) that made their verse more like that of the Germanic languages (see Scott 1990: 297 and Utrera Torremocha 2001: 44–48). The term *vers libre* was first used in its modern sense to describe the verse of the Symbolist poets Emile Verhaeren (b. 1855, d. 1916), Gustave Kahn (b. 1859, d. 1936), and Jules Laforgue (b. 1860, d. 1887).[3] María Victoria Utrera Torremocha traces the evolution of free verse from the numerous poems with a fluctuating number of syllables and/or accents per line (*verso semi-libre*) that had been widely employed in medieval Romance, Germanic, and Russian poetry (2001: 38–56). She places in this category a variety of very different metres, including that of the Pindaric imitations of Friedrich Klopstock (b. 1724, d. 1803) in German, the dolniks adapted from folk verse by Nikolai Karamzin (b. 1766, d. 1826) in Russian, the experiments of Victor Hugo (b. 1802, d. 1885) in French, the *metrica barbara* of Giosuè Carducci (b. 1835, d. 1907) in Italian, and the accentual verse of Rubén Darío (b. 1867, d. 1916) in Spanish.

There were several nineteenth-century precursors of the pioneers of free verse in English: the American poet Walt Whitman (b. 1819, d. 1892) first published his volume *Leaves of Grass* in 1855, thirty years before the poetry of the Symbolists; Gerard Manley Hopkins (b. 1844, d. 1889) composed poetry that was contemporary with theirs, although most of it was unpublished until 1918; Hopkins's friend Robert Bridges (b. 1844, d. 1930) experimented with syllabic irregularity well before 1890, and the Irish poet W. B. Yeats (b. 1865, d. 1939) wavered between more and less regular verse throughout his long career. Their innovations are known as *phrasal metre*, *sprung rhythm*, and *loose iambics* and I shall examine each briefly.

Walt Whitman

Whitman was one of nine children from a working-class New York family; he had little formal education and worked as an editor, teacher, and carpenter, and even tried his hand at politics. Shortly before his thirtieth birthday he travelled to the South and Midwest and found his vocation as America's national poet, although few of his countrymen appreciated his talents in his lifetime. Whitman rejected many of the trappings of Old World culture (Asian as well as European), thus his language was that of the rough American workman, and his metre was derived from the sermons of his time, replete with biblical quotations.[4] As noted above (p. 58), rhythmic liturgical prose had been influential before in moulding English metre, and in Whitman's case it led him to revert to a mode of versifying employed in Ur of the Chaldees.

Whitman's phrasal metre[5]

Whitman regulated his language at phrase level, and combined this with the placing of accents so as to give individual passages either one dominant rhythm or a variety of rhythms. The section of *Leaves of Grass* (Hall 1968) entitled 'Song of Myself' begins with the following lines, which illustrate his method:[6]

(1)	I **ce**-le-brate my-**self**,	|| and <u>sing</u> my-**self**
(2)	And what <u>I</u> as-**sume**	|| <u>you</u> shall as-**sume**
(3)	For **e**-v^ery **a**-tom be-**lo**-nging to <u>me</u>	|| as <u>good</u> be-**longs** to <u>you</u>

Whitman's lines and half-lines have the same parallelism in meaning and language as the poetry of the Old Testament. In these three instances the parallel is between two cola, but the first two lines also present parallels with one another, and the contrasting structure of the third line rounds off what can be termed a rhythmic paragraph. The pattern made by its prominence peaks (2 + 2, 2 + 2, and 4 + 3) is reminiscent of English folk verse: thus while (1) and (2) resemble long measure, (3) has the beat structure of common measure. The offbeats (weak positions) in these lines are represented by between zero syllables, as in position 5 of (2), and three, as in position 3 of (1). From this it can be seen that Whitman's lines contain two types of numerical regulation: colon is balanced with colon, and stress with stress; their metrical structure combines regulation at both phrase and foot level.[7]

Sometimes Whitman creates a three-part structure by subdividing one of his half-lines, as in the following line (11. 10) with its structure of 4 + 2 + 4 beats:

(4)   My **res**-pi-<u>ra</u>-tion and **ins**-pi-<u>ra</u>-tion, || the **bea**-ting of my <u>heart</u>, ||
      the **pas**-sing of <u>blood</u> and <u>air</u> through my <u>lungs</u>

Although most of Whitman's verse has the rhythmic variety found in (1)–(4), resulting from the irregularity in weak-position size, many passages have a strong prevailing rhythm, very often triple time, as in the opening lines of strophe XVI:

(5)   <u>I</u> am of <u>old</u> and <u>young</u>, || of the **foo**-lish as <u>much</u> as the <u>wise</u>,
(6)   Re-**gard**-less of **o**-thers || e-ver re-**gard**-ful of **o**-thers,
(7)   Ma-**ter**-nal as <u>well</u> as pa-**ter**-nal || a <u>child</u> as <u>well</u> as a <u>man</u>,
(8)   <u>Stuff'd</u> with the <u>stuff</u> that is <u>coarse</u> ||
      and <u>stuff'd</u> with the <u>stuff</u> that is <u>fine</u>

Of the nineteen inter-ictic intervals (non-initial weak positions) in this passage, fifteen contain two syllables, giving it a preponderantly triple-time rhythm.

Whitman's impact and influence

Whitman's metre is brilliantly appropriate to his purpose: his frontal attack on literary tradition required a robust assault vehicle, and he found it in this metre derived from Biblical texts and sermons. He had the courage to violate frontiers metrically as well as geographically, and his sure ear for rhythm makes him one of the most important and influential versifiers in the English language. Although Whitman received scant recognition in his lifetime, he never hesitated in his poetic or metrical endeavour; as he says in LII. 3:

(9)   I <u>sound</u> my bar-**ba**-ric <u>yawp</u> || **o**-ver the <u>roofs</u> of the <u>world</u>

Whitman's metrical innovations were unique, and the other major American poets of his time worked within the stress-syllabic and dolnik traditions. Thus, although Edgar Allan Poe (b. 1804, d. 1849) and Emily Dickinson (b. 1830, d. 1886) experimented with new rhythms in their work (see Wilbur 1959 and Johnson 1960), they did so in a way that extended rather than confronted the established metrical norms, and the same can be said of Longfellow's experiments with Classical and Finnish metres. From the middle of the nineteenth century onwards there have been two major centres of verse production in English, one in the USA and the other in Europe. Although the former grew to have around five times the number of English speakers as the latter, the number of individual book titles published in Britain has always been proportionately greater than that in the USA. As a result, a number of American poets have found an audience more rapidly in Europe than in their own country. Longfellow was popular on both sides of the Atlantic, but Poe and Whitman won some of their earliest and most important admirers in Europe, many of them among Swinburne's circle in London and that of the Symbolists in Paris. Most of Dickinson's poems were published only after her death, and in this respect she resembles the most important metrical innovator in nineteenth-century Britain.

Gerard Manley Hopkins

Hopkins was born into a prosperous London family whose interests were literature and religion; at Oxford he excelled academically and converted to the Roman Church. He then decided to become a Jesuit and, when he had completed the long and arduous period of study, was ordained priest and served in some insalubrious parishes. When not serving his parishioners, he taught, and in 1884 he was made Professor of Latin and Greek at University College, Dublin, where he died of typhoid five years later. He published few of his poems, out of deference to his religious superiors, but he sent them to his friends, describing in great detail his versifying method (see Abbot 1935 & 1955). His friend Robert Bridges published these poems in 1918 when he believed that the world was at last ready for their revolutionary form.

Hopkins's sprung rhythm

By 1876 Hopkins was experimenting with a type of metre that he called *sprung rhythm*, consciously derived from earlier English poetry that counted the stresses and not the number of syllables, but also strongly influenced by Hopkins's sense of syllable weight, derived from his Classical studies. Kiparsky 1989 gives a detailed linguistic description of Hopkins's metre, comparing it with the poet's own notes, and Hanson & Kiparsky 1996: 299–325 shows that exactly the same type of metre has been employed in Finnish poetry. It will therefore be sufficient here to summarize Kiparsky's findings and briefly illustrate the way that such a metre works. Sprung rhythm can be seen as an extension of the foot-based stress-syllabic metres that we encountered in Renaissance drama, and its parameters can be summarized as follows.

Hopkins employed a variety of line lengths: their verse templates had between four and twelve positions and could be either left- or right-strong.[8] In sprung rhythm, however, the maximum size of both strong and weak positions is a moraic trochee; a position may contain one syllable (either heavy or light), but it may also contain two light syllables, of which the first is stressed (thus forming a moraic trochee), or a series of (up to four) unstressed light syllables. Hopkins's prominence site is both strong and weak positions, and his prominence type is a mixture of stress and syllable weight. Strong positions must contain a syllable that is either stressed or heavy (or both), while weak ones may not contain prominent syllables (any stressed syllables they contain must be subordinated to an adjacent stress in a strong position). In addition to these five parameters Hopkins's sprung rhythm has two other features, which he termed *overreaving* (the continuation of the metre across line boundaries) and *outrides* (extended weak positions).

The way that all these features come together to create a new type of metre can be seen from the opening lines of 'The Windhover' (Gardner 1953), which is five-ictic:

(10)   I <u>caught</u> this **mor**-ning **mor**-ning's **mi**-nion, **king**-
(11)   dom of **day**-light's **dau**-phin, dap-ple-**dawn**-drawn **Fal**-con,
                                                           in his **ri**-ding
(12)   Of the **rol**-ling le-vel <u>un</u>-der-**neath** him stea-dy <u>air</u>, and **stri**-ding
(13)   <u>High</u> there, how he <u>rung</u> u-pon the <u>rein</u> of a **wim**-pling <u>wing</u>
(14)   In his **ec**-sta-sy! then <u>off</u>, <u>off</u> forth on <u>swing</u>

The size of inter-ictic intervals varies considerably in these lines, particularly (14) in which a trisyllabic interval between the first and second ictuses is followed by two intervals of zero. These trisyllabic intervals may be the result of consecutive positions being disyllabic: thus in (12) 'rolling' may constitute the first strong position and 'level' (a trochee comprising two light syllables) the following weak one. In (11) and (12) similar disyllabic strong–weak contrasts can be found in 'dauphin' / 'dapple', and '-neath him' / 'steady'. Alternatively a trisyllabic interval may represent an extended weak position, as '-con in his' in (11) and '-stasy then' in (14). The trisyllabic weak position 'upon the' in (13) shows that non-trochaic disyllables are allowed to share a position providing they are non-lexical. Hopkins's principle that the scansion of one line should be continuous with the next (*overreaving*) is demonstrated by the split of the word 'kingdom' between (10) and (11), and by the division of the trisyllabic weak position '-ing of the' between (11) and (12). This passage also contains numerous alliterations, emphasizing the poet's aim to return to the left-strong modes of versifying of an earlier era.

Another of Hopkins's early poems, 'The Loss of the Eurydice', employs three- and four-ictic lines, and alliterates even more profusely, as can be seen from the following lines (27–28):

(15)   **Hail**-ropes **hus**-tle and <u>grind</u> their
(16)   **Hea**-ven-gra-vel? **wolf**-snow, <u>worlds</u> of it, <u>wind</u> there?

The similarity to Old and Middle English accentual metres is very clear here and, given the poem's subject, is an important part of the poet's intention. Note that in (16) a disyllabic strong position 1 is followed by a disyllabic weak position 2, both trochaic; and that it is debatable whether a strong position can be void in sprung rhythm: Kiparsky notes just two possible examples, and concludes that if void strong positions are allowed by the metre, they 'must be considered highly marked' (1989: 318).

Sprung rhythm and free verse

Hopkins's innovations, unlike Whitman's, should not be seen as bids for freedom; as a devout Catholic, he greatly prized the acceptance of chains as an act of free will. He argued that sprung rhythm must, if anything, be stricter than conventional stress-syllabic verse (Kiparsky 1989: 305), and sprung rhythm is more rule-bound, since it regulates syllable weight as well as stress, and strong positions as well as weak; it also allows no inversion of lexical stress (1989: 312). Kiparsky demonstrates that Hopkins's new metrics is a logically rigorous construct, and that critics have been wrong to question this. Some popular guides to metre have magnified these doubts by including under the heading 'sprung verse' or 'sprung rhythm' other metres that are not strictly stress-syllabic (see, for example, Hobsbaum 1996: 53–70 and Pinsky 1998: 9). But Hopkins's innovation was specific: he rediscovered that syllable weight can be numerically regulated in English and that, like syllable count, it can be combined with stress. He also developed a distinctive system for doing so that should not be confused with other weight-sensitive metres. I shall therefore not use the term *sprung* indiscriminately in the sections that follow.

Robert Bridges and W. B. Yeats

Although Hopkins's verse was known to only a few of his friends before 1918, the next generation of metrical innovators were influenced by the verse of Bridges and Yeats, whose lines shared some of the characteristics of Hopkins's metrics. If we examine the verse of these two poets, we can see that its metre is transitional between that of Swinburne's verse and that of the verse composed by Eliot and Pound in the first quarter of the twentieth century. This transition begins with a loosening of the iamb, a desire on the poet's part to introduce more rhythmic variety into canonical metres.

Robert Bridges

Bridges studied and practised medicine for some years after leaving Oxford, but abandoned it in 1881 for a full-time writing career. He produced some important criticism and a great deal of poetry: his collected poems appeared in 1912 to great acclaim and he was made Poet Laureate in 1913. Bridges, as Drabble notes, is still respected for 'the simplicity of his diction and his adventurous experiments in metre' (1985: 130). The latter included quantitative dactylic hexameters on the Latin model, and Hobsbaum notes that the results were unimpressive because in the English line the stresses are more easily perceived than the long syllables that are intended to be ictic (1996: 74–76). But Bridges's interest in quantity extended beyond these experiments, and he sought an alternative to the syllabic regularity of the iambic canons. Like his friend Hopkins, he found the effects of varying position size attractive; and he employed in poems like 'London Snow', 'On a Dead Child', and 'Awake, my Heart' (Bridges 1947) a long line that resembled more closely the five-beat ictic verse of earlier centuries than the iambic pentameter. This expansion of position size can be seen clearly in the following lines from 'London Snow':

(17)   In <u>large</u> white <u>flakes</u> [V] **fal**-ling on the **ci**-ty <u>brown</u>   (2)
(18)   The <u>eye</u> [V] **mar**-velled — **mar**-velled at the **dazz**-ling **white**ness   (15)
(19)   No <u>sound</u> of <u>wheel</u> [V] **rum**-bling nor of **foot** [V] **fal**-ling   (17)
(20)   Or **ri**-o-ted in a **drift**, [V] **plun**-ging <u>up</u> to the <u>knees</u>   (22)
(21)   At the <u>sight</u> of the **beau**-ty that <u>greets</u> them,
                                 for the <u>charm</u> they have **bro**ken   (37)

Each of these lines has five ictic syllables, but the interval between them varies between zero (scanned [V]) and three, and in (20) the first interval actually contains four if 'ri-o-ted' is not subject to synaeresis. Bridges here seems to be employing polysyllabic strong as well as weak positions. Thus in (17) 'falling' occupies position 6 and 'on the' position 7, and a similar structure can be observed in each of the other lines: 'marvelled' and 'at the' in (18), 'rumbling' and 'nor of' in (19), 'rioted' and 'in a' in (20), 'greets them' and 'for the' in (21). In employing polysyllabic and void positions, Bridges's intention was to reintroduce the concept of syllable weight into English metrics, but modern generative metrics would describe his experiments as 'foot-based', and the lines so produced have much in common with the dramatic verse of Webster.

Bridges also parted from tradition in another way in 'The Storm Is Over' (Press 1964: 416–17): this poem mixes dolniks of different lengths (two-, three-, four-, and five-ictic) in no fixed order, an experiment in free dolniks which I shall discuss below. In some things, however, Bridges was reluctant to change; for example, he clung to full rhyme even when new alternatives became the vogue. Although his poetic reputation remained high until his death (and he continued versifying until he was well into his eighties), Bridges's poetry received little attention in the second half of the twentieth century, and few critics now rate him as a major poet. Certainly the bleak message, startling diction, and violent imagery of Hopkins are much more to modern tastes. But Bridges was a highly skilled versifier and his innovations in varying position size and the number of beats in each line anticipated subsequent metrical developments.

William Butler Yeats

Yeats was a member of an artistic Dublin family, and at first studied visual art, but soon turned to poetry and politics. He had a long and influential career in both and has a much better claim than Thomas Moore (see Chapter 8, n3) to being Ireland's foremost poet writing in English; certainly, Yeats's poetic reputation remains high in the twenty-first century. But although his poetry (Albright 1990) is considered more modern than that of Bridges, Yeats's versification is no more revolutionary than that of the older poet. Yeats was equally the master of stress-syllabic metres, ballad metres, and dolniks; thus 'Leda and the Swan' is in canonical iambic pentameters, 'An Irish Airman Foresees his Death' is in isosyllabic long measure, and 'Cap and Bells' is a perfect example of a three-ictic dolnik (analysed in detail by Bailey 1976). In one of his most famous poems, 'Byzantium', he mixes three-, four-, and five-ictic lines, but in a fixed order, and, while the longer lines are canonically iambic, the three-ictic ones are dolniks. One of the innovatory aspects of his metre is his use of pararhyme (assonance, consonance, and pararhyme) as an alternative to full rhyme in the manner of French *vers libéré* (see Scott 1990: 302).

Yeats used disyllabic weak positions in his pentameters, as is shown by the following lines from 'Sailing to Byzantium', published in 1927:

(22)   To the **ho**-ly **ci**-ty <u>of</u> By-**zan**-ti-<u>um</u>   (16)
(23)   My **bo**-di-ly <u>form</u> from **a**-ny **nat**[u]-ral <u>thing</u>   (26)

The anacrusis of (22) and the first interval of (23) contain two syllables, But such resolution occurs in only four lines of the thirty-two in this poem and in fewer than 5 per cent of lines in his pentameters as a whole. This is a much more modest scale than we find in some of Bridges's poems. Yeats preferred to achieve metrical variety by mixing line lengths rather than rhythms: for example, the second section of his poem 'The Tower' consists of thirteen strophes, each of eight lines comprising 5–5–5–4–5–4–4–5 iambic feet. The mixed tetrameters of this poem include trochaic, headless lines, and allow the occasional disyllabic interval, as the following lines (ll. 14–15) show:

(24) [V] <u>Ran</u> and <u>with</u> the **gar**-den <u>shears</u>
(25) [V] <u>Clipped</u> an **in**-so-lent **far**-mer's <u>ears</u>

Even more unusual is the following line from 'Nineteen Hundred and Nineteen', which contains both an initial inversion and a proparoxytonic close:

(26) **In**-to the <u>half</u>-de-**ceit** of <u>some</u> in-**to**-xi-cant   (34)

If it had been composed two centuries earlier this line might be interpreted as an alexandrine with a stress on the final syllable, but it occurs in a passage of penta-meters.

Compared with his transatlantic contemporaries, however, Yeats was a metrical conservative: he had an excellent ear for the music of the English language and he found he could obtain all the effects he wished with relatively few departures from the existing system. His view on metrics is summarized in the poem 'Under Ben Bulben' (v. 1–4), which he composed shortly before the Second World War:

(27) **I**-rish <u>po</u>-ets, <u>learn</u> your <u>trade</u>,
(28) <u>Sing</u> wha-**te**-ver <u>is</u> well-<u>made</u>,
(29) <u>Scorn</u> the <u>sort</u> now **gro**-wing <u>up</u>
(30) All <u>out</u> of <u>shape</u> from <u>toe</u> to <u>top</u>.

Instance (30) shows that the metre is the mixed tetrameter of Milton, rather than the trochaic tetrameter, and the consonance linking (29) and (30) reminds us that Yeats was one of the first modern poets to cultivate this device.

The Pioneers of Free Verse in English

Most of the early pioneers were American, although the two most widely read, Ezra Pound (b. 1885, d. 1972) and T. S. Eliot (b. 1888, d. 1965), spent most of their lives in Europe. By the 1920s many other American poets were employing free verse and three in particular were establishing their own distinctive varieties of it: Wallace Stevens (b. 1879, d. 1955), William Carlos Williams (b. 1883, d. 1963), and Marianne Moore (b. 1887, d. 1972). The analysis of free verse that follows is based on some their best-known poems, and their versification differs in so many ways that no simple generalization can accurately cover them all. Although some of these poets tried to explain their own methods, as Hartman notes, 'each poet's system collapses when it attempts to colonize all free verse' (1980: 44). One of my criteria for the selection of these five is that their explanations of free verse were so different, but in this chapter I shall note the features shared by their versifying as well as the features that distinguish them, and I shall try to draw some general conclusions. In my explanation I shall also try to make clear the relationship between the metre of each poet and metres I have already described.

Ezra Pound

Pound was born in the Midwest, graduated from the University of Pennsylvania, and taught briefly in the USA before coming to Europe in 1908. He established himself at the centre of avant-garde literary circles, first in London and then in Paris, before settling finally in Italy. He backed the losing side in the Second World War, for which he was incarcerated between 1945 and 1958. Pound produced a vast amount of poetry (Eliot 1959), translation (Pound 1970), and literary criticism (Eliot 1960). Among much verse that was inconsequential, he produced *Cathay*, his rendering of Chinese classics, *Hugh Selwyn Mauberley*, a lament for a lost world, and the *Cantos*, versified lessons from cultural and economic history (Pound 1975).

Pound's metrical experiments depart from the norms of the stress–syllabic system more radically than those of Hopkins, Bridges, or Yeats. Pound could compose poems entirely in traditional metres (for example, the iambic pentameters of 'Planh for the Young English King', the mixed tetrameters of Milton in 'Dieu qui la faicte', or the triple-time metres of Browning in 'Mesmerism'), but he refused to be contained in any one metrical system. Pound sought to give his lines something that he called 'absolute rhythm', that which most effectively conveys the meaning of the poem (Eliot 1960: 9). This was no more than Pope had advocated in his *Essay on Criticism* two centuries earlier, but Pound's programme for implementing this aim went beyond the subtle manipulation of stress strength and syllable weight, and extended to varying both the number of beats in a poem's lines and the size of the intervals between them. It can be argued that the English stress–syllabic system of versifying suffers from a surfeit of regularity: a regular number of beats per line, a regular size of interval, and in the case of rhymed verse the repetition of all the phonemes after the onset of the final ictic syllable. Although this system had dominated English poetry for more than three hundred years, some poets in every generation had rebelled against it. The most common form of rebellion had been blank verse, which dispensed with rhyme, and the second most common the dolnik, with its varied intervals. A third way had been to vary the number of beats per line, as Restoration and Augustan poets did in their odes; Arnold went a little further in 'Dover Beach' by making its line lengths unpredictable (as noted in Chapter 8), and Dryden even changed the size of the intervals between those beats from one passage of 'Alexander's Feast' to another (as noted in Chapter 7). But to vary both the number of beats and the size of intervals and to dispense with rhyme was revolutionary; yet that was exactly what Pound proposed.

The 'free dolnik'

Russian works on metrics (for example, Smith 2002) describe verse that varies widely in both the number of beats per line and the size of the intervals between them as being in *free dolniks*, and I shall find that term useful to distinguish between this most extreme form of irregularity and other types of metre that are not so variable. Most English critics (and the general public) have been content to label them all 'free verse', but in order to understand modern versifying it is important to separate its very different forms. One of the free dolnik's advantages is that its language sounds natural, almost conversational, but the form's drawback is that it is perilously close to prose, the phrases of which also have a variable number of beats, irregular intervals, and sporadic rhyme. In earlier centuries Blake and Whitman had composed verse with these confusing features, but they found few imitators; Pound's revolution, however, succeeded because of a change in poetry-reading habits. As more people experienced poetry on the page, they were able to see line divisions that only exaggerated pauses could make audible and observe nuances of language that were not immediately obvious. Free verse differs from chopped-up prose only in that its rhythms are carefully crafted, and free-verse poets use a number of devices to obtain the rhythmic effects they desire, many of which require careful reading. These devices include: (1) frequent enjambment (to emphasize the rhythmic structure's precedence over the syntactic); (2) the repetition of some, but not all, of the phonemes in final stressed syllables (making rhyme more subtle and less obtrusive); (3) both extreme contrasts between the length of consecutive lines and also series of lines with the same structure (to provide variety); and (4) occasional lines with very familiar structures (to remind their audiences that they are reading verse). All of these were features of Pound's verse long before they became fashionable.

In order to illustrate Pound's metrics I shall analyse some of his best-known poems in order to quantify their most important metrical features: the number of beats per line, the size of intervals that divide and of the anacruses that precede them, the occurrence of canonical lines, the frequency of enjambment, and the balance between masculine and feminine lines. In this way I hope to build up a picture of Pound's metrical style that can be compared with that of subsequent poets, and the poems I have chosen are 'Sestina: Altaforte', 'E. P. L'Ode pour l'élection de son sépulcre', and two of his *Cantos* (I & XLV). Their line lengths are given in Table L. 'Altaforte' and *Canto* I are predominantly four- and five-ictic poems, while 'L'Ode' and *Canto* XLV are predominantly three- and four-ictic, but contain some longer and shorter lines; in all these poems the number of consecutive lines of the same length rarely exceeds five. Table M, however, shows that these poems differ even more markedly in their other features: 'Altaforte' is a sestina and every line ends with one of six words (four of them paroxytonic): 'peace', 'music', 'clash', 'opposing', 'crimson', and 'rejoicing'. There is hardly any enjambment, and iambic pentameters are avoided; there are also fewer disyllabic intervals than in prose, so the poem is preponderantly in duple time; but there is a very high proportion of zero intervals. In lines like the following, which I have scanned as five-ictic, clashing stresses reinforce the poem's belligerent message:[9]

(31)   And <u>through</u> all the **ri**-ven <u>skies</u> God's <u>swords</u> <u>clash</u>   (12)
(32)   With <u>fat</u> boards, <u>bawds</u>, <u>wine</u> and <u>frail</u> **mu**sic   (17)

'L'Ode' has a more balanced mixture of duple and triple time and far fewer clashing stresses, but it is another rather end-stopped poem. In keeping with the poem's message, its metre moves from order to chaos: the rhymed quatrains of Sections I–III (the 38 per cent of lines in total that have full rhyme) are succeeded by unrhymed strophes of varying lengths in Section IV. The laconic Section V brings a return to regularity, as the poet deplores in eight three-beat lines the culture that failed his generation:

> (33)   For <u>two</u> gross of **bro**-ken statues   (92)
> (34)   For a <u>few</u> **thou**-sand **bat**-tered <u>books</u>   (93)

Once again Pound chose a metre that was admirably suited to his artistic purpose, thus demonstrating his concept of 'absolute rhythm'.

The two *Cantos* that I have selected for analysis both contain significantly more triple time than prose, and the first (*Canto* I) is dactylic, like Homer's *Odyssey*, episodes of which it retraces. The poem's falling rhythm is reinforced by the exceptionally high percentages of zero anacruses and feminine lines, but even masculine lines seem dactylic when they contain a series of paroxytons, as in:

> (35)   I <u>sat</u> to keep <u>off</u> the im-**pe**-tu-ous **im**-po-tent <u>dead</u>   (40)

This line, which paraphrases a Greek line, captures the rhythm of its original and is one of many skilful imitations of the Greek metre in the poem. *Canto* XLV, by contrast, is a strongly anapaestic poem: it begins with a line that it repeats three times, 'With usura' (paroxytonic in Latin because the second -u- is long), and it has a high proportion of such disyllabic anacruses and feminine endings. The poem's exceptional proportion of disyllabic intervals gives its dolnik lines a strong triple-time rhythm, as the following examples show:

> (36)   With u-**su**-ra hath <u>no</u> man a <u>house</u> of good <u>stone</u>   (2)
> (37)   Se-eth <u>no</u> man Gon-**za**-ga his <u>heirs</u> and his **con**cubines   (11)
> (38)   Be-<u>tween</u> the young <u>bride</u> and her <u>bride</u>-groom
>   CON-TRA NA-TURA   (45)

These lines have a number of interesting features: (36) and (37) have disyllabic anacruses that set up an anapaestic rhythm; (37) has the only proparoxytonic ending in the poem; and the break in the triple-time rhythm of (38) echoes the meaning of 'contra natura'.

From this analysis it is clear that Pound's new metrics contained more variety than regularity, offering a different balance between symmetry and surprise from that found in traditional versifying. Subsequent poets were attracted by this rebalancing and by the fact that each poet could choose the amount of variety and regularity in his or her verse. The twentieth century (at least in the West) has often been called the age of the individual, and free verse, the metrics of the individual, was eminently suited to it. Poets with an intuitive ear for rhythm were able to make it as memorable and as aesthetically satisfying as verse in traditional metres; poets without a good ear were able to cut up prose into irrational segments and deceive themselves.

T. S. Eliot

Thomas Stearns Eliot was born in St Louis and educated at Harvard, the Sorbonne, and Oxford, where he completed a doctoral thesis. In 1922 the publication (with Pound's encouragement) of *The Waste Land* won him overnight celebrity, and he dominated English letters for forty years, producing many works of criticism, philosophy, and drama, as well as a series of volumes of verse. Throughout his writing he emphasized the continuity of European literature and sought to identify his own work with its long tradition. Eliot was modest enough to describe his friend Pound as *il miglior fabbro* ('the best craftsman') in his dedication to *The Waste Land*; but, although his published verse (1963) amounted to only a fraction of Pound's, Eliot produced many more poems (and lines) that entered the consciousness of later generations of poets and readers.

Eliot's 'distortions'

Eliot himself stated that the starting points for his metrics were the metrical innovations of Jules Laforgue and the verse of John Webster, which 'stretches, contracts and distorts the blank verse measure' (see Utrera Torremocha 2001: 135). Many passages in Eliot's poetry contain, like Webster's plays, an amalgam of canonical pentameters and five-ictic dolniks, and Hobsbaum (1996: 92–100) argues that Eliot's metre could well be termed 'free blank verse'. Such a term is misleading, however, because Eliot employed rhyme tactically and interspersed many lines of lengths other than five beats and rhythms other than iambic; the range of his 'distortions' therefore goes well beyond blank verse. Thus, for example, he opens Section 1 of *The Waste Land* ('The Burial of the Dead') with seven lines that play with the traditional trochaic tetrameter catalectic, as found in Sidney's lyrics (see p. 128) and Shakespeare's songs (see p. 137), the metre of 'Beauty, music, sweetness, love' (instance (46) in Chapter 6). In lines 1 & 2 of 'The Burial of the Dead' Eliot stretches this metre by adding an extra trochee, thus producing a zero interval and a stress clash; in lines 3, 5, 6, & 7 he distorts the metre by transferring a trochee from the beginning of the line to the end; and in line 4 he contracts the metre by omitting the first trochee. All of these seven lines contain stress clashes and none is a true trochaic tetrameter, but the reader can recognize several regular lines embedded in the passage; he or she has only to disregard the last word in a line or combine it with the opening of the line that follows. For example, adding the word 'stirring' from the previous line would make the following line a trochaic tetrameter catalectic:

> (39)   <u>Dull</u> <u>roots</u> with <u>spring</u> <u>rain</u>   (4)

Standing alone, however, this line's four stressed monosyllables offer four beats in themselves (and two stress clashes), a new and intriguing poetic rhythm.

Another metre that Eliot recruits to his verse on occasion is the common measure of 4 + 3 beats, the metre of 'Sir Patrick Spens' and many other ballads (see p. 64). For example, the following line is one of several longer lines that he includes in his predominantly five-beat poem 'The Love Song of J. Alfred Prufrock' (1917).

(40)   The **yel**-low <u>fog</u> that <u>rubs</u> its <u>back</u>
       u-**pon** the **win**-dow-<u>panes</u>   (15)

The regular metre that Eliot most often distorts, however, is the iambic pentameter, as in the following two lines from the same poem:

(41)   But <u>though</u> I have <u>wept</u> and **fas**-ted, <u>wept</u> and <u>prayed</u>   (81)
(42)   I have <u>seen</u> them <u>ri</u>-ding **sea**-ward <u>on</u> the <u>waves</u>   (127)

The first has a disyllabic second interval and the second line a disyllabic anacrusis, while the following line from 'The Burial of the Dead' closes with two disyllabic intervals:

(43)   Yet <u>when</u> we <u>came</u> back, <u>late</u>, from the **hy**-a-cinth **gar**den   (37)

In order to trace the chronological development of Eliot's metrics and compare it with Pound's, I analyse in Tables L and M selected metrical features of three of Eliot's best-known poems, 'The Love Song of J. Alfred Prufrock', 'The Burial of the Dead' (1922), and the first and last sections of *Ash Wednesday* (1930). Eliot's chief metrical innovation in 'The Love Song of J. Alfred Prufrock' is the use of lines of many lengths where, although 90 per cent of lines have between three and six ictuses, almost 10 per cent are longer. These long lines usually subdivide into 4 + 3, 4, or 5 beats. But overall the poem is very iambic because over 90 per cent of its inter-ictic intervals contain exactly one syllable and stressing clashes are avoided. Moreover, 47 per cent of the poem's lines are either canonical iambic pentameters or vary from the canon only in having one disyllabic weak position, like instance (42) above. In the definition of Tarlinskaja 1976, these lines qualify as 'transitionally iambic', because between 3 and 20 per cent of intervals contain other than one syllable (although Eliot does make full use of the anacrusic principle: more than half this poem's lines precede the first beat by zero or two syllables). The poem is also unadventurous in other metrical features, since there are few feminine lines or enjambments, and more than half of its lines have full rhyme. Other than mixing lines of many lengths, Eliot's versifying, at this stage, was no more innovative than that of Bridges thirty years earlier.

    In contrast, the metre of 'The Burial of the Dead' is a true dolnik: more than a third of its intervals comprise zero or two syllables, and it allows clashing stresses. Other metrical features also show signs that under Pound's influence Eliot's verse was becoming freer: feminine lines and enjambment are frequent, there are far fewer canonical and quasi-canonical lines, and fewer than 9 per cent of lines have full rhyme. After its trochaic opening 'The Burial of the Dead' becomes predominantly iambic, and it closes with a long series of iambic pentameters, increasing the proportion of the poem's lines that are canonical or quasi-canonical to more than one quarter. Robert Pinsky notes that the embedding of such regular lines is a feature of many poets' free verse (1998: 97–116), and this is largely the result of Eliot's influence. Another much-imitated feature is the embedding of quotations from other poets: the close of 'The Burial of the Dead' contains quotations from verse in seven languages. It is tempting to see the metrics of *Ash Wednesday* as a retreat from the extremes of the free dolnik in *The Waste Land*, because the later poem's proportions of many features are midway between those found in the two earlier poems. Those features include short and ultra-short lines, feminine and enjambed lines, non-iambic rhythms, and full rhymes.[10] The proportion of duple time (20.5 per cent of intervals contain other than one syllable) just qualifies the metre as a dolnik,

   In summary, my tables show that Eliot's metrics was undoubtedly more conservative than Pound's. In Eliot's verse canonical iambic pentameters abound, as do lines with only one divergent feature, such as a disyllabic or void anacrusis or interval. Another common deviant is a decasyllable with four beats instead of five, as in the opening line of Section IV of *The Waste Land*, where making 'Phlebas' a 'Phoenician' rather than a 'Philistine' converts an iambic pentameter into a four-beat line with three alliterations, rather like Old English epic metre. This mixture of canonical pentameters, five-beat dolniks, and four-beat decasyllables is sometimes termed a *flexible pentameter* (a term I discussed in relation to Wyatt in Chapter 6). It accounts for a very large proportion of the lines by major twentieth-century poets that the general public considers free verse. But the verse of Pound's and Eliot's contemporary Wallace Stevens provides a better benchmark for modern five-beat verse, one that will enable me to examine the boundaries between the five-ictic dolnik and the flexible pentameter and to develop some useful measures of flexibility.

Wallace Stevens

Stevens was born in Pennsylvania, graduated from Harvard, and worked for most of his life as an insurance executive. He published his verse in a series of volumes between 1923 and 1950 (see Stevens 1965); his poetry is meditative and unostentatious, and much concerned with the difference between appearance and reality. Only in the last years of his life did he gain recognition as a major poet on this side of the Atlantic. Hobsbaum uses one of Stevens's poems, 'The Snow Man', as an example of what he calls 'free verse proper' and he analyses it solely in terms of contrasts between lines (1996: 111–13). But there are distinct patterns in the number of beats per line in this poem, as can be seen from its opening:

   (44)   One <u>must</u> have a <u>mind</u> of **win**ter
   (45)   To re-**gard** the <u>frost</u> and the <u>boughs</u>
   (46)   Of the **pine**-trees **crus**-ted with <u>snow</u>

These lines are three-ictic, as are ten of the poem's fifteen lines, but lines 5–8 are four-ictic, and the poem closes with a single five-ictic line. Like most verse that is termed *free*, Stevens's poems have a predominant line length (measured in ictuses or beats). In his case this is often a four-ictic line, which can be seen as an extension of the short-line canon, but even more frequently it is a line of five beats developed from the canonical long line. Table N gives figures for two of Stevens's best-known poems, 'The Man with the Blue Guitar' (1937), which is predominantly four-ictic, and 'An Ordinary Evening in New Haven' (1950), which is predominantly five-ictic. These figures will facilitate a comparison between Stevens's handling of the two metres, and they will also provide benchmarks for classifying the long-line verse of other twentieth century poets in the next chapter.

Stevens's flexible tetrameter

'The Man with the Blue Guitar' has thirty-three strophes, each containing between four and eight couplets, making 400 lines in total, of which 393 are indisputably four-ictic. Approximately one couplet in five is rhymed, and all but three are oxytonic, and just over half the lines are canonical iambic tetrameters. 'The Man with the Blue Guitar' begins more regularly than it closes: almost two-thirds of the canonical tetrameters in the poem are in the first quarter, which also has fewer enjambments: this part of the poem contains many rhymed sequences of canonical lines, like those that announce the poem's theme:

>   (47)   A tune u-pon the blue gui-tar   (9)
>   (48)   Of things ex-act-ly as they are   (10)

A change in metre seems to reflect the poet's growing uncertainty in the course of the poem: as the poem progresses, the proportion of irregular lines increases, and some lines are in triple time throughout; for example:

>   (49)   Con-cer-ning the na-ture of things as they are   (266)

Approximately one sixth of the poem's anacruses and one seventh of its intervals are disyllabic; zero anacruses, on the other hand, are rare and zero intervals are even rarer. Some lines are made metrically ambiguous by this infusion of triple time, and a few read equally well as pentameters; for example, the following line requires either a trisyllabic second interval or a proparoxytonic ending if it is to have only four ictuses; I have shown it with the second of these options:

>   (50)   To im-prove the se-wers in Je-ru-sa-lem   (195)

In total the poem is a good example of the new 'looser' iambic verse that became increasingly common in the twentieth century; by Tarlinskaja's definition the metre is transitionally iambic but approaching the dolnik. Stevens's metre is a *flexible tetrameter*, and its flexibility is highly appropriate to this poem with its mood shifts, musing, and persistent attempts to grasp the meaning of life. The metre is varied and musical: it helps Stevens to speed up or slow down, to shock or comfort, to soothe or surprise.

The evolution of Stevens's pentameter

Stevens's earliest poems include several in canonical iambic pentameters; for example, there are few metrical irregularities in his 120-line poem 'Sunday Morning' (published in 1923): Stevens avoids full rhyme in the fifteen-line strophes (which seem carefully crafted so as not to be sonnets), but otherwise its form is very conventional. The poem's metrical irregularities amount to one disyllabic anacrusis, four disyllabic intervals, an inversion in positions 6–7 that defies the bracketing condition, a fifth-foot inversion, and some startling enjambments. The following lines show the last two of these features:

(51) E-**la**-tions <u>when</u> the **fo**-rest <u>blooms</u>; **gusty**   (26)
(52) E-**mo**-tions <u>on</u> wet <u>roads</u> on **au**-tumn <u>nights</u>   (27)

Note that the while the second of these lines is canonical the first closes with a stress clash that is reminiscent of the opening lines of Eliot's *The Waste Land*. Although such irregularities are rare in this poem, they show that Stevens was keeping a sharp eye on what his contemporaries were doing and was not afraid to experiment.

When Stevens used this fifteen-line strophe again more than two decades later in 'Credences of Summer' (1947), he also repeated the device of fifth-foot inversion with enjambment (lines 141–42), but his metre has changed significantly: there are more disyllabic intervals in the first five lines of this poem than in the whole of 'Sunday Morning'. Stevens's later style embraced disyllabic intervals, violent enjambments, and the use of atonic monosyllables to provide the line's final ictus, as can be seen from the following lines (112–14) from another late poem, 'It Must Give Pleasure' (from *Notes towards a Supreme Fiction*):

(53) Be-**neath**, far <u>un</u>-der-**neath**, the **sur**-face <u>of</u>
(54) His <u>eye</u> and **au**-di-ble <u>in</u> the **moun**-tains <u>of</u>
(55) His <u>ear</u>, the **ve**-ry ma-**te**-ri-al <u>of</u> his <u>mind</u>

The predominantly five-ictic poem by Stevens that I shall discuss in most detail, however, is 'An Ordinary Evening in New Haven' (1950), because its 198 lines (grouped in eleven strophes, each made up of six tercets) offer a sufficient sample for statistical analysis. The figures in the first section of Table N show the percentages of feminine lines, of canonical lines, of lines with full rhyme, of enjambed lines, and of weak positions containing other than one syllable, and these are compared with the percentages found in 'The Man with the Blue Guitar'.

The lines of 'An Ordinary Evening' are unrhymed, a high proportion (almost one fifth) of them are feminine, and enjambment is even more common than in Steven's earlier four-ictic poem. But far fewer of the lines in 'An Ordinary Evening' are canonical: the proportions of zero and disyllabic anacruses in the two poems are similar, and there is a similar avoidance of zero intervals / stress clashes, but the proportion of disyllabic intervals in 'An Ordinary Evening' (one in four) is far higher. This enables Stevens to introduce sharp rhythmic contrasts, as in the following lines (89–90; I number lines as they appear in Stevens 1965):

(56) The <u>town</u>, the **wea**-ther, <u>in</u> a **ca**-sual **lit**ter
(57) To-**ge**-ther, said <u>words</u> of the <u>world</u> are the <u>life</u> of the <u>world</u>

Here an equally regular triple-time line follows a canonical iambic pentameter, but many lines in this poem have irregular intervals between their beats, and in some cases a four-beat delivery seems to fit the sense better than a five-beat, as in the following lines:

(58) The most **an**-cient <u>light</u> [V] <u>in</u> the most **an**-cient <u>sky</u>   (123)
(59) In <u>things</u> [V] <u>seen</u> and un-**seen**, cre-a-ted from **no**-thing-ness   (149)

I have scanned these lines as five-ictic because the overwhelming majority of the poem's lines have five ictuses and there is no line that lacks a credible five-ictic explanation, but there are more natural alternative deliveries for both lines: in (58) 'most', 'light', 'most', and 'sky' could be made the prominence peaks, and in (59) the stress on 'things' cold be subordinated to that on 'seen'. Delivered in this way, both lines become perfect tumbling verse with a predominantly triple-time rhythm. Many twentieth-century poets cultivated this type of metrical ambiguity, but none more effectively than Stevens.

A comparison of the statistics for the two poems in the first section of Table N shows that the later poem is less regular than the earlier in many respects: it has a far higher percentage of feminine lines, barely half the proportion of regularly iambic lines, and no rhyme (but only slightly more enjambment). In 'An Ordinary Evening' Stevens crossed the boundary from transitionally iambic to dolnik verse (more than 20 per cent of intervals are disyllabic): its metre is not a flexible pentameter, but a five-ictic dolnik. By 1950 Stevens's long-line metre had completed the transition from stress-syllabic (iambic pentameter) to (five-ictic) dolnik, but in 1937 his shorter line was still intermediate between the two types. In the next chapter I shall show that much modern verse that has been called 'free' is better categorized as either flexible pentameters or five-ictic dolniks, and that four-ictic lines are one of the principal sources of metrical variety in both.

William Carlos Williams

Stevens's younger contemporary Williams was born in New Jersey, graduated from the University of Pennsylvania, where he met Pound, and then made a short visit to England. On his return he practised medicine in the town of his birth for the rest of his life but published volumes of verse at regular intervals over a period of more than fifty years (see Litz & MacGowan 1987–88). Much of his poetry is concerned with everyday objects and ordinary people, and many of his poems employ ultra-short lines. Williams also had to wait until the end of his career for recognition this side of the Atlantic, but his reputation as one of the century's major poets is now secure. Williams's verse is of particular interest to metrists for three reasons: (1) he placed himself at the centre of the debate about *variable feet*, (2) a distinguished modern critic has chosen his verse to illustrate a theory of *linear free verse*, and (3) he is the most notable exponent of a important new metre, the *ultra-short line* with predominantly two beats.

'Variable feet' or 'beats'

Some modern works on metrics argue that the lines of free verse differ from those of traditional metres by containing a variable number of variable feet (Preminger et al. 1975: 289), and the *variable foot* has been defined as a unit containing up to four syllables and a single peak of prominence (Hrushovski 1960: 187–89). Attridgean metrists, of course, argue that modern poets have simply rediscovered the art of counting beats instead of syllables. Williams supported the hypothesis of the variable foot, and he believed that his lines were isochronous; that is, they occupied the same time in delivery (Hartman 1980: 35).[11] But delivery instances vary and timing is very much under the control of the performer; moreover, the tendency towards stress-timing in the English language is a tendency, and no more (see

Roach 1980), so while some performances of Williams's lines may be isochronous, others are not. Common to most (but not all) deliveries, however, are the number of prominence peaks and the number of syllables between them, and my analysis of Williams's verse will concentrate on these relatively stable and measurable features of his language.

'Linear free verse'

Philip Hobsbaum offers an alternative analysis of Williams's versification that ignores the rhythms produced by beats and intervals and makes its most important feature the contrast between a line and its neighbours (1996: 111–17). This hypothesis clearly merits careful examination, since one of the distinctive characteristics of free verse is that its lines often contrast with, rather than resemble, their neighbours in structure, and do so in seemingly unpredictable ways. This increased potential for contrast leads Charles Hartman to argue that in free verse the line itself becomes a sort of foot (1980: 66).[12] But Hobsbaum argues that 'free verse proper' always contains a particular sort of binary contrast, that between 'thrusting' and 'receptive' lines (1996: 111), which he compares with the ancient notions of thesis and arsis. He begins by defining thrusting lines as containing heavier stresses (or a higher proportion of them); he also notes the contribution of initial stress to the character of the line (1996: 115–16). In the examples he gives, a thrusting line is usually followed by one or more receptive ones, and he concedes that syntax is involved as well: his thrusting lines are 'declarations' and his receptive ones 'qualifiers' (1996: 117). His examples provide evidence that supports this semantic and syntactic difference: they also show that his thrusting lines usually open sentences or verse paragraphs, while his receptive ones continue and close them. But his view that the weight of stresses is a defining factor invites closer scrutiny, especially since his scansions rely on the obsolete four-levels theory (Trager & Smith 1951).

In Hobsbaum's notation the symbols ≫ indicate a thrusting line, and the symbols ≪ a receptive one, and he applies his scansion to Williams's 'The Widows's Lament in Springtime'. One of his examples of a line with heavy stress is line 7:

(60)   ≫   Thirty-five years

But only in reply to a statement that she had been married, say, 'thirty-four years' would a widow deliver this phrase with a stress on 'five' that matched in weight the ones on 'thirty' and 'years'. It is much more likely that this line should be scanned s w w s, and thus given a triple-time rhythm, especially since it occurs in a sentence (lines 7–10) that is in triple time throughout, as the following scansion shows:

(60)a   **Thir**-ty-five <u>years</u>
(61)   I <u>lived</u> with my **hus**-band.
(62)   The **plum**-tree is <u>white</u> to-day
(63)   With **mas**-ses of **flo**-wers

Instance (63) is repeated minus the initial 'with' in the next line of the poem (11), which Hobsbaum scans as a thrusting line, because of its loss of anacrusis. That he scans almost the same words as a receptive line when they occur later (line 24) shows that his hypothesis makes context more important than content:

(64)   ≫   Masses of flowers
(65)   ≪   Trees of white flowers

The triple-time rhythm of this passage, however, is much more readily apparent than its linear contrasts and may therefore have been the poet's chief aesthetic intention. Even Hobsbaum reveals doubts about the hypothesis he offers, saying that it is only a 'proposed reading', since 'there is always room for debate in the scansion of free verse' (1996: 113).

I find Hobsbaum's hypothesis too limiting: free verse undoubtedly offers more contrasts between lines than traditional metres (see Hartman 1980: 68), but these contrasts are of many types: they may be quantitative (either in length or weight), semantic (as in Hobsbaum's 'declarations' and 'qualifiers'), or structural (for example, lines that are monosyllabic versus those that are polysyllabic). But the most important source of linear contrasts is rhythmic, that provided by the number of beats and size of intervals, and Hobsbaum's analysis fails to recognize this: rhythmic variety is the essence of free verse and he largely ignores it.

Williams's ultra-short line

'The Widow's Lament in Springtime' is only one of many poems in which Williams employed an ultra-short metre in which the majority of lines contain two ictuses. One famous poem in this metre, 'The Crimson Cyclamen' (1936), is long enough (243 lines) to justify statistical analysis, and I have presented my figures for a number of its features in Table N. Williams's metrical intention in this poem seems to have been a high level of variety: no eight consecutive lines are of the same length, and no series of five have the same rhythm. The number of lines of each length according to my analysis is shown in the second section of Table N. Well over half the lines of the poem contain two ictuses and they vary considerably in rhythm, as the following examples show:

(66)   The **co**-lor <u>flows</u>   (141)
(67)   More <u>rose</u> than **crim**son   (2)
(68)   **Strong**-ly <u>marked</u>   (89)
(69)   <u>Stem</u> – the **old**er   (75)
(70)   <u>All</u> [V] <u>rose</u>   (167)
(71)   By its **frail**-ty su-**preme**   (185)
(72)   **Play**-ful-ly **foll**owing   (50)
(73)   They are <u>veined</u> and <u>glow</u>   (183)
(74)   As **al**-ways – the <u>leaves</u>   (33)

Instances (66)–(69) are in duple time: (66) and (67) are iambic, (68) and (69) trochaic, and (70) comprises just two stressed syllables; instances (71) and (72) are in triple time, the first anapaestic and the second dactylic; instances (73) and (74) mix duple and triple rhythms by having two syllables in anacrusis and one in the interval, or vice versa.

In contrast to this variety, the majority of three- and four-ictic lines in the poem are in duple time, like the following:

(75)   The **pe**-tals **fal**-ling <u>down</u>   (201)
(76)   <u>Paints</u> a **dee**-per <u>af</u>-ter-**noon**   (234)

The one-ictic lines in the poem have a variety of syllable lengths and stress contours; examples include '<u>green</u>' (42), '**res**-ting' (108), 'with <u>which</u>' (182), and 'by **flo**-wer' (19). A one-ictic line obviously contains no interval, only an anacrusis and a rhyme, but the 291 intervals in the poem are fairly evenly divided between those in two-ictic lines and those in longer lines. These numbers are sufficiently large for valid statistical analysis, and the third section of Table N compares the rhythms found in Williams's two-ictic lines with those of the longer lines and of the poem as a whole. The majority of anacruses (52.8 per cent) and intervals (70.1 per cent) contain one syllable, and the majority of rhymes (71.8 per cent) are masculine; the figures in the table therefore quantify the exceptions. From these figures it is clear that the metre of this poem is very much more iambic than English prose: the poem's disyllabic intervals represent only one quarter of total, whereas in prose this proportion is close to one third. Since two standard errors on these figures represents 4.6 per cent, the difference is statistically highly significant. Moreover, the poem's longer lines contain far less triple time than its shorter lines: the metre is predominantly iambic and the longer lines seem designed to reinforce this rhythm.

   This analysis of Williams's ultra-short line will be used in the next chapter to assess the changes that this metre underwent in the hands of poets working later in the twentieth century.

Marianne Moore

Moore, like Eliot, was born in St Louis, and he was an enthusiastic admirer of her work. This and her distinguished editing of *The Dial* (1925–29) ensured that she soon became almost as well known in Europe as in the USA. Before that she had worked as a teacher and a librarian, and had published her first volume of poetry in 1921. Her last volume of new verse appeared in 1966, and her complete poems in 1967. While her metrics can be loosely described as free verse, it has three special features: it is asyntactic (she enjambs syntagms), syllabic (she counts syllables), and visual (she makes her audience use their eyes as well as their ears).

Asyntactic verse

In Moore's verse enjambment is the rule rather than the exception and is applied even to syntagms like 'the || star' (Hobsbaum 1996: 79). Such right-boundary flexibility makes counting by eye and finger much easier, because syllables can be moved from one line to another visually after composition. Gasparov describes such freely enjambed verse as *asyntactic* and he notes some of the effects it produces in the verse of Klopstock, one of its early adherents (1996: 285). He also states that Moore's lines often have 'no noticeable rhythm' (1996: 287), and this is because she often abandons a rhythmic pattern established in the earlier part of a line. Since her verse is asyntactic her phrasal stresses often do not coincide with the line end, which may contain syllables that carry no stress at all in normal speech. Such dislocation emphasizes syllables that would otherwise be of little significance and depreciates others that would normally represent peaks in the stress hierarchy. These are effects that a poet may find extremely useful in particular circumstances; for example, ending lines in unimportant words can imitate the habit in informal speech of 'trailing off' and may help poets impart an air of realism and authenticity to their message.[13]

Syllabic verse

Moore varies the number of prominence peaks in her lines but regulates the number of syllables; she makes corresponding lines in each strophe isosyllabic. There are many precedents in Indo-European verse, but the languages concerned had a melodic accent and it is highly probable that they were also syllable-timed, in contrast to English with its strong dynamic accent and stress-timing. Hobsbaum analyses Moore's verse from a syllabic point of view, but does not comment on the peculiar mode of counting she and her imitators adopted (1996: 81–114). French and other Romance poets, aided by their languages' syllable-timing, have always counted syllables by ear to the final stress in the line or hemistich (*rhythmic* counting). By the twentieth century English poets had counted syllables in the Romance way for more than five hundred years; thus an iambic pentameter, like a French *vers de dix*, is a line of 10M or 10F syllables. But Moore and her imitators counted syllables anti-rhythmically: their count included line-final post-tonic syllables, making 9F syllables the equivalent of 10M. They also ignored the rhythmic props on which the intuitive composition of longer lines in Romance relies: either a fixed caesura (like the *alexandrin*'s) or a restricted set of rhythms in the latter part of the line (like the *endecasílabo*'s). But anti-rhythmic counting and the lack of these rhythmic props made it impossible for Moore or her imitators to count their syllables by ear. As Gasparov notes, the syllabic regularity of Moore's verse is apparent only 'on closer scrutiny' (1996: 287), and scrutiny is essentially a visual operation designed to detect auditory events only after they have been transcribed. The most feasible method of producing such verse is to count the syllables on the fingers in the act of composition and check them on the page after it. The syllabism of these experimenters thus depended on counting by eye and fingers and not by ear in the time-honoured (and easiest) manner.

Hobsbaum uses Moore's 'The Steeple-Jack' to exemplify a modern syllabic English poem (1996: 78–79). Each of its strophes contain six lines, of 11, 10, 14, 8, 8, and 3 syllables, in that order, and its lines have neither a fixed caesura nor a restricted range of rhythms. Hobsbaum notes that Moore abandoned her first attempt at this poem, which may be an indication that she found its composition laborious. Thus in strophe 2 of Hobsbaum's text is a line (3) for which Moore's verse design stipulates fourteen syllables:

(77)   Or **sai**-ling <u>round</u> the **light**-house with-out **mo**-ving their <u>wings</u>

But, as the text in the complete poems (1967) shows clearly, Moore used the word 'around' here, not the word 'round', and thus counted her fourteen syllables correctly. Hobsbaum, however, has corrected the grammar and so destroyed the metre — surely proof that the human ear cannot hear the difference between fourteen syllables and thirteen.

Hobsbaum notes that 'the careless reader' may mistake syllabic metre for free

verse, but verse rhythm is an auditory experience, not a visual one, and even the
most careful listeners may come to the same conclusion as careless readers. They
will hear this as a five-beat line and not a fourteen-syllable one, because the human
cognitive process can cope with the first but not the second. And audiences without
the written text, or the means to slow down its delivery, can count only with their
ears, and not their fingers, so they will perceive these lines as free dolniks. Moore's
verse differs from Pound's mainly in that she transfers some syllables between lines
in the interests of numerical tidiness, and thus foregrounds the words and syntagms
so enjambed. The underlying rhythms of her lines are no different from those
of other poets, even though they may be disguised by her adding unimportant
syllables at the line end to make up numbers.

   Moore had lifelong doubts about poetry and, in particular, about its artificiality
and importance relative to life experience. She expressed these eloquently in her
poem 'Poetry', the opening strophe of which can be laid out as follows:

(78)   I <u>too</u> dis-**like** it
              there are <u>things</u> that are im-**por**-tant
                    be-**yond** all this **fid**-dle.
(79)   **Rea**-ding it, ho-**we**-ver,
              with a **per**-fect con-**tempt** for it,
                    one dis-**co**-vers in it **af**-ter all,
                          a <u>place</u> for the **ge**-nu-ine.
(80)   <u>Hands</u> that can <u>grasp</u>, <u>eyes</u>
(81)   that can di-**late**, <u>hair</u> that can <u>rise</u>
(82)   if it <u>must</u>, these <u>things</u>
              are im-**por**-tant, not be-**cause** a

My layout emphasizes the strophe's rhythm, which is based on pairs of strong
stresses, but Moore herself laid it out as five lines, indicated by the numbering here:
(78) contains 19 syllables, (79) contains 19 + 11, (80) contains 5, (81) contains 8,
and (82) contains 13 syllables. I would argue that Moore's ear created this passage's
rhythm and her eye adjusted the syllable count later.

Visual verse

Hobsbaum notes that Moore's visual architecture offers a 'rather restricted form
of verse' (1996: 81), but visual verse, or 'verse for the eye', has a long history, as
Gasparov points out (1996: 288–90). Both Classical and medieval authors composed
verse in which the visual form of the writing on the page signified (figure verse),
and Chinese ideograms convey meaning visually by their very nature (see Pound
1961: 21). Verse for the ear may, of course, include a visual element; for example,
rhymes like 'love/prove' are often described as eye rhymes.[14] The change in
reading habits that I discussed above and the increased importance of the visual
made Marianne Moore's anti-rhythmic syllabics viable, and many subsequent poets
borrowed this technique. Thus, for example, W. H. Auden's poem 'In Memory of
Sigmund Freud' (Auden 1966: 166–70) is syllabic, and the decasyllabic line with four
beats instead of five became a recognized constituent of the flexible pentameter (as
in Heaney's 'Glanmore Sonnets' analysed in the next chapter). But modern English

syllabics defeat the ear for two reasons: they are counted anti-rhythmically, and not to the last stress like the syllables in French verse; Medieval Latin poets counted all the syllables only because they artificially stressed the last syllable in every line, as their rhyming practice clearly shows; and the tendency to stress-timing in English means that a line's length is as much a product of the number of stresses in it as the number of syllables. Modern English syllabic verse is, therefore, a visual device, a game played by the expert and missed by the general audience, and its cultivation is one of the reasons for the rift between the wider poetry-reading public and the subject of verse-craft.

Conclusions

Verse is language divided into lines, units that may match or contrast in length, meaning, and rhythm. Traditionally, poets made their lines match in far more obvious ways than they made them contrast, if only to distinguish their language from prose and normal speech, where contrasts predominate. Regularity has therefore always been the staple of verse, and variability its ornament, so that its symmetries have outnumbered its exceptions, and *sécurité* has outweighed *surprise*. But the more regularities a metrical system has imposed, the more various and ingenious have been the forms of tension that poets have introduced into their lines, and the more determined have been the efforts of some poets to subvert the system. The phenomenon we term *free verse* was a violent rebellion against the excessive regularity of most of the verse composed in Western Europe in the previous centuries. It was not free in the way that prose is free, but it offered a loosening of the old restraints, and a rebalancing of verse's two essential processes, the matching and the contrasting of linguistic units. Free verse became first viable and then fashionable because of a change in poetry-reading habits that promoted the visual to an importance comparable to that of the aural. It became possible for poets to produce sharp rhythmic contrasts without having their verse mistaken for prose, and to compose very short lines without the risk that performance would obscure their boundaries. Free-verse poets were also able to use more subtle devices to convey their meaning and delight their audience: for example, articles could be severed from their nouns by enjambment, words with important interactions could be placed in carefully chosen positions in the line, and the repetition of phonemes in rhyme could be less blatant. Many of the twentieth century's poets were to take all these opportunities.

Free verse allows more contrasts and fewer matches than traditional, but the units of the language that the poet may match or contrast are the same as they have always been in English: phrases, lines, beats, and intervals. Whitman helped later poets rediscover the art of orchestrating phrases and interweaving their structure and meaning; Hopkins led the way in the rediscovery of the importance of beats and of the use of syllable weight, as distinct from number, in crafting the intervals between them. Bridges and Yeats loosened the iambic canons and made a little irregularity respectable. Pound demonstrated that the free dolnik was viable and that whole lines could be used as if they were feet, and Eliot found ingenious ways of wrenching old metres into new. Stevens developed more flexible versions of the English metrical canons and Williams a new ultra-short line that many subsequent poets eagerly borrowed. Finally, Moore demonstrated that lines could be crafted so as to contrast in the ear and match in the eye. Other poets and critics also influenced the advent, establishment, and survival of free verse in English, but the work of these nine poets contributed much towards that enterprise, and many of the poems I have quoted in this chapter are still widely read in the twenty-first century.

Notes to Chapter 9

1. Thus Nigel Fabb reserves the term *metrical* for verse in which the lines contain a fixed number of syllables or moras (2001: 771) and Charles Hartman argues that free verse is not numerically regulated (1980: 17). But he later accepts that many free-verse poets predetermine the number of syllables, stresses, or even putative moras in their lines (1980: 35). Hartman is correct, however, to emphasize that free verse employs rhythmic devices other than regularity.

2. Philip Hobsbaum describes bad free verse and randomly sliced-up prose as lacking 'rhythmic virtues' (1996: 89–92). In most cases it is impossible to hear that they are verse at all unless the line divisions are grossly overemphasized by the performer.

3. One of the immediate precursors of *vers libre* was the *alexandrin libéré* imitated by Dowson, in which the previous generation of French poets had relaxed the rules for caesura and rhyme (see Utrera Torremocha 2001: 76 and Scott 1990: 74–88).

4. Hobsbaum notes Whitman's admiration for the radical freethinker Frances Wright (b. 1795, d. 1852), and quotes a passage in which Whitman seems to be versifying one of her sermons (1996: 107–08).

5. Hobsbaum describes Whitman's metre as *cadenced verse*, noting that it is 'written in long loose lines deriving from lyrical prose' (1996: 104). He also notes that a century earlier this mode of versifying had found its way into Blake's prophetic books from the same source, the Bible (1996: 109). But the term *cadenced verse* risks confusion with the term *verses of cadence*, coined by Southworth 1957 for his interpretation of Chaucer's metre (see Chapter 4, n19). I shall use the term *phrasal verse*, an alternative offered by Scott 1990, to describe Whitman's metre in the remainder of this volume.

6. In scanning verse such as Whitman's, where position number and orientation are variables, I use bold typeface and underlining to indicate strong (bold) and other (underlined) syllables that represent prominence peaks in individual verse instances. As Hartman points out (1980: 53), there is inevitably some subjectivity and imprecision in identifying which stressed syllable should be made prominent in the delivery of both cadenced verse and rhythmic prose.

7. Hrushovski argues of free verse that 'within the line, stresses are conspicuous as the main constituents' (1960: 186).

8. Note that Hopkins himself believed that the feet of his sprung rhythm were all left-strong and that any anacrusis belonged to the final weak position of the preceding line; for some of his initial unstressed syllables, however, there was no preceding line, as in (10) below.

9. Many of the lines in free verse I shall scan contain clashing stresses, and in some cases the clash could be resolved by making one of the syllables involved less prominent than the other in delivery; for example, 'swords clash' can be delivered as a trochee in instance (31) above. I shall scan these lines with clashing stresses whenever such a delivery seems more normal, since there is a long history of zero intervals / void weak positions in English metre. Lines with potentially clashing stresses might be better described as *ambivalent*; for example, (33) and (34) could be scanned as a four-ictic couplet that closes a three-ictic strophe.

10. I shall refer to lines of more than six beats as *ultra-long*, and lines with fewer than three as *ultra-short*, just as I have used the terms *long* to describe lines of five and six beats and *short* to describe those of three and four.

11. Williams's belief that his lines were isochronous in delivery (Hartman 1980: 35) is not supported by a moraic analysis of the instances quoted in this section.

12. Hartman uses the terms *counterpoint* and *symmetry* to describe contrast and parallelism between lines (1980: 24–25 & 61–80); Scott also stresses the rhythmic importance of the line (1990: 299) and proposes three categories of *vers libre*: (1) 'of the measure', (2) 'of the cadence', and (3) 'of the line' (1990: 295).

13. Hobsbaum quotes (1996: 83) an extremely appropriate example of the use of anti-rhythmic counting in the poem 'Considering the Snail' by Thom Gunn (b. 1929, d. 2004). Here the poet emphasizes the hermaphroditic nature of the beast by using lines with an indiscriminate mixture of masculine and feminine endings (6F or 7M).

14. Grammont (1937: 347) ridiculed the concept of rhyme for the eye, but some metrists of the Romance languages continue to use the term (for example, Gallarati 1978: 73). Hanson 2002 argues that a number of English rhymes like 'love/prove' are purely conventional and imply neither a visual matching nor a departure from normal pronunciation. We should also note that what has been called 'eye rhyme' may simply be inexact rhyme, pararhyme, or consonance.

CHAPTER 10

Versifying in English
in the Twentieth Century

The account of the development of free verse in Chapter 9 has taken this narrative well into the twentieth century, at least on the other side of the Atlantic. This chapter will attempt to show how Old World English poets either resisted or accommodated these developments and how by the end of the century poets writing in English, wherever they worked, were making choices from the same menu of metres. They all knew successful examples of stress-syllabic metres, dolniks, and free verse, and they felt at liberty to follow their individual preferences. This individuality makes it difficult to give any shape to my story, but in the space available I shall try to illustrate the variety and richness of twentieth-century metrics by examining the verse of a further seventeen poets. Since Chapter 9 is largely devoted to the work of Americans, ten of the seventeen poets discussed in this chapter will be from the Old World. Depending on the poet concerned, I shall either explore his or her metrical range or examine at least one metrically significant poem in detail. In the case of some poets I shall carry out both exercises, and in the case of two I shall be constrained from quoting actual lines by copyright considerations.

By the twentieth century the populations of Britain and Ireland represented only a small minority of the world's English speakers; there were four times as many in North America alone, and Africa, Asia, and Australasia contained tens of millions more English speakers. Many of the poets discussed in Chapter 9 were born in the nineteenth century but worked in the twentieth, and made free verse their principal mode of versifying. Of these Pound, Eliot, Stevens, Williams, and Moore were all born in the USA, and to that distinguished list we can add the Midwestern poet Carl Sandburg (b. 1898, d. 1967) and the first poet of jazz, Vachel Lindsay (b. 1879, d. 1931). These poets were from different regions and followed very different occupations, but they all embraced free verse more ardently than their European contemporaries, who either rejected it altogether or adopted it as an occasional alternative to more traditional metres. Most of the British and Irish poets of the same generation were more conservative in their metrics; for example, Rudyard Kipling was an extremely versatile metrist, but worked within the existing tradition of stress syllabic verse and the dolnik.[1] Hopkins, Bridges, and Yeats were thus among a minority of poets on this side of the Atlantic who searched actively for major metrical innovations and were prepared to experiment.

I shall exemplify the metrics of Old World poets working in the first quarter of the twentieth century by four studies of specific metrical features: two types of metre employed by Thomas Hardy (b. 1840, d. 1928), the range of metres employed by A. E. Housman (b. 1859, d. 1936), the structure of one of the best-known poems by D. H. Lawrence (b. 1885, d. 1930), and the metrical style of Wilfred Owen (b. 1893, d. 1918). Of these four poets, Hardy and Housman were metrical conservatives, Lawrence a radical, and Owen an innovator who did not live to weld his metrical experiments into a new system.

Old World Versification in the Early Twentieth Century

Thomas Hardy

Hardy was a Dorset man who abandoned a career in architecture to become a successful writer. Although his sixteen novels sold well, they attracted much criticism for their alleged pessimism and immorality. Hardy produced most of his best poetry after the death of his first wife in 1912, and by his own death had become a world-famous man of letters. Many of his poems (Creighton 1977) were in stress-syllabic metres, and his iambic verse was exceptionally regular, for the most part avoiding even initial inversions. His favourite iambic metre was the mixture of tetrameters and trimeters that had long been the chief rival to the short-line canon: 'The Darkling Thrush' and 'When I Set Out for Lyonesse' are notable examples. He also used other line lengths: thus 'Nature's Questioning' is in quatrains comprising lines of 4, 3, 3, and 6 iambic feet, and this metre ingeniously accommodates action in the short lines and reflection in the long, as in the following highly alliterative lines (3–4):

(1)　　All <u>seem</u> to <u>gaze</u> at <u>me</u>
(2)　　Like **chas**-tened **chil**-dren **sit**-ting **si**-lent <u>in</u> a <u>school</u>

　Hardy was also a master of the short line, and his two-ictic dolniks are technically far superior to Skelton's short line; the type of rhythmic effect that Hardy produces by mixing duple and triple time in this metre is shown in the following lines (8–12) from 'I Found Her Out There':

(3)　　I <u>brought</u> her <u>here</u>,
(4)　　　　And have <u>laid</u> her to <u>rest</u>
(5)　　In a **noise**-less <u>nest</u>
(6)　　　　No <u>sea</u> beats <u>near</u>

The weak positions (anacrusis and interval) of (3) and (6) each contain one syllable, those of (4) each contain two, while in (5) the anacrusis contains two and the interval one; note also that the last two lines alliterate very effectively on *n*. Hardy employed this short line in a number of poems, and Table S compares the rhythms found in six of these. The figures show that each poem has its own distinct rhythmic pattern and other metrical features. Thus 'Quid hic agis' has few feminine lines (8.1 per cent) and even fewer zero anacruses (4.1 per cent); its anacruses and inter-ictic intervals are almost equally likely to contain one or two syllables, thus giving an evenly balanced mixture of duple and triple time. In contrast, 'Rain on a Grave' has a high proportion of both feminine lines (38.9 per cent) and zero anacruses (19.4 per cent): it is also predominantly adonic in rhythm [w s w w s (w)], since 75 per cent of anacruses contain one syllable and 91.7 per cent of intervals two. In 'I Found Her Out There' these proportions are almost reversed and there are no feminine lines, which gives the poem a different dominant rhythm [w w s w s]. Two other poems, 'Where the Picnic Was' and 'The Month's Calendar', have more prose-like rhythms with duple time predominating; both also lack feminine lines and the first contains no zero anacruses. 'The Clock-Winder', a much later poem, has feminine lines, but no zero anacruses, and most of its anacruses and intervals contain two syllables, making the line in triple time throughout. As the table shows, Hardy did not allow clashing stresses in his two-ictic dolniks, but he achieved a considerable amount of variety simply by the placement of his unstressed syllables.

It was not only in short-line metres that Hardy mixed duple and triple time to great effect. In the following five-ictic lines, from 'The Voice' (1) and 'Night in the Old Home' (4 & 6), he even found proparoxytonic rhymes so as to continue the ternary rhythm to the very end of the line:[2]

(7)   **Wo**-man much <u>missed</u>, how you <u>call</u> to me, <u>call</u> to me
(8)   My **pe**-rished **peo**-ple who <u>housed</u> them <u>here</u> come <u>back</u> to me
(9)   <u>Now</u> and then **ben**-ding to-**wards** me a <u>glance</u> of **wist**fulness

The first and last two intervals of (8) contain one syllable, and many of the lines of 'Night in the Old Home' contain such duple time; but the two poems leave a very different rhythmic impression because the proportion of disyllabic intervals is 86 per cent in 'The Voice' and 39 per cent in 'Night in the Old Home'. Within these poems there are even more subtle effects: thus, although it is predominantly in duple time, 'Night in the Old Home' closes in a series of triple-time lines. Hardy also sometimes mixes triple-time lines of different lengths, as in 'Throwing a Tree', where each quatrain contains three four-ictic lines followed by a five-ictic line.

It is clear from this analysis that Hardy's remarkable transition from major novelist to major poet was aided by his mastery of a wide range of traditional metres and a willingness to innovate within them.

A. E. Housman

Alfred Edward Housman was born into an affluent Midlands family, but his mother's death on his twelfth birthday left him emotionally scarred. Although a brilliant scholar, he left Oxford without a degree, and spent many miserable years in London. He continued to study while working as a clerk, and was rewarded by chairs in Latin, first in London, then at Cambridge. He published his first volume of poems, *A Shropshire Lad*, at his own expense in 1896. Its fatalistic homosexual love lyrics became increasingly popular and his collected poems were published in 1939. The language of Housman's poetry (Sparrow 1956) was ingeniously artificial: no human being has ever said 'the hue was not the wear', yet his audience understood this line immediately. In his diction he favoured monosyllables (including rare and obsolete ones), and his metrics was equally minimalist, a stress-syllabic version of traditional ballad metres.

Housman's metrical conservatism can be seen from a brief inventory of the forms he employed in *A Shropshire Lad*. Some 87 per cent of the sixty-three poems are in quatrains, and the same proportion of poems employ Housman's favourite rhyme schemes: quatrains rhymed abab (47.6 per cent) or xaxa (15.9 per cent), and couplets rhymed aa bb (23.8 per cent). Similarly, just three line lengths (8M, 7M, and 6M) account for almost 80 per cent of the 1333 lines in the volume, as is shown in the first section of Table P. Housman almost always composed in duple-time metres that allow very few disyllabic intervals. This can be seen from the following four lines, all tetrameters:

(10)	And I <u>wish</u> you <u>luck</u>, come **Lam**-mas-<u>tide</u>	(VIII. 19)
(11)	Oh, <u>look</u> in my <u>eyes</u> then, <u>can</u> you <u>doubt</u>	(V. 25)
(12)	[V] <u>Ale</u>, man, <u>ale's</u> the <u>stuff</u> to <u>drink</u>	(LXII. 23)
(13)	For **fel**-lows <u>whom</u> it <u>hurts</u> to <u>think</u>	(LXII. 24)

Only 2.3 per cent of his total lines open with a disyllabic anacrusis, like instance (10), and only 1.9 per cent contain a disyllabic interval elsewhere in the line, like (11), but 11.6 per cent of his lines have a zero anacrusis, like instance (12), mostly as a result of Housman's predilection for the mixed tetrameter of Milton.

Only three poems in *A Shropshire Lad* are in long-line metres, and none of them is in iambic pentameters (although Housman employed the canon in a few of his later poems). The first, Poem XXIII, is in triple-time pentameters, the rhythm of which is not easily classifiable, as the following two instances demonstrate:

(14)	And <u>there</u> with the <u>rest</u> are the <u>lads</u> that will **ne**-ver be <u>old</u>	(4)
(15)	The **for**-tu-nate **fel**-lows that <u>now</u> you can **ne**-ver dis-**cern**	(10)

The word structure of (14) makes it seem anapaestic, but that of (15) gives a distinctly amphibrachic impression. The second long-line poem, XXXIV, is in double iambic trimeters, of which the first hemistich (invariably feminine) sometimes has a disyllabic anacrusis and the second (invariably masculine) always does. The mixed triple and duple rhythms that result combine with the colloquial diction to make the poem sound very like normal English speech, as the following examples show:

(16)	I will <u>go</u> where <u>I</u> am **wan**-ted, || for the **ser**-geant <u>does</u> not <u>mind</u>;	(9)
(17)	He <u>may</u> be <u>sick</u> to <u>see</u> me || but he <u>treats</u> me **ve**-ry <u>kind</u>	(10)

The third long-line poem, XLVIII, is in iambic alexandrines, many of which subdivide 4–4–4, like the monosyllabic instance (18), rather than 6–6 in the canonical French fashion:

(18)	I <u>pace</u> the <u>earth</u>, and <u>drink</u> the <u>air</u>, and <u>feel</u> the <u>sun</u>	(10)

Only one poem in *A Shropshire Lad*, L, is in dolniks, which are three-ictic, although introduced by a two-ictic folk song; the odd-numbered lines are feminine and the even masculine:

(19)	The <u>lads</u> knew **trou**-ble at **Knigh**-ton	(11)
(20)	When <u>I</u> was a **Knigh**-ton <u>lad</u>	(12)

The disyllabic intervals in this poem appear irregularly and, although its disyllabic anacruses are very few, it is clearly a dolnik. This is a departure from Housman's normal metrical practice: he used sources of variety very sparingly, and thus found a suitably Spartan metrics to help him express his stoic philosophy.

D. H. Lawrence

David Herbert Lawrence came from a mining family and began work in a Nottingham factory, but the success of his novels enabled him to escape this drudgery and travel the world with his German wife. While Lawrence's reputation as a novelist is secure, his poetry (Sola Pinto & Roberts 1964) is more difficult to evaluate. He was a natural rebel, and he wrote and (painted) things that no home-based English poet would have dared. He liked to shock, and it would have been out of character if he had versified conventionally: he embraced free verse, as well as free love, and he did as much as any other English poet to prevent early free verse from being an exclusively American phenomenon. One of his most famous poems, 'Snake', typifies his metrics and its lines can be analysed as free dolniks.

The seventy-four lines of 'Snake' are divided into eighteen strophes of varying lengths; the average length is four lines; only three strophes have the same number of lines as their predecessor, and the distribution of strophe lengths is shown in the second section of Table P. A similar irregularity in the poem's line lengths is demonstrated in the third section of Table P: the poem's lines may contain as few as one ictus or as many as nine. The ultra-long lines in this poem (those with more than six ictuses) are mostly separated from one another, and the ultra-short (fewer than three ictuses) usually open or close a strophe; examples include:

(21)	To <u>drink</u> there	(3)
(22)	For in **Si**-ci-<u>ly</u> the <u>black</u>, black <u>snakes</u> are **in**-no-<u>cent</u>,	
	the **gold** are **ve**-no-<u>mous</u>	(24)
(23)	Of <u>life</u>	(72)

Note that (22) subdivides into three iambic trimeters (with a disyllabic anacrusis) and both (21) and (23) are the result of enjambments that prevent pentameters becoming alexandrines.

The most common line length in the poem is five-ictic, as in the following:

(24)	Was <u>it</u> hu-**mi**-li-<u>ty</u>, to <u>feel</u> so **hon**oured	(33)
(25)	That <u>he</u> should <u>seek</u> my <u>hos</u>-pi-**ta**-li-<u>ty</u>	(39)
(26)	Pro-**cee**-ded to <u>draw</u> his <u>slow</u> length **cur**-ving <u>round</u>	(48)
(27)	[V] <u>O</u>-ver-**came** me <u>now</u> his <u>back</u> was <u>turned</u>	(59)

Instances (24) and (25) would make acceptable iambic pentameters of 10F and 10M syllables respectively, and (27) is a headless iambic pentameter. But the majority of the poem's lines contain at least one disyllabic interval between ictuses, as in the first interval of (26). There are also some good iambic tetrameters and alexandrines, including the following:

(28)	And <u>stooped</u> and <u>drank</u> a **lit**-tle <u>more</u>	(19)
(29)	And <u>climb</u> a-**gain** the **bro**-ken <u>bank</u> of <u>my</u> wall-**face**	(49)

But in total only 18 per cent of the poem's lines are in regular duple time while none contains triple time exclusively. Although the poem's proportion of duple

time (66.9 per cent) is only a little higher than in prose, there is no mistaking
that its language is verse, and that its rhythms are carefully managed. Lawrence
skilfully makes variety the norm in this poem, but there is enough regularity in its
rhythms to please the ear. Often the poet seems to be avoiding regularity by a very
narrow margin; thus, for example, two pentameters lurk behind the opening lines:
★'A snake came to my water trough today | and I in my pyjamas for the heat';[3]
Lawrence produced free verse, not iambic pentameters, by writing 'on a hot, hot
day', rather than 'today', and by not using the possessive pronoun.

Wilfred Owen

Owen was a real Shropshire lad, the son of a railway worker, and he enlisted in the
army and died for king and country a week before the Great War came to its close.
Only five of his poems were published in his lifetime, but his poetic reputation
grew steadily after his death. Owen's poems (Day Lewis 1963), only a handful of
which had been published, were collected posthumously and his fame grew rapidly.
He was an innovative versifier but most of his attention was focused on the contents
of syllables rather than lines. His verse is predominantly the iambic pentameter with
expanded weak positions of Yeats and Bridges. Like Bridges, Owen often employed
disyllabic substitution in this metre, as in the following lines from 'Disabled', which
very appropriately depart from the normal binary gait of the metre:

(30)	He sat in a wheeled chair, **wai**-ting for dark	(1)
(31)	It was **af**-ter **foot**-ball when he'd drunk a peg	(23)
(32)	And soon, he was **draf**-ted out with drums and cheers	(36)

The combination of second-ictus erosion and fourth-foot inversion in (30) invites a
triple-time delivery with 'sat' and 'wheeled' prominent; (31) opens with a disyllabic
anacrusis before becoming iambic; and (32) has a disyllabic first interval to break
up the iambic rhythm.

Owen often used metre to emphasize his meaning; thus he employed an
acatalectic trochaic pentameter, the mirror image of the long-line canon, for one
of his most disturbing poems, 'Mental Cases', where the metre is as disturbed as the
poem's subject:

(33)	These are men whose minds the Dead have **ra**vished	(10)
(34)	**Bat**-ter of guns and **shat**-ter of **fly**-ing **mu**scles	(16)
(35)	**Car**-nage in-**com**-p[a]ra-ble, and **hu**-man **squan**-der	(17)
(36)	Dawn breaks o-pen like a wound that bleeds a-**fresh** [V]	(22)

It is easy to imagine a Welsh delivery of this metre, with a stress accent on the
penults of the polysyllabic words and a tonic accent on the syllables that follow; (33)
confirms the verse design, but (34) requires unusual desyllabifications in its first two
intervals; (35) has a disyllabic first interval, a rarity in trochaic metre; and the metre
finally splits open in (36) with its potential sixth ictus and iambic close.

Owen went much further than Yeats in supplementing full rhyme with assonance, consonance, pararhyme, and weak rhyme. Thus the opening lines of
his poem 'Strange Meeting' end in the words 'escaped' / 'scooped', 'groined' /
'groaned', 'bestirred' / 'stared', 'eyes' / 'bless', 'hall' / 'hell'. The third strophe of

'Miners' is a good example of Owen's weaving together alliteration, pararhyme, and weak rhyme in the Old Welsh manner (cynghanedd; see Chapter 2, n3) so as to create an attractive word music:

(37)   My <u>fire</u> might <u>show</u> steam-**phan**-toms **sim**mer
(38)   From <u>Time's</u> old **cauld**ron,
(39)   Be-**fore** the <u>birds</u> made <u>nests</u> in **sum**mer,
(40)   Or <u>men</u> had **children**

Owen was a tireless experimenter with metre who anticipated, and perhaps helped inspire, the modern vogue for the imaginative use of phoneme repetition.

Old World Versification in the Mid-Twentieth Century

There were many English poets of distinction working in the Old World between 1930 and 1960: of those a few had been born in the nineteenth century, and the most important was Robert Graves (b. 1895, d. 1985). The new generation of poets who joined them found free verse now well established, and could choose between the traditional and new modes of versifying in their own work. Two of these younger poets were not only very popular in this period, but also proved particularly influential in the years that followed: they were W. H. Auden (b. 1907, d. 1973) and Dylan Thomas (b. 1914, d. 1963). The variety to be found in the modes of versifying of this period can be seen from a comparison of some of the differences, and the similarities, between the metrical styles of Graves, Auden, and Thomas.

Robert Graves

Graves came from a middle-class Anglo-German family and left Oxford without a degree to fight in the trenches of the Western Front. He survived and spent much of his life in Majorca where he became a best-selling novelist and respected literary critic. He saw himself, however, primarily as a poet, and his collected poems were first published in 1955; at its best his poetry combines the passion of Donne with the precision of Rochester. I cannot quote any of Graves's lines in this volume because the copyright owners have not given me permission to do so, but the popularity and influence of his poetry, both during his lifetime and since his death, justify a brief note on his metrics. Graves employed a wide range of metres from the iambic canons to free verse, sometimes in the same poem. He was far from impervious to modern trends: for example, in the opening lines of 'From the Embassy' (Graves 1965) he mixes canonical pentameters and free dolniks, and he deploys grammatical anomalies after the manner of Cummings ('otherwhere' and 'here and there' as nouns) and the mixed rhyme typical of Owen.

Graves was fond of very short lines (he praised even Skelton's) and he composed many poems in them; unlike Hardy's, Graves's poems in ultra-short lines usually have a single prevailing rhythm: thus every line of 'In the Wilderness' consists of two dactyls, and the two-ictic lines of 'One Hard Look' are all iambic. Another, much later, poem that is predominantly in triple time is 'The Title of Poet' (which 'comes only with death'): seventeen of its twenty-two lines have an inter-ictic interval containing two syllables. A representative collection of his poems (O'Prey

1986) shows that Graves was capable of composing any type of poem at any time in his career. Nevertheless, some trends can be detected: one is from shorter to longer lines, another from stress-syllabic to free verse, a third from rhyme to unrhymed strophes. Graves sometimes used the freedom that the twentieth century offered poets to innovate, but he just as often chose to versify within long-established conventions.

W. H. Auden

Wystan Hugh Auden was the son of a Birmingham doctor, and his poetry first attracted attention while he was still at Oxford. He became a member of a group of Marxist intellectuals and travelled the world writing and pursuing homosexual love affairs. On the outbreak of the Second World War he moved to the USA, where he found a long-term partner and religion. In the post-war years his status as a major poet was at last recognized, and he became one of the century's most influential poets. His shorter poems (1966) include many on personal subjects, but also many on a variety of political and social themes. Auden greatly influenced his contemporaries and later generations of poets by deploying a language that was very close to sophisticated modern speech, and by tackling the latest and most controversial subjects. He was also a brilliant and versatile metrist, using stress-syllabic metres of every type to create new effects, and employing the four- and five-ictic dolnik of Eliot as skilfully as its originator. Auden also showed that the shorter free-verse line could be an effective vehicle for love poetry, and, like Owen, he often experimented with vowel harmony and weak rhyme, as in the closing trimeter and pentameter of 'On This Island':

(41)   That <u>pass</u> the **har**-bour **mir**-ror
(42)   And <u>all</u> the **sum**-mer <u>through</u> the **wa**-ter **saun**-ter

Auden showed great skill in his use of more complex forms like the sestina, rondeau, and villanelle, and his two sonnet sequences, *Sonnets from China* and *The Quest*, are impressive metrical showcases. Almost every sonnet has a different rhyme scheme, and most have schemes unused previously in English (for example, a sonnet can subdivide 3-3-3-5, or 5-4-5, and one consists of seven couplets). A few sonnets are in tetrameters, alexandrines, dolniks, or a mixture of line lengths, but most are in pentameters. Figures for Auden's sonnets are included in Table Q, which compares a number of twentieth-century poets' iambic pentameters. There is one notable feature of Auden's lines that is not found in those of the earlier poets I have analysed: he sometimes erodes the fifth ictus, as in the following lines from *The Quest*:

(43)   Her **ma**-jes-<u>ty</u> in <u>a</u> bad **tem**-per <u>or</u>   (I. 3)
(44)   That **wai**-ted <u>for</u> her <u>in</u> the **sun**-shine <u>and</u>   (I. 13)
(45)   Had <u>there</u> been <u>si</u>-tu-**a**-tions <u>to</u> be <u>in</u>   (II. 10)

The erosions in (43) and (45) are combined with secondary stresses in other ictic positions, so that the iambic rhythm is very faint and subtle; in (44) there are three erosions, two of them consecutive, a feature that we have noted is avoided by earlier poets. For most of his sonnets Auden relied on the same sources of variety in the long-line canon as his predecessors, but he used them all liberally: feminine lines represent 12 per cent of his total, enjambed lines 15.3 per cent, and 'Italian' lines 40 per cent. He erodes 12.2 per cent of all non-final ictuses, and 21.3 per cent of fourth ictuses, and precedents for these figures can be found in the verse of earlier centuries (see Tables E–J). Auden chose to compose the greater part of his sonnet sequence in canonical pentameters, with no disyllabic inter-ictic intervals, but he achieved a great deal of variety by including sonnets in other metres.

As well as being a highly skilled versifier in canonical metres, he also employed traditional metres, and a variety of metres that can be described loosely as 'free verse'. One of his best-known poems, 'Stop All the Clocks', is in a mixture of metres, including iambic pentameters and hexameters, dactylic and anapaestic tetrameters, and dolniks. As Nila Friedberg notes, 'The fact that one poem includes *many* meters correlates with the idea that the speaker's lover represented *many* things' (2005: 3). Auden was highly aware of the achievements of past generations of English versifiers, and he did more than any other modern poet to ensure that free verse became an addition, not an alternative, to traditional metres. His versifying became a model for that of many of poets writing in the second half of the century, but his skill and versatility have rarely been matched.

Dylan Thomas

Thomas was a Welsh journalist and broadcaster whose poetry and self-indulgent lifestyle brought him fame on both sides of the Atlantic; his early death sealed his reputation, but ensured that his poetic output is relatively modest. His poetry (Thomas 1952 and Davies 1974) was highly rhetorical and romantic, and sometimes his words seem to be generated by other words, not by thoughts. Although he composed some highly effective visual poems (diamond- and X-shaped) in the manner pioneered in French by Guillaume Apollinaire, Thomas's metrics was on the whole rather conservative. His favourite line was the iambic pentameter, and he sometimes combined it with ultra-short lines, as in the octaves, rhymed abca bddc, of 'A Grief Ago', in which lines 1, 4, 6, & 8 are dimeters. He employed the same two line lengths in the five-line strophes of 'The Force that through the Green Fuse Drives the Flower', the first of which is:

(46)   The <u>force</u> that <u>through</u> the <u>green</u> fuse <u>drives</u> the **flo**-wer
(47)   Drives <u>my</u> green <u>age</u>; that <u>blasts</u> the <u>roots</u> of <u>trees</u>
(48)   Is <u>my</u> des-**tro**-yer.
(49)   And <u>I</u> am <u>dumb</u> to <u>tell</u> the **croo**-ked <u>rose</u>
(50)   My <u>youth</u> is <u>bent</u> by <u>the</u> same **win**-try **fe**-ver

These lines show Thomas's strong preference for pararhyme, weak rhyme, and consonance over full rhyme; they are also typical of most of his lines in being very regularly iambic.

Thomas also often employed fixed forms in his poems; and his 'Do Not Go Gentle' is probably the most emotionally powerful villanelle in the English language. Most of these fixed-form poems are sonnets, including his sequence of ten that begins 'Altarwise by Owl-Light', which have a number of unusual metrical features. Their rhyme schemes are novel and varied (most seem to have the sestet before the octave); more than half of the 140 lines are feminine, and it is usually their post-tonic syllables that carry the phoneme repetition (weak rhyme); and in the masculine lines pararhymes outnumber full rhymes. These poems are almost entirely end-stopped and only five of their lines are not canonical pentameters (two headless pentameters and three lines with disyllabic intervals). Thomas seems to have been too busy innovating in other ways to have much time for experimenting with line-structure. His preoccupation with words (rather than feet) is summed up in the following lines (34–36) of 'From Love's First Fever to her Plague':

(51)   To <u>shade</u> and <u>knit</u> a-**new** the <u>patch</u> of <u>words</u>
(52)   Left <u>by</u> the <u>dead</u> who, <u>in</u> their **moon**-less acre,
(53)   Need <u>no</u> word's <u>warmth</u>

These lines demonstrate three features that typify his verse: a regular iambic rhythm, a preacher's gift for choosing words, especially unusual ones, and a chiming musicality based on phoneme repetition, which is almost cynghanedd in the Old Welsh manner. These lines also show something that is not always associated with his poetry: a deep respect for the centuries of tradition that preceded him. Although his reputation has fallen a little since his death, Thomas's influence can be detected in the verse of many modern poets.

New World Versification in the Mid-Twentieth Century

A number of New World poets working in the middle years of the century were of comparable stature to the three Old World poets discussed above, although not all of them became as well known or widely read on this side of the Atlantic. Among them were the Americans Robert Frost (b. 1874, d. 1963) and E. E. Cummings (b. 1894, d. 1962), who were roughly contemporary with Graves, the Australian A. D. Hope (b. 1907, d. 2000), who was much influenced by the work of his contemporary Auden, and another American, Robert Lowell (b. 1917, d. 1977), who was a contemporary of Thomas. The metrics of these four presents an interesting comparison with that of the four Old World poets. In the early part of the century the Old and New Worlds had seemed to be going separate ways metrically, but in this period we can observe them growing closer together. Both groups of poets integrated free verse into their repertoires, along with traditional metres, and developed a new classicism with common standards of excellence. This can be seen from even brief synopses of their metrics.

Robert Frost

Frost spent much of his boyhood in New England farm country, and briefly attended Harvard before coming to England in 1912, where he published his first two volumes of poetry. On his return to the USA he settled in New Hampshire and supported himself by teaching and writing, and his poems of rural life remained popular on both sides of the Atlantic throughout the century. Some of his best poems were among his earliest, and his verse technique changed very little in a career that spanned more than forty years (Frost 1955). I cannot quote any of Frost's lines in this volume because I do not have the copyright holders' permission, but his long and distinguished poetic career merits a short note on his metrics. Although Frost composed many shorter lines and dolniks, as well as some triple-time verse, his favourite line was a pentameter that was not quite perfectly iambic. Like Bridges, he tactically introduced lines with disyllabic weak positions and mixed rhythms into the long-line canon.

Some of his best poems are almost entirely in canonical pentameters (for example, 'Mending Wall'), but many more also contain longer and shorter lines with colloquial but irregular rhythms (for example, 'Death of the Hired Hand' and 'The Witch of Coös'). Frost employed rhyme only when he thought fit (he avoided it in narratives, for example), and he composed only a small minority of his poems in set forms such as the sonnet. But he found a new enthusiasm for rhyme and included very few non-canonical pentameters in the philosophical poems that he composed late in his life. One of these, 'The Lesson for Today', is compared with the pentameters of other twentieth-century poets in Table Q. This poem has a complex but inconsistent rhyme scheme, and it opens with some observations on historical metrics. Its most notable metrical feature is a lack of tension, which suggests that form as well as content contributed to the lukewarm critical reception these poems received. But, for most of his long life, Frost's unostentatious metrics combined with his simple philosophy and diction to win him many admirers in Europe. These included Robert Graves, who considered Frost's verse an excellent model, and Cecil Day Lewis, who rated it amongst the most pleasurable (see Frost 1955: 17–18).

E. E. Cummings

Edward Estlin Cummings, who was born in Massachusetts and educated at Harvard, first achieved fame by his prose work, *The Enormous Room*. He published twelve volumes of poetry between 1923 and his death, and his poetry was always romantic, but also became more reactionary as he grew older. Cummings liked to shock his audience, and to this end he used language in unconventional ways: he employed slang and played tricks with grammar, punctuation, and orthography. An extreme example of his style can be seen in the following iambic pentameter, which he presents as six (somewhat eccentric) lines; it occurs in a poem that begins with the colloquial conversational imperative 'take it from me kiddo' (Cummings 1960):

(54)   [...] for-tis-si-mo A-
        mer
        i
        ca, I
        love
        you [...]

Such effects are amusing but essentially trivial, and Cummings seems to have realized this, since increasingly he came to employ more traditional forms, particularly the sonnet; thus the metre of 'In time's a noble mercy of proportion' could hardly be more canonical, as the following lines (7–8) show:

(55)   — sa-**ha**-ras <u>have</u> their **cen**-tu-<u>ries</u>; ten **thou**sand
(56)   of <u>which</u> are **smal**-ler <u>than</u> a **ro**-se's **mo**ment.

One way in which Cummings's metrics was modern was in his preference for other forms of phoneme repetition over full rhyme; thus he rhymes (55) with 'reasoned' and (56) with 'agreement'.

Cummings also employed occasional short and ultra-short lines in many of his poems, and some are entirely in lines with three or fewer ictuses, including 'i say no world', 'rain or hail', and 'yes is a pleasant country'. He also employed metres that were transitional between iambic and dolnik, as in the four-ictic poems 'anyone lived in a pretty how town' and 'my father moved through dooms of love', and the common-measure poem 'love is more thicker than forget'. These titles illustrate the striking eccentricity of his diction and grammar, but in retrospect it has become clear that Cummings's linguistic innovations were primarily a means of gaining a hearing for reactionary and conventionally sentimental views.

A. D. Hope

A number of Australian poets in this period were accomplished metrical artists and none more so than Alec Derwent Hope, a Canberra professor who had studied in England and whose poetry (Brooks 1992) was most strongly influenced by that of Eliot and Auden. Hope employed the pentameter line far more often than any other and varied its character from poem to poem. Thus in 'Ode on the Death of Pius XII' his iambic pentameter is as canonical as Milton's, but in 'Imperial Adam' and 'Australia' it contains many disyllabic substitutions, and is more like that of Auden at his most adventurous. One of Hope's metrically most interesting poems is the 140-line 'Ode on an Engraving by Casserius' (Heseltine 1972: 203–07); for example, he emphasizes his female cadaver's asexuality by eschewing feminine lines, and the most metrically irregular lines in the poem are those where he challenges scientific method. Hope employs most of the usual sources of variety in the iambic pentameter, and in many respects his metre resembles that of Auden's sonnets, including the frequency of 'Italian' lines, enjambment, initial inversion, and erosion. But, whereas Auden most often erodes the fourth ictus, Hope as frequently erodes the second, and in the following line he combines initial inversion with erosion of both the second and fourth ictuses:

(57)   **Some**-thing of <u>the</u> first <u>Eve</u> is <u>in</u> this <u>pose</u>   (96)

Hope's metre differs from that of Auden's sonnets in one important respect: Hope employs more disyllabic inter-ictic intervals, as in the following line:

(58)   Dragged <u>from</u> the **ri**-ver, <u>found</u> in some **al**-ley at <u>dawn</u>   (71)

In (58) he begins both hemistichs with a monosyllabic initial inversion and ends the line with two disyllabic intervals. The structure of this line helps convey both the bedraggled appearance of its subject, a cadaver, and the violence it has suffered. The proportion of disyllabic intervals in this poem (approximately 5 per cent) makes it transitionally iambic, according to the classification of Tarlinskaja 1976; I have therefore compared it with five-ictic dolniks and other intermediate metres in Table R, rather than with iambic pentameters in Table Q.

Hope employs a somewhat higher proportion of lines that are either not iambic, or not five-ictic, in other poems; thus in 'Letter from the Line' (Heseltine 1972: 195–97) some passages contain so many substitutions that the effect is one of triple time; for example, the following lines (13–16):

(59)   <u>Glad</u> not to **ped**-dle his <u>pres</u>-ti-<u>di</u>-gi-**ta**tion
(60)   Nor <u>sing</u> for his **sup**-per in **is**-lands of a-li-en <u>speech</u>;
(61)   Though the **na**-tives were **friend**-ly e-**nough** in <u>their</u> own **fa**shion;
(62)   Rubbed **no**-ses, <u>hung</u> him with **flo**-wers, and <u>danced</u> with him on
                                                                    the <u>beach</u>

Instance (60) is in a triple time throughout, (59) and (61) move from triple to duple time, and (62) is ambiguous: either a sixth ictus is intended (represented by 'on'), or the last weak position must contain four monosyllables, as in the scansion above (alternatively, 'danced with' can represent a disyllabic strong position followed by a trisyllabic weak position). Note that this passage is set on a rolling ship, and Hope makes it as disorientating metrically as the experience it describes is physically.

Such nuances reveal that Hope was a very skilled and sophisticated metrist: he believed that verse could be never be 'free' in the sense that it was ungoverned (Hartman 1980: 49), and he punctiliously applied a complex set of metrical rules when composing his own poetry. Even critics who accuse Hope's versification of being 'rigid' and 'antiquated' have to admit that it is also 'deft' (see, for example, Goodwin 1986: 125).

Robert Lowell

Lowell was a member of an ancient New England family who converted to Roman Catholicism in 1940 and published his first volume of poetry four years later. He was jailed for being a conscientious objector, he married three times, and he suffered several bouts of mental illness. Lowell's poetry achieved rapid recognition, and he described himself as a writer 'preoccupied with technique, fascinated by the past, tempted by other languages' (Drabble 1985: 590). Until he was forty his versifying was very conservative: many of his poems were in canonical iambic pentameters, and often also in heroic couplets, as is 'Mother Marie Therese', the early poem I have chosen for analysis. Table Q shows that this poem, which has hardly any feminine lines, finds its chief source of metrical variety in a very high proportion of 'Italian' lines (53 per cent, higher than that found in Keats or Gray). Lowell also enjambed more than 18 per cent of lines, a very high proportion for heroic couplets, and one that is matched only for blank verse by Milton and Wordsworth (see Table G, and also the comments of Hobsbaum 1996: 29). In his early poems Lowell employs only the traditional forms of tension in stress-syllabic verse, initial inversion in 8.3 per cent of lines, and the erosion of 9 per cent of non-final ictuses. His strophe design is also usually as regular as his verse design; for example, two of his best-known early poems are odes with nine-line strophes: 'The Ghost', which is an imitation of Propertius, has strophes comprising six pentameters, two tetrameters, and a trimeter, and 'Mr Edwards and the Spider' interweaves four different lengths of iamb in a fixed order. Lowell also sometimes used less regular, but carefully crafted, strophes, as for example, in 'Mary Winslow', where four trimeters and a tetrameter appear at random in a double sonnet that combines an intricate scheme of full rhymes with a scattered series of pararhymes ('cools' / 'bulls' / 'Belles' / 'bibelots') .

At forty, Lowell had a serious mental illness and his poetry changed: he relaxed his pose of austere classicism and began to write more about his own family and personal experience. This change was reflected in his metrics, and from the volume *Life Studies* (1959) onwards he showed a strong preference for free verse and shorter lines; but his language lost none of its precision and rhythmic poise. I shall close this section by illustrating the metrical subtlety that can be found in Lowell's dolniks by a passage from 'For Sale' (lines 11–15), in which he describes the scene after his father's funeral:

> (63)   **Rea**-dy, [V] a-**fraid**
> (64)   of **li**-ving a-**lone** till **eigh**ty,
> (65)   **mo**-ther <u>mooned</u> in a **win**dow
> (66)   as <u>if</u> she had <u>stayed</u> on a <u>train</u>
> (67)   one <u>stop</u> past her <u>des</u>-ti-**na**tion

My scansion shows this as a three-ictic passage with a missing beat / void strong position in the first line, in which Lowell could easily have inserted the word 'and'. But the void is brilliantly appropriate here: his mother was 'ready afraid' with a void inside her. There is also very effective alliteration in this passage ('living' / 'alone', 'mother' / 'mooned', and 'stayed' / 'stop'), and even more impressive is the combination of weak rhyme, assonance, and pararhyme between 'train' and 'destination'. The last word has a full rhyme, 'station', which Lowell, in sympathy with his mother, deliberately misses.

New World Versification in the Late Twentieth Century

The choice of contemporary poets to illustrate recent developments in metre is wider than that for any earlier period, but selection is also more invidious: hitherto I have chosen the poets whose work has stood the test of time, but how well that of any given contemporary poet will wear is less certain. Four hundred years ago it was far from clear that William Shakespeare would be the poet whose reputation would grow and endure; had they been able to gamble on the question, most of his contemporaries would have placed their money on Sidney or Jonson. It is just as difficult to predict which of the many poets active today will be more, and which less, famous in the future. The problem of choice is exacerbated by the fact that the space available limits me to three poets each from the New and Old Worlds. The poets I have selected have all received considerable critical acclaim, and the New World trio are all American. They have very different poetic and metrical styles, and their careers and path to fame were also very different: Allen Ginsberg (b. 1926, d. 1997) was the foremost poet of the iconoclastic 'beat generation' of the 1960s and 1970s; Sylvia Plath (b. 1932, d. 1963) achieved a high public profile following her tragic and early death; and Robert Pinsky (b. 1940) is a poet and translator who has become America's Poet Laureate.

Allen Ginsberg

Ginsberg was the son of a university teacher from New Jersey and, after graduating from Columbia, he produced a series of volumes of verse that made him one of the best-known voices of the 'beat generation'. His poetry, however, outlasted that movement and has remained in print on both sides of the Atlantic (see Corso et al. 1963 and Ginsberg 1996 for popular British editions of his work). Ginsberg employs two very different types of free verse, a shorter line with two to five prominence peaks, and a much longer line that resembles those of Blake's prophetic books and Whitman's *Leaves of Grass*. Whitman is Ginsberg's chief poetic model, and he acknowledges this debt in 'Supermarket in California'; Ginsberg's long line is also reminiscent of liturgical rhythmic prose, but in his case it is that of the Hebrew liturgy, not the Authorised Version.

The resemblance between the metrics of Whitman and Ginsberg can be seen clearly from the latter's early poem 'Howl' (1956), where the lines average well over twenty syllables in length. The following line, which contains fifty-eight syllables, expresses Ginsberg's metrical intention and also his commitment to Pound's principle of absolute rhythm:

> (68)   to recreate the syntax and measure of poor human prose and stand before
> you speechless and intelligent and shaking with shame, rejected yet con-
> fessing out the soul to conform to the rhythm of thought in his naked
> and endless head   (75)

This long line seems to fall naturally into seven rhythmic groups, and for the purposes of rhythmic analysis I would subdivide it as follows.

> ★(68)   to <u>re</u>-cre-**ate** the **syn**-tax and **mea**sure
> of <u>poor</u> [V] **hu**-man <u>prose</u>
> and <u>stand</u> be-**fore** you **speech**less
> and in-**tel**-li-<u>gent</u> and **sha**-king with <u>shame</u>,
> re-**jec**-ted <u>yet</u> con-**fes**-sing <u>out</u> the <u>soul</u>
> to con-**form** to the **rhyth**-m of <u>thought</u>
> in his **na**-ked and **end**-less <u>head</u>.

These subdivisions contain 4, 3, 3, 4, 5, 3, and 3 prominence peaks, respectively, and the line is a series of free dolniks, because the intervals between prominence peaks contain anywhere between zero and two syllables. Each of Ginsberg's long lines has its own structure: the seven subdivisions of this line are not a feature of those that precede or follow it.

Robert Pinsky notes that there are many iambic pentameters 'buried' in 'Howl' (although a better term would be *embedded*), and, amongst other examples, he quotes (1998: 72) the opening of another long line from Ginsberg's poem:

> ★(69)   Who lost their loveboys to the three old shrews

The full line has sixty-three syllables:

> (69)   Who lost their loveboys to the three old shrews of fate the one-eyed
> shrew of the heterosexual dollar the one-eyed shrew that winks out of
> the womb and the one-eyed shrew that does nothing but sit on her ass
> and snip the intellectual golden threads of the craftsman's loom.   (40)

This line falls into six rhythmic groups of syllables, and I would scan it thus, using the same notation as for line 75 above:

> ★(69)   Who <u>lost</u> their **love-**boys to the <u>three</u> old <u>shrews</u> of <u>fate</u>
> the **one-**eyed <u>shrew</u> of the <u>he</u>-te-ro-**se**-xual **dol**lar
> the **one-**eyed <u>shrew</u> that <u>winks</u> out <u>of</u> the <u>womb</u>
> and the **one-**eyed <u>shrew</u> that does **no-**thing but <u>sit</u> on her <u>ass</u>
> and <u>snip</u> the in-tel-**lec**-tual **gol**-den <u>threads</u>
> of the **crafts-**man's <u>loom</u>.

This line thus comprises five five-ictic dolniks followed by a two-ictic dolnik, and these dolniks vary from the perfectly iambic fifth group to the almost perfectly anapaestic fourth. This line provides a good example of how not only pentameters but also other regular lines may be embedded in free verse (see also Pinsky 1998: 97–116). Because Pinsky aims his guide at the general reader, he describes the five-ictic dolnik as an 'iambic pentameter with an anapaest here and there' (1998: 72), a metre he knows well from his own early verse. He points out that the opening line of 'Howl' also consists of two flexible pentameters:

> (70)   I saw the best minds of my generation destroyed by madness, starving
> hysterical naked

Here dividing the line after 'generation' produces a canonical iambic line followed by a line that breaks into triple time. To borrow the metaphor in instance (69), Ginsberg's loom was undoubtedly that of a very intuitive but skilful craftsman. Instance (68), however, shows that Ginsberg did not always construct his lines around the pentameter; thus, although the fifth rhythmic group has the form of a canonical line, the omission of the article before 'measure' in the first group looks like a deliberate attempt to avoid one.

   To summarize, the variety of Ginsberg's metre is more obvious than its regularities, but the latter are also important, and involve two different types of numerical regulation of language: the parallels/contrasts between very long lines, and the stress contrasts within them. 'Howl' is thus a classic example of twentieth-century free verse, or the free dolnik, and demonstrates clearly how Ginsberg's metrics is indebted to both Whitman and Pound.

Sylvia Plath

Plath was the daughter of a German immigrant professor who died when she was eight. On graduating from Smith College, she won a scholarship to Cambridge, where she met and married Ted Hughes, by whom she had two children. She had a history of mental illness and suicide attempts and finally killed herself less than a month after the publication of her first volume of poetry. Her poetry, much of it published posthumously, soon achieved widespread recognition. Even Plath's undergraduate poems demonstrate considerable metrical skill, and at this early stage she had a predilection for rhyme and for fixed forms like the sonnet and villanelle. In the seven years preceding her death Plath's poetry became more distinctive, as her originality and imagination were released by her growing technical mastery. She wrote 224 poems in this period (Hughes 1981), none of them long, but all of them carefully crafted. Her later poems are in dolniks, and in some poems, for example, 'Mystic', 'Balloons', and 'Time Woman', they are free dolniks, because she employed every line length from two- to six-ictic.

In many of her poems, however, five-ictic lines predominate, including 'Above the Oxbow', 'Blackberrying', and 'Mirror'; the closing lines of 'Mirror', which contain a shocking simile that is typical of her poetic style, offer a good example of Plath's subtle use of ictus variation:

> (71)   In <u>me</u> has <u>drowned</u> a young <u>girl</u>, and in <u>me</u> an old **wo**-man
> (72)   **Ri**-ses to-**ward** her <u>day</u> **af**-ter <u>day</u>, like a **ter**-ri-ble <u>fish</u>

Instance (71), like most of the lines in the poem, is five-ictic and predominantly in triple time; Plath maintains this rhythm into (72) but makes it six-ictic, and thus achieves a similar sense of finality to that produced by the extra ictus in the last line of a Spenserian stanza. Plath's fondness for five-ictic lines with a predominantly triple-time rhythm can also be seen in several other poems, including 'Tulips' and 'In Plaster'.

Three- or four-ictic lines predominate in a number of Plath's poems, including 'Daddy', 'Little Fugue', and 'Stings', and among her later poems there are a number where many lines are ultra-short. These include 'Cut', 'Ariel', 'Purdah', 'Brasilia', and 'Thalidomide', and also 'Lady Lazarus', which consists mainly of two- and three-ictic lines, interspersed with one- and four-ictic ones. Once again the following lines (43–45), with their bitter humour, could hardly be mistaken for the work of any other poet:

> (73)   **Dy**-ing
> (74)   Is an <u>art</u> like **e**-v^{e}ry-thing <u>else</u>.
> (75)   I <u>do</u> it ex-**cep**-tion-^{a}lly <u>well</u>

By the 1960s Plath had fully developed an individual voice that was remarkable for its blend of sharp observation with unusual diction, imagery, and rhythms. In the 1950s rhyme in her poems was replaced by intricate patterns of assonance, consonance, and pararhyme, in the manner of Auden or Thomas; but by the 1960s she was avoiding line-end repetition altogether in some poems, and employing full rhyme sporadically and unpredictably in others. In summary, Plath was a metrical artist of the highest calibre: versifying, like everything else, was something she did exceptionally well.

Robert Pinsky

Pinsky was born in New Jersey, educated at Rutgers and Stanford Universities, and has taught at Berkeley, Wellesley, and Boston. As US laureate he has been as passionate an advocate of deism and capitalism as any British laureate of monarchy, and between 1975 and 1996 he produced five major volumes of his own poetry and a widely acclaimed translation of Dante. For most of his poems Pinsky employs a limited range of line lengths, either short or long: thus 'Daughter' (1975) mixes two- and three-ictic dolniks, 'Icicles' (1990) is predominantly three-ictic, and 'Shiva and Parvati in the Rain' (1990) and 'Falling Asleep' (1996) combine two-, three-, and four-ictic dolniks. The form of 'Sonnet' (1990) is particularly innovative: its fourteen lines are subdivided into four tercets and a couplet, and have a rhyme scheme aba cbc ded fef ff; the a, b, and d rhymes are pararhyme, the c and f weak rhyme. The lines are three-ictic dolniks with a boosted proportion of triple-time rhythms: fourteen of the poem's inter-ictic intervals (50 per cent) contain two syllables, seven contain zero, and seven contain a single syllable; only four lines have a (single) syllable in anacrusis. The rhythmic effects of the poem skilfully mirror the content of the poem; thus a predominantly triple rhythm in the opening tercet gives way to a series of stress clashes in the next line:

(76)   **Af**-ter-noon <u>sun</u> on her <u>back</u>
(77)   <u>Calm</u> ir-**re**-gu-lar <u>slap</u>
(78)   Of **wa**-ter a-**gainst** a <u>dock</u>.
(79)   <u>Thin</u> <u>pines</u> **clam**ber

Here the noise of the water is contrasted with the sharp, narrow, monosyllabic feet of the thin pines. Pinsky's verse abounds with such carefully chosen and crafted effects.

The bulk of Pinsky's verse, however, is in longer lines; for example 'Tennis' (1975), his translation of Dante's *Canto* XXXIV, and his longest and most famous poem 'An Explanation of America' (1980). Figures for the last-named poem are included in Table R, where they may be compared with those for the free dolniks of Eliot, the five-ictic dolniks of Stevens, and the five-ictic metres of three of Pinsky's contemporaries, Hope, Hughes, and Heaney. It is clear from these figures that Pinsky's metre must be classed as a transitional iamb, with fewer than 20 per cent of inter-ictic intervals containing two syllables. In 'Tennis' Pinsky employed a proportion of disyllabic intervals not far above the 3 per cent limit by which Tarlinskaja defines the canonical iamb, and *Canto* XXXIV is only slightly less regular. The metre of 'An Explanation of America', however, although still intermediate, is nearer to the five-ictic dolnik of Stevens than to the canonical iamb. Had Pinsky's poem been included in Table Q, it would have been conspicuous only for its high proportion of inter-ictic intervals containing other than a single syllable.

In two of his less regular poems, collected in 1984, Pinsky also employs a six-ictic dolnik: in 'The Unseen' the longer lines form the minority, but in 'The Figured Wheel' they represent the majority. 'The Unseen' contains a great deal of metrical ambiguity, and the poem troubles the reader almost as much by its form as by its subject, the Jewish holocaust. Some lines read more naturally with clashing stresses and, if all the lines of the poem are either five- or six-ictic, then some require a maximum interval of three syllables. The poem's lines seem to be pentameters tortured out of recognition, like the victims of the camp Pinsky visits. The six-ictic structure found in most lines of 'The Figured Wheel' is an even better fit for the poem's theme, because such a line is divisible into hemistichs of equal length, like the spokes of a wheel. A minority of the poem's lines are not six-ictic: thus the following line (45) is divisible into 2 + 2, its four anapaests giving it a rapid and regular motion that emphasizes the inevitability of fortune:

(80)   Of the <u>wheel</u> as it <u>rolls</u> un-re-**len**-ting-ly **o**ver

An equally divisible line offers an opportunity for the poet to mimic rhythmically the contrast that a wheel provides when rotating on a horizontal axis: half always rises while the other half falls. Pinsky takes this opportunity in both the opening and closing lines of the poem; in the former he balances iambs with trochees, and in the latter he speeds up the rhythm with anapaests:

(81)   There, **fi**-gured <u>and</u> pre-**fi**-gured
        in the **no**-thing-trans-**fi**-gu-ring <u>wheel</u>

In this line I have scanned the grammatical monosyllable 'and' as ictic; an alternative scansion would produce a five-ictic line with a trisyllabic interval, and there are a number of lines in the poem where a trisyllabic interval is required to make the line six-ictic; for example, the following line (15), which I scan with three trisyllabic intervals:

(82)   **Ta**-ken from the <u>ten</u> **thou**-sand **sto**-ries
        and the **re**-gi-ster of <u>true</u> **dra**mas

An alternative scansion might make the words 'from', 'and', and 'of' ictic, and the line predominantly trochaic, but would slow down the line. My scansion shows how Pinsky conveys the wheel's rapid, relentless movement throughout the poem, aided by the high proportion of disyllabic (37.5 per cent) and trisyllabic intervals (11.7 per cent). If I am correct, then Pinsky invented an English *taktovik* to serve his purpose.[4] Since good poets versify rapidly and intuitively, there is no reason to presume that he knew the term, or was familiar with Russian poetry: he may simply have been focusing on six strong stresses, and he probably expanded the intervals in order to accommodate his meaning and to give the pace he desired. Another distinctive feature of the poem is its line-end rhythms: over half the lines are feminine and one in seven is proparoxytonic. Expansion in Pinsky's metre is thus not confined to its inter-ictic intervals, but the price paid for the poem's rapid rhythms may be that it is much more end-stopped than most of his five-ictic poems.

   In summary, Pinsky is a poet who most often works comfortably within the modern American tradition, but who can also innovate dramatically when the subject makes other modes of versifying more appropriate.

Old World Versification in the Late Twentieth Century

In 1978 Britain's highest-circulation poetry magazine, Norman Hidden's *New Poetry*, polled its readers on who were the five best living British poets. Ted Hughes (b. 1930, d. 2000) was included in 46 per cent of respondents' lists, and Philip Larkin (b. 1922, d. 1987) in 39 per cent; in third place was the Irishman born in Ulster Seamus Heaney (b. 1939) with 22 per cent, just ahead of Graves and Betjeman (Hidden 1979). In the years that followed the three poets who topped this poll collected many honours, including a Laureateship, a Queen's Gold Medal, and a Nobel Prize. Although their verse differs considerably in both style and content, all three were outstanding metrists, and I shall close my account of the history of versifying in English with a synopsis of their contributions and a few impressive examples of their craftsmanship.

Philip Larkin

Larkin grew up in Coventry and, after graduating from Oxford, had a long and distinguished career as a university librarian; when he abandoned his early ambitions as a novelist he devoted his spare time to jazz and poetry. His verse (Thwaite 1988) offers his readers neither hope nor escape, but brings the consolations of wit and brilliant language. Larkin's metrical versatility is shown by his skilful use of many types of metre: common measure ('After-Dinner Remarks'), trochaic metre ('First Sight'), triple-time metre ('Poem about Oxford'), the transitional iamb ('Faith Healing'), the traditional dolnik ('Wild Oats'), and the free dolnik ('If, my Darling'). But his favourite metres were clearly the iambic canons, and in most of his poems he employed full rhyme in the traditional English manner. In only a few poems did he use pararhyme ('Toads'), or proparoxytonic rhyme ('Good for You, Gavin'), or blank verse ('Autumn').

The majority of Larkin's finest and most memorable lines are canonical, including the following tetrameters taken from 'An Arundel Tomb', 'The Trees', 'This Be the Verse', and 'Ambulances', respectively:

(83)   What <u>will</u> sur-**vive** of <u>us</u> is <u>love</u>   (42)
(84)   Their **green**-ness <u>is</u> a <u>kind</u> of <u>grief</u>   (4)
(85)   They <u>fuck</u> you <u>up</u>, your <u>mum</u> and <u>dad</u>   (1)
(86)   And <u>dulls</u> to **dis**-tance <u>all</u> we <u>are</u>   (30)

Larkin employed equally canonical pentameters in many of his poems, and Table Q compares his iambic pentameter with those of other twentieth-century poets who favoured this metre. The poem analysed is 'The Whitsun Weddings', which contains eight strophes, in each of which the second line is a dimeter and the remainder pentameters. This design, like that of Hope's 'Ode on an Engraving by Casserius', quoted above, is derived from Keats, who employs the rhyme scheme abab cde cde in four of his odes and included a shorter line in one ('Ode to a Nightingale').

Larkin employs most of the traditional sources of variety in 'The Whitsun Weddings', as the following lines illustrate:

(87)   All <u>posed</u> ir-**re**-so-<u>lute</u>-ly **wa**-tching us <u>go</u>   (30)
(88)   As <u>if</u> out <u>on</u> the <u>end</u> of <u>an</u> e-**vent**   (31)
(89)   While <u>girls</u>, **grip**-<u>ping</u> their **hand** bags **tigh**-ter, <u>stared</u>   (54)
(90)   Came <u>close</u> and <u>it</u> was **near**-ly <u>done</u> this <u>frail</u>   (74)
(91)   **Trav**^el-<u>ling</u> co-**in**-ci-<u>dence</u>; and <u>what</u> it <u>held</u>   (75)

Instance (87) contains a disyllabic interval, one of only two in the poem; (88) contains a surfeit of erosions, including the rare consecutive erosion of the first and second ictuses; (89) contains a suitably neurotic inversion in the second foot; and (90) is enjambed with (91), which has an initial inversion. Larkin employs two sources of variety exceptionally often in this poem: medial inversion and enjambment, the latter as often as Milton does in his blank-verse epic. Larkin also employs other less common devices: for example, like Auden, he erodes the final ictus of several lines. He also often employs alliteration in subtle and effective ways, as in the final lines of 'The Whitsun Weddings':

(92)   A <u>sense</u> of **fal**-ling, <u>like</u> an **ar**-row **sho**wer
(93)   Sent <u>out</u> of <u>sight</u>, **some**-<u>where</u> be-**co**-ming <u>rain</u>

Three trochaic words in (92) act like arrows to give the line a strong falling rhythm, while initial inversion in both cola maintain this sense of falling in (93). Even more appropriately, the alliteration of sibilants (with the first spit at the beginning of the previous line) mimics the rain itself. Note that these lines contrast not only semantically (arrows versus rain), but also metrically: a pausing line contrasts with a running, or 'Italian' line, and a masculine ending contrasts with a feminine.

These examples show that, although Larkin may appear a conservative versifier, he applied great metrical inventiveness within the rules as he saw them. He could also innovate highly effectively in strophe design: thus in 'Homage to Government' he produces a reduced sestina that matches and mocks the penny-pinching of his subject. In summary, Larkin was an accomplished metrical artist and he showed his successors that some of the longest-established metres in the twentieth-century repertoire could be made fresh and exciting.

Ted Hughes

Hughes was born in Yorkshire, graduated from Cambridge, and by the time he published his second volume of poems, *Lupercal* (1960), had been married to Sylvia Plath for four years. Following both Plath's and his second partner's suicides, Hughes moved to Dartmoor and, like James Hogg before him, became a farmer. In his forty-year career Hughes produced thirteen volumes of poetry as well as translations, adaptations, and books for children. His love of nature (which for him included caged cats, drowned dogs, flayed foxes, and newly slaughtered pigs) and his fascination with violence was perfectly in tune with his times. Hughes's metrics is very different from Larkin's: even in his earliest published work the younger poet employed mostly the dolnik metres developed in his own century. Table R compares five poems from his first volume, *The Hawk in the Rain* (1957), with the four- and five-ictic verse of four other poets. One feature not included in the comparison is the proportion of full rhyme in these poems; this is 13.5 per cent, which reveals a strong preference for pararhyme. The table shows that Hughes employed a high frequency of enjambment (24.9 per cent) but relatively few feminine lines or canonical iambic pentameters; he also included many four-ictic lines (10.9 per cent). His proportion of disyllabic intervals is very similar to that found in Stevens's 'An Ordinary Evening in New Haven', analysed in Chapter 9, but Hughes used far more clashing stresses (zero intervals) and mixed his five-ictic dolniks with lines of other lengths. The result is as varied and interesting a long line as any to be found in twentieth-century poetry.

The subtle metrical effects that Hughes was able to achieve can be illustrated by two passages, one from an early poem, the other from a late. The following lines (9–12) are from his early poem 'The Jaguar':

(94)   But <u>who</u> runs <u>like</u> the <u>rest</u> past <u>these</u> ar-**ri**ves
(95)   At a <u>cage</u> where the <u>crowd</u> [V] <u>stands</u>, [V] <u>stares</u>, [V] **mes**-me-rized,
(96)   As a <u>child</u> at a <u>dream</u>, at a **ja**-gu-ar **hur**-rying en-**raged**
(97)   Through **pri**-son **dark**-ness **af**-ter the <u>drills</u> of his <u>eyes</u>

The rhythm of each of these lines reinforces the meaning: the alliteration and succession of monosyllables in (94), followed by the triple-time opening of (95) create a sense of rapid movement. This is brought to a halt by the series of stress clashes in the middle of the line, at which point the sibilance that has marked the codas of five syllables captures their onsets as well. The triple-time regularity of (96) then suggests the trance-like quality of the animal's rapid pacing, and the duple time that opens (97) brings a return to grim reality, before the tempo speeds up again for the image of the drill. Note that three of these lines share the same pararhyme and that in the fourth (96) 'enraged' chimes with 'cage' in the preceding line.

Some of Hughes's finest poetry is to be found in his belated tribute to Plath, *Birthday Letters* (1998), and the following passage, which closes the poem 'Fingers', shows that his metrical subtlety did not desert him:

> (98)   I re-**mem**-ber your **fin**-gers. <u>And</u> your **daugh**ter's
> (99)   **Fin**-gers re-**mem**-ber your fingers
> (100) In **ev**^e-ry <u>thing</u> they <u>do</u>.
> (101) <u>Her</u> [V] **fin**-gers o-**bey** and **ho**-nour <u>your</u> [V] fingers,
> (102) The **La**-res <u>and</u> Pe-**na**-tes <u>of</u> our <u>house</u>

The long lines here have ten syllables (counted by ear, 10M = 10F), the number of human digits. Instance (98) is blatantly non-canonical: in my scansion it has four prominence peaks (on syllables 3, 6, 8, and 10), and its rhythm is that which distinguishes the Romance hendecasyllable from the English canon, and comprises two anapaests followed by two iambs (see Dominicy 2003). The next two lines are three-ictic dolniks that contrast strongly with one another: (99) is in triple time and (100) is perfectly iambic. This contrast would provide an effective close to the poem, but like a composer who lulls us with a false climax before adding the final triumphant bars, Hughes continues. Instance (101) is perfectly symmetrical: its verbs (one an iamb, the other a trochee) are transposed from the traditional Christian marriage vows, and it has six significant stresses including the phrasal ones on the pronouns, including peaks on syllables 5 and 7. Then comes the true climax of the poem, in a canonical pentameter; its five weak and five strong positions offer the most perfect analogy for the human hands, which Hughes's words transmute with classical elegance into household gods. The language and the metrical structure of this poem bring many added layers of significance to its message.

Seamus Heaney

Heaney was a Derry Catholic who was educated in a sectarian school and at Queen's University Belfast, where he became part of a circle of young poets. His most productive years coincided with the 'troubles', as the civil war in Northern Ireland was euphemistically called, and he moved to the Irish Republic in 1972. His poetry (1988) has always been widely admired on both sides of the Irish Sea and of the Atlantic, and in 1995 the award of a Nobel Prize recognized his international importance. He has also published literary essays and lectures, and his modern version of *Beowulf*, discussed in Chapter 3, became a best-seller. Like Hughes, he could be described as a nature poet, but the most important features of Heaney's landscapes are people, particularly his long-suffering and violent compatriots.

Heaney employed a wide range of metres, mostly those of the twentieth century, but many of his poems contain a large proportion of canonical lines. His favourite long line was a dolnik in which most of the lines have either four or five ictuses, and he also excelled at the ultra-short line, which most often comprised two. Table R analyses Heaney's 'Glanmore Sonnets', which were published in 1979; their 140 lines are especially interesting because they offer numerous examples of Heaney's both more regular and less regular versifying. Although a substantial proportion of their lines are of other lengths, more than 80 per cent are five-ictic, just over half are canonical pentameters, and many of the apparently irregular lines are headless iambic pentameters, with their typical trochaic rhythm. The proportion of feminine lines in these poems is high, comparable to that found in dramatic verse, but the frequency of enjambment is no more than average for the twentieth century.

Although many of Heaney's lines are iambic, a substantial proportion have a zero anacrusis, and, while only 2 per cent of intervals contain zero syllables, almost 12 per cent contain two. The non-canonical lines in these poems include the following:

(103)   And art a pa-ra-digm of earth new from the lathe   (I. 7)
(104)   [V] Sen-sings, moun-tings from the hi-ding places   (II. 1)
(105)   In Bel-fast han-ke-ring af-ter stone   (II. 6)
(106)   He lived there in the un-say-ab-le lights   (VI. 1)
(107)   This mor-ning when a mag-pie with jer-ky steps   (VIII. 4)
(108)   Where the old one rocked and rocked and rocked   (VIII. 11)

Instance (103) is six-ictic, and has a clash of stressed monosyllables ('earth' / 'new'); (104) is best described as a headless iambic pentameter, and (105) is four-ictic with mixed rhythms. For (106) to have five beats would involve an erosion (on 'in') followed by the wrenching of two weak syllables in 'unsayable', but most performers would give this line four beats and two disyllabic intervals, and I have scanned it in this way. Many of the lines of these poems are decasyllabic but equally irregular, and Sonnet IV is particularly interesting in this respect. At first sight it combines a four-ictic octave with a canonical sestet, but a closer inspection reveals that six of the octave's lines have ten syllables if counted anti-rhythmically. Here Heaney, like many poets before him, has been influenced by Marianne Moore's syllabics; note that a more regular iambic close is a feature of all the sonnets. Many lines are also iambic pentameters but for one feature, including (107) above, which has a disyllabic fourth interval, and (108), which has a disyllabic anacrusis. As the figures in Table R show, Heaney's five-ictic line is intermediate between the dolnik and the canonical iamb, and to distinguish it further from the iambic canon he combines it with other line lengths. He seeks a similar variety in his rhymes: 27 per cent are full rhymes on stressed syllables, but many more involve pararhyme, weak rhyme, or consonance. These sonnets are thus in a modern metre that gives more than a nod to the traditional norms.

Heaney employed the ultra-short line for a number of poems, and Tables S and T give figures for four of these, which show that they varied considerably in rhythm and in other metrical features. Thus, although in all of them fewer than 50 per cent of lines have an iambic opening (an anacrusis consisting of a single syllable), 'Bone Dreams' is the exception in having far more disyllabic and far fewer zero anacruses. 'Viking Dublin', however, is even more exceptional in having a boosted proportion of disyllabic intervals (almost double that found in prose), and 'The Grauballe Man' is the only one of these poems where masculine rhymes constitute more than 80 per cent of total. Table T compares Heaney's ultra-short line with those of two other poets who were fond of this line length: it shows that Heaney's metre resembles Williams's rather than Hardy's in very many ways. For example, Heaney includes many lines with other than two ictuses, tolerates clashing stresses, often gives his lines a trochaic opening, and employs a high number of feminine and proparoxytonic endings. At first sight, however, Heaney is closer to Hardy in the proportion of triple time in his lines; but his percentage of disyllabic intervals, which is slightly above the prose norm, is distorted by the unique rhythmic balance of 'Viking Dublin'.

Heaney employed the two-ictic dolnik for many of the poems in *North* (1975), and this line echoes the half-verse of Old English and Norse epic, and of the earliest Irish poetry (see Meyer 1909: 1–4). The language of Heaney's ultra-short line, however, is much richer in heavy monosyllables than that of the ancient epics, and his zero intervals allow them to clash for dramatic effect. This can be seen clearly from the final strophe of another poem, 'Sunlight':

> (109) And <u>here</u> is <u>love</u>
> (110) Like a **tin**-smith's <u>scoop</u>
> (111) <u>Sunk</u> past its <u>gleam</u>
> (112) In a <u>meal</u>- [V] <u>bin</u>.

In the final line the two stresses of the compound word clash in a way that emphasizes the connection between food and love in the simile. Heaney's ultra-short lines contain many metrical subtleties of this type, and his matching of meaning and metre is a remarkable skill that places him among the century's most accomplished versifiers.

Heaney, who celebrated his sixty-first birthday in the year 2000, is the final poet whose metrics will be discussed in this volume, although there were many distinguished poets among his contemporaries, and a new generation of poets is versifying and innovating in English at this very moment. I have refrained from picking any of these poets' work out for metrical analysis for three reasons: first, because it would be invidious; secondly because it is not clear whose poetry will be read by future generations; and, finally and most importantly, because I know of no poet who has not been strongly influenced by the metrics of those I have already discussed. I believe that I have provided the reader with a history of English metrics that is up to date as far as major developments are concerned, but I have not attempted to cover the metrics of every major poet who has versified in English, either in the twentieth century or any other. The ninety poets whose work I have analysed have been chosen because their work is still readily available, and because, between them, they illustrate all the twists and turns in the story I have to tell. Doubtless I have missed the significance of many recent developments, and they will emerge in the course of the new century; but describing them must remain the task of future literary historians.

Conclusions

For much of the world the twentieth century was a period of immense technological, social, and political change. Although more people wrote poetry than ever before, the audience for it probably declined, and poetry-reading habits changed significantly: families were separated and children were distracted by new studies, and so the audience for poetry now tended to experience it privately and visually rather than aurally and publicly. The visual element in versifying acquired a new importance, and free verse, the craftsmanship of which is often easier to see than to hear, became viable in a way it had not been before.[5] Blake and Whitman had few imitators; Pound and Eliot found many. But, while free verse succeeded in gaining widespread acceptance, it did not replace traditional modes of versifying. The extension of individual choice that characterized Western society in the period was reflected in its poetry, poetics, and metrics: good poets continued to try to perfect form, as well as communicate meaning, and they found their individual ways of doing so. Free verse was integrated comfortably into the existing English metrical system, helped by the fact that the new modes of versifying employed many of the same linguistic features as the traditional. Many poets chose to versify traditionally as well as to explore the new freedom: the canonical metres survived intact in a substantial number of important poems, but the favourite line of most of the century's greatest poets was the five-ictic dolnik. Thus the ancient tendency to perceive lines of verse as a number of beats, feet, ictuses, or prominence peaks survived the imported convention of syllabic regularity.

For five centuries English poets sought and preserved that syllabic regularity by setting the position-size parameter at one syllable in most of their verse, and this produced the stress-syllabic canons. Poets gave this type of verse a measure of rhythmic variety by selectively placing non-stress in strong positions, and stress in weak ones, and by the judicious use of inversion and caesura variation. In the second half of the eighteenth century, however, poets began to seek greater variety than this system allowed, and for many years the rediscovery of folk verse helped satisfy this demand. Nineteenth-century poets revived and developed dolniks and triple-time metres, and in doing so learned how rich and varied rhythms can be created by an inconstant position size. By the end of the century some poets were introducing some variability of position size into canonical iambic metres, but then others discovered an even greater source of rhythmic variety: varying position number from one line to the next. This device enabled consecutive lines either to be contrasted with one another or to be accumulated into a series of similar structures. Meanwhile Whitman had rediscovered the ancient practice of using cola within lines for the same purposes of contrast and parallelism. The most versatile poets of the twentieth century admitted all these innovations into their repertoires along with traditional metres; and, while some poets chose to include regularly iambic lines in their verse to achieve special effects, others composed entire poems in canonical metres.

The integration of so many types of free verse into the English metrical system greatly increased the repertoire of metres available to twentieth-century poets. It also altered the balance between *sécurité* and *surprise*, or regularity and variety, in their verse: any given line could differ from the previous or subsequent line, or both, in more conspicuous ways. The same thing thus happened to metre in the twentieth century as to marriage: short-term relationships, between both lines and people, gradually superseded enduring ones. If metre had previously been a contract between poet and reader that lasted until the expiry of the poem, it was now a bargain to be revoked in the interests of variety. Metrical variety and complexity, however, brought their own problems: as Utrera Torremocha argues, good free verse is not only difficult to write, it is difficult to scan (2001: 28 & 33), and most of the systematic analysis published so far has been of Russian texts (for example, Smith 1989 & 2002). Experienced poets, of course, compose free verse intuitively, as they do other types of verse, and skill in its composition has been acquired largely by trial and error. Although much has been written on the subject, the development of free verse is due more to the example of a few influential poets than to manuals of composition. Metre was clearly of vital concern to all the major poets of the twentieth century, and many played a key role in developing the extremely wide repertoire of modern metres. Today's readers and poets should share that concern. Just as no reader can derive the maximum enjoyment from twentieth-century verse without recognizing the poet's metrical skill, so no new poet can hope to build on that century's poetic achievements unless (s)he understands fully what they were. On that promise of pleasure and that prospect of progress the justification of this volume depends.

Notes to Chapter 10

1. Kipling employed a vast array of different metres with consummate skill; for example, his poem 'We and They' (1990: 631) is probably the liveliest example of poulter's measure in the language.

2. Hardy was perhaps *fool*hardy in employing proparoxytonic rhyme for serious purposes; most other poets have treated it as a joke. Thus John Betjeman (b. 1906, d. 1984) in 'Senex' (Betjeman 1958) wrote: 'Each **sun**-down <u>on</u> my **tri**-cy-<u>cle</u> | I <u>tour</u> the **bo**-rough's <u>edge</u>, | And, **i**-cy <u>as</u> an **i**-ci-<u>cle</u>, | See **bi**-cy-<u>cle</u> by **bi**-cy-<u>cle</u> | Stacked **wai**-ting <u>in</u> the <u>hedge</u>'.

3. Works on linguistic metrics employ asterisks to indicate hypothetic constructs in the same way that other works on linguistics use them to indicate unattested lines.

4. Followers of Attridge's theory also recognize the possibility of triple offbeats, which they denote by the symbol ~o~, making the scansion of instance (82): B ~o~ B ŏ B B ~o~ B ~o~ B ô B o.

5. Free verse when delivered meaningfully tends to sound like prose: only artificially long pauses reveal where the lines end. Verse in which every line is of a different length and is also enjambed is almost impossible for an audience to identify. This elusiveness accounts for both the cultivation of syllabics to provide visual regularity and the popularity of the five-ictic dolnik with its familiar aural pattern.

STATISTICAL TABLES

Table A

Shakespeare and his Predecessors
Percentage of Lines with Various Features

sample	'Italian' caesura	initial inversion	medial inversion	void/ resolution	erosion average
Chaucer *CT*	31	3.7	2.0	<1	11.9
Surrey Rhymed	4	6.3	4.0	2.3	7.6
Surrey *Aeneid*	12	8.3	5.3	2.3	8.8
Sackville 'Induction'	15	2.3	1.7	0.0	7.9
Sidney Sonnets	24	9.3	2.7	<1	7.2
Spenser FQ	30	6.7	<1	0.0	7.5
Shakespeare Sonnets	33	4.7	2.0	0.0	10.6
largest 2σ	± 5.4	± 3.4	± 2.6	± 1.7	± 3.8

All figures in this and subsequent tables are percentages unless otherwise stated; columns headed 'actual' contain numbers (of lines, anacruses, intervals, etc.).

Samples: Chaucer, *CT*: *GP*, 1–300 (Benson 1988); Surrey, *Poems*, 7–14, 17–19, 24–27, and *Aeneid*, II. 1–300 (Keene 1985); Sackville, 'Induction', 1–300 (Campbell 1938); Sidney, *Astrophel and Stella*, II–V, VII, IX–XXV (Bullett 1947), Spenser, *Faerie Queene*, I. 1. 1–334 (Hamilton 1966), Shakespeare, *Sonnets*, 1–22 (Harrison 1949)

Table B

The Dramatic Iambic Pentameter
Percentage of Lines with Various Features

sample	'Italian' caesura	feminine ending	initial inversion	medial inversion	intervals	
					0	*>1*
Sackville 'Induction'	15	0	1.3	1.7	0	0.0
Sackville *Gorboduc*	29	0	2.7	1.0	0	0.7
Norton *Gorboduc*	30	1.0	2.3	4.0	<1	1.3
Marlowe *Tamburlaine*	36	0	7.7	2.7	<1	3.7
Shakespeare *Richard III*	34	17.0	5.0	3.3	<1	4.7
Shakespeare *Ant. & Cleo.*	38	21.7	7.3	4.7	1.7	14.0
Shakespeare Sonnets	33	13.3	4.7	2.0	0	<1
Webster *Duchess*	23	20.4	5.3	8.3	5.7	38.3
largest 2σ	±5.6	±4.8	±3.1	±2.3	±0.3	±4.0

Samples: Sackville, 'Induction', 1–300 (Campbell 1938); Sackville & Norton, *Gorboduc*, I. 1–2 & v. 1–2 (Tydeman 1992); Marlowe, *Tamburlaine the Great*, Part II, I. 1–II. 3 (Steane 1969); Shakespeare, *Richard III*, I. 1–2, *Antony and Cleopatra*, I. 1–5 (Alexander 1959), and *Sonnets*, 1–22 (Harrison 1947); Webster, *Duchess of Malfi*, IV. 1–2 (Lucas 1927)

Table C

The Dramatic Iambic Pentameter
Percentage of Lines with Erosion and Enjambment

sample	erosion of ictus					enjamb.
	1	2	3	4	average	
Sackville 'Induction'	5.0	2.7	12.0	12.0	7.9	12.3
Sackville Gorboduc	9.0	2.7	16.3	6.7	8.7	15.0
Norton Gorboduc	7.0	2.0	10.3	9.3	7.2	10.7
Marlowe Tamburlaine	7.7	2.7	15.3	17.3	10.8	7.3
Shakespeare Richard III	6.7	5.0	13.6	12.0	9.3	8.3
Shakespeare Ant. & Cleo.	7.7	5.3	9.0	10.7	8.2	21.0
Shakespeare Sonnets	14.0	5.3	13.0	10.3	10.6	6.3
Webster Duchess	5.3	5.7	9.3	7.3	7.0	26.7
largest 2σ	±3.3	±2.6	±4.2	±4.4	±1.8	±5.1

Table D

The Non-Dramatic Iambic Pentameter
Percentage of Lines with Various Features

sample	'Italian' lines	initial inversion	erosion of ictuses				
			1	2	3	4	average
Chaucer	31	3.7	7.0	10.7	16.6	13.3	11.9
Shakespeare	33	4.7	4.0	5.3	13.0	10.3	10.6
Milton	41	6.7	14.0	10.3	20.3	13.7	14.6
Dryden	40	3.7	8.3	2.3	14.7	8.3	8.3
Pope	44	3.7	15.3	1.0	23.7	9.3	12.3
Gray	49	2.3	10.2	2.3	18.8	12.5	10.9
largest 2σ	± 3.8	± 2.9	± 4.2	± 4.2	± 4.9	± 4.4	± 4.4

Samples: Chaucer, *CT: GP*, 1–300 (Benson 1988); Shakespeare, *Sonnets*, 1–22 (Harrison 1949); Milton, *Paradise Lost*, I. 1–300 (Leonard 1998); Dryden, *Absalom and Achitophel*, Part I, 1–300 (Sharrock 1968); Pope, *The Rape of the Lock*, Cantos I–III (Probyn 1983); Gray, *Elegy Written in a Country Churchyard* (Reeves 1973)

Table E

Iambic and Trochaic Tetrameters
Percentage of Lines with Various Features

sample	initial inversion	erosion of ictuses				enjambed
		1	2	3	average	
Sidney (trochaic)	0.0	18.8	7.3	8.1	11.4	7.3
Milton (mixed)	3.6	20.8	9.2	8.9	13.0	6.3
Marvell (iambic)	2.7	10.3	5.3	4.0	6.5	9.7
Swift (iambic)	1.0	6.0	8.0	11.1	8.4	14.0
Pope (iambic)	2.6	7.6	8.6	13.5	9.9	4.0
largest 2σ	± 2.2	± 4.7	± 3.9	± 4.6	± 3.9	4.0

Samples: Sidney, *Astrophel and Stella*, six lyrics (Bullett 1947); Milton, 'L'Allegro' and 'Il Penseroso' (Leonard 1998); Marvell, 'Upon Appleton House', 1–300 (Margoliouth 1971); Swift, *Cadenus and Vanessa*, 1–300 (Pollard 1976); Pope, 'Imitations of Horace', Book I, *Epistle VII* and Book II, *Satire VI* (Dobrée 1924)

Table F

Nineteenth-Century Blank Verse
Percentage of Lines with Various Features

sample	'Italian' caesura	feminine ending	initial inversion	medial inversion	enjambed
Shakespeare *Ant. & Cleo.*	38	21.7	7.3	4.7	21.0
Milton *PL*	41	<1	6.7	1.2	39.3
Wordsworth *Prelude*	45	<1	4.7	1.0	33.0
Keats *Fall of Hyp.*	40	0	8.3	2.0	20.7
Tennyson Monologues	32	0	5.3	1.0	23.3
Browning 'Fra Lippo'	31	2.3	6.7	1.3	6.3
largest 2σ	± 5.4	± 4.8	± 3.2	± 2.4	± 5.6

Samples: Shakespeare, *Antony and Cleopatra*, I. 1–5 (Alexander 1959); Milton, *Paradise Lost*, I. 1–300 (Leonard 1998); Wordsworth, *The Prelude*, I. 1–300 (Gill 1984); Keats, *The Fall of Hyperion*, I. 1–300 (Barnard 1977); Tennyson, 'The Lotos-Eaters', 'Ulysses', 'Tithonus', and 'Tiresias', 1–114 (Ricks 1987); Browning, 'Fra Lippo Lippi', 1–300 (Jack 1970)

Table G

Nineteenth-Century Blank Verse
Percentage of Lines with Erosion

sample	erosion of ictuses				
	1	2	3	4	average
Shakespeare Ant. & Cleo.	7.7	2.7	15.3	6.7	8.7
Milton PL	14.0	10.3	20.3	13.7	14.6
Wordsworth Prelude	6.0	15.3	20.7	17.7	14.9
Keats Fall of Hyp.	12.3	6.6	10.3	17.0	11.6
Tennyson Monologues	8.7	12.7	10.3	17.0	12.2
Browning 'Fra Lippo'	8.3	6.7	8.7	14.0	9.4
largest 2σ	±4.0	±4.2	±4.7	±3.9	±1.4

Samples: Shakespeare, *Antony and Cleopatra*, I. 1–5 (Alexander 1959); Milton, *Paradise Lost*, I. 1–300 (Leonard 1998); Wordsworth, *The Prelude*, I. 1–300 (Gill 1984); Keats, *The Fall of Hyperion*, I. 1–300 (Barnard 1977); Tennyson, 'The Lotos-Eaters', 'Ulysses', 'Tithonus', and 'Tiresias', 1–114 (Ricks 1987); Browning, 'Fra Lippo Lippi', 1–300 (Jack 1970)

Table H

Nineteenth-Century Rhymed Pentameters
Percentage of Lines with Various Features

sample	'Italian' caesura	feminine ending	initial inversion	medial inversion	enjambed
Shakespeare Sonnets	33	13.3	4.7	2.0	6.3
Gray 'Elegy'	49	0	2.3	0	1.3
Wordsworth Sonnets	35	0	6.7	0	18.3
Byron Ch. Harold	40	5.0	5.0	1.0	24.3
Shelley Adonais	33	4.7	4.3	4.0	22.0
Keats Sonnets	48	8.3	11.3	1.3	22.7
largest 2σ	± 5.8	± 3.9	± 3.7	± 2.4	± 5.0

Samples: Shakespeare, *Sonnets*, 1–22 (Harrison 1949); Gray, *Elegy Written in a Country Churchyard* (Reeves 1973); Wordsworth, 22 sonnets (Gill 1984: 267–82); Byron, *Childe Harold's Pilgrimage*, I. 1–300 (McGann 1994); Shelley, *Adonais*, 1–300 (Bloom 1966); Keats, 22 sonnets (Barnard 1977)

Table J

Nineteenth-Century Rhymed Pentameters
Percentage of Lines with Erosion

sample	erosion of ictuses				
	1	2	3	4	average
Shakespeare Sonnets	4.0	5.3	13.0	10.3	10.6
Gray Elegy	10.2	2.3	18.8	12.5	10.9
Wordsworth Sonnets	10.7	5.7	9.7	13.0	9.8
Byron Ch. Harold	13.0	9.3	12.3	17.7	13.1
Shelley Adonais	10.3	7.3	17.3	9.7	11.2
Keats Sonnets	12.7	5.3	14.7	9.7	10.6
largest 2σ	± 3.9	± 3.4	± 4.4	± 4.4	± 1.3

Samples: Shakespeare, *Sonnets*, 1–22 (Harrison 1949); Gray, *Elegy Written in a Country Churchyard* (Reeves 1973); Wordsworth, 22 sonnets (Gill 1984: 267–82); Byron, *Childe Harold's Pilgrimage*, 1. 1–300 (McGann 1994); Shelley, *Adonais*, 1–300 (Bloom 1966); Keats, 22 sonnets (Barnard 1977)

Table K

Nineteenth-Century Iambic and Trochaic Tetrameters
Percentage of Lines with Various Features

Sample	initial inversion	enjambed	erosion of ictuses			
			1	2	3	average
IAMBIC						
Swift	1.0	14.0	6.0	8.0	11.1	8.4
Tennyson	<1	11.7	9.0	9.0	12.0	10.0
Browning	4.3	13.3	8.7	13.3	10.0	10.7
TROCHAIC						
Sidney	0	7.3	18.8	7.3	8.1	11.4
Tennyson	0	10.3	25.7	12.3	14.0	17.3
Browning	0	3.7	30.0	4.4	10.0	14.8
Longfellow	0	3.0	50.0	5.3	31.0	28.8
largest 2σ	±2.4	±4.0	±5.8	±3.9	±5.3	±2.6

Samples: Swift, *Cadenus and Vanessa*, 1–300 (Pollard 1976); Tennyson, *In Memoriam*, 300 lines selected by Cecil 1971, and 'Locksley Hall', 1–150 (Ricks 1987); Browning, 'The Italian in England', 'The Confessional', 'Two in the Campagna', 'In Three Days', and 'A Toccata of Galuppi's' (Jack 1970); Sidney, *Astrophel and Stella*, six lyrics (Bullett 1947); Longfellow, *The Song of Hiawatha*, Introduction, I, & II. 1–23 (Byrom 1970)

Table L

The Free Dolnik of Pound and Eliot
Percentage of Lines of Each Length

sample	length in no. of ictuses									actual no. of lines
	1	2	3	4	5	6	7	8	9	
'Altaforte'	0	0	2.6	33.3	59.0	5.1	0	0	0	39
'L'Ode'	0	9.7	54.8	21.5	9.7	4.3	0	0	0	93
Canto I	0	1.4	10.8	29.7	45.9	12.2	0	0	0	74
Canto LXV	8.3	6.3	50.0	22.9	6.3	6.3	0	0	0	48
POUND 4 poems	1.6	5.1	33.1	26.0	27.2	7.1	0	0	0	254
'Prufrock'	0	0.8	16.7	9.1	52.3	11.4	6.8	2.3	0.8	132
'Burial'	0	1.4	5.7	22.9	64.3	5.7	0	0	0	70
Ash W. I & VI	0	9.2	19.7	19.7	39.5	6.6	2.6	2.6	0	76
ELIOT 3 poems	0	3.2	14.7	15.5	51.8	8.6	4.0	1.8	0.4	278
largest 2σ	±8.0	±6.6	±14.4	±15.1	±11.6	±7.6	±4.4	±3.7	±1.5	—

Samples: Pound, 'Sestina: Altaforte' and 'L'Ode pour l'élection de son sépulcre' from *Hugh Selwyn Mauberley* (Eliot 1959), and *Cantos*, I & XLV (Pound 1975); Eliot, 'The Love Song of J. Alfred Prufrock', 'The Burial of the Dead' from *The Waste Land*, and *Ash Wednesday*, Parts I & VI (Eliot 1963)

Table M

The Free Dolnik of Pound and Eliot
Percentage of Lines with Various Features

sample	fem. lines	enjd lines	iambic pents	pents ±1	anacruses		intervals		actual no. of intervals
					0	2	0	2	
'Altaforte'	64.1	2.6	0	12.8	23.1	33.3	24.5	18.9	143
'L'Ode'	39.8	6.5	4.3	2.2	43.0	10.8	6.4	27.9	233
Canto I	56.8	10.8	6.8	0	52.7	5.4	7.6	45.1	264
Canto LXV	72.9	4.2	0	0	22.9	35.4	3.6	73.0	111
POUND 4 poems	54.7	6.7	3.5	2.8	42.0	17.3	9.9	36.2	751
'Prufrock'	8.3	3.0	26.5	20.5	31.1	23.5	0.8	7.8	515
'Burial'	41.4	20.0	17.1	10.0	37.1	11.4	8.2	26.5	257
Ash W. I & VI	15.8	3.9	18.4	3.9	26.3	14.5	5.5	15.0	253
ELIOT 3 poems	18.7	7.6	21.9	13.3	31.3	18.0	3.8	14.2	1025
largest 2σ	±11.5	±9.6	±9.0	±10.7	±13.5	±15.1	±7.2	±8.4	—

Samples: Pound, 'Sestina: Altaforte' and 'L'Ode pour l'élection de son sépulcre' from *Hugh Selwyn Mauberley* (Eliot 1959), and *Cantos*, I & XLV (Pound 1975); Eliot, 'The Love Song of J. Alfred Prufrock', 'The Burial of the Dead' from *The Waste Land*, and *Ash Wednesday*, Parts I & VI (Eliot 1963)

Table N

Stevens's Long-Line and Williams's Ultra-Short-Line Metres

1 Metrical Comparison of Two Poems by Stevens

	lines				anacruses		intervals	
poem	*fem.*	*canon.*	*rhyme*	*enjamb*	*0*	*2*	*0*	*2*
'Guitar'	1.5	53.4	18.8	17.6	5.3	16.5	0.4	14.2
'Evening'	19.2	27.3	0.0	21.2	5.1	19.2	0.9	24.7

2 Line-Length Analysis of Williams's 'The Crimson Cyclamen'

ictuses	1	2	3	4	total
no. of lines	30	141	66	6	243
(% of lines)	(12.3)	(58.0)	(27.2)	(2.5)	(100)
no. of intervals	0	141	132	18	291

3 Interval and Rhyme Analysis of 'The Crimson Cyclamen'

	anacruses		intervals		rhymes	
syllables	*0*	*2*	*0*	*2*	*F*	*P*
two-ictic	34.8	11.3	16.3	23.4	25.5	5.0
3/4-ictic	43.1	5.6	6.0	14.7	23.6	0.0
2–4 ictic total	37.8	9.4	11.0	18.9	24.9	2.4

Samples: Stevens, 'The Man with the Blue Guitar' and 'An Ordinary Evening in New Haven' (Stevens 1965); Williams, 'The Crimson Cyclamen' (Litz & MacGowan 1987–88)

Table P

1 Line Lengths in Housman's *A Shropshire Lad*

8M	8F	7M	7F	6M	6F	other
34.9	1.7	19.6	3.1	24.9	10.7	5.2

2 Strophe Lengths in Lawrence's 'Snake'

no. of lines	2	3	4	5	6	7	8	9
no. of strophes	3	5	4	3	1	1	0	1

3 Number of Ictuses in Lawrence's 'Snake'

no. of ictuses	1	2	3	4	5	6	7	8	9
no. of lines	3	6	10	10	19	12	7	2	5

Samples: Housman, all poems in *A Shropshire Lad* (Sparrow 1956); Lawrence, 'Snake' (Sola Pinto & Roberts 1964)

Table Q

The Twentieth-Century Iambic Pentameter
Percentage of Lines with Various Features

sample	fem. lines	Ital. lines	enjd lines	init. inv.	med. inv.	±1 lines	erosion of ictuses					actual lines
							1	2	3	4	> avge	
Frost 'Lesson … Today'	11.8	37	5.6	<1	<1	<1	5.0	11.2	7.5	10.6	8.5	161
Auden 21 Sonnets	12.0	40	15.3	5.7	<1	<1	7.0	9.0	11.3	21.3	12.2	300
Lowell 'Mother Marie'	1.2	53	18.3	8.3	1.8	<1	5.3	4.7	12.4	13.6	9.0	169
Larkin 'Whitsun Weddings'	5.6	43	33.0	1.4	5.6	1.4	5.6	12.5	6.9	8.3	8.3	72
largest 2σ	±5.4	±11.7	±11.1	±2.8	±5.4	±2.8	±5.4	±7.8	±6.0	±6.5	±6.5	—

Samples: Frost, 'Lesson for Today' (Frost 1955); Auden, 'The Quest' and five 'Sonnets from China' (Auden 1966); Lowell, 'Mother Marie Therese' (Lowell 1963); Larkin, 'The Whitsun Weddings' (Thwaite 1988)

Table R

Twentieth-Century Dolniks and Intermediate Metres
Percentage of Lines with Various Features

sample	fem. lines	enjd lines	iambic pents	length 5-ictic	intervals		actual lines
					0	2	
Eliot 3 poems 1917–30	18.7	7.6	21.9	51.8	3.8	14.2	278
Stevens 'Ordinary Evening'	19.2	21.2	27.3	100	0.9	24.7	198
Hope 'Ode on Casserius'	0	15.7	77.9	99.3	0	4.7	140
Pinsky 'Explan. of America'	36.5	7.9	62.0	100	1.1	13.5	266
Hughes 6 early poems	13.9	24.9	18.4	88.1	1.0	5.4	201
Heaney 'Glanmore Sonnets'	24.2	16.4	52.9	82.1	2.0	11.9	140
largest 2σ	±7.2	±6.1	±8.4	±6.5	±1.2	±2.7	—

Samples: Eliot, 'The Love Song of J. Alfred Prufrock', 'The Burial of the Dead', and 'Ash Wednesday', Parts I & VI (Eliot 1963); Stevens, 'An Ordinary Evening in New Haven' (Stevens 1965); Hope 'Ode on an Engraving of Casserius' (Heseltine 1972); Pinsky, 'An Explanation of America', Part I, 1–300 (Pinsky 1996); Hughes, 'Fallgrief's Girlfriends', 'The Man Seeking Experience Enquires his Way of a Drop of Water', 'Wind', 'Bayonet Charge', 'Six Young Men', and 'The Martyrdom of Bishop Farrar' (Hughes 1995); Heaney, 'Glanmore Sonnets' (Heaney 1990)

Table S

Ten Two-Ictic Dolnik Poems
Percentage of Lines with Various Features

sample	anacrusis		intervals		fem. lines	prop. lines	actual 2-ictic lines	actual other lines
	0	2	0	2				
HARDY 'Quid'	4.1	41.9	0	43.2	8.1	0	74	0
'Rain'	19.4	5.6	0	91.7	38.9	0	36	0
'I Found'	0	75.0	0	37.5	0	0	40	0
'Picnic'	0	46.4	0	25.0	0	0	28	2
'Calendar'	16.7	22.2	0	33.3	0	0	18	2
'Clock-W.'	0	65.9	0	72.7	13.6	4.5	44	4
HEANEY 'Viking'	23.4	29.9	3.9	64.9	26.0	13.0	77	19
'Bone Ds'	42.0	15.9	13.0	27.5	40.6	7.2	69	27
'Grauballe'	19.4	33.3	8.3	41.7	13.9	2.8	36	12
'On Road'	25.3	35.2	0	32.4	40.8	0	71	5
largest 2σ	± 16.4	± 19.6	± 8.1	± 22.2	± 16.2	± 7.7	—	—

Samples: see Table T

Table T

The Two-Ictic Dolnik of Williams, Hardy, and Heaney
Percentage of Lines with Various Features

sample	anacruses		intervals		fem. lines	prop. lines	actual 2-ictic lines	actual other lines
	0	2	0	2				
Williams 'Cyclamen'	34.8	11.3	16.3	23.4	25.5	5.0	141	102
Hardy 6 poems	5.4	45.4	0	52.1	10.8	<1	240	8
Heaney 4 poems	28.5	28.1	5.9	42.3	32.4	6.3	253	71
largest 2σ	± 8.0	± 5.3	± 6.3	± 7.1	± 7.3	± 3.7	—	—

Samples: Williams, 'The Crimson Cyclamen' (Tomlinson 1976); Hardy, 'Quid hic agis', 'Rain on a Grave', 'I Found Her Out There', 'Where the Picnic Was', 'The Month's Calendar', and 'The Clock-Winder' (Creighton 1977); Heaney, 'Viking Dublin: Trial Pieces', 'Bone Dreams', 'The Grauballe Man', and 'On the Road' (Heaney 1990).

Note on statistical significance

The rationale behind the inclusion of figures for two standard errors (2σ) in these tables is as follows: a verse design can only be inferred from all the possible verse instances based upon it, and these represent a population, in the statistical sense, of which the instances in the text are a sample. When comparing texts, therefore, we are comparing samples, and there is an accepted technique for measuring the effect on the figures in such a comparison of *sampling error*, the inaccuracy that arises from choosing one particular sample rather than another. Statisticians measure this in what they term *standard errors* (σ): a difference of ±2σ is termed *statistically significant*, because there is only a 1 in 20 chance of its being the result of sampling error, and a difference of ±3σ is said to be *highly significant*, because that chance is only 1 in 100. To find σ for a text of any length, calculate the square root of ($a \times b$) divided by ($a + b$), where *a* is the number of lines in the text that have the specified feature and *b* is the number that do not.

BIBLIOGRAPHY

ABBOT, J. L., ed., 1935. *The Correspondence of Gerard Manley Hopkins and Richard Watson Dixon* (London: OUP)

——, ed., 1955. *The Letters of Gerard Manley Hopkins and Robert Bridges* (London: OUP)

ABLEY, MARK, 2005. *Spoken Here: Travels among Threatened Languages* (London: Arrow Books)

ABRSM, 1958. *Rudiments and Theory of Music* (London: ABRSM)

ALBRIGHT, DANIEL, ed., 1990. *W. B. Yeats: The Poems* (London: Dent)

ALEXANDER, PETER, ed., 1958. *William Shakespeare: Complete Works*, 4 vols (London: Collins)

ALLEN, ROSAMUND, 2002. '"Nv seið mid loft-songe": A Reappraisal of Lawman's Verse Form', in *Laȝamon: Contexts, Language, and Interpretation*, ed. by Rosamund Allen, Lucy Perry, & Jane Roberts (London: King's College London Centre for Late Antique and Medieval Studies)

ALLEN, W. SIDNEY, 1973. *Accent and Rhythm: Prosodic Features of Latin and Greek: A Study in Theory and Reconstruction* (Cambridge: CUP)

ALLOTT, K., & M. ALLOTT, ed., 1977. *The Poems of Matthew Arnold* (London: Longman)

AMOURS, F. J., ed., 1897. *Scottish Alliterative Poems in Rhyming Stanzas* (Edinburgh: Blackwood)

ANDREW, MALCOLM, & RONALD WALDRON, eds, 1987. *The Poems of the Pearl Manuscript: 'Pearl', 'Cleanness', 'Patience', 'Sir Gawain and the Green Knight'*, 2nd edn (Exeter: University of Exeter Press)

ARBERRY, A. J., 1965. *Arabic Poetry: A Primer for Students* (Cambridge: CUP)

ARCHANGELI, DIANA, & D. TERENCE LANGENDOEN, 1997. *Optimality Theory: An Overview* (Oxford: Blackwell)

ASPIN, ISABEL S. T., ed., 1953. *Anglo-Norman Political Songs*, ANTS, 11 (Oxford: Blackwell)

ASPLAND, C. W., ed., 1979. *A Medieval French Reader* (Oxford: Clarendon Press)

ATTRIDGE, DEREK, 1982. *The Rhythms of English Poetry*, ELS, 14 (London: Longman)

——1987. 'Poetry Unbound: Observations on "Free Verse"', *Proceedings of the British Academy*, 73: 353–74

AUDEN, W. H., 1966. *Collected Shorter Poems, 1927–1957* (London: Faber and Faber)

AVALLE, D'Arco Silvio, 1963. *Preistoria del endecasillabo* (Milan: Riccardi)

BAEHR, RUDOLF, 1970. *Manual de versificación española*, tr. by K. Wagner & F. López Estrada (Madrid: Gredos)

BAILEY, JAMES O., 1968. 'The Basic Structural Characteristics of Russian Literary Meters', in *Studies Presented to Roman Jakobson by his Students*, ed. by Charles E. Gribble (Cambridge, MA: Slavica), pp. 17–38

——1973A. 'The Accentual Verse of Majakovskij's "Раэговор фининспектором о поээии" [Conversation with a Taxman about Poetry]', in *Slavic Poetics: Essays in Honor of Kiril Taranovsky*, ed. by Roman Jakobson, C. H. van Schooneveld, and Dean S. Worth (The Hague: Mouton), pp. 25–31

——1973B. 'The Evolution and Structure of the Russian Iambic Pentameter from 1880–1922', *International Journal of Slavic Linguistics and Poetics*, 16: 119–46

—— 1976. 'Linguistic Givens and their Metrical Realization in a Poem by Yeats', *Language and Style*, 7: 21–33

—— 1987. 'An Exploration in Comparative Metrics', *Style*, 21: 359–76

BALDI, SERGIO, 1953. *La poesia di Sir Thomas Wyatt* (Florence: Le Monnier)

BANDEIRA, MANUEL, 1962. 'Versificação em lingua portuguesa', in *Enciclopedia Delta-Larousse*, VI (Rio de Janeiro: Delta), pp. 3239–49

BARBER, CHARLES, 1993. *The English Language: A Historical Introduction* (Cambridge: CUP)

BARBER, NICHOLAS, & CHARLES BARBER, 1990–91. 'The Versification of the *Canterbury Tales*: A Computer-Based Statistical Study', *Leeds Studies in English*, 21: 81–103 & 22: 57–84

BARKE, JAMES, ed., 1960. *The Poems and Songs of Robert Burns* (London: Tiger Books)

BARNARD, JOHN, ed., 1977. *John Keats: The Complete Poems* (Harmondsworth: Penguin Books)

BAUM, PAULL F., 1922. *The Principles of English Versification* (Cambridge, MA: Harvard UP)

BAWCUTT, P., & F. RIDDY, eds, 1992. *Selected Poems of Henryson and Dunbar* (Edinburgh: Scottish Academic Press)

BAYO, JUAN CARLOS, 1999. 'La teoría del verso desde el punto de vista lingüístico (el sistema de versificación del *Cantar de Mio Cid*)' (unpublished doctoral thesis, University of Barcelona)

BEADLE, RICHARD, & PAMELA KING, eds, 1984. *York Mystery Plays: A Selection in Modern Spelling* (Oxford: Clarendon Press)

BEARE, WILLIAM, 1957. *Latin Verse and European Song: A Study in Accent and Rhythm* (London: Methuen)

BEER, JOHN, ed., 1974. *S. T. Coleridge: Poems*, 2nd edn (London: Dent)

BELTRAMI, PIETRO G., 1981. *Metrica, poetica, metrica dantesca* (Pisa: Pacini)

—— 1986. 'Cesura epica, lirica, italiana: reflessioni sull'endecasillabo di Dante', *Metrica*, 4: 67–103

—— 1991. *La metrica italiana* (Bologna: Il Mulino)

BENNETT, J. A. W., 1986. *Oxford History of English Literature*, I, 2: *Middle English Literature*, ed. & completed by Douglas Gray (Oxford: Clarendon Press)

BENSON, LARRY E., ed., 1988. *The Riverside Chaucer* (Oxford: OUP)

BERNARD, OLIVER, ed. & tr., 1965. *Apollinaire: Selected Poems* (Harmondsworth: Penguin Books)

BETJEMAN, JOHN, 1958. *Collected Poems*, with an introduction by the Earl of Birkenhead (London: Murray)

BIADENE, LEANDRO, 1899. 'Morfologia del sonetto', *Studi di Filologia Romanza*, 4: 1–234

BILLY, DOMINIQUE, 1989. 'Quelques apports récents à la métrique française', *Bulletin de la Société de Linguistique de Paris*, 84: 283–319

—— 1999. 'Le Décasyllabe rénové de Froissart', *Romania*, 117: 508–44

——2000A. 'Le Flottement de la césure dans le décasyllabe des troubadours', *Critica del Testo*, 3: 587–622

——2000B. 'L'Invention de l'*endecasillabo*', in *'Carmina semper et citharae chordi': études de philologie et de métrique offertes à Aldo Menichetti*, ed. by M.-C. Gérard Zai et al. (Geneva: Slatkine), pp. 31–46

—— & MARTIN J. DUFFELL, 2005. 'Le Décasyllabe de John Gower: le dernier mètre anglo-normand', *Revue de Linguistique Romane*, 69: 73–95

BINYON, LAURENCE, ed., 1995. *The Works of Algernon Charles Swinburne* (Ware: Wordsworth Editions); 1st edn 1940

BIRRELL, ANNE, 2004. *Games Poets Play: Readings in Medieval Chinese Poetry* (Cambridge: McGuinness China Monographs)

BLISS, ALAN J., 1958. *The Metre of 'Beowulf'* (Oxford: Blackwell)

—— 1962. *An Introduction to Old English Metre* (Oxford: Blackwell)

BLOOM, HAROLD, ed., 1966. *Percy Bysshe Shelley: Selected Poetry*, Signet Clasics CQ 342 (New York: New American Library)

BOHIGAS (Balaguer), Pere, ed., 1952–59. *Ausias March: Poesies*, 5 vols, Els Nostres Clàssics, A71–73, 77, & 86 (Barcelona: Barcino)

BOLINGER, DWIGHT, 1958. 'A Theory of Pitch Accent', *Word*, 14: 110–49

BOWNAS, GEOFFREY, 1964. 'Background of Language and Prosody', in Bownas & Thwaite 1964: xxxix–lvii

——& ANTHONY THWAITE, ed. & tr., 1964. *The Penguin Book of Japanese Verse* (Harmondsworth: Penguin Books)

BOWRA, MAURICE, 1963. *Primitive Song*, New American/English Library, MT 499 (New York and London: Mentor Books)

BRADLEY, A. C., 1929. 'Monosyllabic Lines and Words', in Bradley, *A Miscellany* (London: Macmillan), pp. 245–67

BRAUNE, WILHELM, & KARL HELM, 1928. *Althochdeutsches Lesebuch*, 9th edn (Halle: Niemeyer)

BRETT, R. L., & A. R. JONES, eds, 1991. *Wordsworth and Coleridge: Lyrical Ballads*, 2nd edn (London: Routledge)

BREWER, R. S., 1925. *Orthometry: The Art of Versification and the Technicalities of Poetry, with a New and Complete Rhyming Dictionary* (Edinburgh: John Grant); 1st edn 1893

BRIDGES, ROBERT, 1947. *The Poetical Works of Robert Bridges, Excluding the Eight Dramas and 'The Testament of Beauty'*, 2nd edn (London: OUP)

BRONOWSKI, J, ed., 1958. *William Blake: A Selection of Poems and Letters* (Harmondsworth: Penguin Books)

BROOKS, DAVID, ed., 1992. *A. D. Hope: Selected Poems* (London: HarperCollins)

BROWER, ROBERT H., 1972. 'Japanese', in Wimsatt 1972: 38–51

BULLETT, GERALD, ed., 1947. *Silver Poets of the Sixteenth Century* (London: Dent)

BURGER, MICHEL, 1957. *Recherches sur la structure et l'origine des vers romans* (Geneva: Droz)

BYROM, THOMAS, ed., 1970. *Henry Wadsworth Longfellow: Poems* (London: Dent)

CABLE, THOMAS M., 1974. *The Meter and Melody of 'Beowulf'* (Urbana: University of Illinois Press)

—— 1988. 'Middle English Meter and its Theoretical Implications', *Yale Language Studies*, 2: 47–69

—— 1989. 'Old and Middle English Prosody: Transformations of the Model', in *Hermeneutics and Medieval Culture*, ed. by Patrick J. Gallacher & Helen Damico (Albany, NY: SUNY Press), pp. 201–11

—— 1991. *The English Alliterative Tradition* (Philadelphia: University of Pennsylvania Press)

CABRÉ, MIRIAM, 1999. *Cerverí de Girona and his Poetic Traditions*, CT, A169 (London: Tamesis)

CAMPBELL, ALISTAIR, 1962. REVIEW OF LORD 1960, *Modern Language Review*, 57: 75

CAMPBELL, LILY B., ed., 1938. *The Mirror for Magistrates* (Cambridge: CUP)

CANO, JUAN, 1931. 'La importancia relativa del acento y de la sílaba en la versificación española', *Romanic Review*, 22: 223–33

CARPER, THOMAS, & DEREK ATTRIDGE, 2003. *Meter and Meaning: An Introduction to Rhythm in Poetry* (New York: Routledge)

CARVALHO, AMORIM DE, 1965. *Tratado de versificação portuguesa*, 2nd edn (Lisbon: Portugália Editora)

CASAS HOMS, JOSÉ MARÍA, ed., 1956. *'Torçimany' de Luis de Averçó: tratado retórico gramatical y diccionario de rimas, siglos XIV–XV*, 2 vols (Barcelona: CSIC)

CAWLEY, A. C., ed., 1956. *'Everyman' and Medieval Miracle Plays*, Everyman's Library, 381 (London: Dent)

CECIL, LORD DAVID, ed., 1971. *A Choice of Tennyson's Verse* (London: Faber and Faber)

CHAMBERS, FRANK M., 1985. *An Introduction to Old Provençal Versification*, Memoirs of the American Philosophical Society, 167 (Philadelphia: American Philosophical Society)

CHAMPION, PIERRE, ed., 1907. *Le Manuscrit autographe des poésies de Charles d'Orléans* (Paris: Honoré Champion)

CHATMAN, SEYMOUR, 1965. *A Theory of Meter* (The Hague: Mouton)

CHICOTE, GLORIA, ed., 2002. *Romancero tradicional argentino*, PMHRS, 25 (London: QMW)

CHILD, F. J., 1863. 'Observations on the Language of Chaucer (Based on Wright's Edition of the *Canterbury Tales*)', *Memoirs of the American Academy of Arts and Sciences*, NS, 8: 445–502 & 9: 265–314

CLARKE, DOROTHY CLOTELLE, 1955. 'Versification in Alfonso el Sabio's *Cantigas*', *Hispanic Review*, 23: 83–98

—— 1964. *Morphology of Fifteenth Century Castilian Verse*, Duquesne Studies, Philological Series, 4 (Pittsburgh: Duquesne UP; Louvain: Nauwelaerts)

—— 1973. *Juan de Mena's 'Laberinto de Fortuna': Classic Epic and 'Mester de clerecía'*, Romance Monographs, 5 (University, MS: Romance Monographs)

CLARKE, G. M., & D. COOKE, 1983. *A Basic Course in Statistics*, 2nd edn (London: Edward Arnold)

COETZEE, J. M., 2002. *Stranger Shores: Essays 1986–1999* (London: Vintage)

COLDWELL, DAVID F., ed., 1957. *Virgil's 'Aeneid' Translated into Scottish Verse by Gawain Douglas, Bishop of Dunkeld* (Edinburgh: Blackwood)

COLE, THOMAS, 1969. 'The Saturnian Verse', *Yale Classical Studies*, 21: 1–73

CORNULIER, BENOÎT DE, 1995. *Art poétique: notions et problèmes de métrique* (Lyon: Presses Universitaires de Lyon)

CORRIENTE, FEDERICO, 1997. *Poesía dialectal árabe y romance en Andalús*, BRH, 2.407 (Madrid: Gredos)

CORSO, GREGORY, LAWRENCE FERLINGHETTI, & ALLEN GINSBERG, 1963. *Penguin Modern Poets*, 5 (Harmondsworth: Penguin Books)

CREED, ROBERT PAYSON, 1966. 'A New Approach to the Rhythm of *Beowulf*', *PMLA*, 81: 23–33

—— 1990. *Reconstructing the Rhythm of 'Beowulf'* (Columbia and London: University of Missouri Press)

CREIGHTON, T. R. M., ed., 1977. *Poems of Thomas Hardy*, 2nd edn (London: Macmillan)

CRESSMAN, RUSSELL RALPH, 1983. 'Gower's *Cinkante Balades* and French Court Lyrics' (unpublished doctoral thesis, University of North Carolina at Chapel Hill)

CRYSTAL, DAVID, ed., 1982. *Linguistic Controversies: Essays in Honour of F. R. Palmer* (London: Edward Arnold)

—— 1985. *A Dictionary of Linguistics and Phonetics*, 2nd edn (Oxford: Blackwell)

CULLER, JONATHAN, 1975. *Structuralist Poetics: Structuralism, Linguistics and the Study of Literature* (London: Routledge & Kegan Paul)

CUMMINGS, E. E., 1960. *Selected Poems 1923–1958* (London: Faber and Faber)

CUNLIFFE, JOHN W., ed., 1912. *Early English Classical Tragedies* (Oxford: Clarendon Press)

CURTIUS, ERNST ROBERT, 1953. *European Literature and the Latin Middle Ages*, tr. by Willard R. Trask (London: Routledge & Kegan Paul)

DAVIES, WALFORD, ed., 1974. *Dylan Thomas: Selected Poems* (London: Dent)

DAVIS, WALTER R., ed., 1970. *The Works of Thomas Campion* (New York: Norton)

DAY LEWIS, C., 1955. 'Introduction', in Frost 1955: 13–18

——, ed., 1963. *The Collected Poems of Wilfred Owen* (London: Chatto & Windus)

DELOFFRE, FRÉDÉRIC, 1973. *Le vers français*, 3rd edn (Paris: SEDES)

DEYERMOND, A. D., 1971. *A Literary History of Spain: The Middle Ages* (London: Ernest Benn)

DOBRÉE, BONAMY, ed., 1924. *Alexander Pope: Collected Poems* (London: Dent)

DOMÍNGUEZ CAPARRÓS, JOSÉ, 2000. *Métrica española*, 2nd edn (Madrid: Síntesis)

——2002. *Métrica de Cervantes*, Bibioteca de Estudios Cervantinos, 10 (Alcalá de Henares: Centro de Estudios Cervantinos)

——, ed., 2001. *Sinibaldo de Mas: Sistema musical de la lengua castellana*, Anejos de Revista de Literatura, 52 (Madrid: CSIC)

DOMINICY, MARC, 1992. 'On the Meter and Prosody of French 12-Syllable Verse', in *Foundations of Verse*, ed. by M. Grimaux, special issue of *Empirical Studies of the Arts*, 10: 157–81

——2003. 'Tendances du décasyllabe espagnol au XXe siècle', in *Le Sens et le Mesure: de la pragmatique à la métrique: hommages à Benoît de Cornulier*, ed. by J.-L. Aroui (Paris: Honoré Champion), pp. 541–67

DONALDSON, E. TALBOT, 1948. 'Chaucer's Final -e', *PMLA*, 63: 1101–24

——1974. 'The Manuscripts of Chaucer's Works and their Use', in *Writers and their Backgrounds: Geoffrey Chaucer*, ed. by Derek Brewer (London: Bell), pp. 85–108

DONALDSON, IAN, ed., 1975. *Ben Jonson: Poems* (London: OUP)

DORCHAIN, AUGUSTE, 1919. *L'Art des vers*, 2nd edn (Paris: Garnier)

DRABBLE, MARGARET, ed., 1985. *The Oxford Companion to English Literature*, 2nd edn (Oxford: OUP)

DRONKE, URSULA, ed. & tr., 1969. *Edda*, 1: *Heroic Poems* (Oxford: Clarendon Press)

DU MÉRIL, EDÉLESTAND, 1843. *Poésies populaires latines antérieures au douzième siècle* (Paris: Brockhaus et Avenarius)

DUFFELL, MARTIN J., 1987. 'The Metre of Santillana's Sonnets', *MAe*, 56: 276–303

——1991. 'The Romance (Hen-)decasyllable: An Exercise in Comparative Metrics' (unpublished doctoral thesis, University of London)

——1994. 'The Metrics of Ausias March in a European Context', *MAe*, 63: 287–300

——1996. 'Chaucer, Gower, and the History of the Hendecasyllable', in *English Historical Metrics*, ed. by C. B. McCully & J. J. Anderson (Cambridge: CUP), pp. 210–18

——1999A. 'Accentual Regularity in the *Sainte Eulalie*', *Rivista di Studi Testuali*, NS, 1: 81–108

——1999B. *Modern Metrical Theory and the 'Verso de arte mayor'*, PMHRS, 10 (London: QMW)

——1999C. 'The Metric Cleansing of Hispanic Verse', *BHS* (Liverpool), 76: 151–68

—— 2000A. 'Lydgate's Metrical Inventiveness and his Debt to Chaucer', in Kennedy 2000b: 227–49

——2000B. '"The Craft So Long to Lerne": Chaucer's Invention of the Iambic Pentameter', *CR*, 34 (1999–2000): 269–88

——2000C. 'The Santillana Factor: The Development of Double Audition in Castilian', in *Santillana: A Symposium*, ed. by Alan Deyermond, PMHRS, 28 (London: QMW), pp. 113–28

——2001. 'From Vidal to Lentini: History, Heresy, and Metrics', in Michaux & Dominicy 2001: 151–71

——2002A. 'Don Rodrigo and Sir Gawain: Family Likeness or Convergent Development?', in *'Mio Cid' Studies: 'Some Problems of Diplomatic' Fifty Years On*, PMHRS, 42 (London: QMW), pp. 129–50

——2002B. 'The Italian Line in English after Chaucer', *Language and Literature*, 11: 291–305

——2003. 'French Symmetry, Germanic Rhythm, and Spanish Metre', in *Chaucer and the Challenge of Medievalism: Studies in Honor of H. A. Kelly*, ed. by Donka Minkova & Theresa Tinkle (Bern: Peter Lang), pp. 105–27

——2005. 'Some Phonological Features of Insular French: A Reconstruction', in *Studies on Ibero-Romance Linguistics Dedicated to Ralph Penny*, ed. by Roger Wright & Peter Ricketts (Newark, DE: Juan de la Cuesta), pp. 103–25

——2007. 'Security and Surprise in the Versification of the *Cancioneros*', in *From the 'Cancioneiro da Vaticana' to the 'Cancionero general': Studies in Honour of Jane Whetnall*, ed. by Alan Deyermond and Barry Taylor, PMHRS, 60 (London: QMW), pp. 161–76

——& DOMINIQUE BILLY, 2004. 'From Decasyllable to Pentameter: Gower's Contribution to English Metrics', *CR*, 38 (2003–04): 383–401

DUGGAN, HOYT N., 1986. 'The Shape of the B-Verse in Middle English Alliterative Poetry', *Speculum*, 61: 564–92

——1987. 'Towards a Theory of Langland's Meter', *Yearbook of Langland Studies*, 1: 41–70

——1988. 'Final -e and the Rhythmic Structure of the B-Verse in Middle English Alliterative Poetry', *MPh*, 86 (1988–89): 119–45

——1996. 'Libertine Scribes and Maidenly Editors: Meditations on Textual Criticism and Metrics', in McCully & Anderson 1996: 219–37

——& THORLAC TURVILLE PETRE, eds, 1989. *The Wars of Alexander*, EETS, SS, 10 (Oxford: OUP)

DUNN, C. J., & S. YANADA, 1958. *Teach Yourself Japanese* (London: Hodder and Stoughton)

DUPARC-QUIOC, SUZANNE, ed., 1976. *La Chanson d'Antioche*, Documents Relatifs à l'Histoire des Croisades, 9 (Paris: Académie d'Inscription et Belles Lettres)

EDWARDS, ROBERT R., ed., 1998. *John Lydgate: Troy Book* (Kalamazoo, MI: Medieval Institution Publications, West Michigan University)

ELCOCK, W. D., 1975. *The Romance Languages*, 2nd edn (London: Faber and Faber)

ELIOT, T. S., 1957. *On Poetry and Poets* (London: Faber and Faber)

——1963. *Collected Poems* (London: Faber and Faber)

——, ed., 1959. *Ezra Pound: Selected Poems* (London: Faber and Faber)

——, ed., 1960. *Literary Essays of Ezra Pound* (London: Faber and Faber)

ELWERT, W. THEODOR, 1965. *Traité de versification française* (Paris: Klincksieck)

——1973. *Versificazione italiana dalle origini ai giorni nostri* (Florence: Le Monnier)

ENDICOTT, ANNABEL M., 1963. 'A Critical Study of Metrical Effects in the Poetry of Sir Thomas Wyatt, with Reference to Analogous Effects in Elizabethan Poetry' (unpublished master's thesis, University of London)

ERNE, LUKAS, 2004. *Shakespeare as Literary Dramatist* (Cambridge: CUP)

EWERT, ALFRED, 1943. *The French Language*, 2nd edn (London: Faber and Faber)

FABB, NIGEL, 1997. *Language in the Verbal Arts of the World* (Oxford: Blackwell)

——2001. 'Weak Monosyllables in Iambic Pentameter Verse and the Communication of Metrical Form', *Lingua*, 111: 771–90

——2002A. *Language and Literary Structure: The Linguistic Analysis of Form in Verse and Narrative* (Cambridge: CUP)

——2002B. 'The Metres of *Dover Beach*', *Language and Literature*, 11: 99–117

——& MORRIS HALLE, 2005. 'Pairs and Triplets: A Theory of Metrical Verse' (unpublished paper presented at the Colloque International, Typologie des Formes Poétiques, CNRS & Université de Paris VIII, 8–9 April)

FAULKES, ANTHONY, ed. & tr., 1995. *Snorri Sturluson: Edda* (London: Dent; Rutland, VT: Tuttle)

FEIN, SUSANNA GREER, 2000. 'The Early Thirteen-Line Stanza: Style and Metrics Reconsidered', in Kennedy 2000b: 97–126

FERGUSON, WILLIAM, 1981. *La versificación imitativa en Fernando de Herrera*, CT, A77 (London: Tamesis)

FLOWER, SIR DESMOND, ed., 1967. *The Poetical Works of Ernest Christopher Dowson* (London: Cassell & Co)

FRANK, ISTVÁN, 1953–57. *Répertoire métrique de la poésie des troubadours*, 2 vols, Bibliothèque de l'École des Hautes Études, Sciences Historiques et Philologiques, 302 & 308 (Paris: Champion)

FRANKEL, HANS H., 'Classical Chinese', in Wimsatt 1972: 22–37

FRASER, G. S., 1970. *Metre, Rhyme and Free Verse*, The Critical Idiom, 8 (London: Methuen)

FRIEDBERG, NILA, 2005. 'How to Translate W. H. Auden into Russian: Translation as Tribute' (unpublished paper presented at the Colloque International, Typologie des Formes Poétiques, CNRS & Université de Paris VIII, 8–9 April)

FROST, ROBERT, 1955. *Selected Poems*, with an introduction by C. Day Lewis (Harmondsworth: Penguin Books)

FRY, DENNIS, 1958. 'Experiments in the Perception of Stress', *Language and Speech*, 1: 126–52

FRY, STEPHEN, 2005. *The Ode Less Travelled: Unlocking the Poet Within* (London: Hutchinson)

FURNIVALL, F. J., ed., 1897. *Hoccleve's Works: The Minor Poems*, II, ed. by I. Gollancz, EETS, ES, 73 (London: OUP)

FUSSELL, PAUL, 1972. 'English: Historical', in Wimsatt 1972: 191–203

GALLARATI, SILVIA BUZZETTI, 1978. 'Artifici metrico-prosodici e versificazione francese antica', *Metrica*, 1: 55–77

GARCIA, MICHEL, 1978. 'Versificación', in Pero López de Ayala, *Libro de poemas, o Rimado de Palacio*, ed. by Michel García, BRH, 4.12 (Madrid: Gredos), pp. 41–58

GARDNER, HELEN, ed., 1972. *The New Oxford Book of English Verse, 1250–1950* (Oxford: Clarendon Press)

GARDNER, W. H., ed., 1953. *Poems and Prose of Gerard Manley Hopkins* (Harmondsworth: Penguin Books)

GARROD, W. H., ed., 1947. *Q. Horatius Flaccus: Opera* , 2nd edn (Oxford: Clarendon Press)

GASPAROV, M. L., 1980A. 'Italianskij stikh: sillabika ili sillabo-tonika? Opyt ispol'zovanija verojatnostnykh modelej stikhovedenii' [Italian Verse: Syllabic or Syllabo-Tonic? An Experiment in Using Probability Models in Metrics], in *Problemy strukturnoj lingvistiki*, V, ed. by P. Grigorjev (Moscow: Nauka), pp. 199–218

—— 1980B. 'Quantitative Methods in Russian Metrics: Achievements and Prospects', in Smith 1980: 1–20

—— 1987. 'A Probability Model of Verse (English, Latin, French, Italian, Spanish, Portuguese)', tr. by Marina Tarlinskaja, *Style*, 21: 322–58

—— 1996. *A History of European Versification*, tr. by G. S. Smith & Marina Tarlinskaja, ed. by G. S. Smith with L. Holford-Strevens (Oxford: Clarendon Press)

—— 1999. *Metr i smysl: ob odnom iz mekhanizmov kul'turnoi parmiati* [Metre and Meaning: On One Mechanism of Cultural Memory] (Moscow: RGGU)

GAUR, ALBERTINE, 1984. *A History of Writing* (London: British Library)

GETTY, PAUL, 2002. *The Metre of 'Beowulf': A Constraint-Based Approach* (Berlin and New York: Mouton de Gruyter)

GIBB, HAMILTON A. R., 1963. *Arabic Literature*, 2nd edn (Oxford: Clarendon Press)

GIEGERICH, HEINZ J., 1980. 'On Stress-Timing in English Phonology', *Lingua*, 51: 187–221

—— 1985. *Metrical Phonology and Phonological Structure: German and English* (Cambridge: CUP)

GILDERSLEEVE, B. K., & GONZÁLEZ LODGE, 1953. *Latin Grammar*, 3rd edn (London: Macmillan)

GILL, STEPHEN, ed., 1984. *The Oxford Authors: William Wordsworth* (Oxford: OUP)

GINSBERG, ALLEN, 1996. *Selected Poems 1947–1995* (Harmondsworth: Penguin Books)

GODLEY, A. D., ed., 1910. *The Poetical Works of Thomas Moore* (London: OUP)

GÓMEZ-BRAVO, ANA M., 1998. *Repertorio métrico de la poesía cancioneril del siglo XV*, Poetria Nova, Serie Maior, 1 (Alcalá de Henares: Universidad de Alcalá)

GOODWIN, KEN, 1986. *A History of Australian Literature* (London: Macmillan)

GORNALL, JOHN, 2000. 'One Summer Does Make a Swallow: Assonance in Galician-Portuguese *Cantigas*', BHS (Liverpool), 77: 397–406

GRAMMONT, MAURICE, 1937. *Le Vers français: ses moyens d'expression, son harmonie*, 4th edn (Paris: Delagrave)

GRAVES, ROBERT, 1961. *The White Goddess* (London: Faber and Faber)

—— 1965. *Collected Poems* (London: Cassell)

——, ed., 1957. *English and Scottish Ballads* (London: Heinemann)

GRAY, J. M., ed., 1935. *Scottish Poetry from Barbour to James VI* (London: Dent)

GRIGSON, GEOFFREY, ed., 1970. *A Choice of Southey's Verse* (London: Faber and Faber)

GROSS, HARVEY, 1972. 'Prosodia come musica', in *La metrica*, ed. by Renzo Cremante & Mario Pazzaglia (Bologna: Il Mulino), pp. 125–30; first publ. in Harvey Gross, *Sound and Form in Modern Poetry* (Ann Arbor: University of Michigan Press, 1964)

——, ed., 1979. *The Structure of Verse: Modern Essays on Prosody*, 2nd edn (New York: Echo Press)

HALL, DONALD, ed., 1968. *A Choice of Whitman's Verse* (London: Faber and Faber)

HALL, JOSEPH, ed., 1901. *'King Horn': A Middle English Romance* (Oxford: Clarendon Press)

HALLE, MORRIS, 1997A. 'Metrical Verse in the Psalms', in *India and Beyond*, ed. by D. van der Meij (London and New York: Kegan Paul), pp. 207–25

—— 1997B. 'On Stress and Accent in Indo-European', *Language*, 73: 275–313

——& SAMUEL J. KEYSER, 1966. 'Chaucer and the Study of Prosody', *CE*, 28 (1966–67): 187–219

——& SAMUEL J. KEYSER, 1971. 'Illustration and Defense of a Theory of the Iambic Pentameter', *CE*, 33 (1971–72): 154–76

HAMER, RICHARD, ed. & TR., 1970. *A Choice of Anglo-Saxon Verse* (London: Faber and Faber)

HAMILTON, A. C., ed., 1966. *Edmund Spenser: Selected Poetry* (London: New English Library)

HAMMOND, ELEANOR PRESCOTT, 1925. 'The Nine-Syllabled Pentameter Line in Some Post-Chaucerian Manuscripts', *MPh*, 23: 129–52

—— 1927. *English Verse between Chaucer and Surrey* (Durham, NC: Duke UP; repr. New York: Octagon, 1965)

HAMMOND, PAUL, 1997. 'Optimality Theory and Prosody', in Archangeli & Langendoen 1997: 33–58

HANSON, KRISTIN, 1991. 'Resolution in Modern Meters' (unpublished doctoral thesis, Stanford University)

—— 1995A. 'Non-Lexical Word Stress in the Iambic Pentameters of John Donne' (unpublished paper, Department of English, University of California at Berkeley)

—— 1995B. 'Prosodic Constituents of Poetic Meter', *Proceedings of the West Coast Conference on Formal Linguistics*, 13: 62–77 (Stanford: CSLI Publications)

—— 1996. 'From Dante to Pinsky: A Theoretical Perspective on the History of the English Iambic Pentameter', *Rivista di Linguistica*, 9: 53–97

—— 2001. 'Quantitative Meter in English: The Lesson of Sir Philip Sidney', *English Language and Linguistics*, 5: 41–91

—— 2002. 'Vowel Variation in English Full Rhymes' (unpublished paper, Department of English, University of California at Berkeley)

——& PAUL KIPARSKY, 1996. 'A Parametric Theory of Poetic Meter', *Language*, 72: 287–335

HANSSEN, FEDERICO, 1913. 'Los endecasílabos de Alfonso X', *Bulletin Hispanique*, 15: 284–99

HARRISON, JOHN, ed., 1949. *William Shakespeare: The Sonnets and 'A Lover's Complaint'*, The Penguin Shakespeare, 18 (Harmondsworth: Penguin Books)

HARTMAN, CHARLES O., 1980. *Free Verse: An Essay on Prosody* (Princeton: Princeton UP)

HASCALL, DUDLEY L., 1970. 'The Prosody of John Lydgate', *Language and Style*, 3: 122–46

HAYES, BRUCE, 1989. 'The Prosodic Hierarchy in Poetic Meter', in *Phonetics and Phonology*, I: *Rhythm and Meter*, ed. by Paul Kiparsky & Gilbert Youmans (San Diego, CA: Academic Press), pp. 201–60

—— 1995. *Metrical Stress Theory: Principles and Case Studies* (Chicago: University of Chicago Press)

HEANEY, SEAMUS, 1990. *New Selected Poems 1966–1987* (London: Faber and Faber)

—— 1999. *Beowulf: A New Translation* (London: Faber and Faber)

HENDERSON, HAROLD H., ed. & tr., 1958. *An Introduction to Haiku: An Anthology of Poems and Poets from Basho to Shiki*, Anchor Books, 150 (New York: Doubleday)

HENDERSON, PHILIP, ed., 1931. *The Complete Works of John Skelton, Laureate* (London: Dent)

HENRY, ALBERT, ed., 1953. *Chrestomathie de la littérature en ancien français* (Bern: Francke)

HESELTINE, HARRY, ed., 1972. *The Penguin Book of Australian Verse* (Harmondsworth: Penguin Books)

HEUSLER, ANDREAS, 1891. 'Zur Metrik des altsächsischen und hochdeutschen Alliterationsverses', *Germania*, 36: 139–79 & 279–307

HIDDEN, NORMAN, 1979. 'The State of Poetry Today', *New Poetry*, 44: 27–32

HIRTZEL, FREDERICK ARTHUR, ed., 1900. *P. Vergilius Maro: Opera* (Oxford: Clarendon Press)

HITCHCOCK, RICHARD, 1977. *The Kharjas*, Research Bibliographies and Checklists, 20 (London: Grant & Cutler)

HOBSBAUM, PHILIP, 1996. *Metre, Rhythm and Verse Form* (London and New York: Routledge)

HOGG, RICHARD M., & CHRISTOPHER B. McCULLY, 1987. *Metrical Phonology: A Course Book* (Cambridge: CUP)

HOLLANDER, JOHN, 1981. *Rhyme's Reason: A Guide to English Verse* (New Haven: Yale UP)

HOLT, ROBERT, ed., 1878. *Ormulum*, with notes and glossary by R. M. White (Oxford: Clarendon Press)

HOPE, A. D., 1966. *Collected Poems* (Sydney: Angus & Robertson)

HOPKINS, KENNETH, 1973. *The Poets Laureate*, 3rd edn (Wakefield: EP Publishing)

HOWELL, A. G. FERRERS, tr., 1973. *Dante Alighieri: De vulgari eloquentiâ* (London: Rebel Press)

HRUSHOVSKI, BENJAMIN, 1960. 'On Free Rhythms in Modern Poetry: Preliminary Remarks towards a Critical Theory of their Structures and Function', in Sebeok 1960: 173–90

HUGHES, TED, 1995. *New Selected Poems 1957–1994* (London: Faber and Faber)

—— 1998. *Birthday Letters* (London: Faber and Faber)

——, ed., 1971. *A Choice of Shakespeare's Verse* (London: Faber and Faber)

——, ed., 1981. *Sylvia Plath: Collected Poems* (London: Faber and Faber)

HURFORD, JAMES R., 1987. *Language and Number: The Emergence of a Cognitive System* (Oxford: Blackwell)

JACK, IAN, ed., 1970. *Robert Browning: Poems 1833–1864* (London: OUP)

JACKSON KNIGHT, W. F., 1944. *Roman Vergil*, 2nd edn (London: Faber and Faber)

JAKOBSON, ROMAN, 1952. 'Studies in Comparative Slav Metrics', *Oxford Slavonic Papers*, 3: 21–66

—— 1960. 'Linguistics and Poetics', in Sebeok 1960: 350–77

—— 1973. 'Principes de versification', in *Questions de poétique*, ed. by T. Todorov, tr. by Léon Robel (Paris: Éditions du Seuil), pp. 44–55

JASINSKI, MAX, 1903. *Histoire du sonnet en France* (Douai: H. Brugère, A. Dalsheimer; repr. Geneva: Slatkine, 1970)

JEFFERSON, JUDITH A., 1987. 'The Hoccleve Monographs and Hoccleve's Metrical Practice', in *Later Middle English Literature*, ed. by Derek Pearsall (Woodbridge and Wolfboro: Brewer)

——2000. 'The Hoccleve Monographs and Hoccleve's Metrical Practice: More than Counting Syllables?', in Kennedy 2000b: 203–26

JOHNSON, THOMAS H., ed., 1960. *The Complete Poems of Emily Dickinson* (Boston: Little, Brown)

JOHNSON, JERI, ed., 1993. *James Joyce: Ulysses* (Oxford: OUP)

JUSTICE, DONALD, 1979. 'Meters and Memory', in Gross 1979: 269–76

KASTNER, L. E., 1903. *A History of French Versification* (Oxford: Clarendon Press)

KEENE, DENNIS, ed., 1985. *Henry Howard, Earl of Surrey: Selected Poems* (Manchester: Carcanet)

KELLY, H. A., 1986. 'Pronouncing Latin Words in English', *Classical World*, 80 (1986–87): 33–37

——1988. 'Lawyers' Latin: *Loquenda ut vulgus?*', *Journal of Legal Education*, 38: 195–207

KENNEDY, GEORGE A., 1980. 'Metrical Irregularity in the Shih Ching', in *Selected Works of George A. Kennedy*, ed. by Tien-Yi-Li (New Haven: Far Eastern Publications, Yale University), pp. 10–26

KENNEDY, RUTH, ed., 1991. 'The Alliterative Katherine Hymn: A Stanzaic Poem of the Late Fourteenth Century' (unpublished doctoral thesis, University of Bristol)

——1999. 'New Theories of Constraint in the Metricality of the Strong-Stress Long Line as Applied to the Rhymed Corpus of Late Middle English Alliterative Verse', in Billy 1999: 131–44

——2000A. 'Strong-Stress Metre in Fourteen-Line Stanza Forms', in Kennedy 2000b: 127–55

——, ed., 2000B. *Medieval English Measures: Studies in Metre and Versification*, special issue of *Parergon*, NS, 18.1

KER, W. P., 1898. 'Analogies between English and Spanish Verse (*Arte mayor)*', *Transactions of the Philological Society*, 113–28

KERKHOF, MAXIM, ed., 1995. JUAN DE MENA, *Laberinto de Fortuna*, Biblioteca Nueva de Erudición y Crítica, 9 (Madrid: Castalia)

KEYSER, SAMUEL J., 1969. 'Old English Prosody', *CE*, 30 (1968–69): 331–56

KIPARSKY, PAUL, 1975. 'Stress, Syntax, and Meter', *Language*, 51: 576–616

——1977. 'The Linguistic Structure of English Verse', *LIn*, 8: 189–247

——1989. 'Sprung Rhythm', in Kiparsky & Youmans 1989: 305–40

——& GILBERT YOUMANS, eds, 1989. *Phonetics and Phonology*, 1: *Rhythm and Meter* (San Diego, CA: Academic Press)

KIPLING, RUDYARD, 1990. *The Complete Verse* (London: Kyle Cathie)

KIRSCHBAUM, LEO, ed., 1961. *Spenser: Selected Poetry*, 2nd edn (New York: Holt, Rinehart and Winston)

KOSTER, W. J. W., 1929. 'Versus saturnius', *Mnemosyne*, NS, 57: 267–346

LAVAUD, RENÉ, & GEORGES MACHICOT, ed. & tr., 1950. *Boecis: poème sur Boèce (fragment): le plus ancien texte littéraire occitan* (Toulouse: Institut d'Études Occitanes)

LÁZARO CARRETER, FERNANDO, 1972. 'La poética del arte mayor castellano', in *Studia hispanica in honorem Rafael Lapesa*, 1 (Madrid: Gredos and Cátedra Seminario Menéndez Pidal), pp. 343–78

LEAVIS, F. R., 1924. *Revaluation* (London: Chatto & Windus)

LEECH, GEOFFREY, 1969. *A Linguistic Guide to English Poetry*, ELS, 4 (London: Longman)

LEGGE, M. DOMINICA, 1963. *Anglo-Norman Literature and its Background* (Oxford: Clarendon Press)

LEHMAN, WINFRED P., 1993. *Theoretical Bases of Indo-European Linguistics* (London and New York: Routledge)

LEONARD, JOHN, ed., 1998. *John Milton: The Complete Poems* (Harmondsworth: Penguin Books)

Levi, Peter, 1985. *A History of Greek Literature* (Harmondsworth: Viking)

Lewis, Charlton M., 1898. *The Foreign Sources of English Versification* (New York: H. Holt)

Lewis, C. S., 1938. 'The Fifteenth-Century Heroic Line', *Essays and Studies*, 24: 28–41

—— 1954. *English Literature in the Sixteenth Century*, Oxford History of English Literature, 3 (London: OUP)

Liberman, Mark Y., & Alan Prince, 1977. 'On Stress and Linguistic Rhythm', *LIn*, 8: 249–336

Litz, A. Walton, & Christopher MacGowan, eds, 1987–88. *The Collected Poems of William Carlos Williams*, 2 vols (Manchester: Carcanet)

Lord, Albert B., 1960. *The Singer of Tales*, Harvard Studies in Comparative Literature, 24 (Cambridge, MA: Harvard UP)

Lote, Georges, 1939. 'Les Origines des vers français', *Annales de la Faculté des Lettres d'Aix*, 21: 219–325

Lotz, John, 1960. 'Metric Typology', in Sebeok 1960: 135–48

Lowell, Robert, 1963. *Selected Poems* (London: Faber and Faber)

Lucas, F. L., ed., 1927. *The Complete Works of John Webster*, 4 vols (London: Chatto & Windus)

Luecke, Jane-Marie, 1978. *Measuring Old English Rhythm: An Application of the Principles of Gregorian Chant to the Meter of 'Beowulf'*, Literary Monographs, 9 (Madison: University of Wisconsin Press)

Macaulay, G. C., ed., 1899. *The Complete Works of John Gower, I: The French Works* (Oxford: Clarendon Press)

——, ed., 1901. *The Complete Works of John Gower, II & III: The English Works*, and IV: *The Latin Works* (Oxford: Clarendon Press)

MacBain, William, ed., 1964. *The Life of St Catherine by Clemence of Barking*, ANTS, 18 (Oxford: Blackwell)

McCabe, Richard A., ed., 1999. *Edmund Spenser: The Minor Poems* (Harmondsworth: Penguin Books)

McConnell, Frank D., ed., 1978. *Byron's Poetry: Authoritative Texts, Letters and Journals, Criticism, Images of Byron* (New York: Norton)

MacCracken, H. N., ed., 1911. *The Minor Poems of John Lydgate, I: The Lydgate Canon and Religious Poems*, EETS, ES, 107 (London: OUP)

McGann, Jerome J., ed., 1994. Lord Byron, *Selected Poetry* (Oxford: OUP)

Mack, Douglas F., ed., 1970. James Hogg, *Selected Poems* (Oxford: Clarendon Press)

Mackenzie, Mackay, ed., 1939. *The Kingis Quair* (London: Faber and Faber)

Macrí, Oreste, 1979. *Ensayo de métrica sintagmática* (Madrid: Gredos)

Margoliouth, H. M., ed., 1971. *The Poems and Letters of Andrew Marvell*, rev. by Pierre Legouis with E. E. Duncan-Jones (Oxford: Clarendon Press)

Marouzeau, Jean, 1931. *La Prononciation du latin* (Paris: Les Belles Lettres)

Marti, Mario, ed., 1970. *Giovanni Boccaccio: Opere minori in volgare, II: Filostrato etc.* (Milan: Rizzoli)

Martínez, H. Salvador, 1975. *El 'Poema de Almería' y la épica románica*, BRH, 2.219 (Madrid: Gredos)

Mazaleyrat, Jean, & Georges Molinié, 1989. *Vocabulaire de la stylistique* (Paris: PUF)

Meillet, P. J. Antoine, 1923. *Les Origines indo-européennes des mètres grecs* (Paris: PUF)

Menichetti, Aldo, 1993. *Metrica italiana: fondamenti, prosodia, rima*, Medioevo e Umanesmo, 83 (Padua: Antenore)

Merrilees, Brian, 2003. 'John Gower's French' (unpublished paper, Department of French, University of Toronto)

Meunier, J.-M., ed., 1933. *La Vie de Saint Alexis: poème français du XIe siècle* (Paris: Droz)

MEYER, BRUNO, 1909. *Primer of Irish Metrics* (Dublin: School of Irish Learning)

MICHAEL, IAN, ed., 1987. *Poema de mio Cid*, 2nd edn, Clásicos Castalia, 75 (Madrid: Castalia)

MICHAUX, CHRISTINE, & MARC DOMINICY, eds, 2001. *Linguistic Approaches to Poetry*, special issue of *Belgian Journal of Linguistics*, 15.1

MIGNE, J. P., ed., 1844. *Gautier de Châtillon: Alexandreis*, in *Cursus Patrilogiae Latinae*, 209: cols 459–74

MILÁ Y FONTANALS, MANUEL, 1893. 'De la poesía popular gallega', in Milá y Fontanals, *Obras completas*, V (Barcelona: Alberto Verdaguer), pp. 363–93

MILLER, GEORGE A., 1956. 'The Magical Number Seven Plus or Minus Two', *Psychological Review*, 63: 81–97

MINKOVA, DONKA, 1987. 'The Prosodic Character of Early Schwa Deletion in English', in *Papers from the 7th International Conference on Historical Linguistics*, ed. by Anna Giacalone Ramat, Onofrio Carruba, & Giuliano Bernini, CILT, 48 (Amsterdam: John Benjamins), pp. 445–57

——1990. 'Adjectival Inflexion Relics and Speeech Rhythm in Late Middle and Early Modern English', in *Papers from the 5th International Conference on Historical Linguistics*, ed. by Sylvia Adamson, Vivien A. Law, Nigel Vincent, & Susan Wright, CILT, 65 (Amsterdam and Philadelphia: John Benjamins), pp. 313–36

——1991. *History of Final Vowels in English* (Berlin and New York: Mouton de Gruyter)

MONTEVERDI, ANGELO, 1939. 'I primi endecasillabi italiani', *Studi Romanzi*, 28: 141–54

——1963. 'Storia dell'iscrizione ferrarese del 1135', *Memorie della Accademia dei Lincei, Classe di Scienze Morali, Storiche e Filologiche*, serie VIII, 11.2: 101–38

MOORE, MARIANNE, 1967. *The Complete Poems of Marianne Moore* (New York: Macmillan)

MUKHERJI, AMULYADHAN, 1976. *Sanskrit Prosody: Its Evolution* (Calcutta: Saraswat Library)

MYNORS, R. A. B., ed., 1958. *C. Valerius Catullus: Opera* (London: OUP)

NAVARRO (Tomás), Tomás, 1973. 'El octosílabo y sus modalidades', in Navarro, *Los poetas y sus versos, desde Jorge Manrique a García Lorca* (Barcelona: Ariel), pp. 36–66

——1974. *Métrica española: reseña histórica y descriptiva*, 4th edn (Madrid: Guadarrama)

NESPOR, MARINA, & IRENE VOGEL, 1986. *Prosodic Phonology*, Studies in Generative Grammar, 28 (Dordrecht: Foris)

NORBERG, DAG, 1958. *Introduction à l'étude de la versification latine médiévale* (Stockholm: Almqvist & Wiksell)

NORTON-SMITH, JOHN, ed., 1966. *John Lydgate: Poems* (Oxford: Clarendon Press)

NOUGARET, LOUIS, 1948. *Traité de métrique latine classique*, Nouvelle Collection à l'Usage des Classes, 36 (Paris: Klincksieck)

NUNES, JOSÉ JOAQUIM, ed., 1926–28. *Cantigas d'amigo dos trovadores galego-portugueses*, 3 vols (Coimbra: University of Coimbra)

OLIVA, SALVADOR, 1980. *Mètrica catalana* (Barcelona: Quaderns Crema)

OMOND, T. S., 1921. *English Metrists, Being a Sketch of English Prosodical Criticism from Elizabethan Times to the Present Day* (Oxford: Clarendon Press)

OPIE, IONA, & PETER OPIE, ed., 1967. *The Oxford Nursery Rhyme Book* (New York: OUP)

O'PREY, PAUL, ed., 1986. *Robert Graves: Selected Poems* (Harmondsworth: Penguin Books)

OWEN, CHARLES A., 1994. 'Notes on Gower's Prosody', *CR*, 28: 405–13

PAETOW, LOUIS J., 1910. *The Arts Course at Medieval Universities with Special Reference to Grammar and Rhetoric* (Urbana-Champaign: University of Illinois Press)

PALGRAVE, FRANCIS TURNER, ed., 1906. *The Poetical Works of Sir Walter Scott, Baronet* (London: Macmillan)

PALMER, L. R., 1954. *The Latin Language* (London: Faber and Faber)

PARKINSON, STEPHEN, 2006. 'Concurrent Patterns of Verse Design in the Galician-Portuguese Lyric', in *Proceedings of the Twelfth Colloquium*, ed. by Jane Whetnall & Alan Deyermond, PMHRS, 51 (London: QMW), pp. 19–38

PAYNE, W., & SIDNEY J. HERITAGE, eds, 1878. THOMAS TUSSER, *Five Hundred Pointes of Good Husbandrie* (London: Trübner)

PEARSALL, DEREK, 1970. *John Lydgate* (London: Routledge & Kegan Paul)

—— 1991. 'Chaucer's Meter: The Evidence of the Manuscripts', in *Medieval Literature: Texts and Interpretation*, ed. by Tim William Machan, MRTS, 79 (Binghamton, NY: MRTS), pp. 41–57

—— 1992. *The Life of Geoffrey Chaucer: A Critical Biography* (Oxford: Blackwell)

—— 1999. 'The Weak Declension of the Adjective and its Importance in Chaucerian Metre', in *Chaucer in Perspective: Middle English Essays in Honour of Norman Blake*, ed. by Geoffrey Lester (Sheffield: Academic Press), pp. 178–93

PEARSON, HESKETH, ed., 1954. *Oscar Wilde: Selected Essays and Poems* (Harmondsworth: Penguin Books)

PECK, RUSSELL A., ed., 1980. *John Gower: Confessio Amantis*, Medieval Reprints for Teaching, 9 (Toronto: Toronto UP)

PENNY, RALPH, 2002. *History of the Spanish Language*, 2nd edn (Cambridge: CUP)

PENSOM, ROGER, 2000. *Accent and Metre in French: A Theory of the Relation between Linguistic Accent and Metrical Practice in French* (Bern: Peter Lang)

PETROCCHI, GIORGIO, ed., 1975. *Dante Alighieri: La 'Commedia' secondo l'antica volgata*, 2nd edn (Turin: Einaudi)

PIERA, CARLOS JOSÉ, 1980. 'Spanish Verse and the Theory of Meter' (unpublished doctoral thesis, University of California at Los Angeles); see *Dissertation Abstracts International*, 42 (1981–82): 197a

—— 2001. 'Intonational Factors in Metrics', in Michaux & Dominicy 2001: 205–28

PIGHI, GIOVANNI BATTISTA, 1970. *Studi di ritmica e metrica* (Turin: Bottega d'Erasmo)

PINKER, STEVEN, 1994. *The Language Instinct: How the Mind Creates Language* (Harmondsworth: Penguin Books)

PINSKY, ROBERT, 1996. *The Figured Wheel: New and Collected Poems* (Manchester: Carcanet)

—— 1998. *The Sounds of Poetry: A Brief Guide* (New York: Farrar, Straus & Giroux)

POLLARD, ARTHUR, ed., 1976. *Silver Poets of the Eighteenth Century* (London: Dent)

POPE, JOHN C., 1942. *The Rhythms of Beowulf: An Interpretation of the Normal and Hypermetric Verse-Forms in Old English Poetry* (New Haven: Yale UP; rev. edn 1966)

——, ed., 1967–68. *The Homilies of Ælfric: A Supplementary Collection*, 2 vols, EETS, OS, 259 & 260 (London: OUP)

POUND, EZRA, 1961. *ABC of Reading* (London: Faber and Faber)

—— 1970. *The Translations of Ezra Pound*, with a foreword by Hugh Kenner (London: Faber and Faber)

—— 1975. *The Cantos of Ezra Pound*, new edn containing 117 cantos (London: Faber and Faber)

PREMINGER, ALEX, with FRANK J. WARNKE & O. B. HARDISON, JR, 1975. *Princeton Encyclopedia of Poetry and Poetics*, enlarged edn (London: Macmillan)

—— & T. V. F. BROGAN, with FRANK J. WARNKE, O. B. HARDISON, JR, & EARL MINER, eds, 1993. *The New Princeton Encyclopedia of Poetry and Poetics* (Princeton, NJ: Princeton UP)

PRESS, JOHN, ed., 1964. *Francis Turner Palgrave: The Golden Treasury, with a Fifth Book Selected by John Press* (London: OUP)

PRICHARD, J. V., ed., 1892–93. *Thomas Percy, Lord Bishop of Dromore: Reliques of Ancient English Poetry, Consisting of Old Heroic Ballads, Songs and Other Pieces of Our Earlier Poets, Together with Some Few of Later Date*, 2 vols, 2nd edn (London: Geo. Bell & Sons)

PURCZINSKY, JULIUS, 1965. 'Germanic Influence in the *Sainte Eulalia*', *Romance Philology*, 19 (1965–66): 271–75

PYLE, FITZROY, 1935. 'The Place of Anglo-Norman in the History of English Versification', *Hermathena*, 39: 22–42

—— 1937. 'The Pedigree of John Lydgate's Heroic Line', *Hermathena*, 50: 26–59

QUILIS, ANTONIO, 1964. *Estructura del encabagliamento en la métrica española: contribución a su estudio experimental* (Madrid: CSIC)

—— 1971. 'Caracterización fonética del acento español', *Travaux de Linguistique et Littérature*, 9: 53–72

RABY, F. J. E., 1934. *A History of Secular Latin Poetry in the Middle Ages*, 2 vols (Oxford: Clarendon Press)

RAFFEL, BURTON, TR., 1963. *Beowulf: A New Translation*, New American Library, MP 531 (New York: Mentor)

RAMÍREZ, PERE, 1985. 'El endecasílabo d'Ausiàs i la recepció de l'"endecasillabo" petrarquista', *Versants: Revue Suisse des Littératures Romanes*, 7: 67–88

RAVEN, D. S., 1965. *Latin Metre: An Introduction* (London: Faber and Faber)

REBHOLZ, R. A., ed., 1978. *Sir Thomas Wyatt: The Complete Poems* (Harmondsworth: Penguin Books)

REEVES, JAMES, ed., 1973. *The Complete English Poems of Thomas Gray* (London: Heinemann)

RENOIR, ALAIN, 1967. *The Poetry of John Lydgate* (London: Routledge & Kegan Paul)

RICKETTS, PETER, 2001. *Concordance of Medieval Occitan* (Turnhout: Brepols)

RICKS, CHRISTOPHER, ed., 1987. *The Poems of Tennyson*, 2nd edn, 3 vols (Harlow: Longman)

RIVKIN, JULIE, & MICHAEL RYAN, 1998. *Literary Theory: An Anthology* (Oxford: Blackwell)

ROACH, PETER, 1982. 'On the Distinction between "Stress-Timed" and "Syllable-Timed" Languages', in Crystal 1982: 73–79

ROBINSON, IAN, 1971. *Chaucer's Prosody: A Study of the Middle English Verse Tradition* (Cambridge: CUP)

ROLLINS, H. E., ed., 1928–29. *Tottel's Miscellany of 1557*, 2 vols (Cambridge, MA: Harvard UP)

ROUBAUD, JACQUES, 1971. 'Mètre et vers', *Poétique*, 2: 366–87

ROWLAND, THOMAS, 1876. *A Grammar of the Welsh Language* (Wrexham: Hughes & Son)

RUSSOM, GEOFFREY, 1987. *Old English Meter and Linguistic Theory* (Cambridge: CUP)

—— 1998. *'Beowulf' and Old Germanic Metre* (Cambridge: CUP)

SAINTSBURY, G., 1906. *A History of English Prosody from the Twelfth Century to the Present Day*, I: *From the Origins to Spenser*; II: *From Shakespeare to Crabbe* (London: Macmillan)

—— 1910A. *A History of English Prosody from the Twelfth Century to the Present Day*, III: *From Blake to Swinburne* (London: Macmillan)

—— 1910B. *A Historical Manual of English Prosody* (London: Macmillan)

SALUS, PETER H., & PAUL B. TAYLOR, 1973. 'Introduction', in *The Elder Edda: A Selection*, tr. by Paul B. Taylor & W. H. Auden (London: Faber and Faber), pp. 13–33

SAMUELS, M. L., 1972. 'Chaucerian Final -E', *Notes and Queries*, 217: 445–48

SANGUINETI, EDOARDO, ed., 1965. *Sonetti della Scuola Siciliana*, 2nd edn (Turin: Einaudi)

SAPORA, ROBERT WILLIAM, JR, 1977. *A Theory of Middle English Alliterative Meter, with Critical Applications*, Speculum Anniversary Monographs, 1 (Cambridge, MA: Mediaeval Academy of America)

SCAGLIONE, ALDO, 1972. *The Classical Theory of Composition from its Origins to the Present: A Historical Survey*, University of North Carolina Studies in Comparative Literature, 53 (Chapel Hill: University of North Carolina Press)

SCHICK, JOSEF, ed., 1891. *Lydgate's 'Temple of Glas'*, EETS, ES, 60 (London: Paul, Trench and Trubner)

SCHIPPER, JAKOB, 1896. *Englische Metrik* (Bonn: E. Strauss)

—— 1910. *A History of English Versification* (Oxford: Clarendon Press)

SCHIRMER, WALTER F., 1961. *John Lydgate: A Study in the Culture of the Fifteenth Century*, tr. by Ann E. Keep (London: Methuen)

SCOTT, CLIVE, 1980. *French Verse Art: A Study* (Cambridge: CUP)

—— 1990. *'Vers libre': The Emergence of Free Verse in France* (Oxford: Clarendon Press)

SCOTT, TOM, ed., 1967. *Late Medieval Scots Poetry: A Selection from the Makars and their Heirs down to 1610* (London: Heinemann)

SCRAGG, DONALD, ed., 1991. *The Battle of Maldon, AD 991* (Oxford: Blackwell and the Manchester Centre for Anglo-Saxon Studies)

SEBEOK, THOMAS A., ed., 1960. *Style in Language* (Boston: MIT Press)

SEYMOUR, M. C., ed., 1981. *Hoccleve: Selections* (Oxford: Clarendon Press)

SIEVERS, EDUARD, 1885. 'Zur Rhythmik des germanischen Alliterationsverses', *Pauls und Braunes Beiträge*, 10: 209–314 & 451–545

SHARROCK, ROGER, ed., 1968. *Selected Poems of John Dryden* (London: Heinemann)

SKEAT, W. W., 1898. 'On the Scansion of English Poetry', *Transactions of the Philological Society*, 484–503

——, ed., 1886. WILLIAM LANGLAND, *'Piers Plowman' in Three Parallel Texts*, 2 vols (Oxford: Clarendon Press; repr. 1954)

SMITH, A. J., ed., 1971. *John Donne: The Complete English Poems* (Harmondsworth: Penguin Books)

SMITH, BARBARA HERRNSTEIN, 1968. *Poetic Closure: A Study of How Poems End* (Chicago: University of Chicago Press)

SMITH, G. S., 1983. 'The Stanza Typology of Russian Poetry 1735–1816: A General Survey', *Russian Literature*, 13: 175–204

—— 1985. 'The Metrical Repertoire of Shorter Poems by Russian Emigres, 1971–1980', *Canadian Slavonic Papers*, 27: 385–99

—— 2000A. 'Russian Poetry: The Lives or the Lines', Presidential Address to the Modern Humanities Research Association, London, 17 March 2000, *Modern Language Review*, 95.4: 29–41

—— 2000B. 'Verse Form and Function in Marina Tsvetaeva's *Tsar'-devitsa*', *Oxford Slavonic Papers*, NS, 33: 108–33

—— 2002. 'The Development of Josef Brodsky's Dol'nik Verse 1972–1976', *Russian Literature*, 52: 471–92

——, ed. & tr., 1980. *Russian Poetics in Translation*, VII: *Metre, Rhythm, Stanza, Rhyme* (Colchester: Department of Language and Linguistics, University of Essex)

SMITH, MILES, et al., ed. & tr., 1611. *The Holy Bible*, the 'Authorised Version' or AV

SOLA PINTO, VIVIAN DE, & WARREN F. ROBERTS, eds, 1964. *D. H. Lawrence: Complete Poems*, 2 vols (London: Heinemann)

SOLOPOVA, ELIZABETH, 2000. 'Computer-Assisted Study of Chaucer's Metre', in Kennedy 2000b: 157–79

SOUTHWORTH, JAMES G., 1957. *Verses of Cadence: An Introduction to the Prosody of Chaucer and his Followers* (Oxford: Blackwell)

—— 1962. *The Prosody of Chaucer and his Followers: Supplementary Chapters to Verses of Cadence* (Oxford: Blackwell)

SPARROW, JOHN, ed., 1956. *A. E. Housman: Collected Poems* (Harmondsworth: Penguin Books with Jonathan Cape)

STANLEY, ERIC GERALD, ed., 1972. *The Owl and the Nightingale* (Manchester: Manchester UP; New York: Barnes & Noble)

STEANE, J. B., ed., 1969. *Christopher Marlowe: The Complete Plays* (Harmondsworth: Penguin Books)

STEELE, ROBERT, ed., 1941. *The English Poems of Charles of Orleans*, I (text), EETS, OS, 215 (London: OUP)

——& MABEL DAY, eds, 1946, *The English Poems of Charles of Orleans*, II: *Notes*, EETS, OS, 220 (London: OUP)

STEVENS, WALLACE, 1965. *The Collected Poems of Wallace Stevens* (London: Faber and Faber)

STEVENSON, W. H., ed., 1971. *The Poems of William Blake*, text by David V. Erdman (London: Longman)

STILLMAN, FRANCES, 1966. *The Poet's Manual and Rhyming Dictionary* (London: Thames and Hudson)

STOCKWELL, ROBERT, & DONKA MINKOVA, 1997. 'The Prosody of *Beowulf*', in *A 'Beowulf' Handbook*, ed. by Robert Bjork & John D. Niles (Lincoln: University of Nebraska Press), pp. 55–83

STRANG, BARBARA M. H., 1980. 'The Ecology of the English Monosyllable', in *Studies in the English Language*, ed. by S. Greenbaum, Geoffrey Leech, & J. Svartvik (London: Longman), pp. 277–93

SUTHERLAND, ROBERT, ed. & tr., 1968. *'The Romaunt of the Rose' and 'La Roman de la rose': A Parallel-Text Edition* (Oxford: Blackwell)

TARLINSKAJA, M., 1976. *English Verse: Theory and History* (The Hague: Mouton)

—— 1993. *Strict Stress-Meter in English Poetry Compared with German and Russian* (Calgary: University of Calgary Press)

TAVANI, GIUSEPPE, 1967. *Repertorio metrico della lirica galego-portoghese*, Officina Romanica, 7 (Rome: Ateneo)

—— 1974. 'Strutture formali e significato en poesia', in *Letteratura e critica: studi in onore di Natalino Sapegno*, ed. by Walter Binni, I (Rome: Bulzoni), pp. 121–43

TAYLOR, BARRY, MARTIN J. DUFFELL, & CHARLES BURNETT, 1998. '*Proverbia Senece et versus Eberardi super eadem*, MS Cambridge, Gonville and Caius College, 122/59, pp. 19–29', *Euphrosyne*, 26: 357–78

THOMAS, DYLAN, 1952. *Collected Poems 1934–1952* (London: Dent)

THOMPSON, JOHN, 1961. *The Founding of English Meter* (London: Routledge & Kegan Paul; New York: Columbia UP)

THWAITE, ANTHONY, ed., 1988. *Philip Larkin: Collected Poems* (London: Faber and Faber)

TODOROV, TSVETAN, ed., 1972. *I formalisti russi* (Turin: Einaudi)

TOLEDO, GUILLERMO ANDRÉS, 1988. *El ritmo en español: estudio fonético con base conputacional*, BRH, 2.361 (Madrid: Gredos)

TOLKIEN, J. R. R., tr., 1975. *'Sir Gawain and the Green Knight', 'Pearl', and 'Sir Orfeo'* (London: Allen & Unwin)

TOMASHEVSKY, BORIS VIKTOROVICH, 1929. *O stikhe* (Leningrad: Priboy)

TRAGER, G. L., & H. L. SMITH, JR, 1951. *An Outline of English Structure*, Studies in Linguistics, Occasional Papers, 3 (Norman, OK: Battenburg Press)

TYDEMAN, WILLIAM, ed., 1992. *Two Tudor Tragedies: 'Gorboduc' and 'The Spanish Tragedy'* (Harmondsworth: Penguin Books)

TYRRELL, ROBERT YELVERTON, ed., 1881. *T. Maccius Plautus: Miles gloriosus* (London: Macmillan)

UTRERA TORREMOCHA, MARÍA VICTORIA, 2001. *Historia y teoría del verso libre*, Cuadernos de Teoría de la Literatura, 1 (Seville: Padilla Libros)

VAN DORSTEN, JAN, ed., 1966. *Sidney: A Defence of Poetry* (Oxford: OUP)

VIANELLO, NEREO, ed., 1966. *Francesco Petrarca: Canzoniere* (Basiano: Bietti)

VIETH, DAVID M., ed., 1968. *The Complete Poems of John Wilmot, Earl of Rochester* (New Haven: Yale UP)

VISING, JOHAN, 1884. *Sur la versification anglo-normande* (Uppsala: Almqvist & Wiksell)

—— 1923. *Anglo-Norman Language and Literature* (London: OUP)

WACKERNAGEL, WILHELM, 1879. *Geschichte der deutschen Literatur*, 2nd edn, 2 vols (Basel: Schweighauserische Buchhandlung)

WADDELL, HELEN, ed. and tr., 1952. *Medieval Latin Lyrics*, Penguin Classics, L29 (Harmondsworth: Penguin Books); 1st edn 1929

WAQUET, FRANÇOISE, 2001. *Latin, or the Empire of a Sign* (London: Verso)

WAVELL, A. P., ed., 1944. *Other Men's Flowers: An Anthology of Poetry Selected by the Field-Marshal Lord Wavell* (London: Jonathan Cape)

WEIL, GOTTHOLD, 1960. ''Arud', in *The Encyclopedia of Islam: New Edition*, I: *A–B*, ed. by Hamilton A. R. Gibb et al. (Leiden: Brill), pp. 667–77

WEISSMILLER, EDWARD R., 1989. 'Triple Threats to Duple Rhythm', in Kiparsky & Youmans 1989: 261–90

WEST, M. L., 1973. 'Indo-European Metre', *Glotta*, 51: 161–87

——1982. *Greek Metre* (Oxford: Clarendon Press)

WHINNOM, KEITH, 1994. *Medieval and Renaissance Spanish Literature: Selected Essays*, ed. by Alan Deyermond, W. F. Hunter, and Joseph T. Snow (Exeter: University of Exeter Press)

WHITNEY, WILLIAM DWIGHT, 1962. *Sanskrit Grammar, including both the Classical Language and the Older Dialects of Veda and Brahmana*, 2nd edn (Delhi: Banarsidass); 1st edn 1888

WILBUR, RICHARD, ed., 1959. *Poe: Complete Poems*, Laurel Poetry Series, D 6962 (New York: Dell)

WILKINS, ERNEST HATCH, 1959. *The Invention of the Sonnet and Other Studies in Italian Literature* (Rome: Edizioni di Storia e Letteratura)

WILKINSON, L. P., 1970. *Golden Age Latin Artistry* (Cambridge: CUP)

WIMSATT, JAMES I., 1982. *Chaucer and the Poems of 'Ch' in University of Pennsylvania MS French 15*, Chaucer Studies, 9 (London: Brewer; Lanham, MD: Rowman & Littlefield)

WIMSATT, W. K., ed., 1972. *Versification: Major Language Types* (New York: MLA and New York UP)

——& MONROE C. BEARDSLEY, 1959. 'The Concept of Meter: An Exercise in Abstraction', *PMLA*, 74: 585–98 [shortened version in Sebeok 1960: 193–96]

WINDEATT, B. A., 1977. '"Most conservatyf the soun": Chaucer's *Troilus* Metre', *Poetica* (Tokyo), 8: 44–60

——, ed., 1984. *Troilus and Criseyde* (London: Longman)

WOLEDGE, BRIAN, ed., 1961. *The Penguin Book of French Verse*, I: *To the Fifteenth Century* (Harmondsworth: Penguin Books)

WRENN, C. L., & W. F. BOLTON, eds, 1988. *'Beowulf' with the 'Finnesburg Fragment'*, 4th edn (Exeter: University of Exeter Press)

WRIGHT, GEORGE T., 1988. *Shakespeare's Metrical Art* (Berkeley: Univ. of California Press)

WRIGHT, ROGER, 1982. *Late Latin and Early Romance in Spain and Carolingian France* (Liverpool: Francis Cairns)

——1994. *Early Ibero-Romance: Twenty-One Studies on Languages and Texts from the Iberian Peninsula between the Roman Empire and the Thirteenth Century*, Juan de la Cuesta Hispanic Monographs, Estudios Lingüísticos, 5 (Newark, DE: Juan de la Cuesta)

——2003. *A Sociophilological Study of Late Latin*, Utrecht Studies in Medieval Literacy, 10 (Turnhout: Brepols)

——, ed. & TR., 1987. *Spanish Ballads* (Warminster: Aris & Phillips)

YOUMANS, GILBERT, 1989. 'Milton's Meter', in Kiparsky & Youmans 1989: 341–79

ZAEHNER, R. C., ed. & tr., 1966. *Hindu Scriptures* (London: Dent)

ZHIRMUNSKY, VIKTOR MAKSIMOVICH, 1966. *Introduction to Metrics: The Theory of Verse*, tr. by C. F. Brown, ed. by Edward Stankiewicz & W. N. Vickery, Slavistic Printings and Reprintings, 58 (The Hague: Mouton)

ZONNEVELD, WIM, 2000. 'The *Ormulum* and the *Lutgart*: Early Germanic Iambs in Context',
   in Kennedy 2000b: 27–52

ZUMTHOR, PAUL, 1970. 'Rhétorique et poétique latines et romanes', *Grundriss der romanischen
   Literaturen des Mittelalters*, I: 57–91

INDEX OF LINGUISTIC AND
METRICAL TERMS

(first, defining, and substantial references)

INDEX OF VERSE TEXTS

❖

INDEX OF SCHOLARS

(whose work is discussed as well as cited)

GENERAL INDEX

❖